I0105061

Shame, Modesty, and Honor in Islam

Also Available from Bloomsbury

Islam as Critique: Sayyid Ahmad Khan and the Challenge of Modernity, Khurram Hussain

Islam, Faith, and Fashion, Magdalena Craciun

Metaphors of Death and Resurrection in the Qur'an, Abdulla Galadari

Shame, Modesty, and Honor in Islam

Edited by
Ayang Utriza Yakin, Adis Duderija, and
An Van Raemdonck

BLOOMSBURY ACADEMIC
LONDON • NEW YORK • OXFORD • NEW DELHI • SYDNEY

BLOOMSBURY ACADEMIC
Bloomsbury Publishing Plc, 50 Bedford Square, London, WC1B 3DP, UK
Bloomsbury Publishing Inc, 1385 Broadway, New York, NY 10018, USA
Bloomsbury Publishing Ireland, 29 Earlsfort Terrace, Dublin 2, D02 AY28, Ireland

BLOOMSBURY, BLOOMSBURY ACADEMIC and the Diana logo are trademarks of Bloomsbury Publishing Plc

First published in Great Britain 2024
Paperback edition published 2025

A catalogue record for this book is available from the British Library.

Library of Congress Cataloging-in-Publication Data
Names: Yakin, Ayang Utriza, 1978– editor. | Duderija, Adis, 1977– editor. | Raemdonck, An van, editor.
Title: Shame, modesty, and honor in Islam / Ayang Utriza Yakin, Adis Duderija, An Van Raemdonck.
Description: 1st. | New York : Bloomsbury Academic, 2023. | Includes bibliographical references and index.
Identifiers: LCCN 2023022918 (print) | LCCN 2023022919 (ebook) | ISBN 9781350386105 (hardback) | ISBN 9781350386143 (paperback) | ISBN 9781350386129 (epub) | ISBN 9781350386112 (adobe pdf)
Subjects: LCSH: Modesty–Religious aspects–Islam. | Shame–Religious aspects–Islam. | Honor–Religious aspects–Islam.
Classification: LCC BP188.16.M6 S526 2023 (print) | LCC BP188.16.M6 (ebook) | DDC 205/.699–dc23/eng/20230626
LC record available at https://lccn.loc.gov/2023022918
LC ebook record available at https://lccn.loc.gov/2023022919

ISBN: HB: 978-1-3503-8610-5
PB: 978-1-3503-8614-3
ePDF: 978-1-3503-8611-2
eBook: 978-1-3503-8612-9

Typeset by Newgen KnowledgeWorks Pvt. Ltd., Chennai, India

For product safety related questions contact productsafety@bloomsbury.com.

To find out more about our authors and books visit www.bloomsbury.com and sign up for our newsletters.

Contents

Acknowledgments

The publication of this volume is the result of transnational collaborative work. The idea of this work originated from my postdoctoral project (Ayang Utriza Yakin) on "Islam and Modesty" at the Chair of Tolerance of the Research Institute "Religions, Spiritualities, Cultures, Societies" (RSCS) of UCLouvain, Belgium. After organizing a workshop on the topic of Islam and modesty, which was mainly restricted to the French academia, I intended to enlarge this project to English-speaking academia. I found two wonderful colleagues as partners and editors to help me realize this: Adis Duderija and An Van Raemdonck.

We, the editors, are very grateful to many individuals who have been part of the journey of completing this volume and would like to sincerely thank them. First, we thank our contributors for accepting our invitation. Furthermore, we are tremendously grateful for their trust in our project since the beginning. Over the years, editors and contributors worked together to sharpen and refine the argumentation of each chapter. We—the editors—are very pleased to have worked with all the contributors with mutual respect and understanding over three rounds of review that took place during the years 2020–2023. Next, we would like to thank sincerely Sophie Rudland, the editor for Islamic Studies at IB Tauris, and Lalle Pursglove, the editor for Religious Studies at Bloomsbury, and her two assistant editors, Lily McMahon and Emily Wootton. We would also like to express our heartfelt thanks to Moch. Nur Ichwan who created the cover art for this book. The image represents calligraphy of the Arabic word *ḥayāʾ* and is painted on batik. Finally, we would like to thank our families for their continued support and love throughout this project.

Ayang Utriza Yakin wants to especially thank Adis Duderija and An Van Raemdonck for agreeing to coedit this volume. Both of them enriched and sharpened this project. Ayang Utriza Yakin is very thankful to Ima Sri Rahmani, his wife, for continuing to support and encourage him in all his academic endeavors and to his four children, Afra Rayhana Yakin, Akhtar Farras Yakin, Ayman Farabi Yakin, and Alifa Fakhira Yakin, for letting him work on the volume. He is also very grateful to Baudouin Dupret who gave him freedom to engage in another project other than his essential postdoctoral research project on law and equality in personal status laws, conducted at SciencesPo Bordeaux, France, and to Louis-Léon Christians for his endless support to enable him to work as a research associate and guest lecturer at UCLouvain, Belgium.

Adis Duderija and An Van Raemdonck would like to extend their thanks to their coeditors and especially Ayang Utriza Yakin for his leadership on this project and for inviting them to be coeditors of this important volume. They are indebted to their institutions—Griffith University and Ghent University, Special Research Fund (BOF)—for supporting their work on this volume.

Ayang Utriza Yakin
Adis Duderija
An Van Raemdonck

Abbreviations

AKP	*Adalet ve Kalkınma Partisi*
ART	Assisted Reproductive Technology
CCP	Chinese Communist Party (CCP)
CNE	*Comité nationale d'éligibilité*
e.g.	*exempli gratia*
et al.	*et alii*
FGC	Female Genital Cutting
HBV	Honor-Based Violence
Ḥ. I.	*Ḥujjat al-Islām*, i.e. a high ranking cleric.
i.a.	*inter alia*
i.e.	*id est*
KUPI	*Kongres Ulama Perempuan Indonesia* (Congress of Indonesian Women Ulama)
LGBTQ	Lesbian, Gay, Bisexual, Transgender, Queer
MAR	Medically Assisted Reproduction
MOE	Ministry of Education
MUIS	*Majlis Ugama Islam Singapura* (Islamic Religious Council of Singapore)
NGO	non-governmental organization
NSFW	Not Safe for Work
NUSMS	National University of Singapore Muslim Society
OLG	OKLETSGO
PERGAS	*Persatuan Ulama dan Guru-Guru Agama Islam Singapura* (Singapore Islamic Scholars & Religious Teachers Association)
SDP	Singapore Democratic Party
UMADD	*Union Malienne pour la Démocratie et le Développement*
UNESCO	United Nations Educational, Scientific and Cultural Organization
UNHCR	United Nations High Commissioner for Refugees

Note on Transliteration

For Arabic transliteration, we followed the *International Journal of Middle East Studies* (IJMES) system and wordlist, while for Turkish, Indonesian, Malay, Persian, and other languages, the authors followed the standardized modern system of each language. For notes and references, we followed the Bloomsbury guidelines. The years are given in the Hijri (A.H.) followed by the Common Era (C.E.) calendar.

Contributors

Alberto Fabio Ambrosio is Professor of Theology and History of Religions at the Luxembourg School of Religion & Society and director of research at the Collège des Bernardins in Paris. He previously spent more than ten years living in Istanbul, where he conducted research on Ottoman and Turkish Islam. He holds a PhD in Modern and Contemporary History from Sorbonne University. His thesis analyzed the practices of whirling dervishes in the Ottoman Empire in the seventeenth century. Among his recent publications on Islam, Sufism, and inter-religious dialogue are *Penser l'islam en Europe. Perspectives du Luxembourg et d'ailleurs* (edited with Laurent Mignon, 2021), and *Liberté de religion et de conviction en Méditerranée* (2020). His recent work focuses on dress and fashion as a system of religious identity, in Islam as well in Western culture.

Muhamad Ali is the Chair of Middle Eastern and Islamic Studies program and an Associate Professor at the Religious Studies Department, and at Southeast Asia: Text, Ritual, and Performance (Seatrip) Program at the University of California, Riverside. He earned a BA. in Islamic studies from the State Institute for Islamic Studies, Jakarta; an MM-CAAE in international management from the University of Indonesia and Grenoble, Paris; an M.Sc. in Middle Eastern and Islamic studies from Edinburgh University, Scotland, and a PhD in history from the University of Hawai`i at Manoa. Dr. Ali published *Islam and Colonialism: Becoming Modern in Indonesia and Malaya* (2015), *Multicultural-Pluralist Theology* (2003), and *Bridging Islam and the West: An Indonesian View* (2009), in addition to several book chapters and journal articles on different aspects of Islam in Southeast Asia.

Souleymane Diallo is a postdoc in the Department of Social Anthropology at the University of Münster, Germany. He earned his PhD in socio-cultural anthropology from the University of Cologne. His publications include the monograph *"The Truth about the Desert": Exile, Memory, and the Making of Communities among Malian Tuareg Refugees in Niger* (2018) and several articles on changing social identities among Tuareg refugees in Niger.

Adis Duderija, PhD (UWA, 2010) is Senior Lecturer in Islamic Studies at Griffith University, Brisbane, Australia. He has published extensively on the theory of progressive Islam, Islamic interpretative tradition with focus on sunna/hadith, gender issues in Islam, religious pluralism, and western Muslim identity construction. His most recent book (co-written) is titled *Islam and Gender: Major Issues and Debates* (2020). Many of his publications can be accessed on Academia.edu.

Marloes Hamelink is a cultural anthropologist, affiliated with African Studies Centre Leiden, the Netherlands, and based in Dar es Salaam, Tanzania. Currently, she is doing research on the online and offline performed lives and moralities of Muslim women in Zanzibar as part of her PhD project. As an ethnographer, she invests in gendered relations and how they get affected by social interactions through hearing and sharing the live stories of different women. Her themes of interest include social media, gender, religion, and morality.

Wai-Yip Ho is Honorary Research Fellow, Institute of Arab and Islamic Studies, University of Exeter. He is the author of *Islam and China's Hong Kong: Ethnic Identity, Muslim Networks and the New Silk Road* (2015). His research interests include Islamic Studies, China's Christian–Muslim relations, New Media and China's Islam, Gulf–China relations and contemporary Muslim youths in the Chinese context.

İrem Özgören Kınlı is an Associate Professor in the Department of Political Science and Public Administration at İzmir Kâtip Çelebi University in Turkey. She graduated from Marmara University (Istanbul), the Francophone Department of Political and Administrative Sciences in 2001. Irem received her first MA from Ege University (Izmir) in international relations in 2004 and another MA from Panthéon-Sorbonne University (Paris) in political sociology in 2005. She obtained her PhD from Panthéon-Sorbonne University in political science in 2011. Her research interests are interdisciplinary and cover the issues of figurational sociology, gender, and political sociology. She is a Fellow of the Norbert Elias Foundation.

John Lever is Reader in the Department of Management at the University of Huddersfield in the UK. He is an interdisciplinary social scientist with a background in sociology and human geography. He has research interests in kosher and halal food markets, refugees, and sustainable food systems. John has published widely on many aspects of halal food production and consumption, notably on the politics of food consumption and practice in religious communities. He is a joint author of *Halal Matters: Islam, Politics and Markets in Global Perspective* (2015) and *Religion, Regulation, Consumption: Globalising Kosher and Halal Markets* (2018). John is a Fellow of the Norbert Elias Foundation.

Danilo Marino is currently associate researcher at the University of Bern, Switzerland. He received a PhD from the University of Naples "L'Orientale" and INALCO of Paris in May 2015 with the thesis "Raconter le haschich dans l'époque mamelouke. Étude et édition critique partielle de la Rāḥat al-arwāḥ fī l-ḥašīš wa-l-rāḥ de Taqī al-Dīn Abū l-Tuqā al-Badrī (847–894/1443–1489)." Between 2018 and 2019, he was a postdoctoral fellow at the Berlin Graduate School Muslim Cultures and Societies with the research project "*Murūʾa* and Masculinity in the Mamlūk Period (1252–1517)." He has published articles on literary renditions of intoxication in medieval Arabic literature and is currently working on the evolution of *murūʾa* in the premodern period as well as on representations of masculinity in Arabic historiography and literature.

Amélie Neuve-Eglise holds a PhD in philosophy from the University of Paris I-Panthéon Sorbonne and the University of Tehran. She has taught at the University of Tehran and is currently a lecturer in Persian Studies at Inalco Paris. She is the co-translator of *L'Aune de la Sagesse* (*The Scale of Wisdom*), a compendium of Shi'a hadith, from Arabic into French. She was the Editor-in-Chief of *La Revue de Téhéran*, a monthly review on Iranian history and culture, in which she has written extensively on Islamic philosophy and mysticism. Her current research focuses on devotional practices and rituals in contemporary Iran and include the study of the place of the body in Shīʿa pilgrimages.

Eva F. Nisa is Senior Lecturer of anthropology in the College of Asia and the Pacific at the Australian National University and an Australian Research Council (ARC) DECRA fellow. She is a scholar of anthropology, Islamic studies, religion, and gender, researching how global currents of Islam are (re)shaping the lives of Muslims in Southeast Asia. Her research and publications focus on the intersections between religious, cultural, political, economic, legal, social, and philosophical aspects of peoples' lives. Currently, she serves on the editorial board of *The Asia Pacific Journal of Anthropology*.

Yanwar Pribadi is lecturer at Indonesian International Islamic University (UIII) and UIN (State Islamic University) Sultan Maulana Hasanuddin Banten, Indonesia. He graduated from Leiden University (MA and PhD). He is the author of *Islam, State and Society in Indonesia: Local Politics in Madura* (Routledge) and several chapters and articles in edited volumes, encyclopaedias, and journals, such as *TRaNS: Trans-Regional and—National Studies of Southeast Asia*; *Bijdragen tot de Taal-, Land- en Volkenkunde*; *South East Asia Research*; *American Journal of Islamic Social Sciences*; *Journal of Muslim Minority Affairs*; and *Encyclopaedia of Islam III*. His research interests include Muslim politics and expressions, Islamic history, religious networks, and citizenship.

An Van Raemdonck is senior postdoc researcher at the Department of Languages and Cultures, Ghent University, Belgium. Her current research project focuses on Islamic ethics in the context of Western urban multicultural life in Belgium. Her doctoral research resulted in the forthcoming monograph *Questioning Female Circumcision as Islamic Practice: Development and Religion in Egypt*. Her research interests include migration, gender, and religion/secularism and are situated at the intersection of Islamic studies and anthropology. She published numerous articles and book chapters and is co-editor-in-chief of *DiGeSt, Journal of Diversity and Gender Studies*.

Norshahril Saat, PhD is Senior Fellow at ISEAS-Yusof Ishak Institute (Singapore) and is Coordinator of the Regional Social and Cultural Studies Programme at the Institute. He is the author of *The State, Ulama and Islam in Malaysia and Indonesia*, and *Tradition and Islamic Learning: Singapore Students in the Al-Azhar University*.

Federica Sona holds a PhD in Law and an International PhD in Law and Society. She is Senior Researcher in the Law and Anthropology Department, Max Planck Institute for Social Anthropology (Halle, Germany). At the time of writing, she is also Visiting Researcher at IALS, University of London (London, UK) and at Harvard Law School, PLS in the Muslim World, Harvard University (Cambridge, USA). Her research interests include (un)official Islamic and Muslim laws; national and international family laws; comparison and interactions between transnational, international, and national legal systems; Western Islam and European Muslim communities; cultural understanding and customary implementation of religious provisions; and sharīʿah-compliant socio-legal cultures and normative orders.

Nur Syafiqah Mohd Taufek is a currently an MA candidate at the Department of Malay Studies, National University of Singapore. She has co-authored several publications, including *The Serious Social Impact of Non-Violent Extremism in Indonesia*; *Indonesian Islam beyond Habib Rizieq Shihab: Deconstructing Islamism and Populism*; and *Rethinking Extremism Beyond Physical Violence: Anti-Shia Hostility in Malaysia.*

Ayang Utriza Yakin is a guest lecturer at the Université Catholique de Louvain (UCLouvain), Belgium, postdoctoral researcher at Sciences-Po Bordeaux, France, and lecturer at the Indonesian International Islamic University (UIII), Depok, West-Java, Indonesia. He was a visiting fellow and postdoctoral researcher in Oxford (2012), Harvard (2013), Tokyo (2016), and UCLouvain (2016–19) and visiting professor in Arabic and Islamic Studies at Ghent University (2019–21). He (co)-authored numerous articles and book chapters and coedited several books: *Rethinking Halal: Genealogy, Current Trends, and New Interpretation* (2021), *Islamic Divorce in the Twentieth-First Century: A Global Perspective* (2022), and *Histoire, Société, et Études islamiques au 21e siècle* (2024).

Introduction

Examining the Concept of *Ḥayā*ʾ: Interpretations of Shame, Modesty, and Honor in Islam

Ayang Utriza Yakin, Adis Duderija, and An Van Raemdonck

This volume focuses on the theme of *ḥayā*ʾ in Islam, which can be translated into English as a combination of the terms shame, modesty, shyness, bashfulness, and honor. The book examines its meanings in medieval Islamic sources as well as in anthropological and sociological research on its different interpretations and conceptualizations in both Muslim majority and minority societies. In Islamic orthodoxy, *ḥayā*ʾ is an ethical and moral value in juridical, mystical, and theological discourses. It is considered to be central to the ethical and moral justifications of every individual—man and woman.[1] The volume aims to demonstrate that the concept of *ḥayā*ʾ has undergone profound conceptual transformations over time and across different geographical regions in specific Islamicate contexts. This, of course, should not be surprising given that the Islamic civilization, which spans almost a millennium and a half, was born in and gave rise to very diverse societies with varying sociocultural realities, practices, and norms that have been associated with *ḥayā*ʾ.

This book brings a unique approach to understanding the questions of shame, modesty, and honor in Islam by bringing together theology and empirical research. Contributions offer historically aware, theologically informed, and empirically grounded analyses of *ḥayā*ʾ in Islam. The book focuses on a specific concept from the Islamic discursive tradition, *ḥayā*ʾ, that is rarely discussed academically. By foregrounding a conceptual study of *ḥayā*ʾ, it is possible to understand well-known themes such as modesty, shame, and honor in a more in-depth and interconnected manner. Furthermore, the empirical case studies have a true global scope, covering Africa, Asia-Pacific Ocean, the Middle East, and Europe as different contexts in which the modesty, shame, and honor nexus has taken shape.

*Ḥayā*ʾ in the Islamic Discursive Tradition

The word *ḥayā*ʾ is not found in the Qurʾan, but its variant is present in two different verses. First, in the Qurʾanic chapter titled al-Ahzab/33:53 in the following phrase: "*fayastaḥyī minkum*," meaning "but the Prophet was embarrassed to dismiss you." Here, *ḥayā*ʾ

(shyness/modesty/shame) appears in the ethical context of the relationship between the Prophet and his companions. Second, it appears in relation to Prophet Shuʿayb's daughters in the following phrase of the Qurʾanic chapter al-Qasas/28:25 "*tamshī ʿalā ʿistiḥyāʾin*": then one of the two women came to him, to Moses, with a shy walk. *Istiḥyāʾ* (shame/modesty/shyness) is situated in the context of a relationship between strangers, without family ties, between Moses and the daughters of Shuʿayb. In these two Qurʾanic verses, *istiḥyāʾ/ḥayāʾ* means modesty of attitude in the interaction between the two sexes.

More generally speaking, *ḥayāʾ* in the Qur'an is related to the ʿ*awra* or the part of the body, both male and female, that should be hidden as well as to the practice of women veiling.[2] Three Qurʾanic verses are often invoked in classical and modern Islamic interpretative traditions as providing the ethical and moral bases that relate to *ḥayāʾ* and ʿ*awra*. Three operative Qurʾanic words that occur in this context are *khimār*, *jilbāb*, and hijab.[3] The first Qurʾanic verse is that of al-Ahzab/33:59, and the operative word in question is *jilbāb* or the long garment going from the head to the foot that covers the whole part of the body of women. The second verse in chapter al-Nur/24:30-31 encourages both sexes to lower their gaze and specifically addresses women to lower (*yudnīna*) their *khimār* (veil) and place them over their bosoms (*juyūbihinna*).

In relation to verse 33:53 where the operative word hijab appears, the meaning of the term connotes the idea of seclusion and physical separation by means of a curtain or similar device. The standard Islamic tradition informs us that this verse specifically applies to the proper conduct male guests are to observe when entering the house of Muhammad and when talking to his wives. According to the same narrative, the historical incident occasioning the verse is well documented in the form of several hadith.[4] There are additional references in the Qurʾan and hadith pertaining to the idea of hijab as the veiling and seclusion of the Prophet's wives, in particular as recognition of their status as Mothers of the Believers, and as a precautionary means believers are advised to adhere to in order to rein in their lust.[5]

It is important to note that all of these key terms—*khimār*, *jilbāb*, and hijab—have not only been subject to various interpretations but also their meanings have evolved over time. Sahar Amer in relation to the meaning of the word *khimār* notes this as follows:

> While in the early tenth century the Qurʾanic injunction for women to cover some of their adornments was interpreted as a call to conceal their bodies except for the hands and face, three centuries later, this same passage was interpreted as a mandate to avoid jewellery and makeup, to cover the neck, ears, and arms, and ultimately for women to disappear entirely from the public sphere. By the early thirteenth century, appropriate Muslim women's dress had already been firmly defined as one that covered the entire body and hair. The only points of debate remained over the face and the hands and whether they too ought to be covered.[6]

The prophetic tradition in the form of hadith has provided additional ideas pertaining to the notion and concept of *ḥayāʾ* in Islam. Several hadiths that have been reported by many narrators mention and explain the subject of *ḥayāʾ* or modesty/shame: for example, the notion that modesty/shame is one of the branches of faith (*al-ḥayāʾu shuʿbatun min al-īmāni*),[7] the idea that the Prophet is more modest than a virgin (*kāna al-nabiyyu ṣalla Allāhu ʿalayhi wa sallam ashadda ḥayāʾan min al-ʿazrāʾi*),[8] the premise that modesty/shame/shyness is a form of ethical discipline (*faʾin lam tastaḥyi fasnaʿ ma shiʾta*),[9] and others. By relying on the textual sources found in the two main normative sources (Qurʾan and hadith) in Islam, jurists, theologians, philosophers, and mystics have conceptualized and developed their own understandings of the meaning of *ḥayāʾ* in their works. Additionally, Muslims across different regions have embraced *ḥayāʾ* as a core ethical value they wish to embody and cultivate.[10]

In classical Islamic philosophy, *ḥayāʾ* is linked to a wide array of synonymous Arabic words, such as *ʿār*, *hishma*, or *tawāḍuʿ*. For example, al-Farabi (d. 950) affirms that man must and can achieve happiness in life by cultivating a good/healthy soul. To attain this soul, one must perfect his behavior in accordance with the values of moderation (*tawassuṭ*) and balance (*iʿtidāl*). One of the virtues to attain this happiness, according to al-Farabi, is *tawāḍuʿ* or modesty. Moreover, for al-Farabi, to be a modest person, one must avoid dissimulation (*taṣannuʿ*) and lie (*mukhriqa*). Instead, one must be genuine (*ṣidq*) in one's efforts at embodying modesty in character and action.[11] Ibn Sina (d. 1037) discussed the term *ʿār*, which has been translated into "shame" in English. He linked this "*ʿār*" or "*shame*" to sexual activities, especially in relation to those women who could not follow reason (*ʿaql*) and are considered to easily succumb to their sexual desire (*shahwa*) to sleep with many men. Accordingly, women's behavior must be "regulated," so that they do not create social "chaos." In his own words:

> Since woman by right must be protected, inasmuch as she can share her sexual desire with many; (and since she) is much inclined to draw attention to herself and, in addition to that, is easily deceived and is less inclined to obey reason; and since sexual relation on her part (with many men) cause great disdain and shame.[12]

Al-Ghazali (d. 1111) also elaborates on the nature and the character of "*hishma*," in the sense of *ḥayāʾ* or shame, linking it to the love for a woman. According to Al-Ghazali, men favor the intellectual to the sensual in their pursuit of pleasure. Otherwise, they will feel ashamed and lose their dignity. He states,

> one desirous of dignity and leadership would hesitate (when confronted with the choice) between the loss of dignity and, for example, attaining his goal with the woman he loves when another (person) would know this and (the affair) would become widely known. He would protect his dignity, abandoning attainment of his (amorous) goal, belittling this for the sake of preserving his honour.[13]

From the classical Islamic legal perspective (*fiqh*), *ḥayāʾ* is, according to Marion H. Katz,[14] the affective trait to proper social functioning and adherence to the law. It is the disposition to form a Muslim moral self and, thus, to obey the law. In other words, *ḥayāʾ* is understood as the affective disposition inhibiting a person from actions that would incur social disapproval or result in loss of esteem. In this sense, *ḥayāʾ* is the combination of physical contraction, emotional discomfort, and social constraint produced by shame/modesty to avoid excessive physical or social self-display and to avoid embarrassment.

In contemporary Islamic philosophy, the Moroccan philosopher Taha ʿAbd al-Rahman is the most significant writer on Islamic modesty. In 2017, he published a trilogy entitled *Din al-Haya'* (The Religion of Modesty), in which he argues for an Islamic modernity. ʿAbd al-Rahman develops Islamic family ethics while critically evaluating Western family ethics and what he perceives as the decline of the family in the West.[15] In his view, family ethics centered around Muslim marriage is crucial for contemporary Islamic ethics. When both spouses live their marital bond based on authentic Islamic values, he argues, "modesty appears on their faces."[16] (See Van Raemdonck's Chapter 14 in this volume for an anthropological discussion of shame and modesty in the frame of Muslim marriage, and Hamelink's Chapter 9 for sexuality outside of Muslim marriages.)

Contemporary Social Scientific Explorations of Shame, Modesty, and Honor

Classical and very influential literature on issues pertaining to honor, shame, and modesty has been primarily written in the context of discussing Mediterranean cultures and societies, some of which focuses on Muslim contexts and therefore warrant a brief discussion. One such very influential scholarly work is *Honour and Shame: The Values of Mediterranean Society*,[17] edited by anthropologist John G. Peristiany. It is a seminal work in the field of anthropology and provides a deep understanding of the cultural values and beliefs of Mediterranean societies. The book examines how these values shape and influence social interactions, family dynamics, and personal identities in countries like Greece, Italy, and Spain. Peristiany argues that the importance placed on honor and shame is deeply ingrained in Mediterranean cultures and can be traced back to ancient traditions and social structures.[18] The book provides a detailed analysis of how these values manifest in various aspects of daily life, including courtship, marriage, gender roles, and political structures. Importantly for the aims of the current volume, Peristiany's book also highlights how the concepts of honor and shame are intertwined with notions of family and community. In Mediterranean societies, family honor is often seen as a collective responsibility, and individuals are expected to behave in ways that reflect positively on their family's reputation. The book examines how these expectations can lead to strict gender roles and expectations, particularly for women, who are often seen as the keepers of family honor. Duderija's Chapter 2 in this volume draws attention to these dynamics. Peristiany also highlights the ways in which honor and shame can lead to conflict and violence in Mediterranean societies. The book explores the cultural practices of vendetta, blood feuds, and honor killings and how these practices reflect the importance of maintaining family honor in these societies. Pribadi's Chapter 6 in this volume also examines the concept of shame and honor through these lenses of community/family and violence in Madura, Indonesia.

Another groundbreaking work on issues pertaining to honor, modesty, and shame is the book *Honour and Shame and the Unity of the Mediterranean*,[19] edited by anthropologist David D. Gilmore. It builds upon the work of Peristiany by examining the concepts of honor and shame in Mediterranean societies from a comparative perspective. Gilmore argues that honor and shame are not unique to Mediterranean societies but are prevalent in many other cultural traditions around the world. This is confirmed in this volume, which looks at cases in West Africa, South East Asia, New Zealand, and China. The book provides a detailed analysis of the cultural values and beliefs that underlie the concepts of honor and shame in Mediterranean societies and how these values are shared across different cultures. Gilmore highlights the importance of family honor and the influence of gender roles in shaping social dynamics in Mediterranean societies. Gilmore's analysis of the relationship between honor and shame and gender has been particularly influential. He argues, in concert with a number of chapters in this volume, that gender plays a significant role in the expression and management of honor and shame in Mediterranean societies and that women are often subject to stricter codes of honor and face greater social and physical consequences for violating these codes. In his words, "Honour is everywhere closely associated with sex." Its basic currency and measurement is the "shame" of women, by which Mediterraneanists mean female sexual chastity. Throughout the Mediterranean area, male honor derives from the struggle to maintain intact the shame of kinswomen, and this renders male reputation insecurely dependent upon female sexual conduct. Men are responsible for the shame of their women, "which is associated with sexual purity and their own honour derives in large measure from the way they discharge their responsibility." When men are unsuccessful in this, they are "shamed," that is, diminished in relation to other men.[20]

Gilmore argues further that the values of honor and shame "are deeply tied up with sexuality and power, with masculinity and gender relations."[21] These themes are discussed in several chapters in this volume. Gilmore's book has also contributed to the broader discussions on culture and morality.[22] This perspective challenges the view that morality is universal and fixed, and instead emphasizes the role of culture in shaping our ethical frameworks. Again, this view is also highlighted in the present volume in the context of many case studies.

The rest of this literature review goes beyond the Mediterranean context and focuses solely on Muslim contexts. Anthropologist Lila Abou-Lughod suggests that to properly understand the meaning of shame/modesty/honor in Islamic contexts, "the word's meaning should be sought not in obscure dictionaries of classical Arabic, but in everyday usage."[23] In line with this, the majority of the chapters in this book take an anthropological approach to understanding what *ḥayāʾ* means in both majority and minority contexts. At the same time, the first section of the book does engage with meanings and conceptualizations as they have been historically transmitted within the Islamic discursive tradition.[24] In fact, this volume's basic premise is that the discursive historical heritage and contemporary uses are interconnected and permanently in dialogue.

The process of transformation of the meaning of the word or the concept of *ḥayāʾ* occurs in specific contexts, where the discourse on modesty/shame is in permanent flux, or what we could describe as "looping" and "fluidity." By "looping," we wish to indicate how people invest *ḥayāʾ* with meanings that produce looping effects between past and future. In other words, behind a term such as *ḥayā'*, there is both a historical discursive reality and a new usage, which opens up future meanings while retaining a memory of the meanings of the past.[25] The contributions in this volume are concerned with religious text and ideas, with the specific aim of understanding how contemporary individuals give meaning to those ideas within their lives.[26] Individuals can rely on what they consider to be Islamic principles consciously, seeking to abide by its tenets both in terms of thought and morality. Others act in ways that are considered socioculturally Islamic but that are firmly incorporated in mundane, everyday social interaction.[27] In sum, the book focuses on how *ḥayā'* is perceived and understood by Muslims, in its relation to theological discourses of the past. Some of the chapters in this book engage with *ḥayā'* in the form of highly contextualized practices and attitudes through ethnography.[28]

Lila Abou-Lughod discusses the idea of honor in her seminal work among the Egyptian Bedouin Awlad Ali.[29] In this context, *ḥayā'* refers to *hishāma*, which consists of two dimensions: an internal state (feeling of shame such as discomfort or shyness and embarrassment/shame) and an external state (a way of acting that arises from these feelings, i.e., self-restraint in the public and private setting).[30] A similar fundamental division between experiencing shame and modesty as an inner state and performing shame and modesty in the form of external, social behavior is made in Chapters 1 and 3 of this volume, which focus, respectively, on crucial Sunni and Shiʿi conceptions within the Islamic discursive tradition. In *Writing Women's Worlds*, Abu-Lughod illustrates the meanings of modesty for the Bedouin Awlad Ali. For instance, for women, it means not wearing a short dress (as it is considered "naked"), not going out to a club, not eating together with men, not watching a movie where people hug and kiss each other, and wearing a headscarf/veil.[31] Women who breach these traditions are deemed immoral and are believed to indulge in shameful acts. Abu Lughod found that the concepts of modesty and shame in this Bedouin society mean following the traditions and customs of the tribes as living values, considering their traditions to stem from the traditions of the Prophet.

A landmark contribution to our understanding of Islamic modesty is found in Saba Mahmood's *Politics of Piety*, where she examines the "pious" practices of the women's mosque movement in Egypt at the cusp of the twenty-first century.[32] Mahmood examined the orthodox Islamic understanding of the virtues of female modesty or piety—of which veiling is an integral part and critical marker—through the lens of the Islamic discursive tradition that is interested in the formation of a particular articulation of embodied ethics. Mahmood explains that this approach to ethical self-cultivation is premised on a markedly different understanding of the concept of "agency, performativity, and resistance presupposed within liberal and poststructuralist feminist scholarship."[33] In this respect, Mahmood's main argument is that to understand the idea of modesty and veiling among these women, we must be attentive to its internal logic that is based on a particular "architecture of the self that undergirds a particular mode of living and attachment"[34] and specific conceptualizations of the notion of "personhood, knowledge, and experience."[35] Mahmood emphasizes that for the women she studied, their concept of modesty is considered divinely prescribed and necessitates the veiling of the woman's body as articulated in orthodox Islam, which considers veiling-based modesty as one of its highest feminine virtues.[36] Moreover,

Mahmood argues that veiling as a form of self-agency in this ethical matrix is regarded as *both* the means *and* the expression of piety and modesty in the process of formation of particular ethical subjects, rather than—as is often considered in liberal feminist or secular discourses—as a marker of women's subordination and passivity and an expression of a patriarchal Islam.

Mahmood's discussion of modesty is set in the context of orthodox women aiming for religious and moral self-improvement. The term *ḥayā'* has similarly been used in revivalist narratives of turning to Islam. For instance, Ellen Anne Mclarney discusses the Egyptian Shams al-Barudi's autobiographical writing on leaving her job as an actress and adopting a more conservative lifestyle. Al-Barudi's narrative speaks of moving from darkness to light, and the notion of *ḥayā'* was for her connected to "sexuality's manifestation in the social institutions of marriage, the family, and childrearing."[37] This volume, in contrast, does not engage with meanings of *ḥayā'* within revivalist movements but is more oriented toward everyday understandings of modesty within a variety of Islamic cultures. Chapter 12 by Nur Syafiqah Mohd Taufek and Norshahril Saat, however, focuses on the Malay minority in Singapore against the background of the South Asian *dakwah* revivalist movement.

International politics, war, and migration and colonial continuities in postcolonial contexts are crucial frameworks to be taken into account in order to understand modesty/shame within both majority and Muslim minority societies. Considerable scholarship has focused on the symbolical politics of the veil among immigrants in Western contexts. Several states promulgate dress regulations to discipline Muslim women's bodies. Annelies Moors analyzed this policy in France as the extension of colonial policies in which women's appearances are politicized in public: unveiled women turned into symbols of support of the French, while veiled women symbolized support for the national fight for an independent Algeria.[38] Until today, the veil in public imagery is associated with religious submission and passivity and unveiling with liberation and adherence to liberal and secular society.[39]

A relevant area of scholarship in this respect is the burgeoning literature on modest/pious fashion. Thimm's edited volume *(Re-)Claiming Bodies Through Fashion and Style Gendered Configurations in Muslim Contexts* seeks to broaden our views on gendered forms of religiosity/spirituality by discussing various ways of dressing, style, and fashion among global Muslim communities.[40] It highlights women's creativity and agency in this respect. Many contributors in the volume explore the link between dress, piety, and modesty, especially the role and function of the hijab. Similarly, Bucar's *Pious Fashion: How Muslim Women Dress*[41] investigates Muslim women's modest clothing in three Muslim majority contexts—Iran, Indonesia, and Turkey. She focuses on the wide range of meanings conveyed by what women in these contexts wear and argues that pious fashion is closely linked to communicating moral beliefs, especially modesty (however, differently understood in different contexts), and the associated cluster of values—namely, "protection, femininity, sexuality, and social order."[42] Pious fashion is also about cultivating ethics and character building. Moreover, Bucar argues that pious fashion can simultaneously both challenge and reinforce dominant sources of moral authority.[43] (See also Chapter 8 by Ambrosio in this volume on the political dimension of pious dress.)

Significant scholarship maintained a focus on Muslim religious agency following Mahmood's lead. Anthropological research showed how women negotiate religious ethical decisions about veiling or unveiling, handshaking or not handshaking, and praying at work within the limiting contours of liberal and secular Western states.[44] Pnina Werbner pointed at the essential role of the migratory context in shaping "normalizing discourses and discursive practices" by *ulama*, scholars, and experts about women as carriers, bearers, and holders of shame and honor of families, groups, and communities.[45] The importance of considering multiple dominant narratives that surround immigrant Muslim women is also emphasized by Jasmin Zine in her work on gendered Islamophobia among young Muslim women in Canada. She argues that women are "subject to patriarchal forms of regulation relating to their body and dress within the Muslim community, on the one hand, and negative stereotypes and gendered Islamophobia within mainstream society, on the other."[46] Indeed, rising xenophobic and Islamophobic sentiment in minority contexts impact on Muslim experience and religious practice (see Chapter 14 by Nisa for an engagement with the veil and modesty after the Islamophobic Christchurch attacks).

The connections between shame, modesty, and honor have been most commonly made in work investigating particular forms of gender violence. Shame is a cultural factor that plays a vital role in legitimizing and perpetrating honor-related violence and killing. In these cases, women are accused of staining family honor and bringing shame to it.[47] Set in the modern Egyptian context, Baudouin Dupret showed in his research on rape and debauchery cases that in common interpretation, "wearing provocatively" is viewed as intrinsically immodest conduct and a shameful act that makes a woman a target for rape or sexual assault.[48] While some authors focus on the connection between Islamic-based understandings of shame and honor and social behavior, other have warned against essentializing and reifying religion and culture, especially in Muslim minority contexts.[49] Jonathan Brown whose work focuses on the Prophetic and Islamic legal tradition argued that the concept of "honor killings" is not endorsed within the Islamic discursive tradition.[50] Oberwittler and Kasselt, in the context of discussing the role of religion, and Islam in particular, in honor killings argue in favor of an indirect role of the former in relation to the latter. In their words,

> Some interpretations of Islamic law, such as those that promote the lawfulness of husbands' physical violence against wives, the criminalization of pre- and extramarital sexual relationships, and the use of flogging or stoning if prosecuted as *ḥadd* (religious) crimes (which does not happen in most Muslim countries), may contribute indirectly to honour killings.[51]

Similarly, Payton and Khan argued that honor-related crimes are most significantly connected to marriage and family systems, rather than gendered and sexual behavior per se. Based on research in Iraqi Kurdistan but drawing from larger historical and anthropological data, Payton and Khan argue that women's honor serves as symbolical capital within complex systems of kin relating.[52] In a similar understanding of honor as symbolical capital, Katherine Ewing analyzed male Muslim experiences in a European context of discrimination and racism as characterized by "stolen honor" because of the effects of stigmatized masculinity.[53]

This volume discusses honor in its various guises and beyond the more common understandings of honor related exclusively to transgressing gender and sexual norms. Chapter 2 by Adis Duderija connects modesty, shame, and honor with Islamic conceptions of masculinity and femininity that have strongly shaped classical Islamic interpretative tradition in the form of what he terms the *gender oppositionality thesis*, which conceptually links male honor to female (sexual) behavior, and argues for a deconnecting and disentangling of this conceptual linking in favor of non-patriarchal gender norms that are characteristic and constitutive of progressive Islam. Danilo Marino argues in Chapter 1 about how the concept of *murūʾa* and *ḥayāʾ* often overlap. *Murūʾa* then refers to self-respect and the ability "to live up to certain standards both in terms of material resources and moral strength." This sense of self-respect and the ability to live up to certain standards is also central to conceptions of honor and masculinity among male Tuareg refugees, as discussed in Chapter 5 by Souleymane Diallo. Chapter 6 by Yanwar Pribadi, on the other hand, contextualizes the concept of honor in the very specific settings of Madura, where it gains specific meanings as appropriate responses to personal insults. Other contexts in which honor is discussed in this book include the clinical setting of undergoing biomedical treatments in Italy (Chapter 10 by Federica Sona) and eating and drinking among South Asian British Muslims (Chapter 11 by John Lever and Irem Ozgoren Kinli).

The originality of this volume lies in combining Islamic studies with other insights from the humanities (history) and social scientific approaches (sociology, anthropology) to discuss Islamic practices and experiences of shame, modesty, and honor. The book engages with historically transmitted ideas within the Islamic discursive tradition as well as contemporary Muslims' grappling with these notions. The book examines the concept of *ḥayāʾ* from multiple perspectives, both in majority and minority contexts and makes, therefore, a valuable contribution to the literature.

Brief Presentation of the Chapters

The chapters in this volume invite readers to see how people perceive *ḥayāʾ* and construct lexicons of modesty in interaction with inherited Islamic tradition and their immediate sociocultural and political environments. Together, the chapters argue for the need to adopt a dynamic understanding of a crucial and highly complex set of Islamic values surrounding *ḥayāʾ*. The book is divided into three parts and consists of fifteen chapters, including an Introduction. The first part consists of three chapters discussing various concepts about *ḥayāʾ* from both Sunni and Shiʿa perspectives. The second part explores shame, modesty, and honor in majority contexts in Jordan, Niger, Indonesia, Malaysia, Turkey, and Tanzania (Zanzibar). The third part includes chapters that explore the same issues in minority contexts in Italy, Great Britain, Singapore, China, and New Zealand.

Reflections on Various Conceptualizations

The first section is theoretical in nature and is devoted to general definitions of the concepts of honor, shame, and modesty and how they were discussed in the classical Islamic tradition. In his chapter, Danilo Marino discusses the meanings and forms of *ḥayā'* (shame/modesty) according to medieval Arabic sources and discusses them in relation to the concept of *murū'a* (honor/dignity). He argues that both concepts can be best understood together. Based on a study of the *makārim al-akhlāq* genre as well as the advice literature, he proposes a definition of *ḥayā'* as "on the one hand the ability to control one's own impulses and desires and from the other it means showing concern, fear, attentiveness over the fact that a potential observer, the people, or God, may express a negative assessment over actions perceived as bad." Whereas *ḥayā'* can be understood as a sense of awareness about one's moral conduct vis-à-vis different entities—namely, oneself, God, and the larger community—*murū'a* refers more specifically to the requirement to maintain a coherence between how one behaves privately and publicly. Finally, Marino argues that *murū'a* and *ḥayā'* were often discussed in medieval Arabic sources in relation to the acquisition and management of personal and material wealth. Both concepts often appeared to talk about proper behaviour in the face of loss of wealth and social status.

In a second conceptual chapter, Adis Duderija bridges historical and contemporary times with a discussion of shame and honor in the mainstream Islamic interpretative tradition, on the one hand, and in theorizing of progressive Islam, on the other. His focus is on analyzing the conceptual relationship between patriarchal (male) honor and so-called female modesty laws. This link is based on dominant constructions of femininity and masculinity within the mainstream Islamic interpretative tradition premised on what he terms the *gender oppositionality* thesis that conceptually links male honor to a particular understanding of femininity, female sexuality, and (perceived) female sexual behavior. Duderija argues for the need to break this conceptual link and proposes alternative views that have been established within his theorizing of progressive Islam over the past decade and a half.

Chapter 3 continues the conceptual and theological discussion of the modesty, shame, and honor nexus, but then with a focus on the Persianate world. In this respect, Amélie Neuve-Eglise examines some uses of the concept of *ḥayā'* in Shi'ite hadiths as well as in theological works and Sufi treatises composed by Muslim scholars of the Persianate world between the tenth and seventeenth centuries. These sources and publications offer a wide range of interpretations of this idea of *ḥayā'* and its subjects, which include human beings, angels, and God. She makes an effort to demonstrate how these evaluations of modesty and shame are characterized by tensions that highlight the hazy and fluid borders between what can be spoken or seen and what should be kept silent and hidden. Despite the fact that *ḥayā'* is frequently portrayed as affects that limit and prevent, some authors contend that they may also be praxis and resources. It establishes a gap between complete transparency and opacity in the interaction between God and humans that can facilitate forgiveness and even salvation.

Shame, Modesty, and Honor in Islamic Environments

The section "Islamic environments" further offers discussions of the notions of shame, modesty, and honor through empirical and anthropological research of contemporary lived experiences in different geographical contexts. Chapters 4 and 5 examine experiences in migration and refugee contexts. An Van Raemdonck examines shame and modesty in the context of marriage by investigating narratives of Syrian refugee women in Jordan. Souleymane Diallo investigates Muslim masculinity among Bellah Tuareg refugees from Mali in Niger. Van Raemdonck argues that dominant understandings of Muslim marriage rely significantly on social values connected to modest behavior and honor, yet the study of Muslim marriage practices has rarely given attention to ethics and morality. She conceptualizes modesty norms in the context of marriage through expectations and performances of gender roles inside and outside the home. Anthropological research with Syrian women in Jordan shows a variety of ways in which women negotiate gendered marital expectations. In both chapters, the context of migration and refuge is crucial for understanding changes of social practice and experiences of modesty, shame, and honor. Refugee family lives are in both cases characterized by men's loss of status, property, and employment. This aspect figures centrally in Diallo's Chapter 5. He addresses how the Bellah articulate local notions of shame and honor in connection to gender, masculinity and Muslim identity, contributing to the scholarship on these previously enslaved people and their descendants. Diallo demonstrates that the Bellah in exile experience a loss in respectability and social status and shows how feelings of shame and dishonor are related to humanitarian aid practices of food distribution and refugee registration in the camp.

Chapters 6 and 7 continue to present research in Muslim majority contexts. Yanwar Pribadi discusses the meanings of *carok* and shame in the island of Madura, Indonesia, and Muhamad Ali's Chapter 7 focuses on local articulations of modesty and *malu* (shame) in the Malaysian context. Pribadi discusses the complexities of *carok* actions, which is a particular social practice specific to the Madurese context that has been decreasing in recent times, yet remains present until today. *Carok* is tightly interwoven with local understandings of shame and honor. It is a violent act of revenge that is undertaken when one needs to overcome shame and feels their honor has been taken away, not rarely resulting in severe violence or killing. Pribadi analyzes *carok* in comparison with and in distinction from honor killings. Additionally, he locates the practice in relation to Madurese gangster and fighting culture, a local political culture of strongmen, dominant and non-dominant forms of Islam, and gender norms. By demonstrating the highly specific characteristics of *carok*—acts of revenge that both men and women can undertake—Pribadi contributes to contemporary understandings of the nexus among shame, modesty, and honor in the Indonesian context. Muhamad Ali's chapter on modesty and *malu* offers another highly contextualized analysis of the use of the term *malu* in Malaysia. This chapter discusses historical constructions of modesty and shame by studying the use of the term *malu* in Malay court chronicles, proverbs, literature, and writings by modern intellectuals. Ali then proceeds to explore different ways in which classic understandings of modesty are contested and negotiated in contemporary times. Modest fashion businesses, for instance, raise the question of whether pious, modestly dressed women ought to be concerned about being fashionable. Activists and social movement groups, such as Sisters in Islam, challenge mainstream understandings of modesty and dress code by emphasizing individual ethics and the equality of women and men when it comes to modest behavior and outlook. The LGBTQ presence in Malaysia poses the highest challenge to mainstream heteronormative gender and modesty norms. Ali concludes with a nuanced analysis of LGBTQ individuals' differentiation from, yet consideration of, dominant social norms.

Chapter 8 by Alberto Ambrosio examines the rhetoric on dress code at the peak of reform in Republican Turkey (between 1925 and 1934). By focusing on an Ottoman pamphlet written by the theologian İskilipli Ātif Hôca (d. 1926) that focuses on the "Hat Act," he argues that a change of paradigm occurred: from modesty as a moral issue to a "political interpretation of modesty as a stronghold against Western culture." As general political reform presented modernization and Westernization, counterarguments against dress reform are "not directly centred on modesty—be it moral or religious—but on the political dimension of such fashionable dress, namely opposing European, and by extension non-Muslim, fashion." Against the historical background of Ottoman dress code regulations that distinguish gender, ethnicity, and religious affiliation, Ambrosio analyzes modesty as an almost neglected aspect in the early Republican debate on dress code.

The last chapter in Islamic environment focuses on Tanzania. "Heshima and Sexuality beyond Marriage: Gendered Interpretations of Morality in Zanzibar" by Marloes Hamelink similarly presents a nuanced discussion of women's negotiation of gender and sexuality roles within dominant social norms. Hamelink contributes to scholarship on women's agency within Islamic legal structures beyond analyses of cultural patriarchy and beyond the binary of female emancipation versus oppression. She sketches the context of Zanzibar as one in which female sexuality and pleasure play a recognizable role in women's personal development. This feature is not in contradiction but rather aligns with the space and roles women navigate within Zanzibari Islamic culture. Hamelink explores on the basis of long-term ethnographic research how women navigate dominant social expectations of female sexuality and respectability by upholding and contesting social norms through secrecy. Women may choose to refuse sex, sexually please their husbands, or seek sexuality outside of marriage.

Shame, Modesty, and Honor in Non-Muslim Countries

The third section of this volume treats non-Muslim countries. Contributions offer fresh approaches to the modesty, shame, and honor nexus by investigating these themes in various contexts, including in biomedical treatments and in everyday life, such as eating and drinking practices. Others show that modesty remains tightly connected to gender and sexuality norms while regaining new meanings connected to their minority status as well. In her chapter "Coping with Honor, Shame and Modesty: Muslims Undergoing Biomedical Treatments in Italy" (Chapter 10), Federica Sona examines Italian Muslim prospective parents visiting fertility clinics. The fertility clinic is the central place in which the views on modesty and shame have been investigated from the perspective of Muslim-intended parents, religious authorities, and non-Muslim medical personnel. She argues that Muslim patients' behavior shows "(anticipatory or hypothetical) shame and the fear of ethical, moral or social disapprobation." In her analysis, Sona identifies three main areas where *ḥayāʾ* is at play in the case of couples undergoing fertility treatment: concerning gender seclusion norms (for instance, female patients consulting male doctors), family honor/masculinity, and social stigmatization.

In Chapter 11, John Lever and İrem Özgören Kınlı discuss the politics of eating and drinking among South Asian British Muslims. Constructions of shame and honor do not center around gender and sexuality norms in this case but are rediscovered and given new meanings in the context of Muslim minority identity politics in the West. The authors rely on Norbert Elias' figurational sociology to analyze the cultural contradictions in eating and drinking practices among second- and third-generation South Asian migrants living in Manchester. Eating and drinking is highly connected to expressions of collective religious identity. Respondents who closely identify with (Muslim) we-groups feel more pressure to follow halal eating and drinking rules, and men tend to feel responsible to protect collective honor. Those who socialize more with non-Muslim communities feel less shame when engaging in non-halal eating and drinking.

Chapter 12 by Nur Syafiqah Mohd Taufek and Norshahril Saat explores modesty in the context of Malay Muslim minority women living in Singapore. This analysis is set against the background of the revivalist *dakwah* movement that emerged in Southeast Asia in the late 1970s. The authors interrogate the current status of the long-time dominant traditionalist-revivalist thought among the Malay minority in Singapore. The focus lies on two episodes in public debate: when Muslim parents started a movement for the right of pupils to wear headscarves in public schools and later of professionals to wear the headscarf in jobs in the public sector, and second, a controversy that was sparked by sexism in a popular podcast. Based on social media analysis of dominant Muslim traditionalist voices, the authors argue that the *dakwah* movement transformed the hijab from a garment important for modesty to one indicative of Muslim identity. They consider that the contemporary dominant voices within the *dakwah* traditionalist movement promote gender inequality and perpetuate sexism.

In Chapter 13 Wai-Yip Ho contextualizes understandings of modesty among Chinese Muslims within the specific context of China and Confucianist values. The author suggests that "the evolving notions of Islamic modesty connect with Muslims' bodies and dispositions regulated under the ideological forces in Chinese history." Three distinct periods are differentiated: premodern Confucianism, modern Westernization, and the more recent patriotism and Sinicization campaign since 2016 under president Xi Jinping. The shift from premodern to modern understandings is characterized by a shift from modesty governed by an invisible and internal morality to a visible, external, and gendered idea of modesty. His analysis recalls the earlier distinction in Chapter 1 of *ḥayāʾ* in front of the self (internal) and *ḥayāʾ* in front of the community (external). In more recent years, Muslim life has been strongly determined and regulated against the backdrop of the Sinicization of religion and minorities. Ho argues that "the government assimilates the Muslim minorities by defining the norm of Islamic modesty and sanctioning the 'abnormal' or 'extreme' practices." Ideology is an important lens in all three historical instances through which to understand dominant conceptions of modesty.

The final chapter (Chapter 14), "The Headscarf and Modesty in Multicultural Aotearoa New Zealand: A Post Christchurch Attack Story" by Eva Nisa, presents a discussion of modesty and the veil in the context of non-Muslims wearing the veil to show solidarity with the Muslim minority after the 2019 Christchurch Mosque attack. Nisa analyzes the aftermath of this Islamophobic violence in multicultural New Zealand. A large part of the population showed support, love, and solidarity with the Muslim minority, including by symbolically wearing the veil in public. Opponents of this act of solidarity, however, "believe this might iconise the headscarf as the sole identifier of their Muslim identity and normalise the practice."

***

Having presented the outline of the chapters it becomes evident that the term *ḥayāʾ* in Islam (shame, modesty, and honor) in both Muslim majority and minority contexts shows a great variety, yet also similarity in meaning across historical periods and geographical areas. The numerous controversies with respect to *ḥayāʾ* are often linked to the different sociocultural, religious, and political layers of meaning attributed to attitudes of shame, modesty, and honor. The volume offers a more precise and better-grounded understanding of the specificity of *ḥayāʾ* in the Islamic tradition, as also its diverse cross-readings, interpretations, and conceptualizations in a great variety of contexts.

Notes

1. Eli Alshech, "Out of Sight and Therefore Out of Mind: Early Sunni Islamic Modesty Regulations and the Creation of Spheres of Privacy," *Journal of Near Eastern Studies* 66 (2007), 267–90; Fedwa Maulty-Douglas, *Woman's Body, Woman's Word: Gender and Discourse in Arabo-Islamic Writing* (Princeton, NJ: Princeton University Press, 1991); Fatima Mernissi, *Beyond the Veil: Male–Female Dynamics in Muslim Society* (London: Saqi, 2011); Fatna Sabbah, *Woman in the Muslim Subconscious* (New York: Pergamon Press, 1984).
2. Alina Alak, Adis Duderija, and Kristine Hissong, *Islam and Gender: Major Issues and Debates* (London: Routledge, 2020), 47–9.
3. Asma Barlas, *Believing Women in Islam: Unreading Patriarchal Interpretations of the Qur'an* (Austin: University of Austin Press, 2002), 53–8.
4. Sahih Bukhari 146, 402, 4891; Sahih Muslim 1428, 2170, 2399, Musnad Ahmad 157, 12023, 25877; Sahih Tirmidzi 3218, see Abubakar al-Qurtubi, *al-Jamiʿ li-Ahkam al-Qur'an* (Beirut: Mu'assasa al-Risala, 1427/2006), vol. 17, 202–3.
5. Emi Goto, "Qur'an and the Veil: Contexts and Interpretations of the Revelation," *International Journal of Asian Studies* 1, no. 2 (2004), 277–95, 286.
6. Sahar Amer, *What Is Veiling* (Chapel Hill: University of North Carolina Press, 2014), 30–1.

7. This hadith was narrated by Muslim, see al-Nawawi, *Sahih Muslim bi-Sharh al-Nawawi* (Cairo: al-Matbaʿa al-Misriyya bi-l Azhar, 1347/1929) vol. 2, 5–7.
8. This hadith was narrated by al-Bukhari hadis no. 5884, see Ibn Hajar al-Asqalani, *Fatḥ al-Bari fi Sharh Sahih al-Bukhari* (Riyad: Maktaba al-Malik Fahd al-Wataniyya, 1421/2001), vol. 10, p. 529 and see also p. 539.
9. This hadith was narrated by al-Bukhari hadis no. 5902, see al-Asqalani, *Fatḥ al-Bari*, vol. 10, 539–40.
10. Zahra Ayubi, Gendered *Morality: Classical Islamic Ethics of the Self, Family and Society* (New York: Columbia University Press, 2019).
11. Al-Farabi, "*Kitab al-Tanbih ʿala Sabil al-Saʿada*," in *Arbaʿ Rasa'il Falsafiyya al-Hakim al-Farabi*, edited by Jaʿfar Al Yasin (Iran: Matba'a Thabathabaʿi, 1371/1951), 47–52.
12. Avicenna, *The Metaphysics of the Healing. Al-Shifā': al-Ilāhiyyāt*, A Parallel Arabic-English Text translated, introduced, and annotated by Michael E. Marmura (Provo, Utah: Brigham University Press, 2005), 373.
13. Al-Ghazali, *The Incoherence of the Philosophers: Tahāfut al-Falāsifa*. A Parallel Arabic-English Text translated, introduced, and annotated by Michael E. Marmura (Provo, Utah: Brigham University Press, 2000), 210.
14. Marion Holmes Katz, "Shame (*Ḥayāʾ*) as an Affective Disposition in Islamic Legal Thought," *Journal of Law, Religion and State* 3 (2014), 139–69.
15. Abdessamad Belhaj, "'The Fall of the Western Family.' Ṭāhā 'Abd al-Raḥmān's Critical Islamic Ethics," *ReOrient* 4, no. 1 (2018), 24–43.
16. Ibid., 38.
17. Julian Pitt-Rivers Peristiany (ed.), *Honour and Shame: The Values of Mediterranean Society* (London: Weidenfeld and Nicholson, 1965).
18. Ibid.
19. David D. Gilmore (ed.), *Honour and Shame and the Unity of the Mediterranean* (Washington, DC: American Anthropological Association, 1987).
20. Ibid., 4.
21. Ibid., 16.
22. Gilmore, *Honour and Shame*.
23. Abu Lughod, *Veiled Sentiments*, 107.
24. Talal Asad, *The Idea of an Anthropology of Islam* (Washington, DC: Center for Contemporary Arab Studies, Georgetown University, 1986).
25. Danièle Hervieu-Léger, "La transmission religieuse en modernité: éléments pour la construction d'un objet de recherche," *Social Compass* 44, no. 1 (1997), 131–43.
26. John R. Bowen, *A New Anthropology of Islam* (Cambridge: Cambridge University Press, 2012).
27. S. Schielke and L. Debevec, *Ordinary Lives and Grand Schemes: An Anthropology of Everyday Religion* (New York: Berghahn Books, 2012).
28. Baudouin Dupret, Thomas Pierret, Paulo G. Pinto, and Kathryn Spellman-Poots (eds.), *Ethnographies of Islam: Ritual Performances and Everyday Practices* (Edinburgh: Edinburgh University Press, 2013).
29. Lila Abu Lughod, *Veiled Sentiments: Honour and Poetry in a Bedouin* Society (California: University of California Press, 2016), see esp. sub-chapter on "Hishama Reconsidered: Deference and the Denial of Sexuality," 152–67, on "Honour: The Moral Basis of Hierarchy," 85–103, and on "Hasham: Honour of the Weak," 103–17.
30. The objective of *ḥayāʾ/hishama* is to teach people to understand social contexts and to act appropriately within them. *Hishama* is emotional discomfort (shame) and active self-control in social contexts, Abu Lughod, *Veiled Sentiments*, 112–17.

31. Lila Abu-Lughod, *Writing Women's Worlds: Bedouin Stories* (California: University of California Press, 1993), ch. 5: Honour and Shame, 175–208.
32. Saba Mahmood, *The Politics of Piety: Islamic Revival and the Feminist Subject* (Princeton, NJ: Princeton University Press, 2005).
33. Ibid., 153.
34. Ibid., 166.
35. Ibid., 16.
36. Ibid., 155.
37. Ellen Anne McLarney, *Soft Force: Women in Egypt's Islamic Awakening* (Princeton, NJ: Princeton University Press, 2015), 164–5.
38. Annelies Moors, "Colonial Traces? Islamic Dress, Gender, and the Public Presence of Islam," in *Colonial and Post-Colonial Governance of Islam: Continuities and Ruptures*, edited by Marce Maussen, Veit Bader, and Annelies Moors (Amsterdam: Amsterdam University Press, 2011), 135–53.
39. Alia Al-Saji, "The Racialization of Muslim Veils: A Philosophical Analysis," *Philosophy & Social Criticism* 36, no. 8 (2010), 875–902.
40. Viola Thimm (ed.), *(Re-)Claiming Bodies through Fashion and Style Gendered Configurations in Muslim Contexts* (New York: Palgrave, 2021).
41. Liz Bucar, *Pious Fashion: How Muslim Women Dress* (Cambridge, MA: Harvard University Press, 2017).
42. Bucar, *Pious Fashion*, 174.
43. Ibid.
44. Nadia Fadil, "Managing Affects and Sensibilities: The Case of Not-Handshaking and Not-Fasting," *Social Anthropology* 17, no. 4 (2009), 439–54; Nadia Fadil, "Not-/Unveiling as An Ethical Practice," *Feminist Review* 98, no. 1 (2011), 83–109; Nadia Fadil, "Performing the Salat [Islamic Prayers] at Work: Secular and Pious Muslims Negotiating the Contours of the Public in Belgium," *Ethnicities* 13, no. 6 (2013), 729–50; Jeanette Jouilli, *Pious Practice and Secular Constraints: Women in the Islamic Revival in Europe* (Stanford, CA: Stanford University Press, 2015).
45. Pnina Werbner, "Veiled Interventions in Pure Space: Honour, Shame and Embodied Struggles among Muslims in Britain and France," *Theory, Culture & Society* 24, no. 2 (2007), 161–86.
46. Jasmin Zina, "Unveiled Sentiments: Gendered Islamophobia and Experiences of Veiling among Muslim Girls in a Canadian Islamic School," *Equity & Excellence in Education* 39, no. 3 (2006), 239–52.
47. Amani M. Awwad, "Gossip, Scandal, Shame and Honour Killing: A Case for Social Constructionism and Hegemonic Discourse," *Social Thought & Research* 24, no. 1/2 (2001), 39–52.
48. Baudouin Dupret, "La typification des atteintes aux bonnes mœurs: Approche praxéologique d'une affaire égyptienne," *Revue Internationale de Sémiotique Juridique* 10, no. 33 (1998), 303–22; Baudouin Dupret, "Normality, Responsibility, Morality: Virginity and Rape in an Egyptian Legal Context," in *Muslim Tradition and Modern Techniques of Power*, edited by A. Salvatore (Münster: LIT Verlag, 2001), 165–83.
49. A. K. Gill, C. Strange, and K. Roberts, *"Honour" Killing and Violence: Theory, Policy and Practice* (London: Palgrave Macmillan, 2014).
50. Jonathan Brown, "Islam Forbids Honour Killing," in *Honour Killings*, edited by Liza Ikdzikowski (New York: Greenhaven, 2018), 71–7.

51. Dietrich Oberwittler and Julia Kasselt, "Honour Killings," in *The Oxford Handbook of Gender, Sex and Crime*, edited by Rosemary Gartner and Bill McCarthy (Oxford: Oxford University Press, 2014), 653.
52. J. Payton and D. Khan, *Honour and the Political Economy of Marriage: Violence against Women in the Kurdistan Region of Iraq* (New Brunswick, NJ: Rutgers University Press, 2019).
53. K. P. Ewing, *Stolen Honour: Stigmatizing Muslim Men in Berlin* (Stanford, CA: Stanford University Press, 2008).

Bibliography

Abu Lughod, Lila. *Veiled Sentiments: Honour and Poetry in a Bedouin Society*. California: University of California Press, 2016.

Alak, Alina, Adis Duderija, and Kristine Hissong, *Islam and Gender: Major Issues and Debates*. London: Routledge, 2020.

Al-Asqalani, Ibn Hajar. *Fath al-Bari fi Sharh Sahih al-Bukhari*. Riyad: Maktaba al-Malik Fahd al-Wataniyya, 1421/2001, vol. 10.

Al-Farabi. "*Kitab al-Tanbih ʿala Sabil al-Saʿada*." In "*Arbaʿ Rasa'il Falsafiyya al-Hakim al-Farabi*. Edited by Jaʿfar Al Yasin, 45–84. Iran: Matba'a Thabathabaʿi, 1371/1951.

Al-Ghazali. *The Incoherence of the Philosophers. Tahāfut al-Falāsifa*. A Parallel Arabic-English Text translated, introduced, and annotated by Michael E. Marmura. Provo, Utah: Brigham University Press, 2000.

Al-Nawawi. *Sahih Muslim bi-Sharh al-Nawawi*. Cairo: al-Matbaʿa al-Misriyya bi-l Azhar, 1347/1929. vol. 2.

Alshech, Eli. "Out of Sight and Therefore Out of Mind: Early Sunnī Islamic Modesty Regulations and the Creation of Spheres of Privacy." *Journal of Near Eastern Studies* 66 (2007): 267–90.

Al-Saji, Alia. "The Racialization of Muslim Veils: A Philosophical Analysis." *Philosophy & Social Criticism* 36, no. 8 (2010): 875–902.

Amer, Samar. *What Is Veiling*. Chapel Hill: University of North Carolina Press, 2014.

Asad, Talal. *The Idea of an Anthropology of Islam*. In Occasional Papers Series. Washington, DC: Center for Contemporary Arab Studies, Georgetown University, 1986.

Avicenna. *The Metaphysics of the Healing. Al-Shifā': al-Ilāhiyyāt*. A Parallel Arabic-English Text translated, introduced, and annotated by Michael E. Marmura. Provo. Utah: Brigham University Press, 2005.

Al-Qurtubi, Abubakar. *al-Jamiʿ li-Ahkam al-Qur'an*. Beirut, Mu'assasa al-Risala, 1427/2006.

Awwad, Amani M. "Gossip, Scandal, Shame and Honour Killing: A Case for Social Constructionism and Hegemonic Discourse." *Social Thought & Research* 24, no. 1/2 (2001): 39–52.

Ayubi, Zahra. *Gendered Morality: Classical Islamic Ethics of the Self, Family and Society*. New York: Columbia University Press, 2019.

Bauer, Karen. *Gender Hierarchy in the Qurʾan: Medieval Interpretations, Modern Responses*. Cambridge: Cambridge University Press, 2015.

Belhaj, Abdessamad. "The Fall of the Western Family. Ṭāhā 'Abd al-Raḥmān's Critical Islamic Ethics." *ReOrient* 4, no. 1 (2018): 24–43.

Bowen, John R. *A New Anthropology of Islam*. Cambridge: Cambridge University Press, 2012.
Brown, Jonathan. "Islam Forbids Honour Killing." In *Honour Killings*. Edited by Liza Ikdzikowski, 71–7. New York: Greenhaven, 2018.
Bucar, Liz. *Pious Fashion: How Muslim Women Dress*. Cambridge, MA: Harvard University Press 2017.
Chaudhry, Ayesha. *Domestic Violence and the Islamic Tradition: Ethics, Law, and the Muslim Discourse on Gender*. Oxford: Oxford University Press, 2013.
Dupret Baudouin, Thomas Pierret, Paulo G. Pinto, and Kathryn Spellman-Poots (eds.). *Ethnographies of Islam: Ritual Performances and Everyday Practices*. Edinburgh: Edinburgh University Press, 2013.
Dupret, Baudouin. "La typification des atteintes aux bonnes mœurs: Approche praxéologique d'une affaire égyptienne." *Revue Internationale de Sémiotique Juridique* 10, no. 33 (1998): 303–22.
Dupret, Baudouin. "Normality, Responsibility, Morality: Virginity and Rape in an Egyptian Legal Context." In *Muslim Tradition and Modern Techniques of Power*. Edited by A. Salvatore, 165–83. Münster: LIT Verlag, 2001 (*Yearbook of the Sociology of Islam* 3).
El Omari Dina, Julia Hammer, and Mouhanad Khorchide (eds.). *Muslim Women and Gender Justice Concepts, Sources, and Histories*. New York: Routledge, 2020.
Ewing, Katherine Pratt. *Stolen Honour: Stigmatizing Muslim Men in Berlin*. Stanford, CA: Stanford University Press, 2008.
Fadil, Nadia. "Managing Affects and Sensibilities: The Case of Not-Handshaking and Not-Fasting." *Social Anthropology* 17, no. 4 (2009): 439–54.
Fadil, Nadia. "Not-/Unveiling as an Ethical Practice." *Feminist Review* 98, no. 1 (2011): 83–109.
Fadil, Nadia. "Performing the *Salat* [Islamic Prayers] at Work: Secular and Pious Muslims Negotiating the Contours of the Public in Belgium." *Ethnicities* 13, no. 6 (2013): 729–50.
Gill, Aisha K., Carolyn Strange, and Karl Roberts. *"Honour" Killing and Violence: Theory, Policy and Practice*. London: Palgrave Macmillan, 2014.
Gilmore, David D. (ed.). *Honour and Shame and the Unity of the Mediterranean*. Washington, DC: American Anthropological Association, 1987.
Goto, Emi. "Qur'an and the Veil: Contexts and Interpretations of the Revelation." *International Journal of Asian Studies* 1 (2004): 277–95.
Hervieu-Léger, Danièle. "La transmission religieuse en modernité: éléments pour la construction d'un objet de recherche." *Social Compass* 44, no. 1 (1997): 131–43.
Howe, Justine. *Routledge Handbook of Islam and Gender*. New York: Routledge, 2020.
Idriss, Maher, and Tahir Abbas (eds.). *Honour, Violence, Women and Islam*. London: Routledge, 2010.
Jouili, Jeanette. *Pious Practice and Secular Constraints: Women in the Islamic Revival in Europe*. Stanford, CA: Stanford University Press, 2015.
Katz, Marion Holmes. "Shame (*Ḥayāʾ*) as an Affective Disposition in Islamic Legal Thought." *Journal of Law, Religion and State* 3 (2014): 139–69.
Lazreg, Marnia. *Questioning the Veil: Open Letter to Muslim Women*. Princeton, NJ: Princeton University Press, 2009.
Mahmood, Saba. *The Politics of Piety: Islamic Revival and the Feminist Subject*. Princeton, NJ: Princeton University Press, 2005.

Maulty-Douglas, Fedwa. *Woman's Body, Woman's Word: Gender and Discourse in Arabo-Islamic Writing*. Princeton, NJ: Princeton University Press, 1991.
McLarney, Ellen Anne. *Soft Force. Women in Egypt's Islamic Awakening*. Princeton, NJ: Princeton University Press, 2015.
Mernissi, Fatima. *Beyond the Veil: Male-Female Dynamics in Muslim Society*. Cambridge, MA: Schekman, 1975.
Moors, Annelies. "Colonial Traces? Islamic Dress, Gender, and the Public Presence of Islam." In *Colonial and Post-Colonial Governance of Islam: Continuities and Ruptures*. Edited by Marce Maussen, Veit Bader, and Annelies Moors, 135–53. Amsterdam: Amsterdam University Press, 2011.
Oberwittler, Dietrich, and Julia Kasselt. "Honour Killings." In *The Oxford Handbook of Gender, Sex and Crime*. Edited by Rosemary Gartner and Bill McCarthy, 652–70. Oxford: Oxford University, Press, 2014.
Payton, Joanne, and Deeyah Khan. *Honour and the Political Economy of Marriage: Violence against Women in the Kurdistan Region of Iraq*. New Brunswick, NJ: Rutgers University Press, 2019.
Peristiany, John G. (ed.). *Honour and Shame: The Values of Mediterranean Society*. London: Weidenfeld and Nicholson, 1965.
Robertson, Roland. "Glocalisation: Time-Space and Homogeneity-Heterogeneity." In *Global Modernities*. Edited by Mike Featherstone, Scott Lash, and Roland Robertson, 25–44. London: Sage, 1995.
Sabbah, Fatna. *Woman in the Muslim Subconscious*. New York: Pergamon Press, 1984.
Sirri, Lana. *Islamic Feminism Discourses on Gender and Sexuality in Contemporary Islam*. New York: Routledge, 2021.
Thimm, Viola (ed.). *(Re-)Claiming Bodies through Fashion and Style Gendered Configurations in Muslim Contexts*. New York: Palgrave, 2021.
Werbner, Pnina. "Veiled Interventions in Pure Space: Honour, Shame and Embodied Struggles among Muslims in Britain and France." *Theory, Culture & Society* 24, no. 2 (2007): 161–86.
Zine, Jasmin. "Unveiled Sentiments: Gendered Islamophobia and Experiences of Veiling among Muslim Girls in a Canadian Islamic School." *Equity & Excellence in Education* 39, no. 3 (2016): 239–52.

Part I

Shame, Modesty, and Honor: Reflections on Various Conceptualizations

1

Shame and *Murūʾa* in Medieval Islam

Danilo Marino

Introduction

In her article about shame in medieval Islamic legal thought,[1] Marion Holmes Katz has demonstrated that *ḥayāʾ* and *murūʾa* functioned in a similar way insofar as both were centered around the attentiveness toward the opinion of others—that is, avoiding blame and social disapprobation. However, she also notes that the sources remain ambivalent as in whether *ḥayāʾ*, understood as "the affective disposition inhibiting a person from actions that would incur disapproval or disesteem"[2] can be always considered relevant from a legal perspective. Similarly, if the adherence to "social standards of dignified comportment"[3] implied by *murūʾa* cannot be ruled out in the legal discussion on bearing witness (*ʿadāla*) in particular, its overall impact in *fiqh* remains still relatively marginal. In other words, if some shame-producing occasions, such as those pertaining to the violation of privacy, are also punishable offenses,[4] others being legally neutral only affect one's reputation and *murūʾa*.

In a similar vein, but with a wider range of sources, Salah Natij published a long article in two consecutive issues of *Studia Islamica* where he thoroughly analyzed the different implications of *murūʾa* in the framework of *adab*. At the end of the first essay, summing up his findings and citing Ricoeur's distinction between acting morally, that is abiding by a set of external rules, and behaving ethically, the self-imposing of a series of obligations considered inherently good, Natij maintains that *murūʾa* clearly pertains to the latter. This is because "l'individu doté de murūʾa est mis en situation de responsabilité non pas devant Dieu ou devant une quelconque autre volonté extérieure, par exemple le contrôle social, mais devant sa propre conscience morale (*ḍamīr*)."[5] Thus, according to Natij, three precepts regulate *murūʾa*: autonomy and independence, coherence and authenticity, and self-control. Therefore, not only did *murūʾa* function independently from religion (*dīn*), but also the latter would not have been understood without the ethical values of *murūʾa*.[6] In his second essay, however, Natij also admits that material conditions are sometimes needed to affirm *murūʾa* and make it visible through acts of generosity that increase one's public standing. Thus, he expanded his early interpretation and provided a new interesting definition of *murūʾa* as "un lieu d'interdépendance entre la respectabilité et la responsabilité."[7]

In this chapter, I intend to follow the same line of thought but from the point of view of premodern Arabic moral literature. In particular, I am interested in understanding how and to what extent *ḥayā'* is relevant for the conceptualization of *murū'a* in the sources of the *makārim al-akhlāq* genre as well as the advice literature. After having compared the definitions of the two terms, I will then discuss the claim that *murū'a* is "the *ḥayā'* before the self," and finally, I will deal with a specific case in which ideas of wealth and the way it is managed are considered central components of *murū'a* because they are also associated to *ḥayā'*.

I argue that *murū'a* is closer to what Western philosophers have defined as self-respect. In his groundbreaking work *A Theory of Justice*, John Rawls assumes that shame results from experiencing an injury to one's self-respect or a blow to one's self-esteem. However, while Rawls seems to treat the two as synonyms, Gabriele Taylor has instead demonstrated that only self-respect is connected to shame, whereas self-esteem is primarily linked to pride and humiliation. *Murū'a* is in my view more similar to self-respect in that both are based on expectations. As Taylor puts it, "to respect oneself is to have a sense of one's own value, and this requires also a degree of self-confidence, a belief that he has got his expectations right."[8]

The Meaning and the Forms of *ḥayā'* according to Medieval Arabic Sources

In his *Tahdhib al-Akhlaq* (*The Refinement of Character*) Miskawayh (d. 421/1030) lists *ḥayā'* among the subcategories of the cardinal virtue of *'iffa* (temperance) and defines it as "the self-restraint of the soul for fear (*khawf*) of committing bad deeds (*qabā'iḥ*), and carefulness to avoid blame and justified insult."[9] Some years later, in his ethical book *al-Dhari'a fi Makarim al-Shari'a* (*The Path to the Virtues of Religious Teachings*) al-Raghib al-Isfahani (d. early fifth/eleventh centuries) probably influenced by Miskawayh gives a very similar definition of *ḥayā'* as "the shrinking of the soul from bad deeds (*qabā'iḥ*)." Then, while adopting what will become the standard connection between *ḥayā'* and *'iffa* (temperance), he interestingly closely associates the concept to cowardice (*jubn*).[10]

These two definitions, which appear to have been clearly influenced by Aristotle's account of *ḥayā'* as the "fear of disgrace" (*al-khawf min al-danā'a*),[11] pivot around two basic ideas: on the one hand, *ḥayā'* is the ability to control one's own impulses and desires and, on the other, it means showing concern, fear, and attentiveness to the fact that a potential observer—the people or God—may express a negative assessment of actions perceived as bad, and therefore the agent is also judged adversely in the light of some moral standards. Moreover, while the most common form of *ḥayā'* is that before the people (*bashar*), al-Raghib argues that one can also feel it with regard to the self (*nafs*) or God. However, he notes that whoever is moved by *ḥayā'* in front of the people but not before the self, clearly considers himself less worthy of respect than the others. Similarly, whoever has *ḥayā'* before the people and the self but not in front of God is ignorant of Him. This is because in al-Raghib's view, human beings feel *ḥayā'* either at what they consider worthy of importance, honor, and respect or when they realize that someone is observing them or listening in on their secrets. Hence, he wonders, "How come a person not knowing God can show respect to Him and knowing that He is looking at him?"[12]

This link between faith (*dīn* or *ʾīmān*) and *ḥayāʾ* appears to be a well-established motif in medieval Arabic sources. Several traditions mostly attributed to the Prophet himself view that *ḥayāʾ* is either part of the faith in God or even "*ḥayāʾ* is *dīn* in its entirety." However, another equally often-cited tradition replicating the syntax of the aforementioned saying reads, "*ḥayāʾ* is good in its entirety."[13] By replacing *dīn* with *khayr*, the message is clear: not only does *ḥayāʾ* mean behaving according to religious values and rules of conduct, but it also has to do with a common sense of what is good and bad, which tends to confirm and eventually overlap with religious morality. Indeed, among the ten qualities of a good Muslim, ʿAʾisha, the Prophet's wife, gives to *ḥayāʾ* the most important position.[14] Therefore, if feeling *ḥayāʾ* is the epitome of goodness, then "if it does not make you ashamed, do whatever you want,"[15] concludes another well-known saying.

The Shafiʿi scholar al-Mawardi (d. 450/1058) also adopts the same mainstream definition of *ḥayāʾ* as "the refraining from doing what is impure and ceasing to act bad publicly." However, he provides a more thorough analysis of the three forms of *ḥayāʾ*. Discussing the first type, the one before God, he uses the same set of sayings linking our concept to faith mentioned earlier, but when it comes to the *ḥayāʾ* before the people, he interestingly says that it is "part of the realization of *murūʾa* and the love for praise."[16] Indeed, continues al-Mawardi, "the *murūʾa* of the man is where he walks, where he enters, from where he goes out, where he sits, the person with whom he be-friends and the person whom he sits with."[17] This means that, as Marion Holmes Katz has correctly noted, *murūʾa* can be understood as the person's social competence, that is, his/her adherence to the custom.[18] Finally, the fact that the third form of *ḥayāʾ*, the one before the self, is also based on temperance (*ʿiffa*) means for the Shafiʿi scholar that one commits to self-monitoring himself in private exactly as if he was in public, because "whoever does in private what he is ashamed to do in public, does not have consideration for himself."[19] This is a very central point that I will discuss thoroughly in the next section.

Murūʾa as the *ḥayāʾ* of the Self

There seems to be a general agreement among Arab as well as Western scholars that *murūʾa* was a sort of unwritten but largely accepted moral code regulating the interaction between individuals in pre-Islamic tribal society.[20] According to Toshihiko Izutsu, after the Revelation, some aspects of this traditional value system, such as blood-vengeance, were rejected altogether, and others, like this unrestrained generosity often drifting into costly extravagance typically associated with the Bedouins, needed to be mitigated in order to fit into the new religion, which was instead exhorting people to adopt a more controlled and sober attitude.[21]

At any rate, like *ḥayāʾ*, *murūʾa* also implies exposure, this constant feeling of being under the gaze of someone else: God, the others, or the self. Al-Mawardi's definition of *murūʾa* in the section about "the rules of conduct according to conventions and accepted practices" attached to the chapter on the "rules of personal conduct" of his *Adab al-Dunya wa-l-Din* recalls indeed the terminology used so far in relation to *ḥayāʾ*: "the consideration (*murāʿā*) for the circumstances (of the action), so that the soul may be in the best condition possible, neither manifesting ill-will deliberately, nor becoming the object of deserved reproach."[22] In other words, not only *ḥayāʾ* but also *murūʾa* pivots around self-restraint from any sort of bad action and fear of public blame, but it is this same *murāʿāt* or the idea of showing sensibility toward a virtuous behavior in public that is itself the definition of *murūʾa* (*wa-ʾinnamā al-murāʿātu hiya al-murūʾa*).[23] However, this attentiveness toward one's irreproachable public image is not enough to ensure one's *murūʾa* unless one commits to do the same in private. Thus, exactly like the *ḥayāʾ* before the self, *murūʾa* means "not doing in private what you are ashamed to do in public."

This is indeed among the most quoted traditions attributed to *murūʾa* in the sources.[24] One anecdote is particular interestingly here: ʿAbd Allah (d. 73/693), the son of the caliph ʿUmar ibn al-Khattab (r. 13–23/634–44), reportedly said, "There is no heavier burden for men than *murūʾa*." One of his companions asked, "That God makes you prosper, describe *murūʾa* for us," and he replied, "I don't have a definition to give." A man insisted and he said, "I don't know what to say except that I was feeling ashamed of something in public only when I was ashamed of it in private."[25] Now, not only does this story tell us how difficult it was to follow a lifestyle based on *murūʾa*, another often quoted motif, it is also because the notion itself seemed to defy any precise definition. Thus, ʿAbd Allah ibn ʿUmar, unable to find the right words, presents his moral integrity as a model of *murūʾa*.

At any rate, this tradition posits that, in order to be entitled with *murūʾa*, one should behave the same in private and in public, avoid hypocrisy, and present before the self the same controlled image he/she is committed to before the people. In other words, it is similar to the situation in the private sphere where one also feels exposed to the critical assessment of his/her own conscience. Interestingly, Ibn Qayyim al-Jawziyya (d. 751/1350) explains this point by stating that it is like having two souls, each one staring at and being ashamed of the other.[26] Thus, what *murūʾa* shares with the *ḥayāʾ* of the self is exactly this idea of constant control over the impulses and appetites, on the one hand, and the extension of the rules of decency into one's private life, on the other. This means that, if one's behavior in public as well as in private is expected to be the same, then what is at stake here is not necessarily one's own privacy, a violation of which would still occasion shame, but rather the effort at self-presenting as a rational and measured human being who, contrary to the animals, has been given an intellect to restrain him/her in all circumstances. In other words, *murūʾa* means preserving one's personhood also before oneself.

This is also the reason why, unlike Miskawayh who, as we have seen, lists *ḥayāʾ* as a subcategory of the cardinal virtue of temperance or *ʿiffa*, al-Mawardi treats the latter as a subcategory of the *murūʾa* in relation to the self.

Murūʾa as *iṣlāḥ al-māl*

This last point allows us to discuss another often quoted tradition: "[Muʿawiya] asked al-Mughira [about *murūʾa*] and he replied: it is the abstention (*ʿiffa*) from what God Almighty has prescribed and the gaining subsistence (*ḥirfa*) from what God Almighty has declared permissible."[27] While the Qurʾanic usage of the root *ʿ-f-f* refers to both chastity and the abstention from wrongdoing in matters of religion, *ʿiffa* was also largely used in works on ethics to translate the Greek cardinal virtue of temperance, the Aristotelian *sōphrosynē*, that is the virtue of self-control and refraining from the satisfaction of unnecessary desires and pleasures.[28] Thus, the convergence between the Qurʾanic concept of abstention and the Greek virtue of self-control may also have helped to mitigate some excessive aspects originally associated with *murūʾa* in the pre-Islamic period, such as the immoderate spending of money. Hence, definitions of *murūʾa* linking the abstention from wrongdoing in matters of religion to making good use of wealth became quite popular in the sources.[29]

As for *ḥirfa*, it is the ability to ensure one's own livelihood and provide for the needs of one's family in a religiously licit way—that is, through an occupation or a profession. Therefore, a young man asserts himself as an adult and claims his place among the "people of *murūʾa*" by getting a *ḥirfa*, which eventually makes him an adequate husband and father:

> A young man was brought before ʿUmar bn al-Khattab who admired his condition and asked: Does he have a *ḥirfa*? It was answered negatively then he said: He has lost my esteem.[30]

In other words, despite inherited status and acquired nobility, *kasal* (inactivity or laziness), which was also stigmatized as "the enemy of *murūʾa* and an obstacle to the acquisition of *futuwwa*,"[31] was definitely considered a failure to reproduce the traditional man's role of the wage earner and eventually a threat to his public image and reputation.

There is indeed evidence suggesting that poverty and the subsequent dependence on financial assistance to provide for the family needs were considered shameful for a man claiming *murūʾa*. Ibn al-Muqaffaʿ (*c.* 102–139/*c.* 720–756) seems to be among the earliest sources presenting this pattern of argument. In his *Kalila wa-Dimna*, he closely connects *ḥayāʾ* to *murūʾa*:

> Poverty is the source of all afflictions: it is a cause of aversion, a deprivation of *ʿaql* and *murūʾa*, a departure from *ʿilm* and *adab*, a source of distress and a concentration of misfortunes. When poverty has fallen on him, there is no other choice than to give up the sense of shame (*ḥayāʾ*) until losing it completely. He who loses his shame loses his distinction (*sarw*) and his *murūʾa*; he who loses his *murūʾa* is hated; he who is hated, suffers; he who suffers, is sad; he who is sad loses his *ʿaql* and disowns his understanding and his memory; and he who is afflicted in all these, every time he speaks he causes more harm to himself than good.[32]

This passage, which appears to have gained some popularity,[33] builds on a chain of losses progressing from a state of material indigence to sadness and mental weakening and possibly displays an ancient belief that wealth and poverty were not just material conditions, but they also had a moral component, from which flowed honor, virtues, the function of reason, and eventually, happiness. Moreover, poverty is something to be ashamed of, because in order to survive and provide for the family's needs, the poor man has no other choice than to overcome the shame of asking for the charity of the others, something that threatens the power inherent in his role and profoundly undermines his *murūʾa*.

The only way to avoid poverty, then, is to manage one's own expenses properly. It is in this perspective that we have to understand another very common description of *murūʾa* as *iṣlāḥ al-māl* or *iṣlāḥ al-maʿīsha*. Traditions pointing at this definition and featuring figures of the early Islamic community are abundant and well represented in sources of different kinds, such as historiographical works, *adab* books, lexicographical writings, advise literature, and ethics spanning from the third/ninth to the tenth/ sixteenth centuries. Therefore, we can safely say that although no variants of this saying are mentioned in the canonical collections of *ḥadīth*, the *murūʾa-iṣlāḥ al-māl* or *al-maʿīsha* equation was particularly well accepted in the normative literature.

But what does this expression really mean? The term *iṣlāḥ*, the verbal noun (*maṣdar*) of the fourth form *aṣlaḥa*, said of things means "restoring," "correcting," "arranging something properly," "ordering," or "repairing." Its moral value includes concepts such as "rendering someone or something good," "right," "incorrupt," "virtuous," or "honest," and in this sense, *iṣlāḥ* replicates some significations of *iḥsān*. Moreover, applied to wealth or possession, it means "rendering it in a good state," "making it prosper," "improving," or "managing it well."[34] As for *māl*, it has been defined as everything that one possesses or acquires such as animals, in particular camels, sheep or goats, provisions, and commodities, but also gold or silver that constitutes one's own wealth and property.[35] Hence, *murūʾa* as *iṣlāḥ al-māl* means that one should ensure that his material resources as well as his possessions are neither consumed nor wasted in useless or reprehensible things, an idea implicit in its contrary *afsada al-māl*, nor greedily accumulated in a way that makes them inefficacious. Rather, one should work for a better use of his wealth by rendering it productive and profitable. *Al-maʿīsha*, and more rarely *al-maʿāsh*, indicates the means of subsistence that make possible the living. Therefore, *iṣlāḥ al-maʿīsha* can be interpreted by analogy with *iṣlāḥ al-māl* as the making "good use" of one's earnings and provisions, for example by donating food in order to cement one's prestige and authority, as well as by "improving" or "cultivating" the livelihood in general, that is, the refinement of one's own manners according to the standard of *adab*.

In the *Kitab al-adab wa-l-muruʾa*, a collection of sayings and poems mostly of a paraenetic nature written by the Damascene poet Salih ibn Janah al-Lakhmi (d. *ca* 81/700), *murūʾa*, *adab*, and *ʿaql* are so linked to each other that the author even employs a telling metaphor to exemplify their mutual dependence:

> The relation existing between man and his subsistence, or between his *ʿaql*, his *adab* and his *murūʾa* is the same existing between the archer and its bow. The

> archer needs the arrow and the arrow needs the bow but the bow needs somebody to string it and, above all, somebody who has the skills and master the art of archery.[36]

In other words, after behaving according to one's mental faculties and following the rules of what is socially acceptable, *murū'a* represents a sort of third way toward moral perfection that consists in applying the same self-reflective approach to one's private life also. This means regarding all occasions as shame producing and thus avoiding being seen in a bad light. Thus, a person having *murū'a* faces continuous public as well as self-induced pressures to show his/her ability to live up to certain standards, both in terms of material resources and moral strength. Evidence suggests that these were indeed two facets of the same concept, as 'Umar bn al-Khattab reportedly said that *murū'a* is a two-fold virtue: the outer (*al-murū'at al-ẓāhira*) and the inner *murū'a* (*al-murū'at al-bāṭina*). The outer *murū'a* is "the comfort of living (*al-riyāsh*), the inner *murū'a* is temperance (*al-'afāf*)."[37] Having discussed the implication of *'iffa* in the acquisition of *murū'a*, we now turn to these "comfort(s) of the living" that are part of the outer *murū'a*.

Markers of *murū'a*

Conceptually, this might appear a little confusing: while *murū'a* in the moral literature refers to abstaining from immoderate expenditures in order to keep one's private sphere away from the humiliation of poverty, historical accounts present instead a different way of negotiating *murū'a* based on abundance and wastefulness. This is the case, for instance, of the story of Jamila (d. 371/981), the daughter of the Hamdanid prince of Mosul Nasir al-Dawla (d. 357/968), who according to Abu Mansur al-Tha'alibi (d. 429/1038), performed the pilgrimage in the year 366/976–7 with a great *murū'a* that no king or queen had ever shown before:

> She displayed great magnanimity of character (*murū'a*), distributed a large amount of wealth, did many pious deeds and performed many acts of liberality—all these to an extent that the charitable works done in the course of the pilgrimage by Zubayda and other daughters of Caliphs and kings, and even by Caliphs and kings themselves, only partially equaled.[38]

Among the acts of generosity and piety, the author was informed that princess Jamila, who arrived in Mecca "with her 400 litters, each lined with satin, so that it was never known in which one she herself was," distributed large amounts of food, both sweets and fresh vegetables, dinars, camels, and robes, and she also freed three hundred male slaves and two hundred female slaves.

Jamila's story reminds the reader of the great generosity of 'Abd Allah ibn Jud'an, a pre-Islamic leading figure of the Banu Taym clan of the Quraysh who died before the Prophet started his prophetic mission. One day he was received by the king of the Persians who said, "I have been informed that you are the greatest in *murū'a* among the Arabs, so tell me about your needs." ʿAbd Allah asked for a cook who could make the *fālūdh* (also spelled *fālūdhaj*, a kind of sweet made of stark, clarified butter and honey), which he then gave to his fellows Quraysh to eat.[39] In doing so, not only did he show his uncommon liberality, but he also demonstrated his high degree of refinement—both elements that made him "the greatest in *murūʾa* among the Arabs." Moreover, it has also been reported that he used to slaughter a camel every day and then distribute the meat and fat among the people. He was, after all, one of the richest merchants in Mecca before the Revelation, something that allowed him to perform such extraordinary acts of generosity and thus enhance his *murūʾa*.

What is interesting here is that both figures are labeled with *murūʾa* on account of the scale of their munificence and on the degree of refinement of their spending, which ultimately became proverbial regardless of their biological gender. Moreover, both ʿAbd Allah and Jamila were members of the wealthy ruling élite, and therefore, the expectations with regard to the way they were using their wealth were particularly high. In other words, the impression is that *murūʾa* is related more to the way in which wealth is managed in order to increase or maintain one's social capital and authority—in a word, *iṣlaḥ al-māl*—rather than on specific gendered roles, and this clearly contradicts the claim made by some moralists like al-Raghib al-Isfahani that *murūʾa* is an exclusively masculine attribute.[40] Now, it is true that in the vast majority of the cases, it was men who had access to resources and were thus able to use them in a certain way. However, the example of Jamila cited above shows that, with financial capacity being equal, women could also be entitled with *murūʾa*, provided that their expenses fulfilled a certain standard.

Thus, it is not surprising that *murūʾa* figures in the advice literature of the Medieval period among the qualities that rulers and vizirs are supposed to earn. The *Mirʾat al-Muruʾat* (*The Mirrors of the Murūʾas*), for instance, a book belonging to the *adab al-wazīr* genre written by Abu Mansur al-Thaʿalibi and probably dedicated to Abu Sahl al-Hamduni, the governor of Nishapur before Masʿud (r. 421–32/1030–40), places a special emphasis on having a large family as well as a large house as markers of *murūʾa*. The author reports the story of a friend of the famous vizir al-Sahib Ismaʿil ibn ʿAbbad al-Talaqani (d. 385/995), who one day asked,

> "What gives evidence of the man's *murūʾa* in his house?" He [the vizir] replied: "A numerous family, some female slaves, servants, wives and riding beasts." And he agreed on this.

Then, al-Thaʿalibi quotes the words of another vizir al-Hasan bn Muhammad ibn Harun al-Muhallabi al-Azdi (d. 352/963), who reportedly said,

> I prefer a numerous household because if it was small, I would be ashamed by my little expenses. For me, there is no pain in spending for their [the family] large number, I rather prefer a life of ease and plenty.[41]

These descriptions are clearly rooted in the Qur'anic verse 18:47: "Wealth and children are adornments of worldly life." In other words, as long as it is legally gained, wealth is neither religiously condemned, nor is its public display morally disapproved of. On the contrary, *murū'a* is the ostentatious display of wealth, as described in these two lines of the fourth-/tenth-century poet Mansur ibn Muhammad al-Kurayzi:

> O ye cheater! You can use all the tricks in your favour.
> *Murū'a* is when wealth (*māl*) is made visible on you.
> How many orators among men,
> but only possessions (*amwāl*) speak for them here.[42]

After the family, the house represents another important marker of socioeconomic success and, as such, is even considered the place where *murū'a* materializes in the most visible way. The *Mirror* devotes a whole chapter on statements about *murū'a* and the house, such as,

> The house of the man is his nest; it is where he has put his living, the resting place for him and the abode of his social life. It is the place that contains all his *murū'a*. How nice is the verse that someone has composed:
>
> It is part of the *murū'a* of the young boy
> the way he lives: a house is what makes him proud.
> Be content with it [the house] in this world
> and prepare yourself for the house of the Heaven.[43]

In another saying, we get specific information on how the house of a person entitled with *murū'a* should look like:

> If in the house are put together the bathroom (*ḥammām*), the *qaṣr* (pavilion or belvedere), the room for the private audience, the room for guests and the library, then the *murū'a* is gathered in it.[44]

This and other similar descriptions of sumptuous palaces are symbols of refinement and wealth. However, the recurrent reference to the private *ḥammām* and the room for guests in the house of a man of *murū'a* suggests that such facilities had a particular social and ethical significance. Thus, while the *ḥammām* points to pleasure and comfort, it also implies that the owner pays greater attention to cleanliness as a marker of status, in general, and to the ritual purity attained by ablutions as an indicator of piety, in particular. This same concern is also formulated in a frequently quoted tradition attributed to 'Umar bn al-Khattab (r. 13/634–23/644), where the external cleanliness of clothes, which mirrors the internal purity and attentiveness toward religious conventions, is also a way in which *murū'a* is publicly displayed: "the visible *murū'a* is clean garments,"[45] a clear reference to Q. 74:4: "Purify your garments."

Having a house large enough to accommodate guests and visitors means that a person is able to perform hospitality in a way that enhances his reputation of a liberal man, as in this saying attributed to the imam Jaʿfar al-Sadiq (d. 148/765):

> A person's happiness is his large house, the elegance of his sitting room and the cleanliness of the room for the ablutions. The most admirable things in the houses are the rooms for guests, which are the indicators of the *murūʾāt*.[46]

While there is no doubt that the reference to the large family and the large house as part of the *murūʾa* of a vizir or of any high-ranking official is a typical feature of the advice literature, a munificence that was expected to grow proportionally to the position in the social hierarchy, all the sources agree, however, that showing generosity through hospitality was the most praiseworthy way to use one's wealth, whatever the amount one possesses. Hence the aphorism attributed to al-Ahnaf ibn Qays (d. 67/686–7): "*murūʾa* altogether is making good use of wealth and spending it in the duties of hospitality."[47]

Conclusion

To sum up our discussion, we have first shown how medieval Arabic sources have often characterized *murūʾa* by reference to *hayāʾ*, and this is because they were both described in terms of anxiety at wrongdoing in matters of religion and being exposed to public blame for lack of adherence to common decency and lack of self-restraint with regard to basic instincts, in public as well as in private. God, the people, and the self were believed to be the three focal points upon which the two notions were founded. Indeed, the concern over being seen in a certain way and thus being vulnerable to disqualification is supposed to guide our everyday living and direct our moral and ethical duties. We have also demonstrated that *ḥayāʾ* was recognized as a central emotional component of *murūʾa* to the extent that a loss of one often affected the acquisition of the other.

While there is no reason to cast doubt on Katz's claim that *murūʾa* is one's "social competence" because it is "grounded in sensitivity to the social perception of one's actions,"[48] the sources also insist on the fact that *murūʾa* is feeling *ḥayāʾ* before oneself. This means that a person having *murūʾa* not only has interiorized a specific set of social moral norms, but he/she also behaves in private according to the same feeling of self-worth that directs his/her actions in public. *Ḥayāʾ* then is meant to protect the integrity of this constructed self from any situation that may occasion a significant loss in one's high moral status. This is particularly evident in the case study described above where wealth and its management were thought to be of such value for one's own sense of worth that a failure to exemplify a model of living according to the relevant standards of *murūʾa* was precisely an occasion for a loss of *ḥayāʾ*.

Notes

1. This chapter is part of an ongoing research project that I started in 2018 when I was a postdoctoral fellow at the Berlin Graduate School Muslim Cultures and Societies (BGSMCS). I would like to thank all the staff and the colleagues at the BGSMCS for their assistance and support and above all Prof. Konrad Hirschler for his valuable insights and inspiration throughout my research in Berlin.
2. Marion Holmes Katz, "Shame (Ḥayā') as an Affective Disposition in Islamic Legal Thought," *Journal of Law, Religion and State* 3 (2014), 164.
3. Ibid., 157.
4. Eli Alshech, "Out of Sight and Therefore Out of Mind: Early Sunni Islamic Modesty Regulations and the Creation of Spheres of Privacy," *Journal of Near Eastern Studies* 66 (2007), 267–90.
5. Salah Natij, "Murū'a, Soucis et interrogations éthiques dans la culture arabe classique (1ere partie)," *Studia Islamica* 112 (2017), 253–4.
6. Natij quite properly concurs with the criticism previously made by Farès, Pellat, and Bravmann of Goldziher's thesis on the conflict between *dīn* and *murū'a*. For an overview of this debate, see Nadia Jamil, *Ethics and Poetry in Sixth-Century Arabia* (Cambridge: Gibb Memorial Trust 2017), 1–64.
7. Salah Natij, "Murū'a, Soucis et interrogations éthiques dans la culture arabe classique (2e partie)," *Studia Islamica* 113 (2018), 18–19.
8. Gabriele Taylor, *Pride, Shame, Guilt: Emotions of self-assessment* (Oxford: Clarendon Press, 1985), 78–9.
9. Ahmad ibn Muhammad Miskawayh, *The Refinement of Character*, translated by Constantine K. Zurayk (Beirut: American University of Beirut Press, 1968), 18. For the Arabic text see Ahmad ibn Muhammad Miskawyh, *Tahdhib al-Akhlaq*, edited by Qustantin Zurayq (Beirut: al-Jami' al-amirikiyya fi Beirut, 1966), 20. See also Katz, "Shame," 142–4 and 146.
10. Abu l-Qasim Husayn ibn Muhammad al-Raghib al-Isfahani, *al-Dhari'a ila Makarim al-Shari'a*, edited by Taha 'Abd al-Ra'uf Sa'd (al-Qahira: Maktabat al-kulliyyat al-azhariyya, 1973), 145–6.
11. Aristotle, *The Arabic Version of the* Nicomachean Ethics, edited by Anna A. Akasoy and Alexander Fidora, translated by Douglas M. Dunlop (Leiden: Brill, 2005), 284–5.
12. Al-Raghib al-Isfahani, *al-Dhari'a*, 147.
13. These sayings appear in the sources as early as the third/ninth century, see for instance Ibn Abi l-Dunya, *Makarim al-Akhlaq*, edited by Muhammad 'Abd al-Qadir Ahmad 'Ata (Beirut: Dar al-kutub al-'ilmiyya, 1989), 64–74; 'Abd Allah ibn Muslim ibn Qutayba al-Dinawari, *'Uyun al-Akhbar*, 4 vols. (al-Qahira: Dar al-kutub al-misriyya, 1925), vol. 1, 278, Abu 'Umar Ahmad ibn Muhammad ibn 'Abd Rabbihi, *al-'Iqd al-Farid*, edited by Muhammad al-Tunji, 7 vols. (Beirut: Dar Sadir, 2001–9), vol. 2, 351. See also Muhammad bn Isma'il al-Muqaddim, *Fiqh al-Haya'* (al-Qahira: Dar al-amal, 2015), 53–6.
14. Ibn Abi l-Dunya, *Makarim al-Akhlaq*, 62: "*ra's makārim al-akhlāq al-ḥayā'*."
15. Ibid., 73. The sources also note that this saying can be interpreted in two different ways, see Katz, "Shame," 145 and al-Muqaddim, *Fiqh al-Haya'*, 67–9.
16. 'Ali ibn Muhammad ibn Habib al-Mawardi, *Adab al-Dunya wa-l-Din* (Beirut: Dar al-kutub al-'ilmiyya, 1987), 214.
17. Ibid.

18. Katz, "Shame," 148.
19. Al-Mawardi, *Adab al-Dunya wa-l-Din*, 214 and Katz, "Shame," 149.
20. Bishr Farès, "Murūʾa," in *Encyclopaedia of Islam*, 2nd ed., edited by Clifford E. Bosworth, Emeri van Donzel, Wolfhart P. Heinrichs, and Charles Pellat, 13 vols. (Leiden: Brill, 1986–2000), vol. 7, 636–8.
21. Toshihiko Izutsu, *The Structure of Ethical Terms in the Quran* (Chicago: ABC International Group, 2000), 49–75.
22. Majid Fakhry, *Ethical Theories in Islam* (Leiden: Brill, 1991), 165. For the Arabic text, see al-Mawardi, *Adab al-Dunya wa-l-Din*, 277.
23. Al-Mawardi, *Adab al-Dunya wa-l-Din*, 277.
24. See, among others, Abu Bakr Muhammad ibn Khalaf ibn al-Marzuban, *al-Muruʾa wa-ma jaʾ fi dhalika ʿan al-Nabi wa-ʿan al-Sahaba wa-l-Tabiʿin*, edited by Muhammad Khayr Ramadan Yusuf (Beirut: Dar Ibn Hazm, 1999), 56.
25. Ibn al-Marzuban, *al-Muruʾa*, 82.
26. Ibn ʿAbd Allah Muhammad ibn Abi Bakr ibn Ayyub ibn Qayyim al-Jawziyya, *Madarij al-Salikin*, edited by Muhammad al-Muʿtasim bi-llah al-Baghdadi, 2 vols. (Beirut: Dar al-kitab al-ʿarabi, 2003), vol. 2, 252.
27. Al-Mawardi, *Adab al-Dunya wa-l-Din*, 310 and 317.
28. See, for instance, Sheila MacDonough, "Abstinence," in *The Encyclopaedia of the Qurʾān* (*EQ*), edited by Jane Dammen McAuliffe, 6 vols. (Leiden: Brill, 2001–6), vol. 1, 19.
29. See for instance definitions of *murūʾa* such as *al-ʿafāf wa-iṣlāḥ al-māl*, *al-ʿafāf fī-l-Islām wa-istiṣlāḥ al-māl* or *al-ʿafāf fī-l-dīn wa-iṣlāḥ al-māl* in Ibn al-Marzuban, *al-Muruʾa*, 45 and 80.
30. Ibn al-Marzuban, *al-Muruʾa*, 39–40.
31. Abu Hatim Muhammad ibn Hibban al-Busti, *Rawdat al-Uqalaʾ wa-Nuzhat al-Fudalaʾ*, edited by Muhammad ʿAbd al-Qadir al-Fadili (Beirut: al-Maktaba al-ʿasriyya, 2014), 203.
32. Abu Muhammad ʿAbd Allah ibn al-Muqaffaʿ, *Kalila wa-Dimna*, edited by ʿAbd al-Wahab ʿAzam (al-Qahira: Dar al-ʿalam al-ʿarabi, 2017), 126. A recent edition of the *Kalila wa-Dimna* based on another manuscript has a slightly different formulation, see Ibn al-Muqaffaʿ, *Kalilah and Dimnah. Fables of Virtues and Vices*, edited and translated by Michael Fishbein and James E. Montgomery (New York: New York University Press, 2021), 198–201.
33. Shortened versions of this passage are found in several sources, among which Ibn ʿAbd Rabbihi, *al-ʿIqd al-Farid*, vol. 2, 454 and al-Marzuban, *al-Muruʾa*, 74–5.
34. Edward William Lane, *Arabic-English Lexicon*, 2 vols. (Cambridge: The Islamic Texts Society, 1984), vol. 2, 1714 and Meïr Moshe Bravmann, *The Spiritual Background of Early Islam: Studies in Ancient Arab Concepts*, 2nd ed. (Leiden: Brill, 2009), 103–6.
35. Lane, *Arabic-English Lexicon*, vol. 2 (Supplement to parts VII and VII), 3026.
36. Salih ibn Janah al-Lakhmi, *al-Adab wa-l-Muruʾa* (Tanta: Dar al-sahaba li-l-turath, 1992), 32.
37. Ibn ʿAbd Rabbihi, *al-ʿIqd al-Farid*, vol. 2, 244.
38. Al-Thaʿalibi, *The Book of Curious and Entertaining Information. The Laṭāʾif al-Maʿārif of al-Thaʿālibī*, translated by Clifford E. Bosworth (Edinburgh: Edinburgh University Press, 1968), 82.
39. Ahmad ibn Yahya ibn Jabir ibn Dawud al-Baladhuri, *Ansab al-Ashraf*, 13 vols., edited by Ihsan ʿAbbas *et alii* (Beirut: Orient Institut, 1979–), vol. 10, 157.
40. Al-Raghib al-Isfahani, *al-Dhariʿa*, 58–9.

41. Abu Mansur al-Tha'alibi, *Mir'at al-Muru'at*, edited by Muhammad Khayr Ramadan Yusuf (Beirut: Dar Ibn Hazm, 2004), 31–2.
42. Ibn Hibban al-Busti, *Rawdat al-Uqala'*, 218.
43. Al-Tha'alibi, *Mir'at al-Muru'at*, 47.
44. Ibid., 49.
45. "*al-murū'a al-ẓāhira al-thiyāb al-ṭāhira*," Ibn Qutayba, *'Uyun al-Akhbar*, vol. 1, 296; Ibn al-Marzuban, *al-Muru'a*, 40 and 41.
46. Al-Tha'alibi, *Mir'at al-Muru'at*, 48.
47. "*al-murū'a kulluhā iṣlāḥ al-māl wa-badhluhu li-l-ḥuqūq*," Muhammad ibn l-Hasan ibn Muhammad ibn 'Ali ibn Hamdun, *Al-Tadhkira al-Hamduniyya*, 10 vols., edited by Iḥsā n 'Abbas and Bakr 'Abbas (Beirut: Dar Sadir, 1996), vol. 2, 193.
48. Katz, "Shame," 148.

Bibliography

Alshech, Eli. "Out of Sight and Therefore Out of Mind: Early Sunnī Islamic Modesty Regulations and the Creation of Spheres of Privacy." *Journal of Near Eastern Studies* 66 (2007): 267–90.

Aristotle. *The Arabic Version of the* Nicomachean Ethics. Edited by Anna A. Akasoy and Alexander Fidora; translated by Douglas M. Dunlop. Leiden: Brill, 2005.

Al-Baladhuri, Ahmad ibn Yahya ibn Jabir ibn Dawud. *Ansab al-Ashraf.* 13 vols. Edited by Ihsan 'Abbas *et alii*. Beirut: Orient Institut, 1979.

Bravmann, Meïr Moshe. *The Spiritual Background of Early Islam: Studies in Ancient Arab Concepts*, 2nd ed. Leiden: Brill, 2009.

Fakhry, Majid. *Ethical Theories in Islam*. Leiden: Brill, 1991.

Farès, Bishr. "Murū'a." In *Encyclopaedia of Islam*, 2nd ed., 13 vols. Edited by Clifford E. Bosworth, Emeri van Donzel, Wolfhart P. Heinrichs, and Charles Pellat, vol. 7, 636–8. Leiden: Brill, 1986–2000.

Ibn 'Abd Rabbihi, Abu 'Umar Ahmad ibn Muhammad. *al-'Iqd al-Farid*. 7 vols. Edited by Muhammad al-Tunji. Beirut: Dar Sadir, 2001–9.

Ibn Abi l-Dunya. *Makarim al-Akhlaq*. Edited by Muhammad 'Abd al-Qadir Ahmad 'Ata. Beirut: Dar al-kutub al-'ilmiyya, 1989.

Ibn Abi l-Dunya. *Islah al-Mal*. Edited by Muhammad 'Abd al-Qadir 'Ata. Beirut: Mu'assasa al-kutub al-thaqafiyya, 1993.

Ibn Hamdun, Muhammad ibn l-Hasan ibn Muhammad ibn 'Ali, *Al-Tadhkira al-Hamduniyya*. 10 vols. Edited by Ihsan 'Abbas and Bakr 'Abbas. Beirut: Dar Ṣadir, 1996.

Ibn Hibban al-Busti, Abu Hatim Muhammad. *Rawdat al-Uqala' wa-Nuzhat al-Fudala'*. Edited by Muhammad 'Abd al-Qadir al-Fadili. Beirut: al-Maktaba al-'asriyya, 2014.

Ibn al-Marzuban, Abu Bakr Muhammad ibn Khalaf. *Al-Muru'a wa-Ma ja' fi Dhalika 'an al-Nabi wa-'an al-Sahaba wa-l-Tabi'in*. Edited by Muhammad Khayr Ramadan Yusuf. Beirut: Dar Ibn Hazm, 1999.

Ibn al-Muqaffa', Abu Muhammad 'Abd Allah. *Kalila wa-Dimna*. Edited by 'Abd al-Wahab 'Azam. Al-Qahira: Dar al-'alam al-'arabi, 2017.

Ibn al-Muqaffa', Abu Muhammad 'Abd Allah. *Kalilah and Dimnah. Fables of Virtues and Vices*. Edited and translated by Michael Fishbein and James E. Montgomery. New York: New York University Press, 2021.

Ibn Qayyim al-Jawziyya, Ibn ʿAbd Allah Muhammad ibn Abi Bakr ibn Ayyub. *Madarij al-Salikin*. 2 vols. Edited by Muhammad al-Muʿtasim bi-llah al-Baghdadi. Beirut: Dar al-kitab al-ʿarabi, 2003.
Ibn Qutayba al-Dinawari, ʿAbd Allah ibn Muslim. *ʿUyun al-Akhbar*. 4 vols. Al-Qahira: Dar al-kutub al-misriyya, 1925.
Izutsu, Toshihiko. *The Structure of Ethical Terms in the Quran*. Chicago: ABC International Group, 2000.
Jamil, Nadia. *Ethics and Poetry in Sixth-Century Arabia*. Cambridge: Gibb Memorial Trust, 2017.
Katz, Marion Holmes. "Shame (Ḥayāʾ) as an Affective Disposition in Islamic Legal Thought." *Journal of Law, Religion and State* 3 (2014): 139–69.
Al-Lakhmi, Salih ibn Janah. *Al-Adab wa-l-Muruʾa*. Tanta: Dar al-sahaba li-l-turath, 1992.
Lane, Edward William. *Arabic-English Lexicon*. 2 vols. Cambridge: Islamic Texts Society, 1984.
MacDonough, Sheila. "Abstinence." In *The Encyclopaedia of the Qurʾān*, 6 vols., edited by Jane Dammen McAuliffe, vol. 1, 19. Leiden: Brill, 2001–6.
Al-Mawardi, ʿAli ibn Muhammad ibn Habib. *Adab al-Dunya wa-l-Din*. Beirut: Dar al-kutub al-ʿilmiyya, 1987.
Miskawayh, Ahmad ibn Muhammad. *The Refinement of Character*. Translated by Constantine K. Zurayk. Beirut: American University of Beirut Press, 1968.
Miskawayh, Ahmad ibn Muhammad. *Tahdhib al-Akhlaq*. Edited by Qustantin Zurayq. Beirut: al-Jamiʿ al-amirikiyya fi Beirut, 1966.
Al-Muqaddim, Muhammad bn Ismaʿil. *Fiqh al-Hayāʾ*. Al-Qahira: Dar al-amal, 2015.
Natij, Salah. "Murūʾa, Soucis et interrogations éthiques dans la culture arabe classique (1ere partie)." *Studia Islamica* 112 (2017): 206–63.
Natij, Salah. "Murūʾa, Soucis et interrogations éthiques dans la culture arabe classique (2e partie)." *Studia Islamica* 113 (2018): 1–55.
Al-Raghib al-Isfahani, Abu l-Qasim Husayn ibn Muhammad. *Al-Dhariʿa ila Makarim al-Shariʿa*. Edited by Ṭaha ʿAbd al-Raʾuf Saʿd. al-Qahira: Maktaba al-kulliyya al-azhariyya, 1973.
Taylor, Gabriele. *Pride, Shame, Guilt. Emotions of self-assessment*. Oxford: Clarendon Press, 1985.
Al-Thaʿalibi, Abu Mansur. *The Book of Curious and Entertaining Information*. Translated by Clifford E. Bosworth. Edinburgh: Edinburgh University Press, 1968.
Al-Thaʿalibi, Abu Mansur. *Mirʾat al-Muruʾat*. Edited by Muhammad Khayr Ramadan Yusuf. Beirut: Dar Ibn Hazm, 2004.

2

Overcoming the Conceptual Link between Patriarchal Honor and Female Modesty Laws in the Islamic Interpretative Tradition

Adis Duderija

In this chapter, I examine the conceptual relationship between patriarchal honor and so-called female modesty laws in the mainstream Islamic interpretative tradition and how this conceptual relationship is justified based on a certain understanding of the concept of masculinity and femininity that were prevalent in this tradition. First, I explain how the concepts of masculinity and femininity are constructed in the mainstream Islamic interpretative tradition and their main delineating features. Next, I explain how such approaches to concepts of masculinity and femininity give rise to the idea of patriarchal/male honor whose linchpins are certain understandings of female modesty, shame, and sexuality. Then, I examine the so-called female modesty laws in the form of practices of veiling and female genital cutting (FGC) as concrete manifestations of this conceptual linking between patriarchal honor and female modesty laws. Finally, I outline alternative approaches to the concept of honor, masculinity, and femininity, as embodied in the theory of progressive Islam, that can break this conceptual link between patriarchal honor and female modesty laws.

Masculinity and Femininity Are Constructed in the Mainstream Islamic Interpretative Tradition

One significant aspect of the mainstream Islamic interpretative tradition[1] as a whole is that nearly all of its discourses are highly gendered. The sources of and powerful influences on this gendered thinking come from both the normative Islamic tradition itself (in the form of its diverse interpretations) as well as the realities of Muslim societies in relation to various assumptions, practices, and beliefs regarding the nature of gender roles and norms.[2]

In addition to the comprehensively gendered nature of the Islamic interpretative tradition, another one of its salient features is its rigid gender-hierarchical structure.[3] Significantly, this gender hierarchical nature of the mainstream Islamic tradition took the form of patriarchy and was forged in patriarchal culture, which privileges and centers the beliefs and experiences of males and the values and norms they construct as superior to those of females.[4] This gender hierarchical and patriarchal nature of the mainstream Islamic tradition will become readily apparent in the kind of conceptual associations that are used as markers of masculinity and femininity as discussed below. Importantly, the gender hierarchical and patriarchal nature of the mainstream Islamic tradition was not problematized as such by those who were responsible for crafting it—namely, the male scholarly elites. For them, this understanding of Islamic normative sources and the accumulated Islamic heritage (*turāth*) was but a "true" reflection of their sociocultural and intellectual milieu as well as an accurate expression of God's will. In other words, the "self-evident" nature of patriarchal and gender hierarchical social order was justified not only based on a particular approach to and interpretation of normative Islamic texts, but also on the basis of the prevalent sociocultural beliefs and what was considered to be scientific knowledge.[5] These beliefs and sources of knowledge themselves were based on hierarchical (in a patriarchal sense) thinking and reflected the hierarchical nature of those societies not just in the realm of gender but beyond, including considerations based on religion- and class-based morality and law.[6] Therefore, the gender hierarchical and patriarchal aspects of the mainstream Islamic interpretative tradition are pervasive and operate at many levels. I refer to this view of gender, for reasons outlined below, as "gender oppositionality."[7] This is so because I wish to draw attention to the fact that the conceptualizations and constructions of masculinity and femininity that underpin the theory of "gender oppositionality" are premised on the idea of opposites, that is, that the conceptual markers constitutive of masculinity are at the opposite end of the spectrum to those of femininity and vice versa.[8]

Conceptual Markers of Masculinity and Femininity in the Mainstream Islamic Interpretative Tradition

What kind of conceptual markers of masculinity and femininity are prevalent in the mainstream Islamic interpretative tradition? The relevant literature[9] informs us that the concept of masculinity and femininity in the mainstream Islamic tradition are primarily conceptually associated with the following set of dichotomies/binaries.

Ontological Superiority/Inferiority

The main argument here is that God had supposedly created the male sex inherently superior and has an inherent preference for males over females. Most classical Muslim scholars identified Adam as the embodiment of the original soul and, thus, as representative of the ideal standard of humanity, whereas Eve's role was merely derivative and inferior. This point is well documented by a contemporary South African scholar of classical Islamic law, Jalajel, who demonstrated how this ontological inequality between genders has translated itself into misogynistic arguments about women that go well beyond matters pertaining to belief and are couched in the form of opinions that view only men as honorable, complete, inherently worthy, and non-deficient.[10] The same tradition views Eve's creation as emphasizing "the secondary, dependent, and imperfect nature of women, and therefore the naturalness of the sexual hierarchy."[11]

Biological Superiority versus Inferiority

The ontological arguments of male superiority are supplemented by those supposedly rooted in biology. There are three main assumptions that are responsible for perpetuating patriarchal and gender hierarchical thinking—namely, (1) the idea that males have a superior role in human reproduction as the life and sex determining element; (2) the notion that women's reproductive function is her primary, if not the only, function in society; and (3) that women/wives are not more than men's tilth, that is, objects of male pleasure, and are disempowered in relation to exercising their reproductive rights.[12]

Ontological arguments in favor of female inferiority are, furthermore, supplemented by those premised on biology. This is particularly so in relation to the role of females in biological conception. The line of argument in this respect is that, unlike that of the male, the female role in conception is considered as less essential for life. It is merely receptive and passive and therefore inferior to that of the role of the male. Moreover, the mainstream Islamic interpretative tradition also conflates the reproductive function of a mother to that of a woman as a whole. One of the consequences of this conflation is that it reduces the concept of femininity to a woman's sexuality and her role in reproduction, over which she does not have much control. As such, female inferiority emerges from both their supposed secondary ontological and secondary biological origin.[13]

Religious/Spiritual and Political Authority versus Lack of Them

The argument of masculine ontological superiority outlined above has been extended into other spheres of human existence and endeavor and how concepts of masculinity and femininity were conceptualized. One such concept that is strongly associated with masculinity is that of men's exclusive entitlement to religious, spiritual, and political authority over women. Across several genres of the mainstream Islamic interpretative tradition, spiritual and religious authority are constructed as quintessentially masculine traits and attributes. Relatedly, access to and engagement with religious knowledge is considered to be the sole prerogative of men.[14]

This gendered spiritual hierarchy engenders and manifests itself also in that of the realm of the mundane. This brings us to the discussion of the nature of political and familial authority in mainstream Islam. One essential component of medieval representations of masculinity is that of the image of a "just" ruler both in the public and private spheres. According to this view, women were essentially considered as subjects of this "just" rulership. In the context of husband–wife relationships, gender hierarchy in the form of masculine authority was associated with concepts of male guardianship (*qiwāma* and *wilāya*) and wifely obedience (*ṭāʿa*) in particular.[15]

Furthermore, masculinity in the context of marriage is linked with concepts such as *tamlīk* (possession), *tamattuʿ* (a man's possession of and unfettered access to his wife's genitalia and enjoyment in the form of sexual intercourse), and *taṣarruf* (sexual conquest), which, in essence, reduce women to objects of male pleasure.[16]

As a corollary, the idea of lack of authority is in fact central to discussions of femininity in the mainstream Islamic interpretative tradition. In other words, women and femininity are thought of in terms of being merely subjects of various forms of male authority and control. This lack of authority is conceptually coupled with the lack of autonomy and control in both the private and public spheres of women's lives as additional conceptual markers of femininity.

Reasoned Discourse and Mind versus Deficiency in Those

Another theme that features prominently in discussions of masculinity in the mainstream Islamic tradition is the idea that only males are capable of rational or reason (*ʿaql*) based discourse and the forming of sound judgment (*raʾy/hazm*). Mainstream Islamic legal and erotic literature has conceptually associated masculinity with, among others, principles of reason.[17] Similarly, in the mainstream Islamic philosophical discourse, masculine traits are associated with concepts such as independence and rationality.[18] The same can be said about canonical hadith literature and Qurʾanic exegesis, where concepts such as rationality and intellect are portrayed as typically masculine and are sites for assertions of male rationality as one of the grounds for their superiority over women.[19] Therefore, rational thought and reason-based discourses are portrayed in the mainstream Islamic interpretative tradition as exclusive markers of masculinity.

On the other hand, femininity is conceptually linked to an irrational predisposition and a strong proclivity for irrational judgment. The idea of women as being the antithesis of knowledge, and religious knowledge in particular, is seen not as an accidental or temporal marker of femininity but an intentional and permanent one.[20] These assumptions are, in turn, used as arguments to justify comprehensive male-based authority over women, both in public and private spheres.[21]

Nature of Male and Female Sexuality

Sexuality is a crucial (but, as we saw above, not the only) marker of what constitutes normative masculinity and femininity. Supposed sexual differences are said to be based on biological and mental functions and capacities that strongly differentiate the sexes. One major concept with respect to the nature of male sexuality is the central position that the concepts of (tribal) female honour (*ʿirḍ*) and its conceptual cognate *ghīra* (jealousy) have in this respect.[22]

Importantly, both these concepts exist in an organic relationship with particular constructions of female modesty (*ḥayāʾ*) as sources of male/family/tribal honor, as will be discussed below. One of the most commonly employed conceptual markers in the mainstream Islamic interpretative tradition used for explaining women's lack of or defective rationality and impaired receptive capacity for knowledge (and therefore illegitimacy of any claims to authority) is that of the particular conceptualization of the nature of female sexuality. In this respect, three concepts—namely *fitna*, *kayd* (trickery), and modesty/shame (*ḥayā'*)—take center stage.[23]

The concept of *fitna* in the context of gender issues in the Islamic tradition can be defined as an irresistible sexual temptation posed by women's active, aggressive, and highly potent sexuality, which can have devastating consequences for the maintenance of the "ideal" and "divinely inspired" Muslim social order. Revealingly, this view of the nature of female sexuality is also reflected by the meaning of the etymological root of the word *fitna* itself. Namely, it is always associated with the women being its subject. The concept of women as sources of *fitna* proceeds from the premise embraced by the mainstream Islamic tradition that the sexual allure of the female for men, and women's reputed looseness, can have catastrophic consequences for the well-being of entire human societies, and even civilizations. In this respect, the supposed inability of women to control their sexual desire and their lack of sexual restraint are also important elements that dominate the mainstream conceptualization of femininity and the nature of female sexuality, in particular. This women-as-*fitna* discourse was also conceptually linked with the idea of sociomoral chaos and the idea of the uncontrollable. One societal consequence of the women-as-*fitna* discourse is the virtually complete exclusion of women from the public sphere as an expression of a religious ideal. The absence of women from the public sphere was justified on the basis of conceptually associating femininity and women with sinfulness and their purported dangerous sexuality embodied in the concept of *fitna*. A particular conceptualization of female modesty/shame (*ḥayā'*) is an additional important conceptual marker that is strongly associated with female sexuality and its nature. *Ḥayā'* is used in the sense of "shyness, diffidence, modesty" as a crucial notion in the mainstream Islamic interpretative tradition and is what a contemporary anthropologist of Islam called "the most feminine of Islamic virtues."[24] One aspect of female *ḥayā'* would entail those behaviors, practices, and attitudes that are in consonance with the idea of women being objects of male authority and control. A contemporary scholar of classical Islamic jurisprudence, Alshech[25] calls these "modesty laws" because they are found in books of Islamic jurisprudence and they are seen as normative at least from the perspective of the Islamic jurists. He includes practices such as the seclusion of women and their complete veiling as examples constitutive of female *ḥayā'*. El Fadl, a leading contemporary scholar of Islamic law, also documents how in contemporary approaches to Islamic interpretative tradition discourses, particular constructions of female "modesty" essentially reduce entire women's bodies, and in some cases even their voices, to that of sexually inciting body parts (*'awrah*). These, in turn, are used to justify women's public invisibility, complete veiling, and comprehensive gender segregation.[26]

The concept of male/family honor (*'irḍ*) and sexual jealousy (*ghīra*) are directly linked to the issues pertaining to the nature of female modesty.[27] Hence, in the context of understanding the nature of female sexuality in the mainstream Islamic interpretative tradition, there is a conceptually organic link between the concept of a particular construction of female *ḥayā'* and the fear of loss of male honor, whose guardians or guarantors are women. In Anwar's words, "Embedded in the masculine concept and practice of honor is the notion of female chastity and decency."[28] Put differently, the above-described conceptualization of female *ḥayāʾ* becomes one of the master signifiers of femininity and female sexuality, in particular.

Another important consideration to keep in mind in the context of discussions on the nature of female *ḥayāʾ* in mainstream Islamic interpretative tradition is the idea of what could be termed female sexual shyness in the context of proper decorum in matters pertaining to licit sexual intercourse and its initiation. This aspect of female *ḥayāʾ* should be interpreted in relation to the point raised above—namely, the idea of sexual conquest being an important marker of masculinity. It is worth noting that this aspect of female *ḥayāʾ* exists in tension with the kind of ideas pertaining to the nature of female sexuality conveyed by the concept of *fitna* discussed above, which view female sexuality as inherently active/aggressive, highly potent, and uncontrollable.[29] Feminist writer and sociologist of Islam Fatima Mernissi (d. 2015) detects this tension between what she terms "explicit" and "implicit" theories of female sexuality that coexist in Muslim cultural contexts.[30] On the one hand, the explicit theory is based on the belief that men are to be aggressive and women passive in their mutual interactions, in general, and in those of a sexual nature, in particular. On the other hand, the implicit theory is premised on the conception of women as embodiments of *fitna*, as explained above. These two theories of female and male sexuality are premised on two very different "logics" and, in fact, endorse conflicting gender roles and norms.

The *fitna*- and *ḥayāʾ*-oriented concept of the nature of female sexuality is further buttressed by the conceptual linking of femininity with that of another concept, *kayd*. *Kayd* can be defined as a kind of trickery or stratagem women resort to in order to manipulate events or men's behavior in a desired direction.[31] The concept has strong sexual overtones and is only applied to women as it implies that their trickery is motivated and manipulated by female sexual desire. Hence, the expression *kayd al-nisāʾ* (the trickery of women). In other words, as in the case of *fitna*, *kayd* as a distinct marker of femininity is associated with all types of anti-divine, negative, and sociomorally eroding forces.[32] Therefore, *kayd*, alongside *fitna* and *ḥayāʾ*, becomes an important conceptual determinant of the nature of female sexuality in the mainstream Islamic interpretative tradition.

In summary, in this section, we highlighted that at the conceptual level, the dominant markers associated with masculinity are overwhelmingly positive and linked with forms of superiority, authority, and control over women, whereas those associated with femininity are its mirror opposites. One could also argue that such conceptualizations of masculinity and femininity could be viewed as the root causes of various forms of marginalization and devaluation of Muslim women's capacities and experiences and a foundation for certain discriminatory practices and societal norms in Muslim (majority) cultural contexts.

The Logic of Patriarchal Honor and Female Modesty Laws

In this section, I explore further the logic and the dynamics behind this conceptual nexus in relation to three practices in which this dynamic plays itself out: (1) veiling/seclusion/gender segregation; (2) FGC; and (3) honor-based violence (HBV), including honor killings. The main argument that is made in the chapter is not whether these practices are "Islamic," but that all these three practices are rooted in the same operative logic—namely, the regulation of female sexuality for the purpose of upholding patriarchal honor. This concept has elsewhere been termed "the logic of patriarchal honor"[33] and will be referred to as such in the rest of this chapter.

In many parts of the world, the upholding of patriarchal honor is directly made contingent on the behavior of their women folk, especially those behaviors that might be interpreted as being sexual in nature.[34] Since the loss of honor is associated with the lowering of the social reputation of the community patriarch, women's behavior in particular becomes subject to communally regulated moral codes. These moral codes differentiate morally praiseworthy from morally repugnant gender roles and norms. Given the organic link between this form of honor and female behavior, moral codes are, in essence, premised on patriarchal notions of ownership of and control of women's sexuality and movement. Although, in theory, moral codes apply to both genders, the patriarchal nature of the concept of honor results in communal incentives to primarily regulate female behavior as women are chiefly considered as the repositories of this kind of honor. The above concept of patriarchal honor is also premised on a certain view of masculinity or "manliness," known in the literature most commonly as hegemonic or traditional masculinity. The above-described concept of patriarchal honor has been an important feature of many (traditional) Muslim-majority cultures.[35] One way in which this appears is through the enforcement of several what could be called sociospatial mechanisms, such as gender segregation and the veiling and seclusion of women.[36]

One important aspect of what I termed the women-as-*fitna* discourse above is that it emerged strongly only in the writings of post-fourth-century Hijri (tenth century CE) Muslim scholars, who, unlike their predecessors, started to increasingly link their explanations and justifications for what Alshech[37] refers to as "modesty laws"[38] (such as gender segregation, seclusion of women, and veiling) to sexual morality rather than social reputation. The process of an increasing conceptual linking between women-as-*fitna* discourse and modesty laws was created, whereby female modesty and female morality became intricately associated with each other. However, this process was, from a historical perspective, only secondary. Prior to the fourth century AH, Muslim scholars' discourse on woman's modesty was primarily linked to that of defending the social status and honor of the family. Given the beliefs and assumptions regarding females' cognitive and emotional predispositions in the mainstream Islamic interpretative tradition discussed previously, the exclusively male Muslim scholars took it upon themselves to put mechanisms in place that would minimize the risk of (free) women putting their own honor and, perhaps more importantly, the honor of the families to which they belonged in jeopardy. The women could compromise the family's honor by, for example, behaving or interacting with the opposite sex in a way that would cause people to doubt their fidelity and purity. Hence, a family's honor and reputation were increasingly linked to the chastity of its women.[39] So, we can conclude that the mainstream interpretative tradition links female modesty laws also to the safeguarding of patriarchal honor, with its attendant negative social and economic implications.

A number of scholars have detected a conceptual link between the concept of aggressive female sexuality, and gender segregation and veiling that is embedded in the logic of patriarchal honor.[40] The same logic is also evident in the manner in which the justifications for FGC—or using the terminology of the mainstream interpretative tradition, *khitān* (female "circumcision")—are proffered. If we examine the nature of the discussions surrounding *khitān* in the mainstream Muslim interpretative tradition, we can clearly detect this logic of patriarchal honor at play. One of the main reasons why FGC was recommended in the Islamic interpretative tradition and practiced in Muslim contexts was to restrain women's sexuality "by limiting their sex drive or, more precisely, by limiting the physical pleasure which they can receive from sexual intercourse."[41] This act of restraining or reducing of women's sexuality in such a manner is premised on the same ideas pertaining to the nature of masculinity and femininity that we described in the previous section. A historian of Islam, Jonathan Berkey writes about female circumcision in Islam:

> The root of the problem lay in certain critical assumptions, common to patriarchal societies, about the nature of female sexuality. In Mediterranean and Near Eastern societies, many shared the misogynistic conviction that women are possessed of an extraordinary sexual appetite, a condition linked to a presumed deficiency in their capacity to reason and consequently, to behave in an ethical fashion.[42]

Furthermore, in these discourses, FGC—unlike male circumcision, which was linked to ritual purity—was considered instrumental to the preservation of female chastity and virtue. Non-circumcised women were viewed as immoral, impure, and incapable of controlling their voracious sexual passions, which, in turn, would compromise the honor of their male patriarch. As in the case of veiling and seclusion, the burden of minimizing the fear of *fitna* falls onto the shoulders of females, in this case by subjecting them to the practice of FGC.

In relation to the link between patriarchal honor and HBV, including honor killings, societies in which HBV occurs most frequently have been described as having highly differentiated gender roles and "emphasize patriarchal rule and control over women and expect female submission and passivity."[43] In many crucial ways, this description of gender roles and norms closely mirrors the conceptual markers of masculinity and femininity in the mainstream Islamic interpretative tradition, as discussed in the previous section.

HBV and honor killings in Muslim contexts could also be indirectly linked to the idea of female sexuality as a male commodity that exists in traditional Muslim cultures. One could argue that the roots of this view are connected to the very nature of the traditional marriage contract, which, in essence, is conceptualized as a form of transaction whereby the husband gains access to the wife's sexual organ and freedom of movement in exchange for having the burden/responsibility of providing for her maintenance (*nafaqa*).[44] Jiwani, a scholar who focuses on HBV, notes that this commodity-like nature of female sexuality underpins the logic of patriarchal honor and can lead to honor killings. In her words,

> Women, as bearers of honor, are regulated by honor codes (e.g., chastity, moral comportment, gender roles). Their sexuality becomes a property that is communally owned and directly related to the social standing of the family and kin. Hence, when a woman has violated such honor codes, she has shamed the family. Her death becomes a vehicle through which the stain of dishonor is removed, and honor restored. It is, therefore, the logic of regulating female sexuality as a repository of patriarchal honour that can lead to honour killings.[45]

In this section, I examined the logic of patriarchal honor in relation to its three major elements that are present in the Muslim context—namely, (1) veiling/seclusion/gender segregation, (2) FGC, and (3) HBV, including honor killings. I demonstrated that all these three practices are embedded in the same operative logic, namely, the regulation of female sexuality for the purpose of upholding patriarchal honor that are intimately linked to the conceptualizations of masculinity and femininity in the mainstream Islamic tradition discussed in the previous section.

Beyond Patriarchal Islam

How can we go beyond these patriarchal interpretations of the Islamic tradition and the concept of patriarchal honor? There are two elements to this question, although there are significant overlaps since conceptual markers of femininity and masculinity are often justified or rationalized through a particular approach to normative Islamic texts.[46] One pertains to interpretational methodology, and the other pertains to issues of conceptual markers of masculinity and femininity that give rise to patriarchal honor as explained above. It is outside the scope of this chapter to deal with the interpretational methodology aspect[47] of this question, but in relation to the latter, the solution, in broadest terms, lies in what is discussed below.

Engendering Alternative Conceptualizations of Gender Cosmologies Based on Reciprocal and Non-hierarchical Relationships

In this respect, it is important to problematize and ultimately destabilize the conceptual prioritizing of masculinity with religious, political, and familial forms of authority and, in turn, conceptually (and actually) strengthening the link between femininity and the religio-political forms of authority. One such initiative that was recently put into practice is to form associations of female Islamic religious leaders (Ulama) such as *Kongres Ulama Perempuan Indonesia* (KUPI) that have the authority to issue fatwas like their male counterparts. The same shift could be achieved through the establishment of religious spaces that affirm female religious and communal authority/leadership. This could be achieved through the establishment and support of women-led mosques (such as the Women's Mosque in America in Los Angeles) or mosques that are run by female imams (as in the case of a Danish female imam of the Mary Mosque in Copenhagen, Sherin Khanakan). The recognition and uplifting of female scholarly authority that engages in the interpretation of normative texts and brings it into fruitful discussion with the existing, male-dominated (and often androcentric) forms of scriptural reasoning are also essential to bring about the necessary paradigm shift in the way gender aspects of religious cosmologies function.

Rethinking the Very Nature and the Conceptual Relationship between Masculinity and Femininity Where Masculinity and Femininity Are Not Considered as Binary Opposites

Traditionalist approaches to the relationship between gender roles, norms, and religion are a by-product of mainstream, patriarchal cultures and cultural value systems that are, to varying extents, either reflected or, in some cases, challenged in the normative religious texts.[48] However, it is important to remember that these normative scriptures provide neither systematic nor comprehensive theories regarding gender roles and norms and that the above-discussed gender oppositionality theory is an outcome of androcentric forms of scriptural reasoning.[49] As such, it is possible to develop alternative conceptual relationships governing the nature of the masculinity–femininity dynamic that are more contextually responsive (i.e., not rooted in supposed biological determinism-based arguments) and are not premised on the logic of complementarity (i.e., oppositionality). The embracing of more dynamic views of masculinity and femininity and the respective gender roles and norms would remove an important element of a patriarchal worldview—namely, the idea of the "naturalness" of male authority, especially in the religious and political realms. This, in turn, would have an emancipatory effect on women's rights, such as in relation to child custody, marriage, and divorce laws, and would help facilitate both a worldview and a world beyond patriarchy in Muslim contexts.

Reconceptualization of the Concept of Honor Itself That Delinks the Honor of Men from the Sexual or Sexually Perceived Behavior of "Their WomenFolk"

As was outlined above, the lowest common denominator of a patriarchal honor-based value system is the conceptual linking of male honor with (perceived) female sexual behavior. In order to engender a world beyond patriarchy, it is essential to, in the short term and at the very minimum, question the rationale behind this form of "honor." In the longer term, it is necessary to shift the very language of honor to that of individual human dignity, where every individual, in their own right, regardless of gender, is considered a source of their own and no one else's honor. This, given our analysis above, would directly contribute to the reduction of HBV in Muslim contexts.

As noted above, the conceptualizations of masculinity and femininity and the concept of patriarchal honor are at times justified on the basis of certain interpretations of Islamic normative texts. Hence, the issue of scriptural reasoning and interpretational methodology is also an important aspect that needs to be considered when developing nonpatriarchal interpretations of Islam.

In this respect, it is important to emphasize that when approached from a certain interpretational framework, the Islamic normative texts can be employed to achieve this paradigm shift from male honor-based to a gender equalitarian dignity-based system of values. There are several scholars, activists, and organizations (myself included) who are associated with the ideas and principles underpinning the theory of progressive Islam working in the field of gender and Islam today. They have, over the past two to three decades, already made important theoretical interventions in relation to the three points outlined above.[50] In what follows, I briefly outline the main elements of their interpretative methodology that can achieve this aim.

One element pertains to the recognition of the influence of the milieu and context that influenced the individual interpreters (most if not all of whom were males) as they relate to the common cultural understandings, societal mores, historical narratives, contemporary scientific understandings, and their own personal biases/subjectivities, which were all significantly shaped by a patriarchal worldview.[51]

An additional characteristic of a non-patriarchal interpretational approach to the Qur'an and Sunna related to the hermeneutical recognition of their need for comprehensive contextualization, especially the ethico-religious and sociolegal injunctions found therein. This means investigating, in a methodical manner, the role of context in the shaping of the very content of the Qur'an and its worldview. For this to take place, we need to recognize the Qur'an's orientation toward the assumed operational discourse of its revelational context that manifests itself in the Qur'anic content and is reflected in the grammatical and syntactical structures employed and embedded in the very language of the Qur'an.[52] This Qur'anically assumed operational discourse must be seen as often reflecting the prevalent religious, cultural, social, political, and economic situation of its direct audience, its first community of listeners and participants rather than introducing them as part of a decidedly new Qur'anic worldview/values. This operational discourse was indeed characterized by patriarchy.[53]

Another feature is based on a thematico-holistic approach to the Qur'an and Sunna, which requires the interpreter to hermeneutically realize that an accurate understanding of a Qur'an- or hadith-based concept is gained only if all the relevant verses dealing with that concept are analyzed and subsequently synthesized into a larger framework of its interpretation by means of a corroborative induction. This is referred to as the thematic and holistic method of interpretation.[54] A thematico-holistic approach to textual evidence concerning the status, position, and the rights of women in the Qur'an and Sunna reveals that sacred texts in fact mitigated existing patriarchal practices and did not initiate them, which is strongly suggestive of the idea that these practices are not integral to their message. A thematic-holistic approach to interpretation suggests that the "comprehensive constant" to all textual evidence uncovered by such an approach amounts to an incremental, progressive improvement of the existing practices pertaining to women.[55]

An additional hermeneutical mechanism that is necessary to overcome patriarchal Islam and the concept of patriarchal honor is *a subscription to a non-salafi-based worldview.* For the purposes of this chapter, we highlight one aspect of this Salafi worldview, namely, its regressive view of the nature of history and time that a priori privileges the interpretative efforts of the early Muslim communities over all others. Thus, Salafism implies a subscription to an epistemologically entirely pre-modern episteme that lacks internal hermeneutical mechanisms to incorporate ethical values and system of ethics that were not prevalent at the time of the formative and classical periods of Islamic thought into its ethical and legal canon. The entire edifice of this traditional/classical/pre-modern Islamic law, legal theory, and ethics was based on an Aristotelian, ethical voluntarist-based system of ethics.[56] This system of ethics, as we saw in the first two sections of the chapter, awarded women an ontologically, ethically, legally, religiously, socially, and politically inferior status vis-à-vis men. It is because of its *salafi weltanschauung* that this approach to the Islamic interpretative system considers this ethical system to be reflective of Divine Will and, as such, the most just system there could ever be.[57] Hence, no evolution of thinking with respect to possible evolution of theories of ethics occurred in classical Islamic thought and its contemporary manifestations.

The next delineating factor is termed purposive and ethico-religious values-based approaches to the interpretation of textual sources (i.e., teleological hermeneutics), and it arises as a direct outgrowth of the previous interpretative tool. The purposive and ethico-religious values-based element of the scriptural hermeneutic is premised on the idea that the actual nature and character of the discourse in the Qur'an and Sunna seek to realize and reach an underlying objective in the form of certain ethico-religious values understood in an ethically objective manner and that are non-patriarchal in nature. In other words, this hermeneutic stipulates that the intended meaning of the text embodies or approximates the spirit or the purpose of the text better than the actual literal meaning itself.[58]

Finally, the last element is premised on the idea of a canon-hadith-dependent Sunna hermeneutics. Sunna, however, differently conceptualized and interpreted, is considered by the majority of Muslims as a source of normative Islamic teachings, including those pertaining to Islamic ethics and law. For a number of reasons examined elsewhere, the concept of a "sound" hadith that consists of a chain of transmitters and a text reportedly traced back to the Prophet's saying or action, or tacit approval of the same, became to a large extent epistemologically and methodologically conflated with the concept of Sunna.[59] Hadith, over time, became an indispensable tool through which the Qur'an was interpreted and provided a large bulk of textual material for the subsequent discourse of Islamic law, theology, and ethics. Much of the hadith literature is patriarchal if not outright misogynist in nature.[60]

However, the concept of Sunna during the formative period of Islam and in non-mainstream approaches to the Islamic interpretative tradition was not conceptualized in such a manner. The concept of Sunna is viewed as a dynamic ethico-religious values-based behavioral concept that is organically linked to that of the Qur'an's *weltanschauung* and is conceptually, hermeneutically, and methodologically independent of the concept of a sound hadith.[61] This conceptual decoupling of hadith from Sunna paves the way to rejection of the normative status of patriarchal and androcentric hadith, which are often used as the basis of patriarchal interpretations of Islam.

Conclusion

In this chapter, I looked at the conceptual relationship between patriarchal honor and female modesty laws in the pre-modern Islamic interpretative tradition and how this conceptual relationship is justified on the basis of a certain understanding of the concept of masculinity and femininity that were embraced in this tradition. I explained how this link between patriarchal honor and female modesty laws gives rise to certain conceptualizations of female modesty, shame, and sexuality and how these modesty laws manifest themselves in the form of practices of veiling, gender segregation, and FGC. In order to challenge such a view of honor and modesty that can still be found in many Muslim cultural contexts, I outlined alternative approaches to gender cosmologies in the Islamic tradition that are based on interpretations of Islamic normative teachings associated with progressive Muslim thought.

Notes

1. By mainstream Islamic interpretative tradition, I mean what today are known as mainstream Sunni and Shi'i expressions of Islam often referred to in form of phrases such as *ahl al-sunna wal jama'a* and Jafari-Twelver Imamism respectively and as delineated in documents such as the Amman Message and as expressed in Islamic jurisprudence, ethics and Qur'ānic exegesis and hadith commentary. https://amman message.com/=. Last accessed June 4, 2021.
2. Adis Duderija, Alina Alak, and Kirstin Hissong, *Islam and Gender: Major Issues and Debates* (New York: Routledge, 2020), 25–43.
3. Chaudhry Ayesha, *Domestic Violence and the Islamic Tradition: Ethics, Law, and the Muslim Discourse on Gender* (Oxford: Oxford University Press, 2013); Ayubi Zahra, *Gendered Morality: Classical Islamic Ethics of the Self, Family and Society* (New York: Columbia University Press, 2019).
4. Ibid.
5. Karen Bauer, *Gender Hierarchy in the Qur'an: Medieval Interpretations, Modern Responses* (Cambridge: Cambridge University Press, 2015).
6. Zahra, *Gendered Morality.*
7. Adis Duderija, "Maqasid al-Shariʿa, Gender Egalitarian Qur'anic Hermeneutics and the Reformation of Muslim Family Law," in *Maqasid al-Shariʿa and Contemporary Reformist Muslim Thought: An Examination*, edited by Adis Duderija (New York: Palgrave, 2014), 193–219.
8. Duderija, Alak, and Hissong, *Islam and Gender*, 25–43.
9. Ibid.
10. David Solomon Jalajel, "Women and Leadership in Islam: A Critical Analysis of Classical Islamic Legal Texts," PhD Thesis, University of Western Cape (2013), 148–61.
11. Bauer, *Gender Hierarchy*, 135.
12. Duderija, Alak, and Hissong, *Islam and Gender*, 25–43.
13. Ibid.
14. Ibid.
15. Ayesha, *Domestic Violence*, 1–20.
16. Hassan Eshkevari, "Rethinking Men's Authority over Women: Qiwāma, Wilāya and Their Underlying Assumptions," in *Gender Equality in Muslim Family Law: Justice and Ethics in Islamic Legal Tradition*, edited by Z. Mir-Hosseini, L. Larsen, C. Moe, and K. Vogt, translated by Ziba Mir Hosseini (London: I.B. Tauris, 2013), 191–211.

17. Jalajel, "Women and Leadership"; Fatna Sabbah, *Woman in the Muslim Subconscious* (New York: Pergamon Press, 1984).
18. Anwar Etin, *Gender and Self in Islam* (Abingdon: Routledge, 2006).
19. Bauer, *Gender Hierarchy*.
20. Duderija, Alak, and Hissong, *Islam and Gender*, 32–8.
21. Ibid., 44–59.
22. Ibid., 31–2, 34–5.
23. Ibid., 34–5.
24. Saba Mahmood, *Politics of Piety: The Islamic Revival and the Feminist Subject* (Princeton, NJ: Princeton University Press, 2004), 155.
25. Eli Alshech, "Out of Sight and Therefore Out of Mind: Early Sunni Islamic Modesty Regulations and the Creation of Spheres of Privacy," *Journal of Near Eastern Studies* 66 (2007), 267–90.
26. Khaled Abou El Fadl, *Speaking in God's Name: Islamic Law, Authority and Women* (Oxford: Oneworld, 2001).
27. Duderija, Alak, and Hissong, *Islam and Gender*, 31–2, 44–58.
28. Anwar, *Gender and Self in Islam*, 129.
29. Sabbah, *Woman*.
30. Fatima Mernissi, *Beyond the Veil: Male-Female Dynamics in Muslim Society* (London: Saqi, 2011).
31. Fedwa Maulty-Douglas, *Woman's Body, Woman's Word: Gender and Discourse in Arabo-Islamic Writing* (Princeton, NJ: Princeton University Press, 1991).
32. Sabbah, *Woman*; Maulty-Douglas, *Woman's Body*.
33. Duderija, Alak, and Hissong, *Islam and Gender*, 44–58.
34. Ibid.
35. In the Arabic speaking world this concept of honour carries the name *'irḍ*, *'irz* in Turkish, *nāmus* in Persian and Kurdish and *'izzat* in the South Asian context.
36. Duderija, Alak, and Hissong, *Islam and Gender*, 44–58.
37. Alshech, "Out of Sight and Therefore Out of Mind."
38. Laws in the sense as found in the discussions of Islamic jurisprudence books.
39. Alshech, "Out of Sight and Therefore Out of Mind."
40. Duderija, Alak, and Hissong, *Islam and Gender*, 44–58.
41. Jonathan Berkey, "Circumcision Circumscribed: Female Excision and Cultural Accommodation in the Medieval Near East," *International Journal of Middle East Studies* 28 (1996), 19–38, 30.
42. Ibid.
43. Dietrich Oberwittler and Julia Kasselt, "Honour Killings," in *The Oxford Handbook of Gender, Sex and Crime*, edited by Rosemary Gartner and Bill McCarthy (Oxford: Oxford University Press, 2014), 653.
44. Abu Hamid Al Ghazali, *Book on the Etiquette of Marriage*, translated by Madelain Farah (Salt Lake City: University of Utah Press, 1984); Ziba Mir Hosseini, "Justice, Equality and Muslim Family Laws: New Ideas, New Prospects," in *Gender Equality and Muslim Family Law: Justice and Ethics in Islamic Legal Tradition*, edited by Z. Mir Hosseini, Lena Larsen, Christian Moe, and Kari Vogt (London: I.B. Tauris, 2013), 7–36.
45. Yasmin, Jiwani, "A Clash of Discourses: Femicides or Honor Killings?," in *Re-Imagining the Other: Culture, Media, and Western-Muslim Intersections*, edited by Mahmoud Eid and Karim H. Karim (New York: Palgrave Macmillan, 2014), 121–52, 125.

46. Adis Duderija, *Constructing Religiously Ideal "Believer" and "Muslim Woman" Concepts: Neo-Traditional Salafi and Progressive Muslim Methods of Interpretation (Manahij)* (New York: Palgrave, 2011).
47. Ibid.
48. Ibid.
49. Ibid.
50. Aysha Hidayatullah, *Feminist Edges of the Qur'an* (New York: Oxford University Press, 2014); Duderija, *Constructing.*
51. Bauer, *Gender Hierarchy.*
52. Adis Duderija, "The Hermeneutical Importance of Qur'anic Assumptions in the Development of a Values Based and Purposive Oriented Qur'an -Sunna Hermeneutic: Case Study of Patriarchy and Slavery," *HAWWA-Journal of Women in the Middle East and the Muslim World* 11 (2013), 58–87.
53. Ibid.
54. Duderija, *Constructing*, 148–50.
55. Ibid.
56. That is, that ethical value terms mean only what is approved or disapproved, commanded or forbidden by God. In terms of Islamic legal theory this would translate into a view that all ethico-moral and legal rules must ultimately be derived from prescriptions enunciated by God.
57. Adis Duderija, *The Imperatives of Progressive Islam* (London: Routledge, 2017), 31–56.
58. Duderija, *Constructing*, 151–5.
59. Adis Duderija, "The Evolution in The Concept of Sunnah during the First Four Generations of Muslims in Relation to the Development of the Concept of an Authentic Ḥadīth as Based on Recent Western Scholarship," *Arab Law Quarterly* 26 (2012), 393–447.
60. El Fadl, *Speaking.*
61. Adis Duderija, "A Paradigm Shift in Assessing /Evaluating the Value and Significance of Hadith in Islamic Thought- From *'ulūm-ul-ḥadīth* to *uṣūl-ul-fiqh*," *Arab Law Quarterly* 23 (2009), 195–206.

Bibliography

Alak, Alina, Adis Duderija, and Kirstin Hissong. *Islam and Gender: Major Issues and Debates*. New York: Routledge, 2020.

Al Ghazali, Abu Hamid. *Book on the Etiquette of Marriage*. Translated by Madelain Farah. Salt Lake City: University of Utah Press, 1984.

Alshech, Eli. "Out of Sight and Therefore Out of Mind: Early Sunni Islamic Modesty Regulations and the Creation of Spheres of Privacy." *Journal of Near Eastern Studies* 66 (2007): 267–90.

Anwar, Etin. *Gender and Self in Islam*. Abingdon: Routledge, 2006.

Ayubi, Zahra. *Gendered Morality: Classical Islamic Ethics of the Self, Family and Society*. New York: Columbia University Press, 2009.

Bauer, Karen. *Gender Hierarchy in the Qur'an: Medieval Interpretations, Modern Responses*. Cambridge: Cambridge University Press, 2015.

Berkey, Jonathan. "Circumcision Circumscribed: Female Excision and Cultural Accommodation in the Medieval Near East." *International Journal of Middle East Studies* 28 (1996): 19–38.

Chaudhry, Ayesha. *Domestic Violence and the Islamic Tradition: Ethics, Law, and the Muslim Discourse on Gender*. Oxford: Oxford University Press, 2013.

Duderija, Adis. "Maqasid al-Shari'ah, Gender Egalitarian Qur'anic Hermeneutics and the Reformation of Muslim Family Law." In *Maqasid al-Shari'a and Contemporary Reformist Muslim Thought: An Examination*. Edited by Adis Duderija, 194–219. New York: Palgrave, 2014.

Duderija, Adis. *Constructing Religiously Ideal "Believer" and "Muslim Woman" Concepts: Neo- Traditional Salafi and Progressive Muslim Methods of Interpretation* (Manahij). New York: Palgrave, 2011.

Duderija, Adis. "The Hermeneutical Importance of Qur'anic Assumptions in the Development of a Values Based and Purposive Oriented Qur'an-Sunna Hermeneutic: Case Study of Patriarchy and Slavery." *HAWWA-Journal of Women in the Middle East and the Muslim World* 11 (2013): 58–87.

Duderija, Adis. "The Evolution in the Concept of Sunnah during the First Four Generations of Muslims in Relation to the Development of the Concept of an Authentic Hadith as Based on Recent Western Scholarship." *Arab Law Quarterly* 26 (2012): 393–447.

Duderija, Adis. "A Paradigm Shift in Assessing /Evaluating the Value and Significance of ḥadīth in Islamic Thought- From *'ulūm-ul-ḥadīth to uṣūl-ul-fiqh*." *Arab Law Quarterly* 23 (2009): 195–206.

Duderija, Adis. *The Imperatives of Progressive Islam*. London: Routledge, 2017.

El Fadl, Khaled. *Speaking in God's Name: Islamic Law, Authority and Women*. Oxford: Oneworld, 2001.

Eshkevari, Hassan. "Rethinking Men's Authority over Women: Qiwama, Wilaya and Their Underlying Assumptions." In *Gender Equality in Muslim Family Law: Justice and Ethics in Islamic Legal Tradition*. Edited by Z. Mir-Hosseini, L. Larsen, C. Moe, and K. Vogt. Translated by Ziba Mir Hosseini, 191–213. London: I.B. Tauris, 2013.

Hidayatullah, Aysha. *Feminist Edges of the Qur'an*. New York: Oxford University Press, 2014.

Jalajel, David Solomon. "Women and Leadership in Islam: A Critical Analysis of Classical Islamic Legal Texts." PhD Thesis. University of Western Cape, 2013.

Jiwani, Yasmin. "A Clash of Discourses: Femicides or Honor Killings?." In *Re-Imagining the Other: Culture, Media, and Western-Muslim Intersections*. Edited by Mahmoud Eid and Karim H. Karim, 121–52. New York: Palgrave Macmillan, 2014.

Mahmood, Saba. *Politics of Piety: The Islamic Revival and the Feminist Subject*. Princeton, NJ: Princeton University Press, 2004.

Maulty-Douglas, Fedwa. *Woman's Body, Woman's Word: Gender and Discourse in Arabo-Islamic Writing*. Princeton, NJ: Princeton University Press, 1991.

Mernissi, Fatima. *Beyond the Veil: Male-Female Dynamics in Muslim Society*. London: Saqi, 2011.

Mir-Hosseini, Ziba. "Justice, Equality and Muslim Family Laws: New Ideas, New Prospects." In *Gender Equality and Muslim Family Law: Justice and Ethics in Islamic Legal Tradition*. Edited by Ziba Mir Hosseini, Lena Larsen, Christian Moe, and Kari Vogt, 7–36. London: I.B. Tauris, 2013.

Oberwittler, Dietrich and Julia Kasselt. "Honour Killings." In *The Oxford Handbook of Gender Sex and Crime*. Edited by Rosemary Gartner and Bill McCarthy. Oxford: Oxford University Press, 2015.

Sabbah, Fatna. *Woman in the Muslim Subconscious*. New York: Pergamon Press, 1984.

3

The Visible and Invisible Kaleidoscope of *ḥayā*ʾ: Theologies and Mystics of Shame and Modesty in the Persianate World (Tenth to Seventeenth Centuries)

Amélie Neuve-Eglise

Introduction

Narrations on *ḥayā*ʾ that were circulating in scholarly circles of the Persianate world in the tenth and subsequent centuries show a plurality of subjects, objects, and shades associated with this notion. A hadith attributed to Jaʿfar ibn Muhammad al-Sadiq (d. 148/765) distinguishes between five different forms of *ḥayā*ʾ, while others encourage practising modesty not only in society but also before God and oneself. In his manual of Sufism, Al-Qushayri (d. 1072) counts up to seven kinds or expressions of shame and modesty,[1] while others discuss the distinct degrees (*darajāt*) and manifestations of *ḥayā*ʾ.

The present chapter is not intended to be a comprehensive inventory of the assessments of *ḥayā*ʾ present in the sacred texts of Islam and writings of major Muslim scholars in the Persianate world. It rather aims to examine some of its uses to underline the complexities and ambivalences of this notion and how it is inhabited by tensions expressed in the frame of anthropologies, theologies, and mystics. Such tensions involve dynamics of veiling and unveiling, enunciations and silences, inner states of contraction and expansion, along with a rich set of emotions that underline the complex and unstable nature of what can be shown, said, and seen in different contexts. To this end, we will examine the way in which the notion of *ḥayā*ʾ and its derivatives are addressed in the Qurʾan, hadiths compiled by Shiʿite theologians from the tenth century onwards, as well as in theological works and treatises on Sufism composed in the Persianate world by Sunni and Shiʿite authors between the tenth and seventeenth centuries. We will also discuss how some of these sources tackle *ḥayā*ʾ not as a fixed concept with a clearly defined moral content, but more as a living phenomenon that springs from movements of the soul, gazes, or glances that constrain as much as instil action.

The dynamics and ambiguities of *ḥayāʾ* make it difficult to provide a single translation of this concept throughout this chapter. Depending on contexts, we will translate it sometimes as modesty and sometimes as shame, bearing in mind that neither term exhausts the semantic richness of *ḥayāʾ*.[2]

Istiḥyāʾ in the Qurʾan

The verbal noun *istiḥyāʾ*, which comes from the same root as *ḥayāʾ*, is mentioned in the Qurʾan to describe the modest gait of Shuʿayb's daughter in her first encounter with Moses (Q. 28:25).[3] This notion here refers to the specific bodily movement of a young woman in the presence of a stranger. In another verse, the conjugated form *yastaḥyī* describes the Prophet Muhammad's discomfort when he shies from asking his chatting guests to leave after a shared meal at his home (Q. 33:53). In this context, *ḥayāʾ* is a form of social propriety that curbs the expression of emotions and involves an attitude of self-restraint in dealing with others. However, after disclosing Muhammad's inner feelings and calling his guests to order, the end of the verse introduces a contrast between the Prophet's bashful silence and the word of the revelation by stating that "God is not ashamed (*lā yastaḥyī*) of [expressing] the truth" (Q. 33:53). Therefore, such verse holds a tension between compliance with social etiquette and the expression of the truth (*al-ḥaqq*). By attributing a form of shame and modesty to the Prophet and denying it to God, it raises the question of the articulation of two fields of communication: that which governs social customs, where non-saying would be appropriate so as not to hurt the other, and that of God with regard to man, based on straightforwardness and acting as a reminder of the rules of courtesy by revealing Muhammad's intimate feelings. The denial of a form of restraint in God in this context also underlines that in the field of revelation, the expression of truth is not limited to strictly theological and legal matters, nor does it avoid what may be labeled by some as semantic triviality. Thus, according to another verse, "God does not shy (*lā yastaḥyī*) from drawing comparisons even with something as small as a gnat, or larger: the believers know it is the truth from their Lord, but the disbelievers say, 'What does God mean by such a comparison?'" (Q. 2:26).[4] The conjugated form of *istiḥyāʾ* also appears in other verses to refer to Pharaoh's sparing the women's lives—and probably chastity—among the people of Moses subjected to his oppression (Q. 28:4). In these different occurrences, the notion of *istiḥyāʾ* is associated with a restraint in body, speech, and deed, although its precise content and contours are not clearly defined.[5]

Facets of *ḥayāʾ* in Shiʿite Hadith and the Writings of Muslim Scholars

Several hadiths mentioning the concept of *ḥayāʾ* have been attributed to Muhammad as well as the Imams of Shiʿism, mainly ʿAli ibn Abi Talib (d. 661) and Jaʿfar ibn Muhammad al-Sadiq (d. 765). Al-Kulayni (d. 941) and Al-Sharif al-Radi (d. 1015) are among the major compilers of such hadiths, which are quoted in later collections.[6]

Ja'far al-Sadiq distinguishes five forms of *ḥayāʾ*: the modesty or shame of sin (*zanb*), deficiency or falling short (*taqṣīr*), generosity (*karāma*), love (*ḥubb*), and awe (*hayba*).[7] Several hadiths present modesty as a disposition inherent to humans and a foundation of morals. In *Ghurar al-Hikam*, which collects the aphorisms of ʿAli ibn Abi Talib, *ḥayāʾ* is described as a beautiful natural disposition (*khuluq jamīl*)[8] as well as the whole magnificence and the best character.[9] It is one of the noble character traits (*makārim al-akhlāq*) with which God endowed the Prophets[10] and is close to the notion of *ḥishma*, which conveys the ideas of decency, deference, and shame.[11]

Among its effects, *ḥayāʾ* guards against morally wrong deeds[12] and acts as a garment that prevents people from seeing the flaws of its wearer.[13] It arouses God's love[14] and is referred to as "the key to every goodness."[15] Modesty and shame are also closely associated with the notion of chastity and self-restraint (*'afāf*).[16] A hadith attributed to ʿAli ibn Abi Talib states that the most chaste is the one who shows more *ḥayāʾ*.[17] Shame is also seen either as the cause[18] or the fruit[19] of chastity. It is opposed to the notions of debauchery (*khana*),[20] indecency (*qiḥa*),[21] and hypocritical ostentation (*riyā'*).[22] While some hadiths clearly relate modesty or shame to female virtue and consider woman as their main subject,[23] most of them are general in scope and seem to concern human beings as a whole.

In several hadiths, *ḥayāʾ* appears as a malleable phenomenon, whose content and intensity vary according to the way it relates with faith (*īmān*) and reason (*'aql*).[24] For ʿAli ibn Abi Talib, "modesty and faith are closely linked together, if either of them is lost, so is the other."[25] Its weakening also leads to a decline in piety. Modesty is therefore not seen as a fixed disposition but as an inclination that can be cultivated, thus acquiring more depth or, on the contrary, disappearing if it is not nurtured by specific beliefs or thoughts. According to another hadith relating an event in pre-eternity, Gabriel descended upon Adam and asked him to choose one thing between reason,[26] modesty, and religion. He chose reason. When Gabriel asked the other two to leave, they replied, "O Gabriel, we have been instructed to remain with reason wherever it may be."[27] Modesty is here associated with a form of common sense. In a similar spirit, ʿAli ibn Abi Talib describes modesty as the fruit of reason[28] and asserts that the most reasonable person is the most modest one.[29] *Ḥayāʾ* is also susceptible to deviations: reasonable modesty/shame should be distinguished from the foolish one[30] when, for instance, a person shies from asking a question for fear of revealing her ignorance.[31] The notion of foolish *ḥayāʾ* echoes the divine condemnation of modesty when it prevents the expression of and access to the truth (Q. 33:53). Several hadiths also strongly condemn it because instead of preserving life, it may prevent sustenance[32] and cause deprivation.[33]

These narrations do not limit *ḥayāʾ* to its social expressions and effects, but also consider it in the frame of an intimate relationship with one's inner self and with God. According to hadiths attributed to ʿAli ibn Abi Talib, the most eminent *ḥayāʾ* consists in being modest to oneself[34] and before God.[35] Faith and following the precepts of a revealed law expand the scope of what may be a source of modesty and shame. *Ḥayāʾ* is therefore designed to embrace the most intimate dimensions of the believer's life, as underlined by the injunction of Musa al-Kazim (d. 799), the seventh Imam of Twelver Shiʿism: "Be modest before God in your inner self as you are in public before people."[36]

Interiority and exteriority are closely interlinked since, according to this aphorism attributed to ʿAli ibn Abi Talib, "he who is not modest before people is not modest before God."[37]

Modesty before God (*ḥayāʾ min Allāh*) involves both a corporal restraint, an attention to body and mind sustenance, and an awareness of the Hereafter, as underlined in this prophetic hadith: "Modesty before God consists in protecting one's mind from what it learns, one's stomach from what it ingests, and in remembering death and the tribulations attached to it."[38] Here *ḥayāʾ* is conceived not only as a regulating principle of individual and social worldly lives, but also as an act of remembrance turned toward the Hereafter. It is also rooted in a theology of the divine gaze, according to which God is infinitely close to His creatures and is aware of their intentions and deeds.[39] Such modesty is endowed with specific effects, such as erasing many sins[40] and preserving from the torment of fire.[41] Some hadiths, which are less frequently quoted and do not appear in the classical collections, also ascribe a form of *ḥayāʾ* to God himself. The idea of a divine modesty, which does not appear in the Qurʾan, raises the question of a possible equivocality of this notion. Such modesty is often associated with the notions of mercy and magnanimity, and among its manifestations is God's refusal to leave empty the hands that a supplicant raises to Him. Islamic and Arabic literary scholar al-Raghib al-Isfahani (d. 1108) also mentions God's reluctance to torment an elderly Muslim for his faults as an illustration of this form of *ḥayāʾ*.[42] The variety of these hadiths provides deeper insights into the various subjects and objects of modesty. However, they don't specify the precise content of this notion and what would distinguish "good" modesty/shame from its "deviant" manifestations. Most of these hadiths are more general statements than peremptory injunctions that would place modesty within a system of rules and laws.

Islamic scholars and theologians have integrated some of these narrations into their reflections on the meaning, scope, and effects of *ḥayāʾ*. While adding some elements of psychology, they have often placed modesty in the field of morality and defined it in contrast to the notion of the vile and ugly (*qubḥ/qabīḥ*). Al-Raghib al-Isfahani defines modesty as the self-restraint or contraction (*inqibāḍ*) of the soul before morally wrong and abominable acts (*qabāʾiḥ*), which leads one to abstain from them.[43] Modesty stems firstly from an inner perception that produces a movement of contraction. However, he does not specify whether such deeds are abandoned because of a repulsive stigma that would be inherent to the nature of certain things or whether such a move occurs as a result of an acquired knowledge of norms and the fear of social disapproval. We are here faced with an ambiguity between *ḥayāʾ* as a disposition inherent to human beings and *ḥayāʾ* as acquired—or strengthened—by faith and the knowledge of a religious morality. Al-Isfahani also specifies the meaning of divine modesty. *Ḥayāʾ* may be ascribed to God not in the sense of a state entailing the contraction of his being (as it would imply a form of pathos incompatible with his omnipotence), but to testify to his mercy with regard to the faults of the weakest among believers. *Ḥayāʾ* may therefore be used to describe him as a virtuous agent free from any despicable deed.[44] In both divine and human realms, modesty is part of a movement of distancing from base acts, either through a refusal to commit them or a will to "cover" them.

The association of modesty with a movement of repulsion and contraction was taken up and completed by other Islamic scholars in the following centuries. The

Shiraz-born Sunni theologian and grammarian al-Jurjani (d. 1414) put forward the idea of modesty or shame as a self-restraint or contraction (*inqibāḍ*) of the soul before something that leads one to abstain from it, and attributed its origin to a desire to protect oneself from the blame (*lawm*) attached to it. He distinguishes between an innate shame pertaining to the soul (*nafsānī*) and deriving from God's act of creation, such as that felt toward exposing one's private parts or having sexual relations in public, and a shame related to faith (*īmānī*), which prevents the believers from engaging in acts of disobedience (*maʿāṣī*) out of fear of God.[45] *Ḥayāʾ* is thus conceived both as a natural disposition regarding the body and its intimacy and as an acquired belief that strengthens the former and ties it to a wider field of prohibitions. Later works have proposed similar definitions while fleshing them out with specific details. In his commentary on a hadith presenting modesty as part of faith, the Twelver Shiʿite scholar Muhammad Baqir al-Majlisi (d. 1699) defines *ḥayāʾ* as a disposition (*malaka*) of the soul that creates a contraction and withdrawal from abominable acts and an aversion (*inzijār*) to what contravenes rules and morals, for fear of blame. For Majlisi, faith in God, His Messenger, and in reward and punishment, coupled with the knowledge of what is defined as morally wrong by the legislator (*shāriʿ*), gives rise to a twofold and complementary phenomenon: modesty before God, the Messenger, and the angels, and the aversion of the soul to evil and illicit things (*muḥarramāt*).[46] Modesty is here clearly inscribed in a religious legal system. It is rooted in a double authority, internal and external, which produces a restraint associated with a fear or concern for the gaze of visible and invisible beings.

Divine and Human *ḥayāʾ* in Sufi Treatises

The topic of *ḥayāʾ* before God is addressed in several Sufi manuals composed between the eleventh and fourteenth centuries in the Persianate world by Sufis and theologians of both Sunni and Shiʿa faith, many of whom are from Khorasan. These treatises are often both didactic and apologetic. They quote the Qurʾan, hadiths, and the sayings of Sufi masters to expose a path, methods, or the different stages of wayfaring toward God. The theme of modesty/shame is often addressed in short chapters, through aphorisms and quotations from sages whose names are not always specified.

In *The Qushayriyyan Epistle on the Science of Sufism* (*Al-Risala al-Qushayriyya fi ʿIlm al-Tasawwuf*), one of the earliest and most comprehensive manuals of Sufism, ʿAbd al-Karim al-Qushayri (d. 1072) devotes a chapter to the concept of *ḥayāʾ* that begins with the quotation of a Qurʾanic verse: "Does he not realise that God sees all?" (Q. 96:14).[47] He thereby links human *ḥayāʾ* to God's omniscient gaze and to the believer's faith in an invisible observing presence enacting good and evil through revelation. He also mentions a hadith of Muhammad mentioned earlier, which associates this form of modesty with the preservation of one's spirit and body as well as with the remembrance of death and resurrection.[48] According to other sayings attributed to sages (*ḥukamāʾ*) and Sufi masters gathered in this chapter, modesty toward God is a modulated reality than can be enhanced if one shares the company of the people who have it. Together with reverential fear (*hayba*), it is described as the "greatest knowledge" (*al-ʿilm al-akbar*) that may be cultivated through asceticism and piety. It remains associated with a movement of contraction of the heart (*inqibāḍ al-qalb*) turned toward the invisible world, which goes along and allows a true glorification of the Lord (*taʿẓīm al-rabb*). Modesty implies a reorientation of the affects, in particular fear, toward God. In turn, it produces a detachment and frees the person from concerns related to worldly matters.[49]

Al-Qushayri also distinguishes between different forms of *ḥayāʾ* by taking elements from a hadith of Jaʿfar al-Sadiq[50] while adding others. According to the distinctions he proposes, *ḥayāʾ* is not only a phenomenon that concerns embodied flesh and blood beings, but it also encompasses angels and, in ways that need to be clarified, God himself. The shame of sin (*ḥayāʾ al-jināya*) is one of its human manifestations. According to the illustration provided by al-Qushayri, its archetypal figure is Adam when, after having disobeyed God and while he was trying to hide himself, God asked him, "O Adam, are you fleeing from Me?" Adam then declared that he was fleeing out of shame before God. Another kind of shame is that of deep humility (*ḥayāʾ al-istiḥqār*), which Moses would have felt when he confided to God that he did not dare to ask Him for a need related to this worldly life. As a response, God gently exhorted him not to exclude daily material sustenance from the scope of invocation: "Ask Me, even for salt for your dough and fodder for your sheep!" Such invitation to set aside this type of shame outlines a theology of intimacy with God. The exchange between God and Moses can also be seen as a kind of courtesy game, where a man humbly acknowledges his indigence toward his self-sufficient Creator, leading the latter to reassert His all-encompassing magnanimity. It also echoes the idea expressed in the Qurʾan that God does not shy from drawing comparisons even with a gnat (Q. 2:26), and consequently, that divine action and words cannot be fathomed through binary categories such as the (human) opposition between the noble and the trivial.

Prophet Muhammad's attitude towards his guests, who lingered in his house after a shared meal and whom he did not dare to dismiss (Q. 33:53), is mentioned as an example of the shame of generosity (*ḥayāʾ al-karam*). Al-Qushayri also places in this category the shame felt by Shuʿayb's daughter toward Moses (Q. 28:25), which he considers to stem from the fear that the latter would decline her invitation.[51] It is interesting to note that the shame of this young woman before this unknown man is not interpreted on the basis of her gender but is linked to issues of hospitality and the concern of being turned down. In these different manifestations, shame brings into play issues related to the upholding of an ontological and social order and serves to reaffirm what it is possible to say and do in the presence of a visible or invisible Other.

According to Al-Qushayri, the experience of *ḥayāʾ* before God is not restricted to humans and may also be shared by angels. Thus, Israfil was subject to the shame of reverence (*ijlāl*) when, faced with a feeling of indigence in the presence of the divine greatness, he draped himself in his wings. Similarly, it was the shame of deficiency or falling short (*taqṣīr*) that gave rise to the angels' exclamation before their Creator: "Glory to You! We have not worshipped You as You deserved to be worshipped." Junayd seems to have this kind of shame in mind in one of his sayings quoted by Al-Qushayri, where he describes it as a state arising from the concomitant vision (*rūʾya*) of the blessings granted by God and of one's own insufficiencies.[52] Shame is thus born out of the experience of a fundamental discordance between an absolute fullness and absolute emptiness, along with a radical impossibility of filling the ontological gap between the divine and the created.

Al-Qushayri also attributes shame to the "Lord" (*rabb*), which is that of the beneficence (*ḥayāʾ al-inʿām*). Here, the subject of shame is not God in His essence, but in His lordship and as a sustainer of His creation. As an illustration, al-Qushayri mentions that in the Hereafter, after the servant has crossed the bridge of the Sirat, the Lord will give him a sealed book and say to him, "You did what you did, but I am ashamed (*qad astaḥyit*) to show it to you. Go, for I have forgiven you."[53] Here, divine shame allows the omniscient gaze of the Lord not to be synonymous with an absolute transparency between Him and His creature, which would condemn the latter to everlasting shame. In this context, divine shame manifests itself through a refusal to mention sin explicitly and to make it seen. It creates a space between absolute transparency and opacity that may allow forgiveness and shape salvation. It also enables parallels to be explored between some manifestations of divine and human *ḥayāʾ*. Thus, the shame of generosity felt by Muhammad in front of his guests may echo divine shame as an act of concealment of human flaws. It also introduces some nuances in a conception of God as saying and showing the true and the real in all circumstances. While this idea is stated in the Qurʾan in the context of revelation (Q. 33:53; 2:26), the narrative mentioned by al-Qushayri allows for other perspectives in the context of an intimate encounter between the Lord and man in the Hereafter.

Al-Qushayri's work posits shame and modesty as states or experiences that inhabit the whole human destiny, from Adam's initial shame to the Lord's final forgiveness, which allows for a liberation from shame. It also outlines a theology that oscillates between apophaticism—as implied in the shame of deficiency or "falling short"—and a closeness and even intimate divine solicitude toward creatures. Nevertheless, his reflection on shame first and foremost reaffirms the incommensurable space between the divine and the created.

Many of the ideas set out in al-Qushayri's manual can be found in later works. This is the case of Rashid al-Din Abu al-Fadl Maybudi's commentary on the Qurʾan (early twelfth century), where the different forms of *ḥayāʾ* are mentioned in very similar terms. Maybudi also endorses the idea that man's shame before God lies in a consciousness of His invisible gaze.[54] Here, again, the implacable dimension of divine omniscience is alleviated by God's *ḥayāʾ* before man, an idea that appears in the frame of an account similar to that of Al-Qushayri, but with a specific emphasis on the link between divine *ḥayāʾ* and love for creatures. According to this narrative, at the door of Paradise, a letter from God entitled "the Eternal love" will arrive. After recalling all the blessings granted by God to man and the little that man does for Him, the Author of the letter states, "My servant! You did what you did, but I am ashamed to chastise you as is worthy for you. Instead I will do what is worthy for Me. Go, for I have forgiven you, so that you will know that I am I and you are you."[55] Here *ḥayāʾ* is inscribed in a complex dynamic that reaffirms the ontological gap separating the Creator from His creature and the rank occupied by each, while at the same time allowing a form of rapprochement through the deployment of a divine magnanimity and love.

Maybudi also envisages divine and humane shame in an economy of concealment of sins, which creates interstices so that what is a source of shame may remain hidden. As an illustration, Maybudi relates a story according to which "the servant will be given his book in his hand and he will see his acts of disobedience. He will be ashamed to read them out. The Real will address him and say, "On the day when you were doing that and you had no shame, I did not disgrace you but instead concealed it. Today when you are ashamed, how could I disgrace you?"[56] Maybudi then mentions a saying attributed to Muhammad according to which "God does not curtain a servant's sin in this world to reproach him with it on the Day of Resurrection."[57] If modesty or shame are initially associated with the believer's awareness of God's gaze upon him, it finds a form of denouement in the fact that God can veil and refuse to show. Complex dynamics are at play, as the human shame that was initially born from the awareness of a divine gaze ultimately entails the turning away of this gaze. Maybudi quotes another narration to underline that divine *ḥayāʾ* is closely linked to a generosity that manifests itself through the answering of invocations: "God is *ḥayy* and generous, he shows *ḥayāʾ* towards His servant if he reaches out to him." Such magnanimity emphasizes again the ontological gap between the Uncreated and the created as well as the discordance and shame it may produce, as Maybudi's mention of this hadith *qudsī* suggests: "My Servant is not fair to Me; He calls me and I am ashamed to turn him down, while he disobeys Me and is not ashamed of Me."[58]

Maybudi also distinguishes three forms of human *ḥayāʾ*: that of the careless ones (*ghāfilān*), who only show modesty or feel shame toward creation and are deemed as unjust and wrongdoers (*ẓālim*); that of the possessors of reason (*ʿāqilān*), who show shame before angels and are moderate (*muqtaṣid*); and finally that of the people endowed with true knowledge (*ʿārifān*), who are ashamed before God and are forerunners (*sābiqān*) in knowledge and good deeds.[59] Such a triad echoes a Qurʾanic verse of Surah Fāṭir, where three kinds of chosen servants to whom the Scripture was given as a heritage are distinguished: "Some of them wronged their own souls, some stayed between [right and wrong], and some, by God's leave, were foremost in good deeds" (Q. 35:32).[60]

Hierarchical classifications of different forms of *ḥayāʾ* are found in various writings of Sufis, including older ones such as *Manazil al-Saʿirin* authored by the Sunni theologian and Sufi ʿAbdullah al-Ansari al-Harawi (d. 1088). He proposes a distinction between three degrees (*darajāt*) of shame or modesty, which vary according to different ways of conceiving and experiencing the divine presence. The first degree is born from the servant's knowledge (*ʿilm al-ʿabd*) that God sees him and causes him to strive to abstain from sins and crimes. The second degree stems from a knowledge of God's closeness to him; it brings about familiarity and love and turns the servant away from worldly life. Finally, the third degree arises from the contemplation (*shuhūd*) of the divine presence. Here, *ḥayāʾ* becomes imbued with reverential awe and erases any form of dispersion (*tafraqa*) in his being. However, such a state does not correspond to the end of the journey and the highest station.[61]

The classification proposed by al-Ansari in this context also outlines a hierarchy of affects, with the idea that increased proximity to God does not give rise to an intensification of love, but rather to a reverential fear that arises from an (always incomplete) vision of the divine incommensurability. Shame as an acute awareness of this ontological cut is a motif that runs through many works, including Iranian Sufi Ruzbihan Baqla Shirazi's (d. 1209) *Mashrab al-Arwah*. While detailing the different states and stations (*maqāmāt*) of the gnostics, he defines modesty in the context of the vision of the divine majesty (*ʿaẓama*). Such vision produces a paradoxical state: it leads to the annihilation of the self (*fanāʾ*) of the gnostic in God, but such annihilation remains incomplete, as the vision also causes an awareness of the limitations of his own existence that gives rise to a form of shame (*khajal*). Ruzbihan does not end his reflection at that point and offers rich considerations on the dynamics of *ḥayāʾ*. In another moment, when the gnostic considers his soul as a sincere servant free of all ambition, then God, in turn, looks upon him with reverence. It is this divine gaze of *ḥayāʾ* on the gnostic who has reached a state of sincerity that produces the "melting" (*ẕawb*) of the individual identity. Shame may here be considered as a first step that allows the self to be polished, such that divine *ḥayāʾ* is aroused, which in turn paves the way for the ultimate encounter. It is in this sense that we can understand a saying attributed to Junayd quoted later by Ruzbihan: "*Ḥayāʾ* removes the bliss of serving God [likely to cause pride or be sought after for its own sake] from the heart of His close friends."[62]

Various sayings attributed to great masters of Sufism gathered in Farid al-Din ʿAttar's (d. c. 1221) *Tazkira al-Owlia* offer other insights into the multiple facets of modesty. Among others, ʿAttar quotes Yusuf ibn Asbat who mentions multiple "signs" or sources of modesty, including—without apparent order—"restraining oneself, contemplating God's majesty, weighing one's words before speaking, avoiding what requires an apology, refraining from engaging in affairs that arouse embarrassment, guarding the tongue, eye, ear, stomach and private parts [from evil], leaving the trappings of worldly life, and remembering death and the dead."[63] Specific attention is devoted to the different variations and effects of shame before God: it is seen as an essential element of worship[64] and, here again, involves a kind of reciprocity, since if a believer shows modesty before God by obeying him, God will shy from punishing him with fire.[65] The ontological distinction between Creator and created is another common pattern that is again emphasized here through the idea that "the *ḥayāʾ* of the servant is the *ḥayāʾ* of remorse (*nadam*), whereas the *ḥayāʾ* of the Most High Creator is the *ḥayāʾ* of generosity (*karam*)."[66]

In the fourteenth century, in his *Misbah al-Hidaya wa Miftah al-Kifaya*, ʿIzz al-Din Kashani (d. 1335) offers his own synthesis of various motifs that run through Sufi thought on *ḥayāʾ*: it signals a state of closeness (*qurb*) to the divine. It also produces a reverential fear and a tenseness of being stemming from the awareness that God knows perfectly well one's inner self and failings. Such shame, described as general (*ʿām*), is called the shame of the people of contemplative vigilance (*murāqaba*) and differs from the shame of the elite (*khāṣṣ*), which is the privilege of those who experience witnessing (*mushāhida*). Here again, the vision of the True is closely associated to a contraction of the self and is a state shared by humans and angels.[67] In these Sufi manuals and writings, *ḥayāʾ* is depicted as a sought-after state, as it is both a sign and a means of fostering a closeness to the divine. Nevertheless, in most cases, the closeness it allows also produces distance and maintains the believer in a state of existential tension. It ultimately gives rise to a desire to drape oneself in a sort of mimicry of Adam or Israfil's gesture.

Leaving the Garment of Shame in Rumi's Poetry

Other scholars, such as the poet Jalal al-Din Muhammad Rumi (d. 1273), have a more ambivalent position on shame and modesty.[68] While he insists on the importance of showing deference to God and His creation,[69] several passages in his writings invite the believer to dispense with shame in his relationship with God. He thereby extends and gives his own interpretation of the distinction between reasonable and foolish *ḥayāʾ* stated in several hadiths. Far from being always closely related to faith, when it prevents one from immersing oneself into a heart-purifying water, shame can obstruct it:

> The water said to the defiled one, "Hasten (to come) into me."
> The defiled one said, "I feel shame before the water."
> Said the water, "Without me how shall this shame go?
> Without me how shall this defilement be removed?"
> Every defiled one who hides from the water is (an example of the saying that)
> "Shame hinders Faith."[70]

For Rumi, the contraction of the self and the fearful shame maintains a veil between the creature and his Creator and prevents the attainment of proximity to Him. *Ḥayāʾ* thus becomes an ontological and epistemological state to be overcome:

> The time is come for me to strip, to quit the (bodily) form and become wholly spirit.
> Come, O Enemy of shame and anxious thought, for I have rent the veil of shame and bashfulness.[71]

For Rumi, only the shedding of shame and a cautious self-restraint allows one to fully immerse oneself in the contemplation of divine beauty. Such vision produces a dilation of being and arouses a feeling of intoxication (*mastī*), ecstasy (*wajd*), or even a state of unconsciousness (*bīkhūdī*) that makes all restraint disappear. Disclosure of divine mysteries and even impertinence and boldness (*gustākhī*), which are seen as vile attitudes and rejected in society, here become seen as the marks of a gnostic elevation:

> I am in love with the art of madness, I am surfeited with wisdom and sagacity.
> When (the veil of) shame is rent asunder, I will publicly declare the mystery (*rāz*):
> how much (more) of this self-restraint and griping pain and tremor?
> I have become concealed in shame, like the fringe (sewn on the inside of a garment):
> I will spring forth of a sudden from beneath this coverlet.[72]

In this context, the "shameless" intoxication of the encounter also entails the abandonment of all worldly ambitions and is associated with purity and sincerity. In his *Divan-e Shams*, Rumi writes, "such drunkenness comes to the head, from such beauty, that the heart doesn't look for a crown or throne. Shame and bashfulness go away."[73] Rumi questions the idea of a harmony and complementarity between shame before God and in society. Here, the relationship to the divine is governed by specific affects that involve the abandonment of any calculating attitude as well as a detachment from conventions and social honors. This idea echoes the Qur᾿anic verse denying shame to God when it comes to expressing the truth. The intoxication produced by the vision also enables a forgetting of the shame born from the awareness of one's own limited being. It allows one to fully immerse oneself in God not only by seeing His majesty, but also by becoming inhabited by His love. Rumi's conception of *ḥayā᾿* presupposes a theology that contrasts with the conception of God's transcendence postulated in certain Sufi treatises.

> When You take the road of separation,
> Lovers lose the glass of mind and intelligence.
> Please tear the curtain of shame and modesty
> That makes the mistake of calling Soul *mind.*
> All modesty and rhymes
> Have been ruined by Your love.
> Since You're gone toward them,
> No curtain is left.[74]

Nevertheless, Rumi's thought on shame and modesty leaves many questions unanswered. The shedding of *ḥayā᾿* is sometimes attributed to the prior will of the believer, sometimes to a divine love that tears its veils away. In all cases, it goes along with the dissolution of calculating reason and pursuit of worldly benefits. The lifting of all curtains nevertheless raises the question of the permanence of a self, endowed with a conscience and a will of its own.

Conclusion

Ḥayā᾿ is the subject of various and complex appreciations in its human and divine manifestations. These different readings share a common idea according to which *ḥayā᾿* is not merely an innate given, but also an acquired and fluctuating state that can be modulated, lost, or strengthened according to the context and the will of its subject. In this context, it lies at the confluence of both a moral code laid down by revelation and a personal ethic. Thus, even though *ḥayā᾿* is often presented as an affect that prevents and limits, some scholars suggest that it may also be a form of praxis and a resource. The multiple interpretations of the subjects of shame and modesty also raises the question of the polysemy of this concept. Divine and human *ḥayā᾿* proceed from and bear the mark of a fundamentally distinct ontological condition. However, they also appear to be deeply interrelated. Both carry a possibility to hide and veil, and thereby to manifest a form of generosity (*karam*). In its divine manifestation, *ḥayā*ʾ weaves a garment and allows the creation of a space between absolute transparency and opacity, which opens up other possibilities and perspectives in the relationship between God and man. In the gnostic realm, the various conceptions of modesty as a state to be preserved or overcome can also be seen as two possible ways to experiment with divine presence and gain access to a knowledge of God's attributes. A self-restraining *ḥayā*ʾ could be the mode of apprehension of His attributes of majesty (*jalāl*), whereas its shedding would enable one to fathom His beauty (*jamāl*). Thus, these writings can also be considered as different experiences and moments of wayfaring involving shifting dynamics and subtle movements between contraction and expansion, awe and intimacy, fearful astonishment and intoxication.

Notes

1. ʿAbd al-Karim Al-Qushayri, *Al-Risala al-Qushayriyya*, edited by Mahmud ibn Sharif and ʿAbd al-Halim Mahmud (Qum: Bidar, 1995), 325–6.
2. *Ḥayā*ʾ can also be translated by the notions of bashfulness, self-restraint, decency, reserve, and shyness. Other terms, such as *sharm* or *ḥishma*, have similar meanings and are sometimes translated equivalently.
3. "And then one of the two women approached him, walking shyly (*ʿalā istiḥyā*ʾ), and said, 'My father is asking for you: he wants to reward you for watering our flocks for us' " (Q. 28:25). *The Qur'an*, translated by M. A. S. Abdel Haleem, 2nd ed. (New York: Oxford University Press, 2005), 246.
4. *The Qurʾan*, translated by Abdel Haleem, 6.
5. Other verses of the Qur'an refer to shame and modesty, such as the passage inviting believers to "lower their glances and guard their private parts," and specifically exhorting believing women not to "display their charms beyond what [it is acceptable] to reveal" as well as to "let their headscarves fall to cover their necklines" (Q. 24:30–31), translated by M. A. S. Abdel Haleem, *The Qurʾan*, 222. However, we here limit our analysis to passages where *ḥayā*ʾ is explicitly named.
6. These include hadith collected in Al-Kulayni, Muhammad ibn Yaʿqub, *Al-Kafi*. 8 vols, 4th ed., edited by ʿAli Akbar Ghaffari and Muhammad Akhundi (Tehran: Dar al-kutub al-islamiyya, 1986), which contains a chapter on *ḥayā*ʾ, vol. 2, 106, as well as in hadith collections such as *Ghurar al-Hikam wa Durar al-Kalim*, which were then taken up by other later compilations such as *Bihar al-Anwar.*
7. Al-Imam Jaʿfar al-Sadiq, *Misbah al-Sharʿia* (Beirut: Muʾassasa al-aʿlamī lil-matbuʿat, 1980), 190; also quoted in al-Majlisi, *Bihar* 71, 336.
8. ʿAbd al-Wahab ibn Muhammad al-Taymimi al-Amadi, *Tasnif Ghurar al-Hikam wa Durar al-Kalam*, edited by Mustafa Derayati (Qum: Maktab al-iʿlam al-islami, 1987), hadith 5434, 256.
9. Al-Taymimi, *Tasnif*, hadith 5437, 256.
10. Al-Kulayni, *Al-kafi*, vol. 2, 56.
11. Ibid., 672.
12. Al-Taymimi, *Tasnif*, hadith 5454, 257.
13. Muhammad Baqir al-Majlisi, *Bihar al-Anwar*, 110 vols, 2nd ed. (Beirut: Muʾassasa al-wafaʾ, 1983), vol. 71, 337.

14. Al-Majlisi, *Bihar*, vol. 71, 334.
15. Al-Taymimi, *Tasnif*, hadith 5453, 257.
16. Al-Kulayni, *Al-Kafi*, vol. 2, 106.
17. Al-Taymimi, *Tasnif*, hadith 5439, 256.
18. Ibid., hadith 5444, 257.
19. Ibid., hadith 5457, 257.
20. Ibid., hadith 5453, 257.
21. Ibid., 257.
22. ʿAli ibn Hasan Tabarsi, *Mishkat al-Anwar fi Ghurar al-Akhbar*, 2nd ed. (Najaf: Al-maktaba al-ḥaydariyya, 1965), 233.
23. Such as this hadith of Jaʿfar al-Ṣadiq: "Modesty has ten parts, nine of which are in women and one in men," Tabarsi, *Mishkat*, 235.
24. On the complexity of this notion in the context of Islam, see Mohammad Ali Amir-Moezzi, *Le Guide divin dans le shiʿisme originel. Aux sources de l'ésotérisme en Islam* (Paris: Lagrasse, Verdier, 1992), 16.
25. Al-Kulayni, *Al-kafi*, vol. 2, 106.
26. On the different possible meanings of this word in this context, see al-Kulayni, *Al-Kafi*, vol. 1, 10.
27. Hadith of ʿAli ibn Abi Talib, quoted in al-Kulayni, *Al-Kafi*, vol. 1, 10–11.
28. Al-Taymimi, *Tasnif*, hadith 5436, 256.
29. Ibid., hadith 5440, 257.
30. Al-Majlisi, *Bihar*, vol. 77, 151.
31. Ibid., vol. 71, 332.
32. Al-Taymimi, *Tasnif*, hadith 5473, 257.
33. Ibid., hadith 5475, 256.
34. [in front of God]. al-Taymimi, *Tasnif*, hadith 5452, 257.
35. Ibid., hadith 5451, 257.
36. Ibn Shuʿba al-Harrani, *Tuhaf al-ʿUqul*, 2nd ed., edited by ʿAli Akbar Ghaffari (Qum: Muʾassasa al-Nashr al-Islami, 1984), 394.
37. Al-Taymimi, *Tasnif*, hadith 5468, 257.
38. Hadith of Prophet Muhammad, quoted in al-Majlisi, *Bihar*, vol. 71, 336, and Tabarsi, *Mishkat*, 234.
39. Hadith of ʿAli ibn Husayn: "Fear God Almighty because of His power over you, and show shame before Him because of His closeness to you," quoted in al-Majlisi, *Bihar*, vol. 71, 336.
40. Al-Taymimi, *Tasnif*, hadith 5455, 257.
41. Ibid., 5456, 257.
42. Quoted in Abu al-Qasim Husayn ibn Muhammad al-Raghib al-Isfahani, *al-Mufradat fi Gharib al-Qurʾan*, edited by Ṣafwan ʿAdnan al-Davudi (Damascus-Beirut: Dar al-qalam, Dar al-shamiyya, 1991), 270. Al-Isfahani mentions that this Prophetic hadith was narrated by ʿAisha, which may explain its absence in Shiʿite collections.
43. Al-Raghib al-Isfahani, *al-Mufradat*, 270.
44. Ibid., 270.
45. Al-Jurjani, ʿAli ibn Muhammad, *Al-Taʿrifat* (Tehran: Naser Khosro, 1991), 42.
46. Al-Majlisi, *Bihar*, vol. 71, 329.
47. *The Qur'an*, translated by M. A. S. Abdel Haleem, 428.
48. Al-Majlisi, *Bihar*, vol. 71, 336; Tabarsi, *Mishkat*, 234.
49. Al-Qushayri, *al-Risala al-Qushayriyya*, 323–5.
50. Hadith quoted *supra*. Jaʿfar al-Sadiq, *Misbah*, 190.

51. Al-Qushayri, *al-Risala*, 324.
52. Ibid., 326.
53. Ibid., 325–6.
54. Rashid al-Din Maybudi, *Kashf al-Asrar wa ʿUdda al-Abrar, The Unveiling of the Mysteries and the Provision of the Pious*. Selections translated by William C. Chittick (Amman: Royal Aal al-Bayt Institute for Islamic Thought, 2015), 184.
55. Maybudi, *Kashf al-Asrar*, translated by Chittick, 79–80.
56. Ibid., 437.
57. Ibid.
58. Rashid al-Din Maybudi, *Kashf al-Asrar wa ʿUdda al-Abrar*, edited by Zahr Khaluʾi (Kitabkhana tasawwuf), 72. http://www.sufi.ir/books/download/farsi/meybodi/kashfol-asrar-kamel.pdf. Accessed February 12, 2023.
59. Maybudi, *Kashf al-Asrar*, edited by Khaluʾi, 72.
60. *The Qurʾan*, translated by M. A. S. Abdel Haleem, 279.
61. ʿAbdullah al-Ansari al-Harawi, *Kitab Manazil al-Saʾirin* (Beirut: Dar al-kutub al-ʿilmiyya, 1988), 54–5.
62. Abu Muhammad Ruzbihan ibn Abi Nasr al-Baqli al-Fasawi, *Mashrab al-Arwah*, edited by ʿAṣim Ibrahim Al-Kayali al-Husayni al-Shazli al-Darqawi (Beirut: Dar al-kutub al-ʿilmiyya, 2005), 154.
63. Farid al-Din ʿAttar, *Tazkira al-Owlia*, edited by Muhammad Adib al-Jadir; translated by Muhammad al-Asili al-Wustaʾi al-Shafiʿi (Damascus: Dar al-maktabi, 2009), 616.
64. ʿAttar, *Tazkira al-Owlia*, 513.
65. Ibid., 385.
66. Quotation attributed to Yahya Moʿaz Razi, ʿAttar, *Tazkira al-Owlia*, 386.
67. ʿIzz al-Din Kashani, *Miṣbaḥ al-Hidaya wa Miftaḥ al-Kifaya*, edited by Jalal al-Din Humaʾi (Tehran: Sokhan, 2015), 420.
68. This chapter examines the example of Rumi, but similar motifs can be found in other Persian language poets such as Hafiz. It is also present, with some specific features, in Sufi *malāmatī* teachings. See Leonard Lewisohn (ed.), *Hafiz and the Religion of Love in Classical Persian Poetry* (New York: Tauris, 2010), 8, 39.
69. For example in Jalaluʾddin Rumi, *The Mathnawi of Jalaluʾddin Rumi*, edited and translated by Reynold A. Nicholson, vol. I (Cambridge: Trustees of the E. J. W. Gibb Memorial, 1926), Book 1, 89.
70. Rumi, *The Mathnawi*, vol. II, Book 2, 291.
71. Rumi, *The Mathnawi*, vol. VI (Cambridge: Trustees of the E. J. W. Gibb Memorial, 1934), Book 6, 291.
72. Rumi, *The Mathnawi*, Book 6, 289.
73. Rumi, *Divan-i Kebir, Bahr-i Recez, Meter 1*, 22 vols., translated from Turkish by Nevit Oguz Ergin [based on Golpinarli's Turkish trans.], vol. 1 (Walla Walla: Current Publishing, Turkish Ministry of Culture, 1995), 36.
74. Rumi, *Divan-i Kebir*, 136. See also Rumi, *The Mathnawi*, Book 6, 368.

Bibliography

Al-Ansari al-Harawi, ʿAbdullah. *Kitab Manazil al-Saʾirin*. Beirut: Dar al-kutub al-ʿilmiyya, 1988.

Amir-Moezzi, Mohammad Ali. *Le Guide divin dans le shiʿisme originel. Aux sources de l'ésotérisme en Islam*. Paris: Lagrasse, Verdier, 1992.
ʿAttar, Farid al-Din. *Tazkira al-Awliyaʾ*. Edited by Muhammad Adib al-Jadir and translated by Muhammad al-Asili al-Wustaʾi al-Shafiʿi. Damascus: Dar al-maktabi, 2009.
Al-Baqli al-Fasawi, Abu Muhammad Ruzbihan ibn Abi Nasr. *Mashrab al-Arwah*. Edited by ʿAsim Ibrahim Al-Kayali al-Husayni al-Shazli al-Darqawi. Beirut: Dar al-kutub al-ʿilmiyy, 2005.
Divan-i Kebir, Bahr-i Recez, Meter 1. 22 vols. Translated by Nevit Oguz Ergin [based on Golpinarli's Turkish translation], vol. 1. Walla Walla: Current Publishing, Turkish Ministry of Culture, 1995.
Al-Harrani, Ibn Shuʿba. *Tuhaf al-ʿUqul*. 2nd ed. Edited by ʿAli Akbar al-Ghaffari, Qum: Mu'assasa al-nashr al-islami, 1984.
Al-Jurjani, ʿAli ibn Muhammad. *Al-Taʿrifat*. Tehran: Naser Khosro, 1991.
Kashani, ʿIzz al-Din. *Misbah al-Hidaya wa Miftah al-Kifaya*. Edited by Jalal al-Din Humaʾi. Tehran: Sokhan, 2015.
Al-Kulayni, Muhammad ibn Yaʿqub. *Al-Kafi*. 8 vols. 4th ed. Edited by ʿAli Akbar Ghaffari and Muhammad Akhundi. Tehran: Dar al-kutub al-islamiyya, 1986.
Al-Majlisi, Muhammad Baqir. *Bihar al-Anwar*. 110 vols. 2nd ed. Beirut: Mu'assasa al-wafaʾ, 1983.
Maybudi, Rashid al-Din. *Kashf al-Asrar wa ʿUdda al-Abrar. The Unveiling of the Mysteries and the Provision of the Pious*. Selections translated by William C. Chittick. Amman: Royal Aal al-Bayt Institute for Islamic Thought, 2015.
Maybudi, Rashid al-Din. *Kashf al-Asrar wa ʿUdda al-Abrar*. Edited by Zahra Khaluʾi. Kitabkhana tassawwuf (online). http://www.sufi.ir/books/download/farsi/meybodi/kashfol-asrar-kamel.pdf. Accessed February 12, 2023.
The Qurʾan. Translated by M. A. S. Abdel Haleem. 2nd ed. New York: Oxford University Press, 2005.
Al-Qushayri, ʿAbd al-Karim. *Al-Risala al-Qushayriyya*, edited by Mahmud ibn Sharif and ʿAbd al-Halim Mahmud. Qum: Bidar, 1995.
Al-Raghib al-Isfahani, Abu al-Qasim Husayn ibn Muhammad. *Al-Mufradat fi Gharib al-Qurʾan*. Edited by Safwan ʿAdnan al-Davudi. Damascus-Beirut: Dar al-qalam, Dar al-shamiyya, 1991.
Rumi, Jalaluʾddin. *The Mathnawi of Jalalu'ddin Rumi*. Edited and translated by Reynold A. Nicholson. Vol. I, II and VI. Cambridge: Trustees of the E. J. W. Gibb Memorial, 1926 (for Vol. I, II), 1934 (for Vol. 6).
Al-Sadiq, Jaʿfar [al-Imam]. *Misbah al-Shariʿa*. Beirut: Mu'assasa al-aʿlami lil-matbuʿat, 1980.
Tabarsi, ʿAli ibn Hasan. *Mishkat al-Anwar fi Ghurar al-Akhbar*. 2nd ed. Najaf: Al-maktaba al-ḥaydariyya, 1965.
Al-Taymimi Al-Amadi, ʿAbd al-Wahab ibn Muhammad. *Tasnif Ghurar al-Hikam wa Durar al-Kalam*. Edited by Mustafa Derayati. Qum: Maktab al-iʿlam al-islami, 1987.

Part II

Shame, Modesty, and Honor in Islamic Environments

4

Understanding Shame and Modesty in the Context of Muslim Marriage: Narratives of Syrian Refugee Women in Jordan

An Van Raemdonck

Introduction

Practices of modesty and shame among Muslims have often been related to Islamic values and norms. Muslim women and men often organize their lives to Islamically inspired understandings of male and female modest behavior either consciously or unwittingly. Modesty is ultimately connected to the expression of gender and sexuality norms in ways perceived as religiously and socially acceptable. Marriage and marital relationships are important social institutions in which modesty is not only performed and practiced but also challenged and contested. Spouses' understandings of modesty contribute to shaping interactions within intimate relationships as well as social exchanges with relatives, neighbors, organizations, and society at large.

This chapter examines expressions and performances of modesty and shame by Syrian refugee women in Jordan in the context of their marital relationships. In doing so, the chapter's novelty lies in its focus on Muslim marriage—as a crucial Islamic social institution—for understanding articulations of shame and modesty. Interestingly, modesty as an Islamic ethical value has rarely been studied in relation to marriage, although predominant understandings of Muslim marriage contain significant social values connected to modest behavior and honor.

The first section of this chapter establishes how Muslim marriage mobilizes specific gendered norms that have been inspired by both historical Islamic traditions and the introduction of modernist family ideology. The second section presents Muslim marriage as a contemporary institution that is currently associated with spouses' shared sexual and gendered moral values that are appreciative of shame, modesty, and honor values. Together these two sections provide the theoretical background against which I introduce my anthropological material and analysis of Syrian refugee women in Jordan in the second part of this chapter. The context of refuge and migration adds another interpretative dimension to the narratives of these women.

In this chapter, I argue that Islamic modesty norms in the context of marriage mainly appear through expectations of gender roles inside and outside of the home. These expectations relate to interactions between spouses as well as women's social interactions with relatives and with society at large. In other words, modesty within marriage relates to women's abilities to study, work, or spend time outside of the home. The context of migration often causes ruptures within family relations as well as opportunities for change in previous gender dynamics. A host of factors, such as the loss of property, unclear and unstable residency status, difficulty finding and retaining jobs, and overall socioeconomic precarity, alter spouses' interactions with each other and their social environment. Men often fail to provide for the household, and women adopt new roles as workers, providers and caretakers, and social mediators. In sum, the migration context often leads to modified performances of socioreligious expectations of modesty.

I draw from ethnographic research and twenty in-depth interviews collected over two years (2017–19) in the cities of Zarqa and Amman. All interviews were conducted in Levantine colloquial Arabic by the author with the assistance of a Palestinian native speaker research assistant. This research forms part of a larger collaborative anthropological research project on the shifting meanings and contexts of (early) marriage practices among Syrian refugee communities in Jordan.

Characterizing Muslim Marital Relationships

Muslim marriages have long been the subject of scholarly inquiry, but remarkably few studies investigated the meanings and values understood in contemporary marriage.[1] Scholarship focuses rather on legal, unregistered, and illicit forms of marriage and Islamic and modern law regulating marriage and divorce practices.[2] More recently, attention has been given to certain institutionalized practices such as arranged, early (underage), and forced marriages, often inspired by development and humanitarian initiatives aiming to drive social change.[3] Insights remain scarce when it comes to the socioreligious meanings of being married; characterizations of desired, expected, and existing spousal relationships; and how gender roles are articulated and taken up between spouses. This is, in certain ways, surprising given the central role of Muslim marriage in organizing gender and sexuality norms.

The idea of practicing sexuality within the boundaries of marriage has been discussed widely. For example, Fadwa el Guindi explained, when studying practices of veiling in the 1980s in Egypt and Bahrain, that "sex is to be enjoyed in matrimony" and that social behavior between men and women outside of marriage ought to be desexualized.[4] She argued that women become *sitt al-bayt*, or "the lady of the home," a term that she employed to "stress an autonomous managerial role, not domesticity."[5] A married woman is the "senior woman of the household" and indicates "the premise of an adult woman's role of guardianship." More recently, Julianne Hammer studied Muslim marriages in the United States and stated that "Muslim marriage norms regulate sexual access and practice and provide Muslims with guidelines for sexual and gender norms."[6]

The development of Islamic marriage and family law, or Personal Status Law, is deeply interwoven with modern and postcolonial conditions across the MENA region. Historian Kenneth Cuno finds that recent changes in the Egyptian constitution made in the aftermath of the 2011 uprising still "express a family ideology constructed by modernist intellectuals beginning in the late nineteenth century."[7] Indeed, the current public, intellectual, and legal debate on marriage is still shaped by the colonial, modern visions of the family and women's and men's proper gender roles. Circumscribed social roles for women as caretakers and domestic managers who play a crucial role in child-rearing form part of modernist notions of gender and family norms and are not necessarily Islamic, that is, historically transmitted in Islamic scripture and law. Historians and Islamic law scholars have demonstrated how modernist visions relate to and differ from various historical and precolonial principles of Islamic law.[8] Often, current arrangements and ideals of family, marriage, gender, and motherhood are, therefore, the result of both cultural (modern) and religious (Islamic) entanglements.

Some historians and scholars of Islamic law proposed to conceive of women's role in marriage as a "maintenance-obedience relationship," referring to a husband's responsibility to maintain his wife in return for his wife's duty to obey.[9] This reflects previous understandings of marriage as a particular "gender contract"[10] and of the centrality of the notion of *nushuz* or (the wife's) disobedience to the Islamic marital contract.[11] Cuno argues how this ideal was equally shaped as a combination of precolonial Muslim thought, on the one hand, and modern European and Middle-Eastern reformist visions of the conjugal family, on the other.[12] This resulted in a "hybrid family ideology" that retains elements from all those sources until today.[13] Social scientists have shown that, in reality, women have been doing work outside of the home throughout history because this is more often than not a simple economic necessity.[14] The "maintenance-obedience relationship" is therefore variously interpreted and put into practice differently across time and across socioeconomic classes. This insight reaffirms the call for research that combines the study of contemporary Islamic law with social history and the examination of women's and men's narratives and actual social practices.[15] Finally, some scholars of contemporary Islamic law have been analyzing classic *fiqh*, gender relations and marriage through the lens of human rights, justice, and progressive values.[16] This work promotes the dissociation of modesty and honor principles from dominant gender concepts and marriage and family ideology.

Contemporary Marital Values: Shared Gendered and Sexual Morality

If a Muslim marriage contract is classically characterized as a spousal "maintenance-obedience relationship," then which values are prominent within marital relationships? How do marital and family values relate to social understandings of women's modesty, shame, and men's honor? Marriage assumes a central role in the social organization of sexuality and women's and men's social roles. Egyptian middle- to upper-class women in the 1990s seeking a potential spouse on the marriage market tended "to present themselves in a modest, moral manner to make themselves appealing."[17]

Anthropologist Bahira Sherif Trask explains that young women and men in Egypt put a great emphasis on following dominant codes of sexual morality and modesty before marriage. They show disapproval of dating before marriage and ambiguity concerning working outside of the home for women after marriage. Women's higher education and ability to find work are valued, but at the same time, dominant norms prioritize women's marital duties as spouses and mothers.

Sharing similar moral values, such as ideas of what constitutes modesty, is often an important aspect of young women's and men's ideas of marriageability. For some in Muslim American communities, sharing an Islamic background means sharing moral values and is, therefore, the most significant aspect of their search for a spouse. For them sharing faith-based values is more important than sharing with their spouse the previous nationality of their families.[18] "In this unstable world, one's values are the only things one has to hang on to" is an often-heard comment by Sherif.[19] Indeed, also in Egypt, the feeling that rapid global changes and demands affect local communities can reinforce interest in maintaining dominant social norms such as modesty and codes of sexual morality.[20] The act of marriage itself forms part of this set of shared social and religious values as opposed to other forms of sexual relationships and cohabitation. Marriage regulates sexuality and protects morality and modesty. A modern theorist of Islamic orthodoxy, Abul Ala Mawdudi, sees the limits set on sexuality as "set by God" and considers marriage, therefore, as a "religious duty."[21]

Numerous Qur'anic verses bearing on modesty are addressed to the Prophet's household, who are considered as examples to be followed by the community of believers.[22] These Qur'anic injunctions relate to going out, greeting, and having social interactions with nonrelatives inside and outside of the house. The Prophet's wives were to shun adornment (Q. 33:33) and lewdness. For the Prophet's wives, punishment for lewdness was double (Q. 33:30), but so was a reward for right-doing (Q. 33:31).[23] Similar and more general exhortations of modesty were directed to the entire community of believers. The gravest violation of modesty for both women and men is having illicit sexual relationships outside of marriage. In sum, modesty for spouses relates to bodily sexual behavior as much as to traits of character.

Modesty norms between spouses are least explicit within the Islamic discursive tradition and can, therefore, vary greatly across cultures, geographical regions, and times.[24] I will argue that in my research with married Syrian refugee women in Jordan, modesty norms among spouses are most prominently articulated through the performance of gender roles within marriage and in the spouses' dealings with their communities. This finding has been observed in several other contexts as well.

In a study of contemporary US Muslim marriages, "the most obvious dimension of marital dynamics is a debate about gender hierarchy versus gender equality within marriage."[25] Hammer found a variety of positions taken among Muslim married couples: from complete egalitarianism, through gender complementarity ideas, to forms of marital hierarchy in which the husband takes the leading position and where he is financially responsible and the main decision-maker. Discussions about working outside of the home for women equally result in positions across the entire spectrum: not working outside at all to working full time and sharing home responsibilities, mirroring larger (non-Muslim) American marital differences.

Highly educated British Muslims are shown to have a different set of priorities than their parents when seeking a potential spouse. They, too, are concerned that their potential spouses may have different expectations of gender roles within marriage.[26] Similarly, Muslim communities in Java, Indonesia, experienced widespread economic and educational changes, leading to more freedom in following gender and sexual norms. This led to a discrepancy between those embracing more liberal gender norms, prolonged courtship, and delayed marriage and those seeking fast marriages with no courtship and familiarization periods.[27] In Muslim minority contexts such as Belgium, understandings about gender hierarchy or gender equality between spouses are visible in debates about concluding a civil marriage in comparison to a religious marriage.[28]

This brief review aims to establish the importance of modesty and honor in classic understandings of Muslim marriage and in contemporary lived experiences among Muslims across the globe. Many prefer to marry as a way of expressing a religious duty or as showing a shared set of moral values in gender and sexuality. Modesty norms within marriage are most often expressed through the performance of gender roles. Differences and tensions among spouses occur around understandings of gender complementarity or gender hierarchy and in the choice of women to work or have social activities outside of the home. In the following sections, I will discuss different cases of such contestations of modesty and honor in the context of Syrian refugee women living in Jordan. My discussion will first summarize and thematize more general findings concerning (early) marriage and, second, highlight four different narratives of married women through in-depth accounts of how modesty and honor play central roles in these women's marital lives.

Narratives of Syrian Women Refugees Living in Jordan

A Variety of Marriage Practices

During the period of empirical research between 2017 and 2020, women were asked to share their opinions and lived experiences of (early) marriage in ten participatory action research discussion group talks, twenty in-depth interviews, and two focus group discussions. These findings point to the difficulty of discussing early marriage as a singular well-defined social practice. Instead, women discussed the diversity of early marriage practices and found it hard to contain them in one generalized category. Possible practices include cousin marriage, arranged marriage by family (both forms are also referred to as "traditional marriage"), large and small age gaps between spouses, partners of the same or different nationalities, and marriages involving cross-border migration or among communities of the displaced. The degree of social and family pressure to marry and the available space for negotiation concerning partner choice and marriage timing can differ greatly. Parents may or may not accept romantic love to play a role in the selection of a suitable spouse. Some women value romantic love and personal choice greatly, while others prefer to rely on the family-based judgment of who would be a good partner. Additionally, young women who fled and migrated and found themselves living isolated from their own (extended) families have different experiences from women who continue to live in relative proximity to their own family members and not only their in-laws. Many women considered a small age gap between partners the most suitable. A large age gap would easily lead to conflict and disagreement, because in their view, young wives are considered vulnerable and more easy to be taken advantage of by her husband and in-laws.

Tafāhum: Mutual Understanding

When asked what women find most important in a marriage or what makes a marriage successful, a great majority mentioned *tafāhum* or "(good) mutual understanding and agreement." This refers to the couple's ability to reach agreement and to find paths toward reconciliation after disagreement. It entails trust and respect as underlying principles. The topics about which to reach an understanding can be very diverse and include behavior inside and outside of the home, and interactions with extended families and in-laws. Topics that easily cause disagreement relate to working outside of the home or going out to visit family, neighbors, or NGOs. Often, women attended meetings organized by NGOs on topics such as child upbringing, education, and reproductive health, especially during the early years of the Syrian refugee crisis. Men at times object when their partners want to join meetings and have to travel across the city and take public transport. Mutual understanding and support can help to solve disagreements and smooth out differences concerning expectations of gendered behavior. Women stressed the importance of understanding for a good, long-term marriage and blamed failing relations for a lack of it. An example of a positive relationship filled with "mutual understanding" is Hanan's story.

Hanan was nineteen when she fled her home city of Homs with her family because of increasing bombings and violence. She had just entered university. A few months later, in Jordan, her life felt meaningless and empty. She felt depressed at losing all her friends, and in her words, "all my 13 years of education evaporated into thin air." What started as a new phase in her life and an exciting journey of higher education became forcefully interrupted. Very soon after fleeing, her future husband showed interest and proposed. She explained, "I told my mother at the time that I wanted to finish my studies first. I didn't need the headache." She knew him from university, and they met and talked at her brother's (who was his friend) house. She agreed to marry, bearing in mind the advice that "it is best to marry the one who loves you" rather than pursuing the one you love. Four years and two children later, she is convinced that she made the right choice. Feeling loved and happy, she stresses their good mutual understanding that shows particularly in his ongoing encouragement of her pursuing her life ambitions, which is to go back to university and graduate. As soon as circumstances allow, she plans to continue higher education, knowing that her husband supports her fully.

I have argued above that modesty in the context of Muslim marriage appears foremost in terms of gender roles, such as both partners' ideas about gender hierarchy and gender complementarity in and outside the home. Acting modest includes dedicating time and attention to the household, husband, and children, rather than to other affairs outside of the home. Hanan's narrative exemplifies how *tafāhum* includes the variety of roles spouses take up in their lives. Hanan's husband agrees that she seeks further personal development by pursuing higher education, probably followed by working outside of the home, as soon as their new post-migration circumstances allow. He does not have expectations of gender roles that are more typical of a marital "obedience-maintenance" relation in which the husband is the sole family provider and the wife takes up a caring and nurturing role. Hanan is not expected to modestly limit her worldly activities outside of the home.

Mediating the Lack of Understanding and Conflict

Positive understanding is of course not always present among spouses. In some cases, women who participated in this research sought to circumvent the lack of sympathy and agreement by creatively finding a *modus vivendi* with their husbands. Abeer, who was twenty-one at the time of our meeting, had married a cousin of her father's at the age of seventeen. She was already familiar with him but was taken aback by her husband's behavior after marriage. He did not like her going out and talking to strangers. After two months of marital life, she left the house and moved back in with her family for six months. She discovered that she was pregnant in this period. For the sake of their child and the community, she reconciled with her husband and continued life with him. She said that

> he acted as the great leader. He told me that I should fear him, that I should be afraid of him, but I am not afraid, and I believe that he talked nonsense and acted very old-fashioned. (Abeer, 21)

Abeer started to verbally show agreement and willingness to meet his demands while continuing to do as she wanted in reality. This appeasing attitude was working well. She lived on the outskirts of the city of Zarqa but traveled to the city center and visited the market and NGOs as she pleased. They both embraced different ideas and preferences about how spouses should behave with each other and society. He expected her to act in accordance with old-fashioned gender roles in which he was the head of the household and family provider. Abeer managed to circumvent this difference and navigate around the lack of *tafāhum*.

It is not always possible to reconcile conflicting expectations of gender roles and modest behavior among spouses. Manal, for instance, grew up in a large household of thirteen children where she "was spoiled by her father," living in a family that she calls ordinary as they were neither rich nor poor. She received very good grades at school but dropped out because her brothers thought it would be best for her to marry early.

> I finished school at age 13, and then about a year later I got engaged at 14. At the beginning of age 15 I was married. I want to secure everything for my children, and I want them to go to school, especially the girls. I want them to have a good education, and I don't want them to marry early like me. I want them to have certificates so that they are strengthened and not taken advantage of when they grow up and even if they get married that their husbands don't take advantage of them. (Manal, 28)

She is determined to offer her daughters more opportunities in life. Manal did not want to get married and did not accept her husband during the first weeks of marriage. She says that "[she] did not give him his rights as a husband" and "would not go near him and push him away." Her refusal determined the course of events in the following years. Their relationship was characterized by disagreement and negativity, which caused her great pain and sadness since the start. They led almost separate lives while living in the same house in Syria. Manal believes that her initial refusal to have sexual intercourse in the first weeks of marriage left a lasting imprint on her husband's behavior. Her refusal may have left him feeling humiliated and not respected. Consequently, he started to engage in seemingly similar disrespectful behavior toward his wife.

She explains that they never went together on excursions and family visits in prewar Syria as a couple. She visited relatives alone, and her husband did not pick her up at night to accompany her back home as is expected. He refused to join his wife on visits, even when her family invited him during Ramadan. Consequently, relatives took up the role of accompanying her back home at night, highlighting his absence, and in turn leaving her feeling embarrassed and ashamed. She explains that "he also does everything without consulting me and I have to hear from other people what he did, and that is very embarrassing and makes me feel small." His neglectful behavior is experienced as irresponsible and disrespectful toward her, the children, and her family. Both partners felt being treated in unusual ways that did not correspond to their gendered understandings of spousal interaction and codes of morality, causing feelings of shame and dishonor. The lack of feeling like a real married couple that engages in activities together saddens her most and pushes her to wanting a divorce. She says,

> It was wrong to have stayed together from the beginning. We should have left each other. What was wrong here is that I lived for the dignity of my family (*anā ʿasht ʿalā ḥisāb karamāt ahlī*) and not myself, and I did not want to upset my father, and I did not want anyone to talk about my family or us. Now I feel that I should have just gotten a divorce and have a natural marriage (*tazawajt ṭabīʿy*). But those were the days, and now I have children, and we want to leave each other, but we don't want to do that to our children. So we stay together for the sake of the children. (Manal, 28)

Her desire to divorce is balanced by feelings of responsibility and care toward the children. They continue their marriage but spend most of the time separate, in some periods even living in different places. The ill fortune and lack of understanding that Manal experienced in her marriage are complemented, however, by a growing social life in Jordan that has offered her emotional comfort and social support.

Marriage, Migration, and Changes in Gender Roles

A growing body of literature gives attention to the different effects on women and men that war, flight, and post-migration life bring about. War and migration may disrupt established patterns of gender roles.[29] The Syrian women interviewed explained how these changes played out in their families. A major factor is the loss of property in Syria, which causes families to hire houses while having insecure jobs, unstable (humanitarian) financial assistance, and unpredictable income. All interlocutors deplored the high rental prices and high costs of electricity, water, and gas. Most struggled to make ends meet. Husbands who were successful family providers in prewar Syria were faced with unemployment because of illness or inability to find jobs. Manal's husband, who was already suffering from a heart condition, did not find suitable work in Jordan. His absence as a family provider was a motivation for her to develop strong social networks and participate as much as possible in her new host society. She calls herself "active, strong and participating," "in contrast to [her] husband." She selects schools for her children and does all upbringing and care work herself. It is obvious that she loves to be around people and easily makes new friends. She explains that she sought such opportunities whenever possible, also by participating in NGO activities:

> Everyone has a different life, and this is why I like to meet different people because you learn so much from each other and learn from mistakes. So, when you express yourself to your friends, and they share experiences, you learn. For example, I learn a lot from meeting people, and in the past, I used to be very shy. If I went to a [NGO] workshop or session, I would look at the ground and be very shy to talk or participate. But the more I went and the more I did, the less shy I became. I learned so much about life from them, and also my attitude is teaching them about life. (Manal, 28)

Several women spoke in similar ways about experiencing personal growth after migration despite the many hardships that were associated with leaving their home countries. Reem's life narrative resembles Manal's in several ways. She married at the age of fifteen while she was not willing and ready to marry and has had a contentious relationship with her husband, characterized by a lack of understanding. After her father died due to war-related violence, her husband's behavior changed and became more demanding. She spent long periods in pain trying to appease him and enduring harsh treatment, including physical violence. While she is living in the same apartment building as her in-laws in Jordan, her husband mainly resides in Syria with his sister and visits her during certain periods of the year. His unusual behavior—letting his wife live alone with their children in a different country—and abusive treatment were hurtful. At the same time, through life in Jordan, she managed gradually to find more strength to confront him.

> I used to be naïve and not know things. He would say horrible things, and I remained quiet and did not say anything to my family. Only recently, I decided to start telling them. Had I been more mature, I would have left him immediately. (Reem, 25)

Only with the passing of time and through living almost independently in Jordan, sharing a flat with her sister-in-law, did she gain more strength and confidence when her husband expected obedience and silence.

> For example, [in the past] I used to wear trousers and all of sudden he said I was forbidden to wear trousers and that I had to wear a long dress (*abāya*). I ended up listening to him because I was unaware, naïve and young. … I first thought [the abuse] was normal. Then I started feeling it more, and then I started understanding right from wrong in life. (Reem, 25)

Also, for Reem, life in Jordan offered many difficulties and hardships. Many women went through feelings of social alienation and had to adapt to Jordanian communities where, often, they did not feel welcome. Street vendors at times treated them differently, or they used to be called out on the streets. Living through those difficulties caused them to feel more decisive and more assertive. As Mona phrased it, "we are 20 years old, but we feel as if we are 40." Also, the increase of opportunities in Jordan to meet other women outside of the family circle and make new friends—during NGO activities for instance—was often experienced as helpful and supportive.[30] Reem explains,

> When I started attending these meetings and meeting other women and seeing that there is a whole different life out there and a whole different way of living, I started to wonder, where have I been? Then I bought nicer clothes and started dressing up and socializing more. … I became stronger and stopped following orders, and I told them [her in-laws], like they have their life and conditions, so do I. In the past, they would make me do the cleaning while their daughters were sleeping. I stopped that and started focusing on my own life and my own home. … Now also, I dare to talk back. In the past, I never talked, but just as they have rights, I have rights. (Reem, 25)

While Reem's struggle is about coping with or leaving an abusive relationship, many other women expressed experiencing greater personal strength and more confidence due to life in Jordan as a refugee. Life in exile can increase women's mobility and opportunities to meet other people outside of the family. In cases of disagreement concerning appropriate gendered roles and behavior, these women learned to express themselves more strongly rather than trying to live according to their husbands' gender role expectations in marriage.

Conclusion

This chapter sought to conceptualize and discuss the notions of modesty, shame, and honor in the context of Muslim marriage. Muslim marriage has been studied extensively in the scholarly literature by historians and scholars of Islamic law. This led, for instance, to great attention to different types of marriage: informal, legal/registered, and religiously ambiguous or contested forms of marriage. Less attention has been given to lived experiences and accompanying sets of values associated with (love and) marriage in everyday life. This chapter sought to connect scholarly knowledge on characterizations of marriage in the Islamic discursive tradition with contemporary social scientific insights on gendered values that Muslims associate with marriage.

My discussion focused on how modesty norms are understood within the context of Muslim marital relationships. In addition to limited social scientific literature, my argument is based on findings of a two-year anthropological research project on (early) marriage practices among Syrian refugees in Jordan. The chapter aimed to show that intertwined cultural–religious notions of modesty, shame, and honor in a marital context mainly appear through understandings of gender roles. Literature shows how expectations of gender roles inside and outside of the home are significant in selecting spouses. Partners may have differing opinions about suitable gender roles and differing ideas about gender hierarchy, complementarity, and equality in marriage. Classic understandings of the Muslim marriage contract cast husbands in the role of family providers and wives as "obedient" carers and nurturers.

Anthropological findings among Syrian refugees in Jordan confirm and illustrate the centrality of gender role expectations within marriage. This chapter showed that couples may share similar gender expectations and have an overall good "mutual understanding" (*tafāhum*) in their relationship or, indeed, may lack this overall sense of agreement and sympathy. By highlighting four in-depth narratives of Syrian women, I aimed to show how modesty norms and marital gender expectations figure prominently in these women's lives and how widely they can vary. In cases of disagreement, husbands often prefer their wives not to spend time or work outside of the home. Some women are resourceful and manage to navigate conflicting expectations by deception. Others face domestic conflict and confrontation and suffer from abusive relationships. Finally, the context of migration and adjustment to a new host society offers another interpretative layer to women's experiences. It is well established that post-migration life often alters established gender patterns. Among our research participants, it was seen that life in Jordan offered more opportunities for women to reevaluate their marital relations, socialize more with nonfamily members, and experiment with different gendered behaviors.

Notes

1. See, among others, Juliane Hammer, "Marriage in American Muslim Communities," *Religion Compass* 9, no. 2 (2015), 35–44; Fauzia Ahmad, "Graduating towards Marriage? Attitudes towards Marriage and Relationships among University-Educated British Muslim Women," *Culture and Religion* 13, no. 2 (2012), 193–210; Corinne Fortier, Aymon Kreil, and Irene Maffi, "The Trouble of Love in the Arab World: Romance, Marriage, and the Shaping of Intimate Lives," *Arab Studies Journal* 24, no. 2 (2016), 96–101; Enaya Hammad Othman, "Muslim Women in the Diaspora: Shaping Lives and Negotiating Their Marriages," in *World of Diasporas: Different Perceptions on the Concept of Diaspora*, edited by Harjinder Singh Majhail and Sinan Dogan (Leiden: Brill, 2018); Bahira Sherif, "The Prayer of a Married Man Is Equal to Seventy Prayers of a Single Man: The Central Role of Marriage among Upper-Middle-Class Muslim Egyptians," *Journal of Family Issues* 20, no. 5 (1999), 617–32.
2. See, among others, Kenneth M. Cuno, *Modernizing Marriage: Family, Ideology, and Law in Nineteenth- and Early Twentieth-Century Egypt* (Syracuse: Syracuse University

Press, 2015); Nadia Sonneveld, *Khulʿ Divorce in Egypt: Public Debates, Judicial Practices, and Everyday Life* (Cairo: American University in Cairo Press, 2012); Annelies Moors, "Debating Women in Islamic Family Law: Legal Texts and Social Practices," in *The Social History of Women and Gender in the Middle East*, edited by Margaret Meriwether and Judith E. Tucker (London: Routledge, 1999), 141–74; Judith E. Tucker, *Women, Family, and Gender in Islamic Law* (Cambridge: Cambridge University Press, 2008).

3. An Van Raemdonck, "A Desire for Normality: (Early) Marriage among Syrian Refugees in Jordan between Waiting and Home-making," *Social Anthropology* 29, no. 1 (2021), 174–87; An Van Raemdonck and Marina de Regt, "Early Marriage in Perspective: Practicing an Ethics of Dialogue with Syrian Refugees in Jordan," *Progress in Development Studies* 20, no. 4 (2020), 312–327; Dina Zbeidy, "Marriage, Displacement and Refugee Futures: Marriage as Aspiration among Syrian Refugees in Jordan," *Etnofoor* 32, no. 1 (2020), 61–76; Michelle Lokot, " 'Blood Doesn't Become Water'? Syrian Social Relations during Displacement." *Journal of Refugee Studies* 33 no. 3 (2018), 555–76.
4. Fadwa El Guindi, *Veil: Modesty, Privacy and Resistance* (New York: Berg, 1999), 136.
5. Ibid., 82.
6. Hammer, "Marriage in American Muslim Communities," 35.
7. Cuno, *Modernizing Marriage*, 1.
8. Ibid.
9. Sonneveld, *Khulʿ Divorce in Egypt.*
10. Annelies Moors, *Women, Property and Islam: Palestinian Experiences, 1920–1990* (Cambridge: Cambridge University Press, 1995).
11. Tucker, *Women, Family, and Gender in Islamic Law.*
12. Cuno, *Modernizing Marriage.*
13. Ibid., 12.
14. Diane Singerman and Homa Hoodfar (eds.), *Development, Change, and Gender in Cairo: A View from the Household* (Bloomington: Indiana University Press, 1996).
15. Moors, "Debating Women in Islamic Family Law."
16. See, among others: Ziba Mir-Hosseini, "Justice and Equality and Muslim Family Laws: New Ideas, New Prospects," in *Sharia and Justice: An Ethical, Legal, Political, and Cross-cultural Approach*, edited by Abbas Poya (Berlin: De Gruyter, 2018); Kecia Ali, *Sexual Ethics & Islam. Feminist Reflections on Qur'an, Hadith and Jurisprudence* (Oxford: Oneworld, 2006); Adis Duderija, *The Imperatives of Progressive Islam* (London: Taylor & Francis, 2017).
17. Sherif, "The Prayer of a Married Man Is Equal to Seventy Prayers of a Single Man."
18. Othman, "Muslim Women in the Diaspora."
19. Sherif, "The Prayer of a Married Man Is Equal to Seventy Prayers of a Single Man," 622.
20. An Van Raemdonck, "Challenging Global Gender Politics: Egypt's Islamist Experience," in *Institutionalizing Gender Equality. Historical and Global Perspectives*, edited by Yulia Gradskova and Sara S. Sanders (London: Lexington Books, 2015).
21. Mawlana Abul Aʿla Maudoodi, *The Laws of Marriage and Divorce in Islam* (Kuwait: Islamic Book, 1983), 6–7 cited in Bahira Sherif, "The Prayer of a Married Man Is Equal to Seventy Prayers of a Single Man."
22. Richard T. Antoun, "On the Modesty of Women in Arab Muslim Villages: A Study in the Accommodation of Traditions," *American Anthropologist* 70, no. 4 (1968), 672.

23. Ibid.
24. Ibid., 673–6; Musawa, *Who Provides? Who Cares? Changing Dynamics in Muslim Families.*
25. Hammer, "Marriage in American Muslim Communities," 40.
26. Ahmad, "Graduating towards Marriage?"
27. Nancy J. Smith-Hefner, "The New Muslim Romance: Changing Patterns of Courtship and Marriage among Educated Javanese Youth," *Journal of Southeast Asian Studies* 36, no. 3 (2005), 441–59.
28. Kim Lecoyer, "Marriage Conclusion in Belgian Muslim Families: Navigating Transnational Social Spaces of Normativity," *Migration Letters* 14, no. 1 (2017), 11–24.
29. See, among others: Lewis Turner, "Are Syrian Men Vulnerable Too? Gendering the Syria Refugee Response," *Middle East Institute*, 2016; Elena Fiddian-Qasmiyeh, "'Ideal' Refugee Women and Gender Equality Mainstreaming in the Sahrawi Refugee Camps: 'Good Practice' for Whom?" *Refugee Survey Quarterly* 29, no. 2 (2010), 64–84; Elena Fiddian-Qasmiyeh, "Gender and Forced Migration," in *The Oxford Handbook of Refugee and Forced Migration Studies*, edited by Elena Fiddian-Qasmiyeh, Gil Loescher, Katy Long, and Nando Sigona (Oxford: Oxford University Press, 2014); Jane Freedman, Zeynep Kivilcim, and Nurcan Ö. Baklacıoğlu, *A Gendered Approach to the Syrian Refugee Crisis* (London: Taylor & Francis, 2017).
30. Van Raemdonck and de Regt, "Early Marriage in Perspective."

Bibliography

Ahmad, Fauzia. "Graduating towards Marriage? Attitudes towards Marriage and Relationships among University-Educated British Muslim Women." *Culture and Religion* 13, no. 2 (2012): 193–210.

Ali, Kecia. *Sexual Ethics & Islam. Feminist Reflections on Qur'an, Hadith and Jurisprudence.* Oxford: Oneworld, 2006.

Antoun, Richard T. "On the Modesty of Women in Arab Muslim Villages: A Study in the Accommodation of Traditions." *American Anthropologist* 70, no. 4 (1968): 671–97.

Charrad, Mounira. *States and Women's Rights: The Making of Postcolonial Tunisia, Algeria, and Morocco.* Berkeley: University of California Press, 2001.

Cuno, Kenneth M. *Modernizing Marriage: Family, Ideology, and Law in Nineteenth- and Early Twentieth-Century Egypt.* Syracuse: Syracuse University Press, 2015.

Duderija, Adis. *The Imperatives of Progressive Islam.* London: Taylor & Francis, 2017.

El Guindi, Fadwa. *Veil: Modesty, Privacy and Resistance.* New York: Berg, 1999.

Fiddian-Qasmiyeh, Elena. "'Ideal' Refugee Women and Gender Equality Mainstreaming in the Sahrawi Refugee Camps: 'Good Practice' for Whom?" *Refugee Survey Quarterly* 29, no. 2 (2010): 64–84.

Fiddian-Qasmiyeh, Elena. "Gender and Forced Migration." In *The Oxford Handbook of Refugee and Forced Migration Studies.* Edited by Elena Fiddian-Qasmiyeh, Gil Loescher, Katy Long and Nando Sigona, 395–408. Oxford: Oxford University Press, 2014.

Fortier, Corinne, Aymon Kreil, and Irene Maffi. "The Trouble of Love in the Arab World: Romance, Marriage, and the Shaping of Intimate Lives." *Arab Studies Journal* 24, no. 2 (2016): 96–101.

Freedman, Jane, Zeynep Kivilcim, and Nurcan Ö. Baklacıoğlu. *A Gendered Approach to the Syrian Refugee Crisis*. London: Taylor & Francis, 2017.
Hammer, Juliane. “Marriage in American Muslim Communities.” *Religion Compass* 9, no. 2 (2015): 35–44.
Lecoyer, Kim. “Marriage Conclusion in Belgian Muslim Families: Navigating Transnational Social Spaces of Normativity.” *Migration Letters* 14, no. 1 (2017): 11–24.
Mir-Hosseini, Ziba. “Justice and Equality and Muslim Family Laws: New Ideas, New Prospects.” In *Sharia and Justice: An Ethical, Legal, Political, and Cross-cultural Approach*. Edited by Abbas Poya, 73–104. Berlin: De Gruyter, 2018.
Moors, Annelies. “Debating Islamic Family Law: Legal Texts and Social Practices.” In *A Social History of Women and Gender in the Modern Middle East*. Edited by Margaret Meriwether and Judith E. Tucker, 141–74. London: Routledge, 1999.
Moors, Annelies. *Women, Property and Islam: Palestinian Experiences, 1920–1990*. Cambridge: Cambridge University Press, 1995.
Musawa. *Who Provides? Who Cares? Changing Dynamics in Muslim Families*, 2018. https://www.musawah.org/wp-content/uploads/2018/11/WhoProvidesWhoCares_En.pdf (accessed June 14, 2023).
Othman, Enaya Hammad. “Muslim Women in the Diaspora: Shaping Lives and Negotiating Their Marriages.” In *World of Diasporas: Different Perceptions on the Concept of Diaspora*. Edited by Harjinder Singh Majhail and Sinan Dogan, 92–101. Leiden: Brill, 2018.
Sherif, Bahira. “The Prayer of a Married Man Is Equal to Seventy Prayers of a Single Man: The Central Role of Marriage among Upper-Middle-Class Muslim Egyptians.” *Journal of Family Issues* 20, no. 5 (1999): 617–32.
Singerman, Diane, and Homa Hoodfar (eds.). *Development, Change, and Gender in Cairo: A View from the Household*. Bloomington: Indiana University Press, 1996.
Smith-Hefner, Nancy J. “The New Muslim Romance: Changing Patterns of Courtship and Marriage among Educated Javanese Youth.” *Journal of Southeast Asian Studies* 36, no. 3 (2005): 441–59.
Sonneveld, Nadia. *Khulʿ Divorce in Egypt: Public Debates, Judicial Practices, and Everyday Life*. Cairo: American University in Cairo Press, 2012.
Tucker, Judith E. *Women, Family, and Gender in Islamic Law*. Cambridge: Cambridge University Press, 2008.
Turner, Lewis. “Are Syrian Men Vulnerable Too? Gendering the Syria Refugee Response.” Middle East Institute, 2016. https://www.mei.edu/publications/are-syrian-men-vulnerable-too-gendering-syria-refugee-response (accessed June 14, 2023).
Van Raemdonck, An. “Challenging Global Gender Politics: Egypt’s Islamist Experience.” In *Institutionalizing Gender Equality: Historical and Global Perspectives*. Edited by Yulia Gradskova and Sara S. Sanders, 243–72. London: Lexington Books, 2015.
Van Raemdonck, An. “A Desire for Normality: (Early) Marriage among Syrian Refugees in Jordan between Waiting and Home-Making.” *Social Anthropology* 29, no. 1 (2021): 174–87.
Van Raemdonck, An, and Marina de Regt. “Early Marriage in Perspective: Practicing an Ethics of Dialogue with Syrian Refugees in Jordan.” *Progress in Development Studies* 20, no. 4 (2020): 312–27.
Zbeidy, Dina. “Marriage, Displacement and Refugee Futures: Marriage as Aspiration among Syrian Refugees in Jordan.” *Etnofoor* 32, no. 1 (2020): 61–76.

5

Shame, Exile, and Muslim Masculinity among the Bellah Refugees from Mali in Niger

Souleymane Diallo

Introduction

This chapter stresses the centrality of Tuareg cultural notions of shame and honor to the ways in which the Bellah refugee men understand their gender and religious identities in the refugee camp of Abala near the Nigerien/Malian frontier. By discussing this, the chapter adds to the existing robust theoretical accounts that explore how cultural and religious norms are intersected and intermingled.[1] The Bellah identity marks a social status group perceived to be of inferior status. They stand at the bottom of a hierarchically ordered Tuareg society below a set of lineages or clans composed of the "noble" warriors and religious experts at the top and the vassal social groups in the middle.[2] In contrast to Bellah, conceived as racially Black, and of unfree birth,[3] both noble and vassal groups are perceived racially as "white" or "red," and of free birth. Ideally, while freeborn men occupied themselves with pastoral affairs, trade, religion, and warfare, the Bellah, considered as unable to understand religious duties, performed menial tasks, domestic work, and herding for their masters.[4]

This social division of labor rests on widespread local ideas that associated menial work with formerly enslaved persons and their descendants. They are conceived of as those who don't know shame and honor because they don't know their genealogy.[5] In contrast to the Bellah, the freeborn Tuareg know their genealogies.[6] Knowing one's genealogy, as documented by scholars of the Tuareg societies, forms the cornerstone of the Tuareg's notions of shame and honor. This is captured by the following depiction of the notion of *temushagha* suggested by Lecocq. He notes that

> [the] *imushagh* distinguish themselves by a culture of honour and shame, quite common among the Mediterranean cultures most anthropologists classify them amongst, precisely on the grounds of this particular trait. This culture is called *temushagha*, "the way of the *imushagh*." It consists first of all of the knowledge of honour and shame—*eshik* and *takaraket* respectively in Tamasheq—and second in the knowledge of one's *temet*—one's lineage and ancestry—which form the basis of

political organisation and which are kept closed off from strong political and social mobility through marriage strategies.

The term *imushagh* refers to the freeborn noble and politically dominant clans in Menaka, where the refugees under study here came from in northern Mali. Like the above account, scholarly literature on honor and shame among the Tuareg has mostly empirically focused on the perspective of the freeborn.[7]

This chapter shifts the empirical focus from the freeborn to the Bellahs. It discusses the Bellah's understanding of shame and honor and how this informs their self-understandings as Muslim men in Abala and vice versa. By addressing how the Bellah articulate local notions of shame and honor as well as their gender and Muslim identity, the chapter contributes to the few studies that paid attention to the religious life of the formerly enslaved people and their descendants.[8]

The argumentation is based on a two-step analysis. First, the chapter discusses the changing conditions of household economies and family relations and reflects on how men's sense of honor has been affected in Abala. Second, it delves into how women and men evaluate male honor and religious identity in the light of these adverse conditions of exile. My interpretations of the Bellah's notions of shame and honor draw on works of anthropologists who discuss shame and honor as an instance of social evaluation or measurement of the personalities of the actors according to the ideal standards of their societies.[9]

The Changing Conditions of Bellah Post-Slavery Household Economies and Family Relations in Abala

To understand the broader social implications of how the Bellah men relate their cultural notions of shame and honor to their religious identity, we need to view these narratives as further developments in the reformulations of Bellah's gender relations that began in the mid-twentieth century after most of them left their former masters.[10] Indeed, historically informed scholarly accounts distinguish several types of Bellah in northern Mali.[11] One group of Bellah consists of those who, under colonial rule, practiced agriculture for part of the year and owed their freeborn masters a share of the harvest (*iklan n eguef*). Another category of Bellah are those who constitute autonomous groups of herders (*iklan n tenere*). A third subgroup of Bellah are those who live with the masters in domestic settings (*iklan daw ehan*). The fourth category of Bellah are those who left their masters to settle in towns.[12] Hall reports that the French colonial administration (1894–1960) feared that these people acted as advocates for other Bellah, influencing them to leave their masters. For example, in a report on the Tuareg Kel Sidi Ali in 1950, the French administrator Henri Leroux indicated that "the emancipated and settled elements [of the Bellah] in Timbuktu rapidly became the champions of Bellah emancipation and the counselors for their brothers still in the tribe. It is they who gave the first asylum and assured the subsistence of the new fugitives."[13]

As a result, the social status of the formerly enslaved Bellah underwent significant transformations under French colonial administration. According to Denise Bouche, these resulted from the drastic measures that French administrators adopted to weaken the rebellious nobles, the Tuareg, who resisted colonial presence in Timbuktu and Gao.[14] In this process, the colonial government dispersed slave families and provided the family heads with a proper identity card.[15]

Although these processes mostly took place in the Timbuktu and Gao regions, among clans who had mounted resistance to the French colonial powers, the Kel Adagh warrior clans in the Kidal region were also affected by these measures[16]. The leaders of *imghad* vassal groups were placed under the direct authority of colonial administrators. This deprived the politically dominant clans (the Ifoghas) of any opportunity to assume a role as political brokers between formerly dependent clans and the colonial state; these clans of the Tuareg nobility lost much of their former political legitimacy. This development and subsequent urban settlements[17] marked the onset of the former slaves' autonomous household formations.[18] This chapter presents further developments of these historical processes of the reformulations of the Bellah family structure, relations, and household economy. In particular, it points to how the living conditions in the refugee camp of Abala have affected the Bellah men's self-esteem as heads of family and the sense of Muslim masculinity.

The Bellah formed 68% of the refugee population in Abala.[19] They came from various factions based in the area around Menaka in northern Mali.[20] These Bellah explained the reasons for their exile as follows. They contended that the Tuareg of free birth had singled them out and subjected them to collective violence in 2012 in Mali. They explained that in order to understand the roots of the current conflict between them and the freeborn Tuareg in Menaka, it is important to reflect upon the political processes that have been at work since the early 1990s.[21] For instance, some informants stressed the importance of the formation of a political party (UMADD, *Union Malienne pour la Démocratie et le Développement*) in 1992 and later the creation of a radio station by Bellah in Menaka.[22] The radio station had introduced a weekly public discussion program that centered on the history of the desert. More specifically, the radio program called *tessayt n-Azawagh* (meaning "assessing the history of Azawagh," read "desert") called for critical conversations about the historical status of social groups in northern Mali. These actions began to undermine the domination of the freeborn Tuareg. For example, the Bellah organized themselves and succeeded in electing Aghamad ag Azam-zim as Deputy of Menaka between 1992 and 1997, which marked a victory for the former slaves over the former masters as Aghamad ag Azam-zim had defeated the noble free Tuareg, Bajan ag Hamatou, the leader of the Tuareg's sociopolitical organization (federation) in Menaka.[23] Others still pointed to the creation of the association *Temedt* (placenta) as another major event that exacerbated the tension between the free- and unfree-born Tuareg in the area around Menaka. This tension stemmed in particular from the fact that the association took on the role of a human rights activist by fighting for the Bellah's freedom from domestic or herding slavery, which is still practiced by some Tuareg of free birth in northern Mali. The prizes Ibrahim ag Idbaltanat, the leading figure of this Bellah human rights association, received from Anti-Slavery International in 2012 and UNESCO in 2014, respectively, illustrate some wider political effects that *Temedt* produced since its creation. Taken together, as the informants argued, these events and processes invigorated the tension between the Bellah and the freeborn Tuareg, motivating the latter to attack and expel the former from Menaka and its surrounding area in 2012 and the following years.

There are several refugee camps in southern Niger, and among these are that of Abala where I conducted fieldwork among these Bellah as a part of my doctoral (2012–16) and subsequent research (in total twenty-four months). Fieldwork methods consisted of participant observation, narrative interviews, and focus group discussions. I conducted narrative interviews and focus group discussions in Tamasheq, French, and occasionally in Bamanankan (a local language spoken in southern Mali) with Bellah who spent some years in southern Mali. The research stays in Niger were built on previous fieldwork carried out between 2007 and 2011 in Djecbok (Gao), Kidal town, Essuq, and Adiel hoc in the region of Kidal (in total nine months). In Abala, I stayed in the guesthouse rented by the UNHCR. I spent the day time in the refugee camp and the night at the guesthouse. That put me in an optimal position to have equal access to humanitarian workers and the Bellah refugees.

Between 2012 and 2021, the refugee men met every day from 8.00 am to 1.00 pm, and again from 3.00 pm to 6.00 pm, to socialize and have informal conversations under the hangar in front of the NGOs' offices in the camp.[24] Their themes centered on news from home; their living conditions in Abala, Bellah history and identity, and their differences from the Tuareg. In their everyday conversations I followed on a daily basis, the refugee men who joined the informal conversations under the hangar in the refugee camp between 2012 and 2021 reflected on their living conditions in exile as a situation that had turned them into "nothing," *adinat n bànan*,[25] or "zero." Before their exile, this term was a commonly used insult indicating someone's loss or lack of status, whether age related or linked to gender.[26] The fact that refugees used this term so profusely to characterize their own situation in Abala reflected their sense of crisis as well as a widespread perception that the exile came with a loss in respectability and social status. Below, I explore how the informants related their loss in respectability and social status to food distribution registration processes in the refugee camp of Abala.

Provisioning Food, Shifts in Bellah Gendered Roles, and Family Relations

The food distribution policy implemented by humanitarian workers is one site where the refugee men experience their loss in respectability and social status. For example, one informant, Assaley, in his late fifties,[27] disliked that he could no longer speak to his second wife in the following terms:

> Whenever I speak to her since we arrived in this camp, she always reminds me that I am not the one who feeds her. She said that it is rather Sarmaji[28] who feeds her who could to talk to her but not me. … In reality we men just became "nothings" in this camp. Look for example, you cannot even raise your voice to your family anymore.

Understanding the full implication of this statement requires that we look into Assaley's family situations before, and in the context of exile in Abala. Assaley was born in 1956 in Andéramboukane near Menaka. Originally, his late father was enslaved by a family of the Kel Agayok, a grouping of the Dawsahak, a subgroup of the freeborn Tuareg in the area of Menaka.[29] Since Assaley went to school in his early years, he was able to escape domestic work with the Dawsahak. He dropped out of formal education just after elementary school and has since then moved from one temporary job to another, including working at the community health center in Andéramboukane for several years and working as a translator for NGOs near Andéramboukane[30] and Menaka at other times. Assaley is married with two wives and nine children with whom he moved together from Andéramboukane to Abala. Two children were born in the refugee camp between 2012 and 2020, which takes the total to eleven.

When I arrived in the refugee camp in Abala in August 2014 for my second stay, Assaley had ceased to stay overnight with his second wife living in the second quarter. For him, this was the only option because it had become difficult to speak to her. Assaley complained that whenever he attempted to make conversation with her, she reacted vehemently, telling him that it is no longer he who is feeding the family. Instead, it is rather the NGOs operating in the camp. Assaley interpreted his wife's reaction as a result of the food distribution regulations introduced by UNHCR in Abala. He explained that the UNHCR set the individual food ration to 12 kg of rice per person per month and also held women responsible for their children's food ration. In Assaley's family, every wife cooked for herself and her children. As a result, whenever he went to see his second wife, he has to purchase extra food provisions and bring this over to her. The days he did not have money to purchase extra food, she did not cook for him. Alternatively, she suggested sometimes that he cook using the food that she had received from the UNHCR, but Assaley would have to pay it back whenever he got some money. Moreover, she insisted that it is Assaley's duty to feed his family at all costs.

For Assaley, the UNHCR's policies contradicted the Bellah conventional gender relations within "post-slavery" families:

> Our ... women are made for home where they cook, take care of children and old parents. ... in contrast, we, men, go and search for food, money, and cultivate and take care of animals. In the case of danger, we stood for our wives, fought for them; and they respected us. This gave sense to our existence as men.

This quoted passage enables us to understand that it was precisely their submission to Assaley's demands prior to exile that explained their changing attitudes toward him in Abala.[31] Assaley therefore interpreted the change in his wives' attitudes as evidence of their loss of respect for him. To conclude, Assaley's account reveals that men felt like nothing because they lost their status, identity, role, and respectability (recently acquired since about the 1950s) as heads of families in Abala partly due to the NGOs' inversion of domestic roles. As the account shows, initially, men controlled family resources; in Niger, however, women were in control.

Assaley's situation in the refugee camp in Abala is similar to the experience of those men in Turner's account on how the relief operations' policy of equality driven by the UNHCR challenges older hierarchies of authority among Burundian refugees of Lukole in Tanzania.[32] Turner argues that

> A recurring subject would be the men lamenting that the women no longer respect them. The reason allegedly being that the men no longer can provide for their wives and children. It is the UNHCR-or merely … that provides food, medicine and plastic sheeting for building blindés (huts). And UNHCR provides the same amount to men, women and children alike. "The UNHCR is a better husband" the women say, according to the men at least.[33]

In a similar way, Assaley's statement reveals that men felt like nothing because they lost their status identity and respectability as heads of families in Abala partly due to the fact that their role as fathers and sole providers could no longer be achieved under conditions of lasting exile.

The Registration: Refugee Subject versus Family Member

In the UNHCR camp in Abala, all refugees have to register upon arrival, which ensures that the UNHCR has a count of the exact number of refugees and is able to provide them with food and health care. The registration comprises three steps. First, registration at the International Office of Immigration requires that refugees declare themselves as displaced people fleeing war in Mali. In cases in which those declaring their refugee status do not have identity documents, knowledgeable, educated refugees such as Assaley (introduced earlier) and Ehatt (a sixty-year-old man, descendant of formerly enslaved parents) act as witnesses. At the end of this step, the refugee applicants receive the official documents they need for the second step. This takes place at the CNE,[34] the representative of the Government of Niger as the host country. The document issued there bears witness to and acceptance of the refugees' legal status in Niger. At the final step, the refugees are required to present the records they receive earlier at the International Office for Migration and the CNE to the UNHCR. It is at this final stage that food ration cards are delivered to them.

Ehatt, a man in his late fifties, and several other Bellah men I met in Abala explained that this registration was in itself a humiliating process for family fathers. For instance, he described his own experience in his daughter's case in the following terms:

> My daughter was ill. As we were queuing several days here, I went to ask if she could stay in the tent, and that I could provide her details at the registration desk; they refused as if I am not her father. I am wondering what she could tell them about herself that I, as her father, cannot say. I could not register her until she recovered. Four months later, there was a second registration campaign, and then I succeeded in registering her. But before, we did not receive anything from NGOs on her behalf. That means that the family fathers became useless people in this camp.

There is evident tension between Ehatt's self-perception as a father and the NGOs' regulations at the camp. Ehatt viewed his suggestion to stand at the desk instead of his daughter as just a way to allow her to get some rest since she was ill. As a father, he perceived doing so as a parental role. The way in which he felt his status as a father was threatened echoes the observation by Liisa Malkki that humanitarian interventions rest on a perception that depersonalizes and dehistoricizes the refugees.[35] Humanitarian workers with whom I engaged in nightly conversations justified their measures regarding the registration, maintaining that they operated in the context of international law. Accordingly, women and children should be considered refugees in need of protection as they have rights that should be promoted independently before situating them within a web of affiliation in the family. Ehatt called this NGO interference "with family affairs."[36] For him, anything between a father, a mother, and a child should be primarily considered a family affair. It is only the head of the family who is responsible for such matters. He stated this more explicitly in the following terms: "Since I am no longer able to lead matters concerning my family, this means that I am no longer the one leading my family. It is UNHCR that does everything concerning our families here." As a result, family fathers like Ehatt felt that they have become useless people in exile.

To understand the social implications of why Ehatt and Assaley felt that they became useless people in exile (*adinat n bànan*), we need to relate their arguments to local cultural notions of shame and honor through the lens of which they experienced being reduced to nothing. In Tamasheq, the language spoken by Tuareg, these notions are respectively shame (*takarake*t) and honor (*eshik*). The Bellah men used the notion of (*takaraket*) to refer to someone's loss in status as a result of his or her failure to live up to local conventional expectations that mediate his/her social status whether linked to birth, age, or gender. Seen in this light, Assaley's and Ehatt's status as fathers and husbands are mediated through the roles linked to these positionalities. This understanding is, respectively, reflected in how they interpret their roles as husbands and fathers as those entitled to control domestic resources and stand on the family's behalf. It is this situation that generates their experiences of *takaraket*. Taken in this sense, *takaraket* implies the lack of and longing for honor (*eshik*). For the Bellah men, one's honor results from how one fulfills conventional social roles linked to one's status, whether linked to age or gender. In this way, Asseley and Ehatt, experienced *takaraket* (shame) as an incapacity to have honor (*eshik*) that goes with their social positionalities as fathers and husbands. Below, I explore the ways in which they relate their situations of being reduced to "nothing" in Muslim masculinity.

The Bellah's Loss in Respectability and the Status of Muslim Masculinity in Abala

As I have observed in Abala, the Bellah's understanding of male status in Islam intersects with their cultural interpretations of shame and honor. For them, their state of being useless persons (*adinat n bànan*), which can be understood as "ashamed people," does not imply that they have lost in status as fathers and husbands only. It also involved the loss in status as Muslim men. This implies that male honor (*ahalis wan tidit*) mediates men's Muslim gender identity. Central to the Bellah men's and women's understandings of Muslim masculinity is the capacity to provide for the family and to be held accountable for their family members.[37] As a result, the man of the household, the father, would expect obedience while the mother as well as their children would heed his demands in return for his "providing" for the family. For instance, Assaley's first wife, named Taouket, forty-eight years old with four children, once explained to me why she kept aside the food received from the UNHCR and asked her husband to provide them with food supply in the following terms:

> In Islam, women are not the ones who should provide for the family but men. If a man does not feed his family, he cannot expect and does not deserve to be called a man, a head of family. Also, this man cannot be a proper Muslim man. It is God who made men heads of the household. For this reason, God also assigned them the task to provide for their family. If they don't do this, they cannot call themselves Muslim men. That's the reason that I sell out the food received from the UNHCR and used that money for my own needs. It is the husband who should bring food home not me. If he does not do this, he cannot expect to be respected.

This statement spells out the centrality of providing for the family in local understandings of religious duties. Here, providing for the family is taken to be a religious duty and performative practice of that identity. The statement also points to the precarity of this identity. For instance, a man's failure to meet the expectations to provide for the family calls his masculine identity into question. As a result, the family members may contest the authority of the father. This complex provision–obedience dynamic within slave domestic relations contrasts and highlights significant post-slavery social changes in conventional nomad household economies in which Bellah mothers, children, and fathers were all placed under the authority of the masters for whom they performed menial tasks.[38] Here it should be remembered that the enslaved men did not have the responsibility of feeding their wives and children. This was the task of their masters. As such, the Islamic association of males as family providers has the connotation of an emancipated view of gender relations after the end of slavery in most individual cases in the 1950s.

It is not only the women who relate men's respectability and masculinity to their understanding of Islam and masculinity, but men also do it. For instance, on several occasions, Assaley put to me that

> The situation turned us (men)into bad Muslims. Imagine, in Islam, I am supposed to provide for my family. I did so in Mali. But I am unable to do it here in Niger. I don't have work, therefore, I cannot generate the financial means for this. The food supplies provided by the UNHCR is not seen by my wives as my own efforts to feed them. That's our challenge here.

This account illustrates how Assaley equates his incapacity to provide for his family with loss in status as a Muslim man. This unearths his understanding that exile came with loss in respectability and status of religious subjectivity. Ehatt also further explained to me that

> In Islam, the duty of the father is not only to provide the family with food. He is the one who speaks for the family. When he is present, the mother and the children don't have a word to say. He is the one who represents the family. But what we saw here is that the humanitarian workers interviewed me, recorded my details to register me. Next to me was my family. They asked individually everyone as we did have something to do with each other.

The failure here to perform their roles as fathers is captured through local conceptions of masculine honor (*ahalis wan tidit*). For them, the male honor is a status that implies being respected (*anhidj id semghar*) and considered (*anhidj id timhar*). As men felt that they were less considered and not respected by women, it made them feel that their honor was lost. This conception of honor and shame provide the *terrain* to capture how loss in respectability and Muslim men's status is empirically lived by the Bellah in Abala.

Altogether, the examples discussed above also shed light on the ways in which my informants longed for masculine honor under conditions of shame and humiliation in Niger. Men's self-evaluations in light of their capacities to provide for their families offer a new and useful way of understanding honor among the Tuareg. According to Lecocq[39] and Murphy,[40] honor in Tuareg society was less based on obedience than it was on a sense of composed self-habitus. One's honor is in how one behaves oneself, not in how others behave toward you, which is only a derivative of one's behavior (the idea being that if you behaved honorably, people would treat you with deference). The complex idea of "respect in exchange of provision" in Niger prompts us to consider the relevance of political economy to honor as well as to shift analytical focus from the self-habitus to evaluations that others make of the performance of this habitus.

Conclusion

This chapter has sought empirically to cast light on the ways in which the Bellah men and women understand their gender and religious identity in Abala. The discussions have shown how the Bellah men articulated their gender and religious identity with local cultural notions of shame and honor. As a result, the chapter analytically furthers scholarly understandings of the relevance of cultural notions of shame and honor to constructions and contestations of the religious identity.

Notes

1. Emile Durkheim, *Les forms élémentaires de la vie religieuse* (Paris: Presses Universitaires de France, 1968); Clifford Geertz, *The Interpretations of Cultures* (New York: Basic Books, 1973); Talal Asad, *Genealogies of Religion, Discipline*

and Reasons of Power in Christianity and Islam (Baltimore, MD: Johns Hopkins University, 1993).

2. Georg Klute, *Die Schwerste Arbeit der Welt. Alltag von Tuareg Nomaden* (München: Trickster Verlag, 1992a); Baz S. Lecocq, "The Bellah Question: Slave Emancipation, Race and Social Categories in Late Twentieth-Century Northern Mali," *Canadian Journal of African Studies* 39, no. 1 (2005), 42–68; Baz S. Lecocq, *Disputed Desert: Decolonisation, Competing Nationalisms and Tuareg Rebellions in Mali* (Leiden: Brill, 2010).
3. Lecocq, "The Bellah Question"; Bruce S. Hall, "The Question of 'Race' in the Pre-colonial Southern Sahara," *Journal of North African Studies* 10, nos. 3–4 (2005), 339–67; Bruce S. Hall, "Bellah Histories of Decolonization, Iklan Paths to Freedom: The Meanings of Race and Slavery in the Late-Colonial Niger Bend (Mali), 1944–1960," *International Journal of African Historical Studies* 44, no. 1 (2011), 61–87.
4. Gunvor Berge, "In Defence of Pastoralism: Form and Flux among Tuaregs in Northern Mali." PhD diss. Museum of Anthropology, Oslo University, 2000; Lecocq, "The Bellah Question."
5. Lecocq, *Disputed Desert: Decolonisation*, 4.
6. Lecocq, "The Bellah Question."
7. Robert Francis Murphy, "The Social Distance and the Veil," *American Anthropologist* 66, no. 6 (1964), 1257–74; Dominique Cajasus, "The Wedding Ritual among the Kel Ferwan Tuaregs," *Journal of the Anthropological Society of Oxford-Online* 14, no. 2 (1983), 227–37; Nicolaisen, Johannes and Nicolaisen, Ida. *The Pastoral Tuareg, Ecology, Culture, and Society* (Copenhagen: The Carsberg Foundation/Rhodos, 1997).
8. Hall, *Bellah Histories of Decolonization*; Souleymane Diallo, *The Truth about the Desert: Exile, Memory, and the Making of Communities among Malian Tuareg Refugees in Niger* (London: Modern Academic Publishing-Ubiquity Press, 2018).
9. John George Peristiany, *Honour and Shame: The Values of Mediterranean Society* (Chicago: University of Chicago Press, 1966); Michael Herzfeld, "Honour and Shame: Problems in the Comparative Analysis of Moral Systems," *Man, New Series* 15, no. 2 (1980), 339–51; Jean Pierre Olivier De Sardan, *Concepts et Conceptions Songhayzarma: Histoire, Culture, Société* (Paris: Nubia, 1982); Jean Pierre Olivier De Sardan, *Les sociétés Songhayzarma (Niger/Mali). Chefs, guerriers, esclaves, paysans* (Paris: Karthala, 1984); Fatoumata Ouattara, "Savoir-vivre et honte chez les Senufo Nanerge (Burkina Faso)," thèse de doctorat (École des Hautes Études en Sciences Sociales Paris, 1999).
10. Annemarie Bouman, "The Price of Marriage: Shifting Boundaries, Compromised Agency and the Effects of Globalization on *Iklan* Marriages," in *Tuareg Society within a Globalized World: Saharan Life in Transition*, edited by Ines Kohl and Anja Fischer (London: I.B.Tauris, 2010), 109–24.
11. Hall, "Bellah Histories of Decolonization"; Benedetta Rossi, *Reconfiguring Slavery: West African Trajectories* (Cambridge: Liverpool University Press, 2009); Benedetta Rossi, "Tuareg Trajectories of Slavery: Preliminary Reflections on a Changing Field," in *Tuareg Society within a Globalized World: Saharan Life in Transition*, edited by Ines Kohl and Anja Fischer (London: I.B. Tauris, 2010), 89–108.
12. Hall, "Bellah Histories of Decolonization."
13. Ibid.
14. DeniseBouche, *Les Villages de Liberté en Afrique Noire Française, 1887–1910* (Paris: Edition Mouton, 1968).
15. Ibid.

16. Pierre Boilley, *Les Touaregs Kel Adagh. Dépendances et Révoltes: Du Soudan Français au Mali Contemporain* (Paris: Karthala, 1999).
17. See Martin Klein, *Slavery and Colonial Rule in French West Africa* (New York: Cambridge University Press, 1998); Florence Boyer, "Le projet migratoire des migrants touaregs de zone de Bankilaré: la pauvreté désavouée," *Stichproben: Wiener Zeitschrift für kritische Afrikastudien* 8 (2005), 47–67; Hall, "The Question of Race."
18. Susan Rasmussen, "Within the Tent and at the Crossroads: Travel and Gender Identity among the Tuareg of Niger," *Ethnos* 26, no. 2 (1998), 153–82; Susan Rasmussen, "The Slave Narrative in Life History and Myth, and Problems of Ethnographic Representation of the cultural Predicament," *Ethnohistory* 46, no. 1 (1999), 67–108. Formerly, slaves registered on the identity cards of their masters as their part of their family.
19. According to the census conducted by UNHCR between 2012 and 2014, an estimated number of 11,795 persons lived in the refugee camp of Abala. The findings stemming from this survey classified 68 percent of refugees in the camp as Tuareg former slaves or Bellah followed by 19 percent of Hausa, 10 percent Songhay, and 2 percent Fulani; 1 percent were freeborn Tuareg.
20. They are from the following fractions: Dabakkar, Kel Talatayt, Ishadenharen, Kel Abaket, Kel Essuq, Kel Tabonant Bellah, Tagassassante, Elhadji Moussa, Ikarkawane, Tarbanassa, Tamizguida Bellah. Ibhawane, Kel Tabonanate Imajorène, Tamizguida Imajorène. Igueressanane-Tabaho, Kel Tessayt, Targuitamant Wan Adrar, Targuitamant Wan Agayok, Zamburuten, Kel Talamin, Ikarabassan.
21. For a more historical understanding of Bellah and freeborn conflicted relations, see Lecocq, "The Bellah Question"; Hall, "Bellah Histories of Decolonization," 67–9.
22. The radio station is called "radio Adrar." Although the informants claimed that the Bellah created the radio station, it should be noted it was actually created by Moulaye Touhami Haidara, an Arab, son of the (former) Imam of Menaka, who, as member of the Bellah's political party UMADD (*Union Malienne pour la Démocratie et le Développement, UMADD*) was and is still supportive of the Bellah's political actions toward their emancipation in northern Mali.
23. The same argument has been used to support Mossis Bocoum, the former Mayor of Menaka. However, unexpectedly (from the unfree's side) since 1997, the former political dominant clans have won the other parliamentary elections.
24. The refugee camp is still there and the refugee men continue to meet up under the hangar on daily basis.
25. Adinat in bànan can be translated both as "useless persons" or "nothing" in plural, and in awadim in bànan in the singular.
26. For example, according to Ehatt, as way to stress the noble Ifoghas, Idaraggagan, Ikarabasan, Ibhawan, Kel Tabonant, Tamisguida's loss in power and status, and their intermediary social position below politically dominant nobles and above the vassals and the Bellah, the noble Kel-Talatayt, Kel Ahara and other fractions composing the noble warriors' groups known as the Kel-Akaimed, ironically refer to them as win bànan: nothing.
27. I nicknamed all informants throughout this chapter, except Ahiyou who passed away on August 23, 2015, before the end of their exile in Abala.
28. Sarmaji was the camp manager in Abala. Thus, by saying that it was Sarmaji who feeds them, the women wanted to mention that they were fed by NGOs and not by their husbands.

29. For further details on the Dawsahak, see Clarles Grémont, "Dans le piège des offres de violence. Concurrences, Protections et Représailesdans la region de mènaka (Nord-Mali, 2000–2018)," *Hérodote* 172 (2019), 43–62. According to French historian Charles Grémont, some of the Dawsahak trace their genealogy back to the ancestor of the Ifoghas, Aita, the ruling clans of the Kel Adagh in the Kidal region, see Charles Grémont, *Les Touaregs Iwellemmedan (1647–1896): Un Ensemble Politique de la Boucle du Niger* (Paris: Karthala, 2010), 117. Other references to them, based on linguistic characteristics, evoke a possible connection between the Dawsahak and the Songhay as their language, called tadagsahak (the language of the Dawsahak) has a similar vocabulary and syntax to the Songhay, the language of the Songhay ethnic group in Timbuktu and Gao regions. During some of my own earlier stays in northern Mali between 2007 and 2011, I heard some oral accounts saying that the Dawsahak are of Israelite origin. However, Grémont presents them as an important social group in the Tuareg social and political constellation in Menaka.
30. This is the formal spelling on the map. Otherwise, people say it differently. Originally the name is Ader n bokar, valley of bokar, which refers to the hausa cloth sold on the market by Haussa traders. The French couldn't pronounce it and garbled the name.
31. What Assaley represents here should be, seen, as [traditional] gender relations that had been reformulated as such only in the mid-twentieth century after they had left their former masters.
32. Simon Turner, "Angry Young Men in Camps: Gender, Age and Class Relations among Burundian Refugees in Tanzania," *New Issues in Refugee Research*, Working Paper 9 (Geneva: UNHCR, 1999).
33. Ibid., 1.
34. Commission Nationale d'éligibilité au Statut des Réfugiés.
35. Liisa Malkki, *Exile and Purity: Violence, Memory, and National Cosmology among Hutu Refugees in Tanzania* (Chicago: University of Chicago Press, 1995).
36. In French: "les affaires de familles."
37. Dorothea Schulz and Souleymane Diallo, "Competing Assertions of Muslim Masculinity in Mali," *Journal of Religion in Africa* 46 (2016), 219–50.
38. Clare Oxby, "Women and the Allocation of Herding Labour in a Pastoral Society (southern Kel Ferwan Twareg, Niger)," in *Le fils et le neveu. Jeux et Enjeux de la parenté touarègue*, edited by S. Bernus, P. Bonte, L. Brock, and H. Claudot (Paris: Maison des Sciences de l'Homme and Cambridge University Press, 1986), 99–128; Georg Klute, "Le Travail chez les Kel-Adagh," *Journal des Africanistes* 62 (1992), 200–5; G. Spittler, "La notion de travail chez les Kel Ewey," *Revue du monde musulman et de la Méditerranée* 57, no. 3 (1990), 89–98.
39. Lecocq, *Disputed Desert.*
40. Robert Francis Murphy, "The Social Distance and the Veil," *American Anthropologist* 66, no. 6 (1964), 1257–74.

Bibliography

Asad, Talal. *Genealogies of Religion, Discipline and Reasons of Power in Christianity and Islam.* Baltimore, MD: Johns Hopkins University, 1993.

Berge, Gunvor. "In Defence of Pastoralism: Form and Flux among Tuaregs in Northern Mali." PhD Diss., Museum of Anthropology, Oslo University, 2000.

Boilley, Pierre. *Les Touaregs Kel Adagh. Dépendances et Révoltes: Du Soudan Français au Mali Contemporain*. Paris: Karthala, 1999.
Bouche, Denise. *Les Villages de Liberté en Afrique Noire Française, 1887–1910*. Paris: Edition. 1968.
Bouman, Annemarie. "The Price of Marriage: Shifting Boundaries, Compromised Agency and the Effects of Globalization on Iklan Marriages." In *Tuareg Society within a Globalized World: Saharan Life in Transition*. Edited by Ines Kohl and Anja Fischer, 109–24. London: I.B. Tauris, 2010.
Boyer, Florence. "Le projet migratoire des migrants touaregs de la zone de Bankilaré: la pauvreté désavouée." *Stichproben: Wiener Zeitschrift für kritische Afrikastudien* 8 (2005): 47–67.
Casajus, Dominique. "The Wedding Ritual among the Kel Ferwan Tuaregs." *Journal of the Anthropological Society of Oxford-Online* 14, no. 2 (1983): 227–37.
Diallo, Souleymane. *"The Truth about the Desert": Exile, Memory, and the Making of Communities among Malian Tuareg Refugees in Niger*. London: Modern Academic Publishing-Ubiquity Press, 2018.
Durkheim, Emile. *Les forms élémentaires de la vie religieuse*. Paris: Presses Universitaires de France, 1968.
Geertz, Clifford, *The Interpretations of Cultures*. New York: Basic Books, 1973.
Grémont, Charles. *Les Touaregs Iwellemmedan (1647–1896): Un Ensemble Politique de la Boucle du Niger*. Paris: Karthala, 2010.
Grémont, Charles. "Dans le piège des offres de violence. Concurrences, Protections et Représailles dans la region de mènaka (Nord-Mali, 2000–2018)." *Hérodote* 172 (2019): 43–62.
Hall, Bruce S. "The Question of 'Race' in the Pre-colonial Southern Sahara." *Journal of North African Studies* 10, nos. 3–4 (2005): 339–67.
Hall, Bruce S. "Bellah Histories of Decolonization, Iklan Paths to Freedom: The Meanings of Race and Slavery in the Late-Colonial Niger Bend (Mali), 1944–1960." *International Journal of African Historical Studies* 44, no. 1 (2011): 61–87.
Herzfeld, Micheal. "Honour and Shame: Problems in the Comparative Analysis of Moral Systems." *Man, New Series* 15, no. 2 (1980): 339–51.
Klein, Martin. *Slavery and Colonial Rule in French West Africa*. New York: Cambridge University Press, 1998.
Klute, Georg. *Die Schwerste Arbeit der Welt. Alltag von Tuareg Nomaden*. München: Trickster Verlag, 1992a.
Klute, Georg. "Le Travail chez les Kel-Adagh." *Journal des Africanistes* 62 (1992): 200–5.
Lecocq, S. Baz. "The Bellah Question: Slave Emancipation, Race and Social Categories in Late Twentieth-Century Northern Mali." *Canadian Journal of African Studies* 39, no. 1 (2005): 42–68.
Lecocq, S. Baz. *Disputed Desert: Decolonisation, Competing Nationalisms, and Tuareg Rebellions in Mali*. Leiden: Brill, 2010.
Malkki, Liisa. *Exile and Purity. Violence, Memory, and National Cosmology among Hutu Refugees in Tanzania*. Chicago: University of Chicago Press, 1995.
Murphy, Robert Francis. "The Social Distance and the Veil." *American Anthropologist* 66, no. 6 (1964): 1257–74.
Nicolaisen, Johannes, and Nicolaisen Ida. *The Pastoral Tuareg, Ecology, Culture, and Society*. Copenhagen: The Carsberg Foundation/Rhodos, 1997.
Olivier De Sardan, Jean Pierre. *Concepts et conceptions songhay-zarma: histoire, culture, société*. Paris: Nubia, 1982.

Olivier De Sardan, Jean Pierre. *Les sociétés songhay-zarma (Niger/Mali). Chefs, guerriers, esclaves, paysans*. Paris: Karthala, 1984.

Oxby, Clare. "Women and the Allocation of Herding Labour in a Pastoral Society (southern Kel Ferwan Twareg, Niger)." In *Le fils et le neveu. Jeux et Enjeux de la parenté touarègue*. Edited by S. Bernus, P. Bonte, L. Brock, and H. Claudot, 99–128. Paris: Maison des Sciences de l'Homme and Cambridge University Press, 1986.

Ouattara, Fatoumata. "Savoir-vivre et honte chez les Senufo Nanerge (Burkina Faso)." Thèse de doctorat. *École des Hautes Études en Sciences Sociales Paris*, 1999.

Peristiany, John George. *Honour and Shame: The Values of Mediterranean Society*. Chicago: University of Chicago Press, 1966.

Rasmussen, Susan. "Within the Tent and at the Crossroads: Travel and Gender Identity among the Tuareg of Niger." *Ethnos* 26, no. 21 (1998): 153–82.

Rasmussen, Susan. "The Slave Narrative in Life History and Myth, and Problems of Ethnographic Representation of the Cultural Predicament." *Ethnohistory* 46, no. 1 (1999): 67–108.

Rossi, Benedetta. *Reconfiguring Slavery: West African Trajectories*. Cambridge: Liverpool University Press, 2009.

Rossi, Benedetta. "Tuareg Trajectories of Slavery: Preliminary Reflections on a Changing Field." In *Tuareg Society within a Globalized World: Saharan Life in Transition*. Edited by Ines Kohl and Anja Fischer, 89–108. London: I.B. Tauris, 2010.

Schulz, Dorothea, and Souleymane Diallo. "Competing Assertions of Muslim Masculinity in Mali. *Journal of Religion in Africa* 46 (2016): 219–50.

Spittler, Georg. "La notion de travail chez les Kel Ewey." *Revue du monde musulmane et de la Mediterranée* 57, no. 3 (1990): 89–98.

Turner, Simon. *Angry Young Men in Camps: Gender, Age and Class Relations among Burundian Refugees in Tanzania*. Geneva: UNHCR, 1999.

6

The Ultimate Vindication of Honor: *Carok*, Shame, and Islam in Madura, Indonesia

Yanwar Pribadi

Introduction

This chapter discusses *carok* and its uneasy relationships with honor, shame (*malo*), and Islam in the Indonesian island of Madura. In many Muslim contexts, honor and shame are closely related to *ḥayāʾ* (in Islamic teachings it is mostly used in the context of modesty and shame). In many cases, *ḥayāʾ* in Islam is considered as fundamental to Muslims' faith and a way to guide them to practice modest behavior and proper conduct.[1]

The concept of honor and shame is very important in order to understand *carok*. *Carok* is a distinctive Madurese form of fighting using sharp weapons, which often leads to the death of the perpetrators and that serves as the last resort in terms of overcoming shame and defending one's honor. Any Madurese can commit *carok*, and their motives are predominantly driven by attempts to take their honor back after they were made to be *malo* (ashamed). Madurese who commit *carok* believe that their honor, taken away by insults, will be regained if they take a revenge action. However, it does not mean that *carok* can be committed indiscriminately. The main reason is certainly the need to defend honor and to overcome shame (the feeling of *malo*).[2]

Carok may be related to honor killing, a term to denote murders of an individual or individuals, either outsiders or members of a family, by people intending to protect what they view as the honor of their family.[3] The killings are generated by the perpetrators' loss of honor that eventually causes shame. *Carok* may lead to blood feuds, feuds with a cycle of retaliatory violence, with the families, friends, or associates of someone who has been killed or injured or otherwise wronged or dishonored, seeking vengeance by killing or injuring the offenders or their families.[4]

Despite the decreasing trend for *carok* actions in daily life today, the tradition is still widely perceived as a legitimate demonstration of honor in Madura. So, why does the tradition still exist in modern times? What is the relationship between *carok*, honor, and shame? What is the relationship between *carok* and Islam? The answers to the questions are the focus of this chapter.

In terms of honor killing, religion sometimes becomes the motive, although cultural factors are obviously the main driving forces. Most frequently, honor killing involves the murder of a woman or girl by male family members, due to the perpetrators' belief that the victim has brought dishonor or shame upon the family name, reputation, or prestige.[5]

Meanwhile, blood feuds are parts of a larger concept called revenge. Blood feuds may begin if one party (correctly or incorrectly) perceives itself to have been attacked or insulted by another. Conducting a blood feud is important as the avenging of family honor is imperative. The practice of blood feuds is associated with the ancient idea of purification of honor.[6]

Carok, despite its close relations to honor and shame, has its distinctive characteristics. Sociologist Abdur Rozaki argues that there are at least two cultural processes in which someone can be regarded as a *blater* (local Madurese strongmen/gangsters). Firstly, his ability in martial arts, daring attitudes, networks, and victories in *carok*. Secondly, his involvement in criminality and direct and indirect violent actions.[7] The anthropologist A. Latief Wiyata also argues that someone will not be considered a *blater* if he has not committed *carok*,[8] and that *carok* is considered by some perpetrators as a tool for obtaining a higher position or social status as a *blater* in their community.[9] He also says that *carok* actions are only committed by men, never by women.[10]

I would argue that *carok*, however, is not simply a form of honor killing and blood feuds. Most victims of honor killing are women. Even though both men and women can commit and can become victims of honor killing, in many places, conformity to moral standards implies different behavior codes for men and women, including stricter standards for chastity for women. In many cases, the honor motive is used by men as a pretext to control women and their sexuality, and in general the rights of women. Some of the important points in upholding honor include chastity, having no premarital and extramarital relations, dressing properly, conducting oneself according to expectations, and knowing one's duties according to traditions.[11] Meanwhile, *carok* is not a procedure to control the rights of women even though both honor killing and *carok* involve the notions of honor and shame. *Carok* is not simply a form of blood feud either. In many places, the revenge killing can be carried out against any member of the relatives or kin groups of the perpetrator and has serious implications. It means that revenge can be taken against minors for offenses committed by adult relatives.[12] In fact, *carok* killings do not target any relatives of the perpetrator, let alone minors.

Moreover, I will also demonstrate that the winner of a *carok* fighting is not automatically regarded as a *blater*, contrary to what Rozaki notes.[13] In principle, the *blater* are not criminals, though some of them may be involved in criminal activities. They are local strongmen/gangsters who resemble the mafiosi in Sicily, Italy, in that they offer protection to those who need it or those who are thought to need it.[14] In addition, contrary to what Wiyata notes,[15] I will show that *carok* is not a distinctive characteristic of the *blater*. In Madura, anyone, including women, can commit *carok* if they feel insulted and wish to regain their honor by killing or injuring their adversary.

Based on ethnographic fieldwork consisting of extensive interviews, casual chats, hangouts, and observations in Madura, Indonesia (in the Regency of Bangkalan and Sampang), between 2009 and 2011 as well as on newspaper sources, this chapter aims to contribute to the wider discussions on preserving honor and overcoming shame through the use of violence in a Muslim community. It builds on the idea put forward by Pribadi that piety, tradition, and violence are highly apparent in everyday life in Madura.[16] While staying in Madura, I not only dealt with the experience of the people at the particular point in time when I was staying there, but also concentrated on past events within living memory. The narratives I obtained on *carok* were mostly based on this situation. I never witnessed any *carok* fighting because it was not meant for public display (although many were often conducted in open spaces), and so only the perpetrators and people around them knew about the *carok* fighting plans. Moreover, it was difficult to approach the best direct sources or to gain access to the most interesting areas of enquiry since many perpetrators of *carok* and their families initially refused to talk to me. Only after I was represented or accompanied by "trustworthy" intermediaries or informants was I able to approach several sources.

The chapter suggests that in terms of *carok* in Madura, *malo* can be viewed as how people carry and properly maintain their code of honor, conduct, and ethical foundations. As such, many Madurese consider the violent action of *carok* neither to be a breach of Islamic teachings nor a violation of law, but as an ultimate vindication of honor and overcoming shame. Therefore, I maintain that *carok* is deeply institutionalized in Madurese society, and since *carok* is frequently approved by the social environment and the righters of wrongs dare to challenge the weak law enforcement, *carok* actions have often been seen as an answer in matters of regaining the loss of honor and overcoming shame. While there are few low-level Islamic preachers who give indirect approval to those who wish to commit *carok*, most high-ranking *ʿulamāʾ* (Islamic religious scholars), however, reject it. This ambiguous relation between honor, shame, and Islam is exemplified by the saying "better dead than ashamed/dishonoured" ("*ango'an poteya tolang etembang poteya mata*") that appears to legitimate the phenomenon within an Islamic community. This chapter is thus a vital addition in the literature of *ḥayāʾ* in Islam that mostly focuses on physical modesty of women's clothing.

This chapter proceeds as follows. In the next section, I explore multiple aspects of the setting—the island of Madura—that include piety, tradition, and violence. Subsequently, the next section elucidates multiple aspects of honor in various countries and those of shame in Madura. Then, I discuss how *carok* is committed as a way to regain honor and to overcome shame. After this, I analyze the relationship between *carok* and Islamic traditions. The last section is the conclusion.

Piety, Tradition, and Violence in Madura

The island of Madura is located off the eastern part of Java. It consists of four regencies (*kabupaten*), from west to east: Bangkalan, Sampang, Pamekasan, and Sumenep. Madura comprises an area of approximately 4,250 km^2. According to the official statistics, the island has a population of 3,963,814 (2020), most of whom are Muslims.[17]

In the map of Indonesian Islam, Madura has long been regarded as one of the principal centers of Islam in the country, besides Aceh, Banten, West Sumatra, and South Sulawesi. However, Madura is not only known as an island of Islamic piety, but also an island of cultural tradition and cultural violence. In terms of Islamic piety, the island is well known for the presence of numerous Islamic centers, such as Islamic boarding schools (*pesantren*), and the frequency of the holding of Islamic rituals, such as annual celebrations held on the anniversaries of the death of religious leaders (*ḥaul*). In terms of cultural tradition, the people are accustomed to hold on to syncretic traditions that are a mix of Islamic and local Madurese cultures, such as various *rokat* festivities (rituals asking for protection from the spirits of the ancestors and avoiding calamities). In terms of cultural violence, the island is notorious for local cultural forms associated with violence and other aspects, such as fraternity, wealth, and status that include *carok*, bull racings (*kerapan sapi*), cock fightings (*sabung ayam*), and feasts characteristic to the *blater* community (*remo*).[18] Consequently, piety, tradition, and violence have been visible in the everyday life of the people.

In terms of Islamic piety, a strong religious tradition appears to have emerged as a result of a long-term Islamization process in Madura, where there are at least two forms of Islam: the *santri* culture and the non-*santri* culture. In the *pesantren* tradition, *santri* mean pupils of *pesantren*. However, in addition to this meaning of the term *santri* in the *pesantren* tradition, it is used primarily to refer to the majority of Madurese Muslims who are proponents of a more orthodox Islam based on the global influences of Sunni Islam. In comparison, people of the non-*santri* culture are in the minority among Madurese Muslims. While this last group also adheres to Sunni Islam, they are proponents of a less orthodox form of the religion that is influenced more by local mystical belief systems.[19]

In terms of cultural tradition, while *kiai* (religious leaders/teachers) as the core of the *santri* culture sustain close connections with Islam, Madurese at the grassroots level also recognize supernatural powers of spirits that mediate between them and God. From this point of view, many Madurese believe that several events occur because of God's will, while others occur according to a set of unknown powers or according to the laws of nature. As a result, in order to put everything in order, the supernatural spirit powers have to be gratified regularly. For that reason, the Madurese frequently hold collective ritualistic festivities.[20]

In terms of cultural violence, Madurese people have traditionally been stereotyped and associated with violence, touchiness, suspiciousness, being temperamental, fierceness, vengefulness, and combativeness.[21] These stereotypes stem from colonial times and were used by the Dutch. However, they have survived to this day, reinforced by other ethnic communities in Indonesia, particularly those in neighboring Java who consider themselves to be "more refined."

As mentioned before, local cultural forms associated with violence, fraternity, wealth, and status, such as *remo*, *kerapan sapi* (bull racings), *sabung ayam* (cock fightings), and *carok*, have provided the Madurese with opportunities to signify their traditions that preserve cultural violence. In a wider context, sociologist Johan Galtung defines cultural violence as

> [a]ny aspect of a culture that can be used to legitimize violence in its direct or structural form. Examples of cultural violence are indicated, using a division of culture into religion and ideology, art and language, and empirical and formal science.[22]

We can see that in Madura, violence is legitimized by certain aspects of culture, such as in *carok* fightings. It also holds true for *blater* traditions such as *remo*. In *remo*, a *blater* can commit acts of violence if he is interrupted by another *blater* when he is dancing with a dancer. This act of violence is legitimized by a set of rules for *remo* that all *blater* are expected to follow.[23]

Honor and *Malo*

In many Muslim societies, honor is a key part of a Muslim's identity and self-worth and is highly regarded in the community's values and norms. Before we see what honor and shame mean for the Madurese, we will look at the attributes in other communities. For instance, among Turkish people, honor is identified as *namus*. For women, *namus* means chastity, while for men it means having chaste female family members. A man is expected to preserve the *namus* of his family based on the conduct of the family's womenfolk. This means that women cannot have illicit sexual relationships, are expected to maintain their virginity prior to marriage, and thereafter need to remain sexually faithful to their husband.[24]

In Pakistan, honor is defined as a multidimensional term that includes familial respect (*izzat*) and social prestige (*ghairat*). Honor can be described as a relation between a person's own feelings of self-esteem and that of the peer group (honor group). Because honor is socially bestowed, it is transient and can be lost because of acts that are considered shameful. Adultery, romance, and even flirting compromise female chastity and create shame on the offender and his/her family. Consequently, losing honor leads to disgrace and shame for the family.[25]

Honor is a key element of the northern Gheg society in Albania. When a person is made to be ashamed/dishonored, for instance by a violation of his private property, his honor will be restored only through the death of the offender. As the tradition of *gjakmarrja* (literally means blood taking) explains, Albanians will prefer to die because they believe that insults must be avenged and family honor must be upheld.[26]

In general, honor is defined as virtue on the one hand and as dominance or hierarchy on the other. In both cases, honor is considered as a gendered value system. Honor as virtue is mostly associated with women, while honor as dominance or hierarchy is related to men. Honor is thus a public representation of masculinity–femininity relations. However, honor also simultaneously involves a concern of the kinship group. The necessity to regain and protect one's honor is judged by the community as a whole, and because honor expresses the kinship group's highest values, honor killing is an important method to restore honor in many "honour and shame" societies.[27]

Honor is also often regarded as a central element in the social standing and position of a family within a community.[28] Factors such as gender, age, place of residence, education, and tribal and kinship relations crucially affect how honor is perceived in many Muslim societies. They see honor as the meaning and the purpose of life, something for whose sake people can be killed.[29]

Let us now discuss Madura. In Madura, all *carok* cases are caused by conflicts due to various matters. All of them are triggered by the feeling of *malo* due to the loss of honor. To restore honor that has been abused, Madurese will commit *carok* that receives support from the community. While in Indonesian language (*bahasa Indonesia*) shame is translated as *malu*, in Madurese it is translated as *malo* and *todus*. There are certainly differences between the two. *Todus* is a feeling that arises from within a person's mind as a result of his/her own actions that deviate from normative rules. *Malo* appears as a result of people's actions that disrespect one's existence and honor. Madurese who are treated in this way are bound to feel ill-treated, which in turn will make them take actions in an effort to restore their honor.

There are four main motives behind *carok* cases; the most notorious is adultery, followed by misunderstandings, land disputes, and unpaid debts. Adultery in this case does not exclusively involve sexual intercourse. Flirting with someone's wife or partner can be considered as a serious offence and will provoke *carok*. The feeling of *malo* due to harrassment to one's wife is not only felt by the husband, but also by his relatives and the community. This happens because invading one's honor is regarded as an act that damages social order.[30]

In general, Madurese view that any offence to one's wife is seen as an insult to honor that eventually generates a feeling of *malo* for the husband, the husband and wife's family, and the community. The husband feels *malo* because his role and function to protect his wife is considered a failure. Furthermore, because pestering another person's wife is considered as an act that damages social order, other relatives and close members of the community will feel the same way. If there is a *carok* because of this issue, it is understandable if they support it.[31]

A man whose honor is abused but does not dare to commit *carok* will be ridiculed as not being a man. Some people even consider this kind of man as not being a real Madurese. Therefore, the Madurese who commit *carok* will do it not only because they do not want to be seen as a coward, but also because they still want to be seen as Madurese. If this is the case, then *carok* also means an essential way for them to express their ethnic identity. All these aspects reinforce the notion that *carok* is not an act of ordinary violence, but an act of cultural violence that has complex sociocultural meanings.

Carok as a Way to Regain Honor and to Overcome Shame

There is perhaps no single thing more notorious, more violent, and more associated with crime in Madura than *carok*. For instance, a series of 1980s editions of an East Java newspaper was frequently bombarded with reports on *carok*. What was more remarkable was the fact that police officers always stated that the numbers of *carok* actions were declining at that time.[32] Despite these police officers' unsubstantiated reports, it seems very likely that the numbers of *carok* actions in earlier periods were even higher.

In colonial records in terms of *carok*, Dutch sources mention, "When a Madurese was made to be ashamed, he pulled his knife and immediately avenged the insult or waited until an opportunity arose to avenge himself." Fights, murder, and homicide (*carok*) were the order of the day, if one can believe it. One assumed the adage "an eye for an eye, a tooth for a tooth," and "even 'small insults' were 'answered with a knife' "[33] and "before the prohibition of carrying weapons in 1863, *carok* was also committed with spears, lances, swords, broadswords, and kris."[34]

Madurese use sickles and other sharp weapons to kill, or at least attempt to injure, their adversary in *carok* fighting. According to oral tradition, the act of *carok* was usually performed like a real duel, one side against the other. In later periods, attempts to kill or to injure adversaries when they were unprepared or unarmed were also considered to be *carok* as long as the main reason was to defend one's honor. In contrast, when a crime is committed where the victim is injured or killed but the main reason is not defending one's honor, the act cannot be considered *carok*. At this point, we can say that *carok* is not simply a criminal action, as many outsiders see it.[35]

Carok is normally, but not exclusively, committed by men. There are at least two *carok* cases—in my findings—that involved women as the perpetrators. In the first case, it was reported that two women, Hosni and Erru, residents of the subdistrict of Bluto in Sumenep, committed *carok* because of a misunderstanding over garbage. As a result, Hosni was severely wounded and received medical treatment.[36] Eight years earlier, in 1984, a certain T assassinated S in a bloody duel in the subdistrict of Konang, Bangkalan. T killed S because she was convinced that the latter had had an affair with her husband, who was actually S's uncle.[37] *Carok*, for Madurese, whether committed by men or women, is considered to be the ultimate vindication of honor following an insult.

Not all *carok* cases are triggered by "more serious" events, such as adultery or unpaid debts. In fact, many cases show that *carok* is triggered by disputes over insignificant matters, such as the dispute over garbage mentioned above,[38] a misunderstanding over cow dung that led to a murder,[39] or an insult generated by flatulence.[40] These three cases, along with many others, which may seem trivial to outsiders, are taken very seriously by many Madurese. These apparently insignificant causes all led to an insult to one's honor in which s/he was made to be *malo*, which for Madurese is a serious harassment, and so the loss of honor had to be avenged with a fight.

However, it does not mean that *carok* can be committed indiscriminately. There always has to be a reason to perform *carok*. The most important reason, as stated, is the need to defend honor when, for instance, one's spouse has been pestered. Incidentally, how the spouse reacts to this attention, favorably or otherwise, is irrelevant. For many Madurese, harassment of a spouse is considered to be an extremely serious offence.

> I did not wish to commit *carok* with Mat Kani. He is known as a *blater* in his village. My friends kept telling me that I had to commit *carok* against him in order to solve the problem [of indebtedness] between us, because he did not show good faith in paying his debt. I was still hesitant due to the fact that the amount of money he borrowed was not much. But when my friends persistently reminded me that he was a *blater*, and that by killing him I would be considered as a *blater* too, I began to think about it earnestly ... now, even though he was not killed and he will almost certainly take revenge, I have more courage to show him that I am capable of challenging him.[41]

As Wiyata argues, sometimes people come to *kiai* to receive a blessing and an amulet when they want to commit *carok*.[42] Nevertheless, it seems that it is only low-level *kiai* in villages who give approval to those who wish to commit *carok*. A number of high-ranking *kiai* who I have spoken to reject the idea of *carok*, or at least do not overtly support the violent action. The anthropologist Iik Mansurnoor also reveals that a high-ranking *kiai* in Bettet, Pamekasan showed his disapproval of *carok*. In 1984, a young man Muja wanted to take revenge because he had a quarrel with another young man, Barlekeh, over an insignificant matter. Muja went to see a *kiai* who had been his teacher and complained about the way he was made to be *malo* and insisted that the *kiai* should provide him with a formula to retain his confidence. The *kiai* agreed to bless Muja but issued a warning of excommunication against Muja if he should decide to commit *carok* against Barlekeh. For some time, the *kiai*'s threat against Muja succeeded in preventing the imminent *carok*. Not so long after the quarrel between Muja and Barlekeh, the *kiai* died. When the *kiai* went for treatment, Muja and his core kinsmen attacked those of Barlekeh, killing two and seriously injuring one.[43] Here, we see that an influential *kiai* remains an effective deterrent for some villagers, but when he is absent, the *kiai*'s disapproval has little effect. The late *Kiai* Nuruddin (d. 2021), a prominent *kiai* in Madura, and also East Java in general, told me that he would never give blessings to anyone who wished to commit *carok*. He insisted that conflicts that led to the loss of honor could be solved only in a consensual (*kekeluargaan*) way and that the *kiai* must play an important role in the problem-solving.[44]

It is clear that for many Madurese, honor is considered very essential in their life. In my fieldwork, I had a number of casual chats with housewives and young females in villages in Bangkalan. They stress the importance of fighting for honor as a true indication of "real human beings" (*manusia sesungguhnya*) and good Muslims. When asked about honor, they are convinced that it is a highly important aspect that must be respected, and when honor is violated, either men or women have to defend it. The reason for talking to these women is obvious. If women have a strong tendency to emphasize the significance of the popular saying, then it follows that men, as the main actors of forms of violence in Madura, are highly likely to believe in this maxim,[45] as shown in the interview below:

> We are called hotheads by Dayak people and Javanese; Malay and Buginese confirm the viewpoint. We never want to have disputes with those people but we cannot just remain silent if we are bothered. For us, it means someone is threatening our existence and our existence means our honour. If someone violates our honour, no matter where we live, we have to defend it. We would rather die than lose face (*malo*). We are always Madurese, wherever we live. There is nothing else we can do [to overcome the shame] than committing *carok*.[46]

Carok, when committed by the Madurese, always originates from feelings of being *malo* because their honor is harassed by others. Harassment of honor is tantamount to the feeling of being abused. In fact, one's existence and honor cannot be separated from her/his role, function, and status in the social structure of the Madurese. In practice, one's role, function, and social status are not only to be recognized by her/himself, but must also receive recognition from other people. The feeling of *malo* appears when people disrespect one's existence and honor, so that they feel meaningless. Madurese who feel offended will be highly likely to undertake violent actions against the harassers as an effort to regain their honor and to overcome shame.

Carok and Islam

Before we proceed to *carok*, I will first describe the relationships between Islam and honor killing in other countries. The anthropologist Are Knudsen has suggested that religion plays a significant role in honor killing in Pakistan. This is mainly because religion is the ultimate arbiter of sexual chastity and prescribes harsh punishments for those who compromise it. The state-sponsored Islamization program that began under Zia-ul-Haq's regime (1979–88) promoted Islamic orthodoxy and conservatism and made adultery a criminal offence by turning sections of Islamic law into statutory law. The growing orthodoxy and conservatism in the country made the protection of honor not only a social duty but also a religious duty, thereby spurring homicide of men and women.[47] In Turkey, many pious Turkish Muslims do invoke their faith when committing an honor killing. Honor killing is said to be *sevap*, or meritorious according to Islam, a deed for which the perpetrator will be rewarded by God in life and the afterlife.[48]

Nevertheless, Niaz A. Shah Kakakhel, a reader in law, argues that honor killing has nothing to do with the teachings of Islam. He asserts that Islam provides strict evidential prerequisites for punishing the adulterous: testimony of four witnesses before the *qāḍī* (magistrate or judge of a *Sharia* court) is to be provided and the man and woman are certainly given an opportunity of leading evidence to prove themselves innocent.[49] The Qur'an also indicates that no one can take the law into one's own hands since it is against the grain of the criminal justice system of Islam. The only way allowed to take life by the Qur'an is according to law.[50] In fact, honor killing and "honour and shame cultures" are also found in countries with strong Christian traditions, such as in the Mediterranean region and Latin America, or among Hindus in India, and is not linked exclusively to Islam.[51]

It is important to note, however, that honor killing is rooted in the regulation of women's sexuality with the aim to uphold patriarchal honor. Even though there is no text in the Qur'an that can be used to justify the practice of honor killing, there is in fact one hadith (reports of the words, actions, and tacit consent of the Prophet Muhammad) that indicates that if one witnesses an adulterous wife and in a state of anger kills both parties, his act will not be considered as murder in the legal sense. Despite the sporadic application of this reasoning in Muslim history/Islamic law and the existence of competing interpretations, it still informs legal codes in some Muslim countries. In societies where this code of law applies, perpetrators of honor killing are usually given very lenient sentences. Honor killing in Muslim contexts can also be indirectly linked to the notion of female sexuality as a male commodity that exists in traditional Muslim culture.[52]

In Madura, although Islamic teachings stress that *malu or malo* starts from a Muslim's heart and that in a *hadith* the Prophet Muhammad said that the strong is not the one who overcomes people by his strength, but the strong is the one who controls himself while in anger,[53] for many Madurese, *ḥayā'* can have another meaning, particularly when it is a question of regaining honor and overcoming shame. In this case, Madurese can be culturally violent if their honor, particularly when they are made to be *malo*, is insulted, harassed, or violated. Consequently, in order to regain their honor and to overcome shame, they may commit *carok* that is considered to be the ultimate vindication of honor. In this case, honor is considered to be more important than anything else, even when compared to Islamic teachings that stress the importance of *ḥayā'* for Muslims to avoid anything considered to be distasteful, abominable, or violent.

Conclusion

In many cases, *ḥayā'* is considered fundamental to Muslims' faith and a guidance for modest behavior and proper conduct. *Ḥayā'* can thus be defined as the means by which morals and ethics in society are maintained and pursued. However, the concept of *ḥayā'* may vary greatly from one place to another. In certain places, for instance, *ḥayā'* is seen more as a form of honor that must be defended when it is challenged. Therefore, while in most Muslim communities violent actions such as *carok* may be considered as an immodest behavior and improper conduct, in Madura, the situation is much more complex.

Carok tradition has existed until today because many Madurese neither consider the violent action of *carok* to be a breach of Islamic teachings nor a violation of law, but as an ultimate vindication of honor, particularly when they are made to be *malo*, where in the broad concept of *ḥayā'*, *malo* and honor are two of the key meanings. As a result, *carok* is deeply institutionalized in Madurese society, and the action has often been seen as an answer in matters of regaining the loss of honor and overcoming shame. Therefore, in terms of *carok* in Madura, *malo* (shame) can be viewed as how people carry and properly maintain their code of honor, conduct, and ethical foundations. This circumstance in relation to honor, shame, and Islam is exemplified by the popular saying "better dead than ashamed/dishonoured" that appears to legitimate the phenomenon within a Muslim society that shows piety, tradition, and violence at the same time.

This chapter has shown that shame and honor are considered as fundamental in Muslims' code of conduct in Madura. Regaining the loss of honor and overcoming shame are seen as a way to consider the perpetrators of *carok* as "real human beings," good Muslims, and real Madurese. These three elements show that *carok* also figures as an essential way for them to express their cultural, religious, and ethnic identity. This chapter is a vital addition to the literature of *ḥayā'* in Islam by contributing to the discussions on honor, shame, and violence in a particular Muslim society. By highlighting the close connection between the three aspects—of being "real human beings," good Muslims, and real Madurese—this chapter supports the proposition put forward by Pribadi that piety, tradition, and violence are highly apparent in everyday life in Madura.[54]

Notes

1. Adis Duderija, Alina Isac Alak, and Kristin Hissong, *Islam and Gender: Major Issues and Debates* (London: Routledge, 2020), 44.
2. Yanwar Pribadi, "Islam and Politics in Madura: Ulama and Other Local Leaders in Search of Influence (1990–2010)," PhD diss., Faculty of Humanities, Leiden University, Leiden (2013a).
3. Ursula Smartt, "Honour Killings," *Justice of the Peace* 170 (January 7 and 14, 2006), 4–7; Niaz A. Shah Kakakhel, "Honour Killings: Islamic and Human Rights Perspectives," *Northern Ireland Legal Quarterly* 55, no. 1 (2004), 78–89; Clementine van Eck, *Purified by Blood: Honour Killings amongst Turks in the Netherlands* (Amsterdam: Amsterdam University Press, 2003); Are Knudsen, *License to Kill: Honour Killings in Pakistan* (Bergen: Chr. Michelsen Institute Development Studies and Human Rights, 2004).
4. Rolf Kuschel, "Killing Begets Killing: Homicides and Blood Feuds on a Polynesian Outlier," *Bijdragen tot de Taal-, Land- en Volkenkunde*: Politics, Tradition and Change in the Pacific 149, no. 4 (1993), 690–717; Mirjona Sadiku, "A Tradition of Honor, Hospitality and Blood Feuds: Exploring the Kanun Customary Law in Contemporary Albania," *Balkan Social Science Review* 3, no. 1 (2014), 93–115; Katerina Standish, "Understanding Cultural Violence and Gender: Honour Killings; Dowry Murder; the Zina Ordinance and Blood-feuds," *Journal of Gender Studies* 23, no. 2 (2014), 111–24; Muhammad Azam Chaudhary, "The Ways of Revenge in Chilas, Gilgit-Baltistan, Pakistan: Shia-Sunni Clashes as Blood Feuds," *Ethnoscripts: Zeitschrift für aktuelle ethnologische Studien* 16, no. 1 (2014), 97–114.
5. Smartt, "Honour Killings"; Kakakhel, "Honour Killings"; Van Eck, *Purified by Blood*; Knudsen, *License to Kill.*
6. Kuschel, "Killing Begets Killing"; Sadiku, "A Tradition of Honor, Hospitality and Blood Feuds"; Standish, "Understanding Cultural Violence and Gender"; Chaudhary, "The Ways of Revenge in Chilas, Gilgit-Baltistan, Pakistan."
7. Abdur Rozaki, *Menabur Kharisma Menuai Kuasa: Kiprah Kiai dan Blater sebagai Rezim Kembar di Madura* (Yogyakarta: Pustaka Marwa, 2004), 11–12.
8. A. Latief Wiyata, *Carok: Konflik Kekerasan dan Harga Diri Orang Madura* (Yogyakarta: LKiS, 2006), 114.
9. Ibid., 230.
10. Ibid., 176–7 and 184.
11. Filiz Kardam, *The Dynamics of Honor Killings in Turkey: Prospects for Action* (Ankara: Population Association, 2005); Emily Dyer, *"Honour" Killings in the UK* (London: The Henry Jackson Society, 2015).
12. Peter Kreuzer, *Political Clans and Violence in the Southern Philippines*, PRIF Report No. 71 (Frankfurt: Peace Research Institute Frankfurt, 2005); Sandra F. Joireman, "Aiming for Certainty: The Kanun, Blood Feuds and the Ascertainment of Customary Law," *Journal of Legal Pluralism and Unofficial Law* 36, no. 2 (2014), 1–14.
13. Rozaki, *Menabur*, 11–12.
14. Pribadi, "Islam and Politics in Madura," 6.

15. Wiyata, *Carok*, 176–7 and 184.
16. Pribadi, "Islam and Politics in Madura."
17. https://jatim.bps.go.id/indicator/12/375/1/jumlah-penduduk-provinsi-jawa-timur.html (accessed January 4, 2021).
18. *Remo* is an exclusive all-*blater* feast that also serves as a rotating savings and credit association. A guest has to give money to the host and, in return, when he becomes a host, he will receive money from the former host and other guests, who will eventually become hosts as well. In principle, when he becomes a guest for a *remo* being held by a fellow *blater*, he has to provide the host (who was himself a guest at an earlier occasion) with more cash than he received from him before. If he gives the same amount of money or even less, the host may consider this as an insult. Consequently, he may be removed from the membership of *remo*. However, exceptions frequently do occur, as many hosts show no real objection if they receive the same amount of money, taking into consideration the possibility that some people may not have sufficient funds to attend a *remo*. See Pribadi, "Islam and Politics in Madura," 93.
19. Yanwar Pribadi, "Religious Networks in Madura: Pesantren, Nahdlatul Ulama and Kiai as the Core of Santri Culture," *Al-Jami'ah: Journal of Islamic Studies* 51, no. 1 (2013b), 1–32.
20. Pribadi, "Islam and Politics in Madura."
21. Huub de Jonge, "Stereotypes of the Madurese," in *Across Madura Strait: the Dynamics of an Insular Society*, edited by Kees van Dijk, Huub de Jonge, and Elly Touwen-Bouwsma (Leiden: KITLV Press, 1995), 13.
22. Johan Galtung, "Cultural Violence," *Journal of Peace Research* 27, no. 3 (1990), 291.
23. Pribadi, "Islam and Politics in Madura."
24. Van Eck, *Purified by Blood*, 9.
25. Knudsen, *License to Kill*, 3–4.
26. Sadiku, "A Tradition of Honor, Hospitality and Blood Feuds," 106.
27. Alina Zvinkliene, "'Honour Killings' in Modern Societies: A Sociological Perspective," *ICR Journal* 1, no. 3 (2010), 532; Maliha Zia Lari, *"Honour Killings" in Pakistan and Compliance of Law* (Islamabad: Aurat Publication and Information Service Foundation, 2011), 21–2.
28. Dyer, *"Honour" Killings in the UK*, 11.
29. Kardam, *The Dynamics of Honor Killings in Turkey*, 60.
30. Wiyata, *Carok*, 170–5. Due to the word limit, see Wiyata's *Carok* and Pribadi's *Islam* for the exemplary cases of *carok* in more detail.
31. Wiyata, *Carok*, 175.
32. See for instance, *Jawa Pos*, January 3, 1983 and *Jawa Pos*, April 11, 1984.
33. *De Java-Post* 1911, 9–22: 345 and Wop 1866: 284, both are quoted in De Jonge, "Stereotypes," 13.
34. Huub de Jonge, "Rather White Bones Than White Eyes: Violent Self-Help among the Madurese," in *Violence and Vengeance: Discontent and Conflict in New Order Indonesia*, edited by Frans Hüsken and Huub de Jonge (Saarbrücken: Verlag für Entwicklungspolitik Saarbrücken, 2002), 147.
35. Pribadi, "Islam and Politics in Madura."
36. *Jawa Pos*, August 12, 1992.
37. *Jawa Pos*, May 4, 1984.
38. *Jawa Pos*, August 12, 1992.
39. *Jawa Pos*, November 21, 1992.

40. *Jawa Pos*, September 1, 1983.
41. Interview with B in Bangkalan on February 12, 2011.
42. Wiyata, *Carok*, 50.
43. Iik Mansurnoor, *Islam in an Indonesian World: Ulama of Madura* (Yogyakarta: Gadjah Mada University Press, 1990), 360.
44. Interview with *Kiai* Nuruddin on December 1, 2009.
45. Pribadi, "Islam and Politics in Madura," 106.
46. Interview with MZ, a Madurese from Palangkaraya, Central Kalimantan, who now resides in Bangkalan, on December 3, 2009.
47. Knudsen, *License to Kill*, 6–7.
48. Van Eck, *Purified by Blood*, 39.
49. Kakakhel, "Honour Killings," 82.
50. Zvinkliene, "Honour Killings' in Modern Societies," 535.
51. Van Eck, *Purified by Blood*, 37; Zvinkliene, "Honour Killings' in Modern Societies," 535; Duderija, Alak, and Hissong, *Islam and Gender*, 52.
52. Duderija, Alak, and Hissong, *Islam and Gender*, 44 and 53.
53. See https://sunnah.com/bukhari:6114 (accessed October 16, 2021).
54. Pribadi, "Islam and Politics in Madura."

Bibliography

Chaudhary, Muhammad Azam. "The Ways of Revenge in Chilas, Gilgit-Baltistan, Pakistan: Shia-Sunni Clashes as Blood Feuds." *Ethnoscripts: Zeitschrift für aktuelle ethnologische Studien* 16, no. 1 (2014): 97–114.

Duderija, Adis, Alina Isac Alak, and Kristin Hissong. *Islam and Gender: Major Issues and Debates*. London: Routledge, 2020.

Dyer, Emily. *"Honour" Killings in the UK*. London: The Henry Jackson Society, 2015.

Eck, Clementine van. *Purified by Blood: Honour Killings amongst Turks in the Netherlands*. Amsterdam: Amsterdam University Press, 2003.

Galtung, Johan. "Cultural Violence." *Journal of Peace Research* 27, no 3 (1990): 291–305.

Joireman, Sandra F. "Aiming for Certainty: The Kanun, Blood Feuds and the Ascertainment of Customary Law." *Journal of Legal Pluralism and Unofficial Law* 36, no. 2 (2014): 1–14.

Jonge, Huub de. "Stereotypes of the Madurese." In *Across Madura Strait: the Dynamics of an Insular Society*. Edited by Kees van Dijk, Huub de Jonge, and Elly Touwen-Bouwsma, 7–24. Leiden: KITLV Press, 1995.

Jonge, Huub de. "Rather White Bones than White Eyes: Violent Self-Help among the Madurese." In *Violence and Vengeance: Discontent and Conflict in New Order Indonesia*. Edited by Frans Hüsken and Huub de Jonge, 143–56. Saarbrücken: Verlag für Entwicklungspolitik Saarbrücken, 2002.

Kakakhel, Niaz A. Shah. "Honour Killings: Islamic and Human Rights Perspectives." *Northern Ireland Legal Quarterly* 55, no. 1 (2004): 78–89.

Kardam, Filiz. *The Dynamics of Honor Killings in Turkey: Prospects for Action*. Ankara: Population Association, 2005.

Knudsen, Are. *License to Kill: Honour Killings in Pakistan*. Bergen: Chr. Michelsen Institute Development Studies and Human Rights, 2004.

Kreuzer, Peter. *Political Clans and Violence in the Southern Philippines*. PRIF Report No. 71, Frankfurt: Peace Research Institute Frankfurt, 2005.
Kuschel, Rolf. "Killing Begets Killing: Homicides and Blood Feuds on a Polynesian Outlier." *Bijdragen tot de Taal-, Land- en Volkenkunde*: Politics, Tradition and Change in the Pacific 149, no. 4 (1993): 690–717.
Lari, Maliha Zia. *"Honour Killings" in Pakistan and Compliance of Law*. Islamabad: Aurat Publication and Information Service Foundation, 2011.
Mansurnoor, Iik. *Islam in an Indonesian World: Ulama of Madura*. Yogyakarta: Gadjah Mada University Press, 1990.
Pribadi, Yanwar. "Islam and Politics in Madura: Ulama and Other Local Leaders in Search of Influence (1990–2010)." PhD diss. Faculty of Humanities, Leiden University, 2013.
Pribadi, Yanwar. "Religious Networks in Madura: Pesantren, Nahdlatul Ulama and Kiai as the Core of Santri Culture." *Al-Jami'ah: Journal of Islamic Studies* 51, no. 1 (2013b): 1–32.
Rozaki, Abdur. *Menabur Kharisma Menuai Kuasa: Kiprah Kiai dan Blater sebagai Rezim Kembar di Madura*. Yogyakarta: Pustaka Marwa, 2004.
Sadiku, Mirjona. "A Tradition of Honor, Hospitality and Blood Feuds: Exploring the Kanun Customary Law in Contemporary Albania." *Balkan Social Science Review* 3, no. 1 (2014): 93–115.
Smartt, Ursula. "Honour Killings." *Justice of the Peace* 170 (January 7 and 14, 2006): 4–7.
Standish, Katerina. "Understanding Cultural Violence and Gender: Honour Killings; Dowry Murder; the Zina Ordinance and Blood-feuds." *Journal of Gender Studies* 23, no. 2 (2014): 111–24.
Wiyata, A. Latief. *Carok: Konflik Kekerasan dan Harga Diri Orang Madura*. Yogyakarta: LkiS, 2006.
Zvinkliene, Alina. "'Honour Killings' in Modern Societies: A Sociological Perspective." *ICR Journal* 1, no. 3 (2010): 532–5.

Newspapers, online sources, and attributed and unattributed interviews

Jawa Pos, January 3, 1983.
Jawa Pos, September 1, 1983.
Jawa Pos, April 11, 1984.
Jawa Pos, May 4, 1984.
Jawa Pos, August 12, 1992.
Jawa Pos, November 21, 1992.
Badan Pusat Statistik Provinsi Jawa Timur (2020), "Jumlah Penduduk Provinsi Jawa Timur (Jiwa), 2018–2020." https://jatim.bps.go.id/indicator/12/375/1/jumlah-penduduk-provinsi-jawa-timur.html https://sunnah.com/bukhari:6114 (accessed June 11, 2023).
Interview with B in Bangkalan on February 12, 2011.
Interview with *Kiai* Nuruddin on December 1, 2009.
Interview with MZ, a Madurese from Palangkaraya, Central Kalimantan, who now resides in Bangkalan, December 3, 2009, Bangkalan, Indonesia.

7

Islam, Modesty, and Dignity in Malaysia

Muhamad Ali

Introduction

Modesty in the Malay–Indonesian contexts has only recently received scholarly attention, although the concepts of modesty and shame have been used in the past. Modesty has complex meanings and applications, and some see it as a virtue of being disposed to underestimate one's self-worth.[1] In Malay cultures, modesty is conceptualized through shame or *malu* in Malay, which can be defined as a self-conscious emotive quality or an affective disposition that has a core meaning in relating individuals to wider social groups—real or imagined.[2] A related concept "*murū'a*," originally translated in gendered terms as "manhood," has been used to refer to "honour" or "dignity."[3] From the Malay perspectives, *malu* functions more often as a social good, something akin to a sense of propriety (*adab*), although it is also used in negative connotations, such as being passive, introverted, or shy of doing certain things in life. The feeling of *malu* may be invoked in different situations: doing or thinking of doing something perceived to be inappropriate or foolish; having a shameful personal characteristic, such as ugliness, deformity, or poverty; feeling *malu* on account of the shameful deed or character of a family member; and being teased, criticized, or complained about because of one's shameful deed or character.[4] The feelings of *malu* serve as the cohesive force that maintains, or even constitutes the community consensus of primarily the Malay village, which lacks formal authority structures,[5] although *malu* prevails in middle- and upper-class society as well. More recently, Elizabeth F. Collins and Ernaldi Bahar used a cognitive approach to explore the changes and variations in the uses of *malu* among Malay Indonesian men and women in the past and during the New Order era (1966–98). In the article, Collins and Bahar explore the gendered uses of *malu* shaping male aggression and female self-restraint and the culture-specific syndromes of *amuk* (anger and indiscriminate attack) among the men and *latah* (compulsive utterance of obscenities) among the women and point to the decline of such syndromes in contemporary times. They argue that some people call for a particularly Islamic morality of haram (forbidden) and halal (permitted), whereas others call for a more culturally pluralistic morality based on *malu* itself. They claim that wearing of the veil or *jilbab* by women involves a reinforcement of *malu*'s tendency and "an implicit acceptance of subordinate gender roles that limit the women's public activity and freedom of choice."[6]

In contrast to the Indonesian context in which Islam is the majority but not the state's religion and Malays are not the majority, this chapter considers Malaysia where a Malay is defined as "an individual who professes the religion of Islam, habitually speaks the Malay language, and conforms to Malay customs."[7] The present chapter refines some of the arguments made regarding the uses of *malu* among men and women and considers the contemporary cases of contestations of modest fashion, unveiling, and the LGBTQ (Lesbian, Gay, Bisexual, Trans, and Queer) movement. It will briefly explore the way in which Malay authors used shame, modesty, and dignity in the Malay court chronicles, proverbs, and literatures. Then it will discuss the way in which modesty and dignity operate in the contentious domains of fashion, veiling, and non-heterosexual orientations in contemporary Malaysia.

Construction of Shame and Dignity in the Past

The concept of *malu* has been used in the Malay court chronicles, proverbs, and literature. The *Malay Annals* (*Sejarah Melayu*), the early literary work that gives a mythical history of the Melaka sultanate from between the fifteenth and sixteenth centuries, uses *malu* to mean being shameful, shy, or embarrassed as a punitive or anticipatory mechanism of keeping one's honor within the court and before the people. For an instance of *malu* as an outcome of something that has been done, Sultan Muhammad Shah (r. 1424–44) was made personally ashamed when he knew that his words were not obeyed by his own brother.[8] For an example of an anticipatory *malu*, Sultan Manshur Syah (r. 1459–1477) felt ashamed of thinking that he would be potentially succeeded by a queen to keep his courtly honor and dignity.[9] Beyond the court, the Malay proverbs, such as those collected in the nineteenth century, link the notion of shamelessness to societal dishonor, although without the sense of belonging to a court or an imagined Malay community. For example, a proverb says, "Like the shark is a person witty a character for sponging shamelessly on his neighbors."[10] Here one would be without shame if they took advantage of someone else's generosity, charity, or hospitality to obtain things such as money and food. According to another proverb, when someone exposes the faults of his own household, he puts himself to open shame and publishes his own dishonor, just like a maxim "will a man put his salt out in the rain?"[11]

As authors and intellectuals began to imagine a Malay community within the wider Eastern Islamic community (*umma*), they used shame, modesty, and dignity as a collectively ethnic and religious virtue. Abdullah bin Abdul Kadir (1796–1854), an author of Malay–Tamil descent and a teacher, interpreter, and writer who worked for British colonial official Thomas Raffles (1781–1826) during his posting in Singapore, uses *malu* in terms of the ethnic, communal, and social as well as individual and religious. For instance, Abdullah noted *malu* as shame and fear of committing wrongs among the Malay elite and also his fellow Malays:

> There was in Malacca among all races a feeling of shame and fear between one man and another. If, for instance, a Malay child did a wrongful act or anything bad of that kind to a Chinese or a man of any other race seeing it could correct him or strike him and would receive the approbation of the child's parents.[12]

But Abdullah also imagined how other Malays thought of him as causing shame to other people as he positioned himself in between the Malay subjects and the British. He said, "They called me Padre Abdullah which they thought was a discreditable and shameful designation. They reviled me because I stood in well with the white people and considered it a sin that I should teach men our language."[13] Abdullah also made some reference to the idea of being shameful in front of Allah. He recorded a story about a Malay owner of women slaves: "The man who owned these slaves behaved like a beast, shameless and without fear of Allah. The younger girls hung around him while he behaved in a manner which it would be improper for me to describe in this book."[14] He used Islam also to criticize a Malay sultan and a prince for being overly respected regardless of their bad behaviors: "The prince, who had no shame of fear of Allah and His creatures, of eating things forbidden by Islam, did whatever pleased them."[15] Moreover, Abdullah was critical of the inability of the Malay elite to teach manners to their children:

> They allowed them to do anything they like, give in to their every wish, and pay no attention to instructing them in the humanities, in modesty, or a sense of shame, or in the elements of culture and courteous behavior.[16]

Here, Abdullah expressed his view of Islam in condemning the bad manners of the Malay elite and people for not acting piously before God and other people.[17]

During the transition period from the British to Malay sovereignty, intellectuals began to construct and develop religious, cultural, and nationalistic perspectives to modesty and dignity. For example, an author of Malay-Arab descent, Alwi bin Sheikh Al-Hady (1892–1970), who titled his booklet "Western and Malay mannerisms," wished to call the Malay elite and the commoners to embrace Islamic—often framed as Eastern—ways of behavior. Based on his observation, bad manners were offensive, disrespectful, and shameful.[18] He was critical of other Malays who did not observe etiquette like keeping promises and being on time. He was concerned about the negative identification of Malays with "oriental punctuality." He maintained that although Malays had a good reputation of being "smart and fast" in imitating other peoples and cultures, they unfortunately often followed these cultures improperly. Malays followed the Western lifestyle concerning dressing and dancing, but what was shameful was that they did not observe punctuality and promise keeping, which were more in line with Islamic ethics.[19]

Other Malay intellectuals placed emphasis on the human body and clothing in their formulation and differentiation of the Eastern and Western cultures. Malay author Zainal 'Abidin bin Ahmad, known as Za'ba (1895–1973), framed the notion of modesty in terms of the Eastern and Western attitudes toward the male and female body and clothing as well as other domains of familial and social life. He contends that to dress in such a way as to not cover the immodest or private parts of the body in public, in ordinary encounters with other men, and during prayers is a sin against the unwritten rules of Malay propriety as well as Islam. He subscribed to the rules of Islam, which stipulated that the private part of the body for a man comprises all the area between the navel and the knees and for a woman the whole of the body and limbs except the face, hands, and feet.[20] Based on his observation, religious conservatives even objected to the men's use of shorts open at the knee because it leaves a part of the lower thigh exposed to view and so gives offense to pious eyes. In addition, the practice of wearing a bathing suit that covers the private parts was observed in public places, and women had to hide the outline of their figure and form, unlike the bathing suit worn by Western women. In this regard, the Malay seems to say to the Westerner, "That face of yours is equivalent in dignity to this shameful part of mine!"[21]

For Za'ba, the proper relationship between man and woman as observed by the Malays are patterned on "the best traditions of the East."[22] Being modest means safety for women, and honor for men, he says. Woman is the sacred treasure and man the guardian protector and supporter not as the West has so often charged the East with, that "woman is regarded as a mere plaything, chattel and slave, and man the lord and master though abuse has corrupted that pure ideal as it has corrupted many other ideals in human relations."[23] To support his observation, Za'ba cited the Qur'anic verses that regulate men's attitudes toward women (Q. 2:228; Q. 2:187; and Q. 4:34). To Za'ba, although Malays see that men and women are spiritually and morally equal before God, they are not only biologically different but should be socially differentiated as well. The boundaries of their private parts are different, and their dresses are and should remain distinct. Men and women should dress differently. The regulations are regarded as "the common instinct among most Eastern people everywhere" as "mothers, sisters, wives and daughters, both one's own and those of others, are treated with respectful modesty and bashfulness by the men."[24] The association of Malays with Islam and Eastern "shy" culture continues to be constructed and becomes a subject of contestation as in the cases of modest fashion in contemporary Malaysia to be discussed in what follows.[25]

Contestation of Modest Fashion

After the Iranian revolution in 1979 and the global revival of Islam, the issue of veiling—especially the female—increasingly became the fundamental mark of an ideal society for many Muslims across the globe.[26] For women, modesty is constructed and contested in different forms: hijab, *jilbab*, or *tudung*. More recently, fashion designers have become new icons of Muslim pop culture in local and global markets.[27] Fazrena Aziz, for example, started her TudungPeople while studying at the International Islamic University Malaysia. Fazrena believed that the headscarf or *tudung* is more than just a piece of clothing to cover a Muslim woman's head and ears—it also serves to beautify the woman. She considers her fashion business her *da*ʿ*wa* or call to Islam.[28] On the one hand, the current trend of hijab or *tudung* fashion in Malaysia as elsewhere indicates Muslim women's sense of agency in participating in the global market.[29] On the other hand, controversies are sparked over whether or not "modest fashion" is a contradiction.[30] Contestation occurs over whether or not women should support the conservative interpretation of modesty in dressing within global consumerism rather than becoming pious and modest before God and the society.

For those who don the hijab, fashion affects the meaning and expression of modesty in different, personalized ways. For many, wearing the hijab means following religious obligations rather than just following fashion. For others, following fashion means disregarding the religious notion of modesty—in the sense of simplicity and moderation.[31] The conformity to class standard and the need for uniqueness in hijab consciousness among the Malay women are some of the factors more important than simplicity and moderation implied in modesty.[32] The traditional meanings of being embarrassed for not covering the private parts of the body have become minimized, and even neglected. It is no longer shameful to show off one's social standing by wearing the fashionable dress with hijab.[33] Modest fashion is about social class and social mobility. It greatly varies between poor and ordinary Malay women who show simplicity and the elite Malay women from the middle and upper classes who show a modern and even luxurious lifestyle. For most, modest fashion belongs to the elite middle class and high class. The self-representations of these elite Muslim women going fashionable and global, however, increase their sense of pride of being both Muslim and modern. The fashionable hijab has become a new symbol of wealth and status.[34]

For other women, being religiously modest and being fashionable are not an either/or question. It is a matter of degree and context, and hybridity. A Malay female academician said,

> The new styles of hijab are elegant and sophisticated but allows me to be confident in my appearance as an academician, therefore I want to be a role model and show some good example so that maybe when teenagers took at me, they can don hijab and still do fashion as the same time but in a proper way and presentable.[35]

Malay Muslim women dress in diverse styles of fashion according to the trends while observing the physical association of modesty as *aurat*, covering certain private parts of the body. The extent to which a dressing style conforms to shariʿa law and ethics, or fits the modern culture, or is a combination of both, is dependent on the individuals and their circumstances.[36]

Contestation of Modesty through Unveiling and among LGBTQ Malays

Beyond modest and modern fashion, the challenge to the mainstream interpretation and practice of veiling comes from among Muslim women who maintain that veiling is a cultural expression rather than a religious obligation. They distinguish between a universal Islamic ethics of modesty and the particular Arabic culture of veiling. They question why the veil covering the hair has become a mark of modesty.[37] Can one unveil and still be modest and pious? How does a women reconcile the modesty of the veil with the modesty of character? Prominent female politicians and activists do not cover their heads. Activist Maryam Lee, who wrote the book *Unveiling Choice*, said,

> All my life, I had been told that wearing the headscarf is mandatory and if I don't wear it, it's sinful. And then I found out that it actually wasn't, so I felt very cheated—like all your life you've been told one thing, and it turns out to be a lie.

Maryam feels that unveiling would mean getting bullied and harassed even though she does not feel less Muslim by removing her hijab.[38] But many other women are not veiled. In an interview, a Malay woman said,

> I cannot wear it any longer because what I know makes me a hypocrite. The *tudung* is not who I am. I put it on because I wanted to fit in with others and I listened to what my *ustaz* (teacher) told me. It was not 100 percent my decision. I have been there, so now I can share my story with other people. Maybe they can learn from my experience and not make the same mistakes. It is better not to wear it rather than selectively wearing it depending on my mood or when the situation calls for it.[39]

Sisters in Islam, the nongovernmental organization founded by Muslim women in 1988, which promotes the rights of women in Malaysia, has actively criticized the state and mainstream patriarchal culture of controlling women's bodies and dress. Sisters in Islam contend that girls are outperforming boys in schools and women make up the majority of undergraduates in public universities. Women represent more than fifty percent of the labor force in Malaysia. But the operations such as the crackdown by the religious police undermine women's position and reduce their worth to just their bodies and clothing. On their part, they reason that the Qur'an passages on how men and women should dress focus on modesty as an avoidance of access and the covering of nakedness and clothing as a beauty. Qur'an 7:26 and 49:13 state that the garment of piety or consciousness of God (*taqwa*) is the best of all. For them, modesty should mean moderation and piety, and it should apply to men and women. They say the campaigns circulated in print and online via social media have been designed to "unfairly target, vilify, and warn women—and not men—of their modesty." They cite the Qur'anic verse 24:30 calling men to guard their modesty by lowering their gaze. They maintain that the state's discrimination against women is an outcome of "male-centric interpretations influenced by cultural practices and values of a patriarchal society."[40]

Other Malay individuals have identified themselves with the lesbian, gay, bisexual, transgender, and queer (LGBTQ) culture and have more at stake to challenge the mainstream heterosexual culture and yet continue to negotiate their sexual and gender orientations by adjusting aspects of their appearances and behaviors to the religious practice, familial norms, social pressures and stigmatization, and state's control and criminalization.[41] For the mainstream culture, to be gay in Malaysia is a sin (*dosa*) and causes shame to the family. Individual stories from among LGBTQ Malays reveal that they fear the negative reactions to their gender orientations of family members and the public. One individual says,

> My partner and a close friend traveled with me to visit my family in Malaysia. They were introduced as close friends, and even though the experience there was positive, I felt as if I was keeping a secret from them. I wanted my family to meet the woman I loved, but I was fearful of negative reactions if I revealed my relationship.[42]

The cancellations of some events planned to show LGBTQ pride in Kuala Lumpur in 2011 and in Penang in 2014 were seen as public reactions against "immoralities" aimed at poisoning the Malay youth. Disclosing their identity threatens relationships and causes shame and grief to the family. Some individuals even received death threats when they came out to reveal their non-conforming sexual orientation in front of their family and publicly in social media.[43]

The mainstream views are based on the conceptions of the *fitrah* as the innate and unalterable natural disposition, and the acts of *liwat* (sodomy) and *musahaqah* (lesbian sex) are sinful.[44] The Malaysia' National Fatwa Council ruled that women who dress like men and possess male characteristics and sexual desire are against *fitrah* and the Law of God (*sunnatullah*). The Council states that Western manners in dress, hairstyle, speech, and accessories lead to homosexuality.[45] In this difficult circumstance, LGBTQ individuals feel obliged to cover their true identities and negotiate their roles before others, adjust their ways of speaking and their behavior, and decide if it is safe to reveal their sexual orientation in a manner that feels appropriate to their culture, family, and the society. Some project a heterosexual public image while concealing their homosexual identity. For example, Mahmud, a gay character in a contemporary Malaysian novel says,

> There is something nice about not having too many *Melayu* about; they are always so disapproving—all that *tak boleh, tak halus, tak manis* (forbidden, inappropriate, impolite)—it makes me sick.[46]

Other gay Malays find that their faith and sexuality are not in contradiction: being gay is "a perfection in God's eyes." Still others find their gay sexuality punishable in Islamic law and wish to be released from it, but they cannot do anything about it. Other lesbians put on headscarves (*tudung*) covering their *aurat* as a way of fulling their religious obligation to protect their modesty while still desiring only women in their private life. Some of them have gone for the hajj pilgrimage to Mecca and use the *hajjah* title and remain lesbian. In other cases, Malay lesbians feel under pressure to get married to protect themselves from being portrayed as shameless and immoral.[47] In still other cases, they negotiate their sexual orientations by "being tactful in carrying oneself" (*pandai membawa diri*) in ways deemed "not vulgar" or "not overdone." For instance, they avoid public display of affection. Others wear fashion ambiguous enough for others to judge who they really are by having a stylist haircut and wearing sunglasses and necklaces, which is uncommon for Malay men. Still others wear typical fashionable male attires. Some limit their interactions in beauty salons, cafes, or other spaces considered safe for them to sustain their friendships.[48] In these uneasy situations, different LGBTQ individuals still wish to observe *malu* sensitivity in the public and preserve their honor or *murūʾa* by knowing what and when to conceal and reveal.

Conclusion

This chapter explores the way in which Malay authors and activists in the past and the present have constructed and contested modesty in terms of shame and dignity in a variety of ways. The Malay courts and commoners' uses of shame signify courtly or individual embarrassment without imagining a distinct Malay identity. The Malay intellectuals constructed shame and modesty in terms of eastern Islam versus the western in the domains of life, involving racial, cultural, and gendered difference and hierarchy as manifested through men and women's bodies and ways of dressing.

In contemporary times, public debates over modesty in fashion and veiling still touch upon the question of which parts of the body should be covered and whether modesty and fashion are a paradox or a combination. Veiling and unveiling among Malay women become subjects of renewed interpretation of what modesty really means as they contest over a universalized Islamic modesty and a particular piece of Arab cultural clothing. Many maintain that one can unveil and be pious, whereas others see veiling as the only norm for Muslim women. Within the patriarchal culture, organizations like Sisters in Islam promote gender justice for women—including the right to unveiling—and they call for modesty and moral standards for everyone, not merely for women. Moreover, LGBTQ Malays face stigmatization and heterocultural challenges but they are mindful of the mainstream, albeit conservative, interpretations of modesty, dignity, and the innate nature of human beings and creatively negotiate their identities and behaviors in public. In all the various cases under discussion, modesty and dignity remain an important, albeit constructed and contested, emotive lexicon and affective disposition. They serve as an anticipatory or punitive mechanism for behaving appropriately and ethically in a predominantly Muslim, religiously conservative, yet multicultural Malaysia.

Notes

1. Julia Driver, *Uneasy Virtue* (Cambridge: Cambridge University Press, 2001), 21; Scott Woodcock, "The Social Dimensions of Modesty," *Canadian Journal of Philosophy* 38, no. 1 (2008), 1–29; Muhamad Ali, "The Interplay between *Adab* and Local Ethics and Etiquette in Indonesia and Malaysian Literature," in *Piety, Politics and Everyday Ethics in Southeast Asian Islam*, edited by Robert Rozehnal (London: Bloomsbury Academic, 2019), 19–39.
2. Peter A. Stearns, *Shame: A Brief History* (Illinois: University of Illinois Press, 2017), 1–9, 10–48, 96–130.
3. See Marion Holmes Katz, "Shame (*Ḥayāʾ*) as an Affective Disposition in Islamic Legal Thought," *Journal of Law, Religion and State* 2 (2014), 139–69; Ahmed El Shamsy, "Shame, Sin, and Virtue: Islamic Notions of Privacy," in *Public and Private in Ancient*

Mediterranean Law and Religion. Edited by Clifford Ando and Jörg Rüpke (Berlin: De Gruyter, 2015), 237–48.

4. Cliff Goddard, "Social Emotions of Malay (*Bahasa Melayu*)," *Etho* 24, no. 3 (1996), 432–60.
5. Narifumi Maeda, "Family Circle, Community, and Nation in Malaysia," *Current Anthropology* 16, no. 1 (1975), 166.
6. Elizabeth Fuller Collins and Ernaldi Bahar, "To Know Shame: Malu and Its Uses in Malay Societies," *Crossroads: An Interdisciplinary Journal of Southeast Asian Studies* 14, no. 1 (2000), 35–69.
7. This does not necessarily mean fixity and consensus on what it means to be Malay. See, for example, Timothy P. Barnard (ed.), *Contesting Malayness: Malay Identity Across Boundaries* (Singapore: Singapore University Press, 2004).
8. Richard Olaf Winstedt, "The Malay Annals of Sejarah Melayu," *Journal of the Malayan Branch of the Royal Asiatic Society* 16, no. 3, 132 (1938), 89.
9. Winstedt, "The Malay Annals," 90.
10. William Edward Maxwell, "Malay Proverbs (Continued)," *Journal of the Straits Branch of the Royal Asiatic Society* 2 (1878), 139.
11. Maxwell, "Malay Proverbs," 157.
12. Abdullah bin Abdul Kadir, translated by A. H. Hills, *The Hikayat Abdullah* (Kuala Lumpur: Oxford University Press, 1970), 46.
13. Ibid., 128.
14. Ibid., 183.
15. Ibid., 272.
16. Ibid., 311.
17. Contemporary scholar Syed Hussein Alatas criticized Abdullah for failing to see the responsibility of the British for allowing inhuman treatments of slaves in Singapore. Syed Hussein Alatas, *The Myth of the Lazy Native: A Study of the Image of the Malays, Filipinos and Javanese from the 16th to the 20th Century and Its Function in the Ideology of Colonial Capitalism* (London: Frank Cass, 1997), Note 30, 145.
18. Alwi bin Sheikh Al-Hady, *Malay Customs and Traditions* (Singapore: D. Moore for Eastern Universities Press Ltd, 1962), 67.
19. Alwi bin Sheikh Al-Hady, *Adab -Tertib (Dalam Pergaulan dan Champoran) Chara Barat dan Chara Melayu* (Singapore: Malaysia Publications Limited, 1965), 9–10. Elizabeth Collins and Ernaldi Bahar claim that in contrast to Western culture, the Malays use *malu* to constrain individualism and support hierarchy and deference. The view forwarded by Alwi Al-Hady here suggests a case of intersection of aspects of the Western and aspects of the Eastern as well as contradictions, real or imagined. Collins and Bahar, "To Know Shame," 37.
20. On the religious references to which parts of the male and female body are forbidden to be revealed in public (*aurat* or *ʿawra* in Arabic), among Malay authors themselves, please see, for example, Aisha Wood Boulanouar, "The Notion of Modesty in Muslim Women's Clothing: An Islamic Point of View," *New Zealand Journal of Asian Studies* 8, no. 2 (December 2006), 134–56.
21. Alwi Al-Hady, *Adab - Tertib*, 67, 68.
22. Ibid., 71.
23. Ibid.
24. Ibid.
25. For example, Zarina Muhammad, Akmaliza Abdullah, and Ratna Roshida Ab Razak, "Sifat Malu dalam Kerangka Akhlak Melayu," *Jurnal Hadhari* 11, no. 2 (2019), 231–44.

26. See Khairuddin Aljunied, *Muslim Cosmopolitanism: Southeast Asian Islam in Comparative Perspective* (Edinburgh: Edinburgh University Press, 2016), 102–4.
27. Nurzihan Hassim and Nur Leila Khalid, "'Stailo & Sopan': Modesty and Malay-Muslim Women," conference paper presented at the International Conference on Trends in Social Sciences and Humanities, August 19–20, 2015, Bali, Indonesia.
28. New brands have emerged, such as TudungPeople, PopLook, EVBasics, MimpiKita, Thavia, and Olloum. Kasmiah Mustapha, "Balancing Fashion with Modesty," https://www.nst.com.my/lifestyle/flair/2018/08/403881/balancing-fashion-modesty (accessed January 21, 2021); Santriani Bohari, "8 Modest Malaysian Labels Every Muslimah Needs to Know;" https://www.havehalalwilltravel.com/8-modest-malaysian-labels-every-muslimah-needs-to-know (accessed January 21, 2021).
29. The Su Yen, Gan Pei Lee, Bazlin Darina Binti, and Tajudin Ahmad, "A Conceptual Paper on Modest Wear for Malaysia Muslim Women in Contemporary Hijab Fashion," *Journal of Islamic, Social, Economics and Development* 3, no. 8 (March 2018), 41–9.
30. Hafsa Lodi, *Modesty: A Fashion Paradox: Uncovering the Causes, Controversies, and Key Players behind the Global Trend to Conceal, rather Than Reveal* (London: Neem Tree Press, 2020).
31. Nurzihan Hassim, Shahreen M. Nayan, and Md Sidin A. Ishak, "Hijabistas: An Analysis of the Mediation of Malay-Muslims and Modesty," *Jurnal Pengajian Media Malaysia (Malaysian Journal of Media Studies)* 17, no. 2 (2015), 10–25.
32. Siti Hasnah Hassan and HusnaAra, "Hijab Fashion Consciousness among Young Muslim Women in Malaysia," *European Journal of Molecular & Clinical Medicine* 7, no. 8 (2020), 446–67.
33. Bazlin Darina Binti, Tajudin Ahmad, The Su Yen, and Gan Pei Lee, "Hijab Styling Is It Fashion or Modesty? Its Portrayal in Three Popular Hijab Brands in Malaysia," *International Journal of Modern Trends in Business Research* 2, no. 7 (April 2019), 58–65.
34. Lee Lian Kong, "Forget Supreme, Hijab Is the New Symbol of Wealth and Status in Malaysia." https://www.vice.com/en/article/vbwwzm/luxury-hijab-malaysia-wealth-status-malaysia (accessed January 21, 2021).
35. Tajudin Ahmad et al., "Blending or Adjusting Modesty in Styling Fashionable Hijab? A Study among Malay Women Academicians at a Private University in Perak," *International Journal of Modern Trends in Social Sciences* 2, no. 8 (June 2019), 62.
36. Zulina Kamarulzaman and Nazlina Shaari, "A Comparison Framework on Islamic Dress Code and Modest Fashion in the Malaysian Fashion Industry," *PalArch's Journal of Anthropology of Egypt/Egyptology* 17, no. 7 (2020), 7063–72.
37. On other Muslim contexts, such as Morocco, see Fatima Mernissi, *The Veil and the Male Elite: A Feminist Interpretation of Women's Rights in Islam* (New York: Basic Books, 1992) and Algeria, see Marnia Lazreg, *Questioning the Veil: Open Letters to Muslim Women* (Princeton, NJ: Princeton University Press, 2009).
38. "Unveiling: Malaysian Activist Fights for Hijab Freedom," *Bangkok Post*, September 21, 2020, https://www.bangkokpost.com/world/1989067/unveiling-malaysian-activist-fights-for-hijab-freedom (accessed January 22, 2021).
39. Azza Basarudin, *Humanizing the Sacred: Sisters in Islam and the Struggle for Gender Justice in Malaysia* (Seattle: University of Washington Press, 2016), 196–7.
40. "Sisters in Islam: In Search for Peace," April 27, 2015. https://togethermag.eu/sisters-in-islam-in-search-of-peace/ (accessed January 22, 2021); "Sisters in Islam: Don't Judge Women for Their Clothing," Wednesday, April 18, 2018 (accessed January 22,

2021); "Obsession with Controlling What Women Wear Needs to Stop," May 13, 2019 https://www.malaysiakini.com/letters/476002 (accessed January 22, 2021).
41. A 2013 Pew Research Center opinion survey showed that 9 percent of the Malaysians contend LGBTQ peoples should be accepted in society while 86 percent believe they should not. https://www.pewresearch.org/global/2013/06/04/the-global-divide-on-homosexuality/ (accessed November 1, 2021).
42. Hemla Singaravelu and Wai Hsien Cheah, "Being Gay and Lesbian in Malaysia," in *LGBTQ Mental Health*, edited by Nadine Nakamura and Carmen H. Logie (Washington, DC: American Psychological Association, 2020), 122.
43. Singaravelu and Hsien Cheah, "Being Gay," 126–9.
44. Collin Jerome, "Queer Malay Identity Formation," *Indonesia and the Malay World* 41, no. 119 (2013), 101.
45. "Isu Transgender, Tasyabbuh atau Penyerupaan: Hukumnya (Edisi Kemasakini)." https://muftiwp.gov.my/artikel/bayan-linnas/1820-siri-5-isu-transgender-tasyab buh-atau-penyerupaan-hukumnya-edisi-kemaskini (accessed November 3, 2021); see also Basarudin, *Humanizing the Sacred*, 67.
46. Cited in Jerome, "Queer Malay," 103.
47. Jerome, "Queer Malay,"109–10.
48. Chua Hang-Kuen, "*Malu* Sensitivity and the Identities of Non-Heteronormative Malay Muslim Men in Peninsular Malaysia," *Kajian Malaysia* 37, no. 1 (2019), 109–30.

Bibliography

Abdul Kadir, Abdullah bin. Translated by A. H. Hills, *The Hikayat Abdullah*. Kuala Lumpur: Oxford University Press, 1970.

Ahmad, Tajudin, Bazlin Darina Binti, Yen The Su, and Lee Gan Pei. "Hijab Styling Is it Fashion or Modesty? Its Portrayal in Three Popular Hijab Brands in Malaysia." *International Journal of Modern Trends in Business Research* 2, no. 7 (April 2019): 58–65.

Ahmad, Tajudin, Bazlin Darina Binti, Darren Yoong Wei Tung, Goh Chun Ghee, Lee Jia An, Lee Pui Yee, Lee Zheng Da, and Teh Su Yen. "Blending or Adjusting Modesty in Styling Fashionable Hijab? A Study among Malay Women Academicians at a Private University in Perak." *International Journal of Modern Trends in Social Sciences* 2, no. 8 (June 2019): 55–63.

Alatas, Syed Hussein. *The Myth of the Lazy Native: A Study of the Image of the Malays, Filipinos and Javanese from the 16th to the 20th Century and Its Function in the Ideology of Colonial Capitalism*. London: Frank Cass, 1997.

Ali, Muhamad. "The Interplay between Adab and Local Ethics and Etiquette in Indonesia and Malaysian Literature." In *Piety, Politics and Everyday Ethics in Southeast Asian Islam*. Edited by Robert Rozehnal, 19–39. London: Bloomsbury Academic, 2019.

Aljunied, Khairuddin. *Muslim Cosmopolitanism: Southeast Asian Islam in Comparative Perspective*. Edinburgh: Edinburgh University Press, 2016.

Barnard, Timothy P. (ed.). *Contesting Malayness: Malay Identity across Boundaries*. Singapore: Singapore University Press, 2004.

Basarudin, Azza. *Humanizing the Sacred: Sisters in Islam and the Struggle for Gender Justice in Malaysia*. Seattle: University of Washington Press, 2016.

Bohari, Santrianii. "8 Modest Malaysian Labels Every Muslimah Needs to Know." https://www.havehalalwilltravel.com/8-modest-malaysian-labels-every-muslimah-needs-to-know (accessed January 21, 2021).
Boulanouar, Aisha Wood. "The Notion of Modesty in Muslim Women's Clothing: An Islamic Point of View." *New Zealand Journal of Asian Studies* 8, no. 2, December (2006): 134–56.
Collins, Elizabeth Fuller, and Ernaldi Bahar. "To Know Shame: Malu and Its Uses in Malay Societies." *Crossroads: An Interdisciplinary Journal of Southeast Asian Studies* 14, no. 1 (2000): 35–69.
Driver, Julia. *Uneasy Virtue*. Cambridge: Cambridge University Press, 2001.
El Shamsy, Ahmed. "Shame, Sin, and Virtue: Islamic Notions of Privacy." In *Public and Private in Ancient Mediterranean Law and Religion*. Edited by Clifford Ando and Jörg Rüpke, 237–48. Berlin: De Gruyter, 2015.
Goddard, Cliff. "Social Emotions of Malay (Bahasa Melayu)." *Ethos* 24, no. 3 (September 1996): 432–60.
Hang-Kuen, Chua. "*Malu* Sensitivity and the Identities of Non-Heteronormative Malay Muslim Men in Peninsular Malaysia." *Kajian Malaysia* 37, no. 1 (2019): 109–30.
Hassan Siti Hasnah, Ara Husna. "Hijab Fashion Consciousness among Young Muslim Women in Malaysia." *European Journal of Molecular & Clinical Medicine* 7, no. 8 (2020): 446–67.
Hassim Nurzihan, Khalid Nur Leila. "'Stailo & Sopan': Modesty and Malay-Muslim Women." Conference paper presented at the International Conference on Trends in Social Sciences and Humanities, August 19–20, 2015, Bali, Indonesia.
Hassim Nurzihan, Nayan Shahreen M., and Ishak Md Sidin A. "Hijabistas: An Analysis of the Mediation of Malay-Muslims and Modesty." *Jurnal Pengajian Media Malaysia (Malaysian Journal of Media Studies)* 17, no. 2 (2015): 10–25.
"Isu Transgender, Tasyabbuh atau Penyerupaan: Hukumnya (Edisi Kemasakini)." https://muftiwp.gov.my/artikel/bayan-linnas/1820-siri-5-isu-transgender-tasyabbuh-atau-penyerupaan-hukumnya-edisi-kemaskini (accessed November 3, 2021).
Jerome, Collin. "Queer Malay Identity Formation." *Indonesia and the Malay World* 41, no. 119 (2013): 97–115.
Kamarulzaman Zulina, Shaari Nazlina. "A Comparison Framework on Islamic Dress Code and Modest Fashion in the Malaysian Fashion Industry." *PalArch's Journal of Anthropology of Egypt/Egyptology* 17, no. 7 (2020): 7063–72.
Katz, Marion Holmes. "Shame (*Haya'*) as an Affective Disposition in Islamic Legal Thought." *Journal of Law, Religion and State* 2 (2014): 139–69.
Lazreg, Marnia. *Questioning the Veil: Open Letters to Muslim Women*. Princeton, NJ: Princeton University Press, 2009.
Lian Kong, Lee. "Forget Supreme, Hijab Is the New Symbol of Wealth and Status in Malaysia." https://www.vice.com/en/article/vbwwzm/luxury-hijab-malaysia-wealth-status-malaysia (accessed January 21, 2021).
Lodi, Hafsa. *Modesty: A Fashion Paradox: Uncovering the Causes, Controversies, and Key Players behind the Global Trend to Conceal, rather Than Reveal*. London: Neem Tree Press, 2020.
Maeda, N. "Family circle, Community, and Nation in Malaysia." *Current Anthropology* 16, no. 1 (1975): 166.
Maxwell, W. E. "Malay Proverbs (Continued)." *Journal of the Straits Branch of the Royal Asiatic Society* 2, December (1878): 136–62.

Mernissi, Fatima. *The Veil and the Male Elite: A Feminist Interpretation of Women's Rights in Islam*. New York: Basic Books, 1992.
Muhammad Zarina, Abdullah Akmaliza, and Ab Razak Ratna Roshida. "Sifat Malu dalam Kerangka Akhlak Melayu." *Jurnal Hadhari* 11, no. 2 (2019): 231–44.
Mustapha, Kasmiah. "Balancing Fashion with Modesty." https://www.nst.com.my/lifestyle/flair/2018/08/403881/balancing-fashion-modesty(accessed January 21, 2021).
"Obsession with Controlling What Women Wear Needs to Stop." May 13, 2019, https://www.malaysiakini.com/letters/476002 (accessed January 22, 2021); https://www.pewresearch.org/global/2013/06/04/the-global-divide-on-homosexuality/ (accessed November 1, 2021).
Sheikh Al-Hady, Alwi bin. *Malay Customs and Traditions*. Singapore: D. Moore for Eastern Universities Press Ltd, 1962.
Sheikh Al-Hady, Alwi bin. *Adab -Tertib (Dalam Pergaulan dan Champoran) Chara Barat dan Chara Melayu*. Singapore: Malaysia Publications Limited, 1965.
Singaravelu, Hemla, and Wai Hsien Cheah, "Being Gay and Lesbian in Malaysia." In *LGBTQ Mental Health*. Edited by Nadine Nakamura and Carmen H. Logie, 121–35. Washington, DC: American Psychological Association, 2020.
"Sisters in Islam: In Search for Peace." April 27, 2015. https://togethermag.eu/sisters-in-islam-in-search-of-peace/ (accessed January 22, 2021).
"Sisters in Islam: Don't Judge Women for Their Clothing." Wednesday, April 18, 2018. https://www.thestar.com.my/news/nation/2018/04/18/sisters-in-islam-dont-judge-women-for-their-clothing (accessed January 22, 2021).
Stearns, Peter A. *Shame: A Brief History*. Illinois: University of Illinois Press, 2017.
Su Yen, The, Lee Gan Pei, Tajudin Ahmad, and Bazlin Darina Binti. "A Conceptual Paper on Modest Wear for Malaysia Muslim Women in Contemporary Hijab Fashion." *Journal of Islamic, Social, Economics and Development* 3, no. 8 (2018): 41–9.
"Unveiling: Malaysian Activist Fights for Hijab Freedom." September 21, 2020, https://www.bangkokpost.com/world/1989067/unveiling-malaysian-activist-fights-for-hijab-freedom (accessed January 22, 2021).
Winstedt, R. O. (ed.). "The Malay Annals of Sejarah Melayu." *Journal of the Malayan Branch of the Royal Asiatic Society* 16, no. 3, 132, December (1938): 1–226.
Woodcock, Scott. "The Social Dimensions of Modesty." *Canadian Journal of Philosophy* 38, no. 1, March (2008): 1–29.

8

Fashion, Clothing, and Modesty in Republican Turkey (1925–34)

Alberto Fabio Ambrosio

Introduction

This chapter examines the rhetoric that certain dress reforms provoked in Republican Turkey—a revolution that peaked between 1925 and 1934, years that marked the period when the reform model was developed. Although it may not seem directly and explicitly linked to a modesty rhetoric, the issue at the heart of this revolution is nevertheless related to establishing a dress code that reflects Western fashion. Therefore, this chapter deals with the absence of a profound theological reflection on modesty and modest vestment during the new course of the Turkish Republic, rather than on modesty in fashion in itself. This is compensated by a new kind of a discourse: a policy of modesty in garments to maintain a traditional style as opposed to a Western one. In other terms, the moral dimension of modesty becomes a political issue in social debates. The Ottoman pamphlet studied in this chapter is a manifesto that shows the change of paradigm: from modesty as a moral issue to the political strategy. The result of this inquiry leads to affirm, as we will see, that the moral and religious discourse on modesty is replaced by a political interpretation of modesty as a stronghold against Western culture. The question of modesty arises merely as an afterthought. However, it is not this theme's moral dimension that is attributed to the rhetoric accompanying the dress reform but rather that of mushrooming Westernization. If, on the one hand, the reform is implemented with the aim of modernizing the country by opening the door to Westernization, the counter-rhetoric is not directly centered on modesty—be it moral or religious—but on the political dimension of such fashionable dress—namely, opposing European, and by extension non-Muslim, fashion.

Modesty has not been of much interest to Turkish scholars researching the Republican period when the dress reform was introduced. Since then, no real literature on *hayâ*[1] and dress in the Turkish Republican period has existed, neither in Turkish literature nor in European languages, except those on the body and gender.[2] But even in these systematic monographs, the interaction between moral modesty and dress code is underexplored, other than for the veil. In fact, the veil is the major focus of all the attention on modesty and dress, and the literature is so abundant that it represents a field in itself.[3] The literary and academic Turkish corpus that this research explores—which focuses on modesty (*hayâ*)—is limited, even though there are some modern religious pamphlets welcoming this concept. Research focuses more on a related term, *tesettür*,[4] which defines modesty of dress, and by extension preferentially refers to the "fashion" of veiled women.

Because of this lack of a deepening research on the interaction between the idea of modesty and dress reform, this chapter focuses on the meaning of modesty in the new Turkish Republican era with an interpretation of the social impact of the political hermeneutics of modesty. Therefore, after briefly identifying the historical antecedents of various Ottoman reforms, this chapter will analyze a pamphlet written by a theologian of the time—İskilipli Âtif Hôca (d. 1926)—that focuses on the "Hat Act." This analysis helps to identify what is meant by the concept of modesty, which was not treated as such at the time of the reform. As we will see, no place is given to the above-mentioned term, *hayâ*, used here to mean modesty, in this short pamphlet.

In modern Turkish history, the issue of modesty seems to be more related to the issue of the "veil," *tesettür*, a word in the Turkish language that covers a rather broad semantic field, including meanings such as "modest fashion" and "attire for those who are veiled." Although similar, the two concepts go far beyond the simple act of dressing. Indeed, depending on how it is approached, modesty itself could refer to the idea of simple perception or to virtue. It could be said that the issue of modesty—a theme that has also seen many different guises throughout European history—is an issue in modern Turkey relating to the history of attire, its revolution, and ultimately its use for political purposes.

Ottoman-Style Sumptuary Laws

The Ottoman Empire underwent an evolution in dress from the sixteenth century, or from when the relationships between European dress cultures began to penetrate Ottoman countries.[5] This evolution affected both its internal development and the way in which its relationship changed with an emerging French institution—namely, fashion.[6] If, under the Old Regime in France, that is, before the French Revolution, sumptuary laws were enacted to adapt clothing style to match one's rank—measures that gave clothing a societal dimension—from the sixteenth century onward, Ottoman society also knew a period in which fatwas issued by the Mufti of Istanbul, *şeyh'ül-islâm*, stigmatized the ethnic origin. Zilfi declared,

> As a rule, the Ottoman Empire did not impose a comprehensive directory of sartorial dos and don'ts on its non-Muslim subjects, though in general non-Muslims' clothing was mandated to be differentiated from that of Muslims in terms of restricted colours and access to status goods.[7]

Nora Şeni also highlights the stigmatization of minorities in her research when she states that while the issue of modesty was key among Muslims, in practice, each community set out what it deemed respectable for its women.[8]

What makes the issue of modesty so crucial when exploring the history of dress during the Ottoman Empire, and subsequently during the young Republic of Turkey, is that it was contextualized in relation to Europe. Şeni continues,

> Opening up to Europe was a game-changer. All the elite who went to Europe to study in the mid-19th century returned with a different dress culture—and many European images reached Istanbul.[9]

Moreover, orders issued by the kadi of Istanbul[10] from the end of the sixteenth century were all designed to discourage women from dressing too similarly to European fashion, even though dress codes were not considered to have religious significance.[11] During the Ottoman Empire, these laws—which can be compared to those described as sumptuary laws in Europe—were not only intended to create gender differences, but also to draw a distinction between communities marked by an ethnic or, first and foremost, a particular religious affiliation. The main mark is still the one left by religious identity, further influenced by fashions originating in Europe, as observed by European travelers too. Reminders about dress rules issued by Muslim jurists in the sixteenth to eighteenth centuries, which were primarily aimed at Muslim women who were commanded not to dress in foreign ways, help us to understand the origins of the reforms introduced in Turkey from 1923, the year in which the Republic was proclaimed.

For example, a law applying to the male dress code and headwear, in particular, was passed in 1829 during the Ottoman Empire under Sultan Mahmud II, who reigned from 1808 to 1839. It stipulated that all men were obliged to wear a fez, while the general wearing of a turban (*türban*) was banned and henceforth reserved for the religious elite only. This decision preceded by ten years the Gülhane Edict, which ushered in an era of reforms (*Tanzimat*, 1839–76) that were rooted in a strong sense of equality among the Sultan's subjects, based on common citizenship. In fact, attempts at reform had been made in the army since the end of the eighteenth century, but without any real success.[12] The Janissaries, otherwise known as the Sultan's army corps, were not blameless in resisting all forms of progress, and it is not surprising that the law banning the turban was introduced after this army corps had been disbanded in the Hippodrome Square in 1826.

Both the issue of male headwear and that of the female veil assume the value of a true political stake in Republican history. With the Ottoman Empire gone and the Republic only emerging, fashion originating from Europe posed a problem during the transition between the regimes. This is evidenced by a great number of articles in the Ottoman press harshly criticizing this fashion export on religious grounds.[13] It is on this basis—historical and political as much as sartorial—that the legislative work undertaken by Republican Turkey as the heir to the Empire must at times simply be seen as a counterpoint.

Dressing the Republic

Following the Turkish War of Independence fought against occupying European powers that began in 1919, it was evident from the moment the emerging Republic of

Turkey was proclaimed on October 29, 1923, that it had a pressing need to establish a framework regarding dress codes. According to Mustafa Kemal Paşa (d. 1938), it was a question of founding a new nation, built on references other than those that had been used by the Ottoman Empire. A cultural and political program was needed to lay the foundations for this undertaking in the aftermath of the War of Independence. What's more, during his 36-hour speech (*Nutuk*) to the National Assembly, the father of the new homeland, Atatürk, spelled out the founding elements of the new Turkey (*Yeni Türkiye*), based on modernity. Implementing modernity would go far beyond a politics inspired by a scientific analysis of society by not only investing in the symbols of culture—a dress code being one of them—but also in the very structures of the social system, such as national education, whose broad outlines are shaped by the criteria of a secular country.[14] Such is the famous *nutuk* (speech) during which the father of the Turks proposed a new culture, while wearing a suit that squarely broke with the old Ottoman way of dressing under the guise of its being his official outfit. It was an irrefutable sign that Ottoman culture was now over.

The attention Atatürk paid to the dress code, for both himself and the fledgling Republic, allows us to rethink contemporary Turkish history in terms of the rhetoric of dress. Even before the debates concerning the "veil issue," which only emerged from the moment a political Islam was established in the 1950s, it was the "Hat Act" of 1925 (*şapka kararnamesi*) or, better still, the dress revolution, that ushered in the reform.[15]

Like the sumptuary laws proclaimed throughout the Ottoman Empire's history, the new Turkey had its own dress laws that reflected the revolutionary idea that all citizens of this single and indivisible Republic were equal. Having been debated by the Turkish Grand Assembly chaired by Atatürk on September 2, 1925, the "Hat Act," law no. 671, was enacted within this socio-historical framework on November 25 of the same year and subsequently published in the *Official Gazette* on November 28.[16] From then on, men were to abandon the vestige of Ottoman dress practices—the fez—in favor of a European-style hat. This act was debated on the same day as law no. 677, which was subsequently adopted on November 30 and published on December 12 of the same year. This particular law will be remembered for its radical reforms concerning the banning of all Sufi orders, the abolition of all the religious titles and the obligation for all former order members to be named according to the traditional lexicon rather than according to their former titles.[17] On the surface—but only on the surface—these two laws have nothing to do with one another, yet the dress element brings them together.

When out in public, men now had to wear a European-style suit that varied depending on the time of day. Evening dress must differ from work wear, and each outfit must be complemented by a hat that matches the suit; the letter of the law states,

> Suits worn by State employees must be identical to those worn by civilised people on Earth. To clarify, these individuals must wear a different suit and hat depending on what the time of day, night or official celebration requires.[18]

When inside a public place, men would no longer be allowed to wear hats:

> Inside [State] buildings, it is stipulated that men should not have their heads covered. A nod of the head would be a sufficient greeting.[19]

This, therefore, contradicted a central tenet of Muslim practice, since the head had to be covered as much as possible as a sign of social prestige, on the one hand, and as a mark of religious affiliation, on the other.[20] Moreover, the final paragraph of the law declares that "the people must also be obliged to wear 'hat'-like headwear, or face prosecution by the government."[21]

This law marked a step toward shifting mentalities, clearly inspired by practices introduced during the French Revolution, which aimed to entrust democratic behavior with the task of standardizing social appearances.[22] As for the issue of gender, the law does not directly affect women's clothing practices since they only have to adjust to changes in men's fashion. However, female civil servants eventually also complied with the legal restriction of not covering their heads or faces when in a public space.[23] This ban on women wearing the veil in public spaces is rooted in a law primarily aimed at men's clothing intended to impose the wearing of a European-style hat, as Turkish historian Ayten Sezer observes in her book:

> With the landmark law of 1926 on male-female equality relating to political voting and the enactment of the 1925 "Hat Act," which banned both the fez and the turban, regional approaches and the press also encouraged the veil to be abandoned and modern dress practices to be adopted. Since the law established gender equality long before other European countries, women in Turkey were granted the right to vote in municipal elections in 1930 and legislative elections in 1934.[24]

It was as a result of law no. 2596 of December 3, 1934, prohibiting certain types of dress in public spaces that the issue of the veil was raised in legal terms. However, this law targets all religious attire, especially outfits worn by minorities. Christians were, therefore, obliged to comply with the law, unless a formal agreement had been reached, particularly in the case of minorities who were fully recognized by the Turkish state, such as the Armenian, Greek Orthodox, and Catholic communities.[25] Appearance mattered a great deal to this new Republic, which wanted to "impose," also legally, a new mentality.

There is so much literature on the subject that we will limit ourselves solely to the criticisms of the 1925 law to explore the paradigm that gave rise to and established a new sense of modesty. While trivial at first glance, following further examination, the *diktat* could not remain in force in its present form since it was indeed a decree that men's heads, and soon—by way of the imitation effect—women's heads, would be uncovered in public spaces and that the fez, the last remnant of an Arab-Muslim culture, was to disappear forever in favor of a "simple" European-style hat (*şapka*). The etymology of the word *şapka* itself was used in the sixteenth century—according to Filippo Argenti (1533[26])—to refer to the headwear worn by the Greeks, who were Christians. The "Hat Act" of 1925 looked toward Europe, and more precisely toward another religious culture; at the very least, using the word *şapka* meant the Turkish people understood the connection with Christian headwear rather than that favored by

Muslims. This is precisely the reason why this law was not supported unanimously but, rather, gave rise to detractors and opponents, among them İskilipli Mehmed Âtıf Hoca.

Old-Fashioned Capital Punishment

The pamphlet of İskilipli Âtıf Hoca, titled "Imitating the Franks and the hat," which carried great weight in political debates, put the issue of modesty on the agenda. As a matter of fact, it is not really a philosophical or theological argument *per se*, but rather the absence of such argument that results in this text being a reflection on modesty. Indeed, the contrary argument is crucial since the author, far from basing his discussion of the dress code on what is obvious—modesty relating to dress—engages in a political confrontation between a European dress culture that clashes with the one in vogue at the end of the Ottoman Empire and whose end is decreed by Republican Turkey. If, by presenting this pamphlet, we cannot extensively explore the concept itself of modesty or of shame, we can nevertheless introduce a new criterion for comprehending it: the political use of a traditional dress code versus the novelty of the Western dress code in Turkish society.

It is in this respect that the Muslim theologian's opposition to the famous "Hat Act" merits study: there is no monograph-length research on the subject, and it led to him being hanged. İskilipli Mehmed Âtıf Hoca (d. 1926[27]) was a very high dignitary within the religious sphere of the Ottoman Empire. His supporters saw him as an envoy of God, whereas those who penned the Kemalist Reform rhetoric considered him to be a dictator.[28] Despite being cleared of any charges, he was put under the spotlight because he disagreed with the new regime established under Mustafa Kemal at a time when the latter led the Council of Religious Affairs, succeeding Mustafa Sabri Efendi (d. 1954), the last *şeyh'ül-islâm* in Ottoman history. In fact, in the very early months following the proclamation of the Republic of Turkey, Mehmed Âtıf published a pamphlet with an eloquent title: *Frenk Mukallitliği ve Şapka* ("Imitating the Franks and the hat"[29]). This controversial pamphlet, which was published on July 12, 1924 (10 *zilhicce* 1343) and written in Ottoman[30] is allegedly based on Muslim theological interpretation and criticizes the notion of imitating (*taklit*) European fashion in and of itself. On December 7 the following year, the pamphlet led to his arrest, and he was sentenced to be hanged by the "Freedom Courts" (*Istiklâl Mahkemesi*); he subsequently died by hanging in 1926. If the general opinion immediately establishes a link between capital punishment and his case against European fashion, a truly historical reconstruction of these events still remains to be undertaken.

As a matter of fact, having published his pamphlet the year before the "Hat Act" was introduced, Mehmed Âtıf had the opportunity to plead "not guilty" and avoid the harsh sentence handed to him. But he renounced this right—in keeping with his inner convictions—a safeguard that he could have legitimately provided for himself, thus adopting an unprecedented stance in the face of the new policy:

> Disregarding his right to defend himself and ignoring a dream he had, İskilipli, as an individual concerned with embracing his religion in the social order, shows that the despair of being unable to hold his own had considerable influence.[31]

The pamphlet that is said to have condemned him to death was not his only piece of writing to focus on the issue of dress. A book from 1920, *Tesettür-ü Şer'i* (The Veil of the Law), as well as articles published in a religious journal—*Mahfil*, edited by the last commentator of the *Mesnevî*, Tahirülmevlevî (d. 1951)—illustrate that he concerned himself greatly with this topic. His articles on the veil, *tesettür*, which he submitted to *Mahfil* from 1922 to 1923, covered interpretation in its entirety, from a purely sartorial question and the modesty of the veil to the metaphor of the veil. This can be seen from the translated titles: "The Veil and the encounter between men and women,"[32] "The wisdom of the law of the veil,"[33] "The heart of the law of the veil,"[34] and "The body of laws and religious truths in the divine wisdom and adamic style of intelligence."[35]

The short pamphlet we are interested in covers five chapters ranging from the question of imitating others, the Westerner, the clothing accessories considered ungodly because they are inspired by European dress styles, and the final answer. It also includes an interesting compendium of Muslim theology relating to Muslim believers' dress. As the first chapter in the pamphlet reminds us, imitation is impossible for Muslims: they are forbidden to imitate anything foreign to the culture of the Prophet Muhammad. Moreover, the only possible imitation in Islam is of the Prophet, and any innovation that violates this principle is to be condemned as *bid'ah* or "blameworthy." Imitation of appearances, including in the field of dress, does not reflect the spirit of Islam and must be rejected all the more forcefully if it involves recreating appearances derived from a culture that is both foreign and unholy (*küfür*):

> In summary, it is not permitted to imitate the novelties or innovations and the manners and mores of civilizations that contradict the sharia. It is most certainly unlawful to adopt the customs and usages of non-Muslim nations. Therefore, it is forbidden by the sacred law of the sharia for a Muslim to dress like a non-Muslim in order to appear like one of them. Our Prophet stated, "those who try to adopt the mores of a people [who try to be like them] is actually one of them" [related by Imam Ahmad and Abu Davud].[36]

Although during the Prophet's time he allowed his followers to dress like other believers—notably Christians and Jews—this subsequently changed when the more established Muslim community had to distinguish itself from others. The short second chapter focuses on Muslims who must distinguish themselves from other civilizations, even if they can draw on positive aspects from the said civilizations:

> Materially and spiritually, the Western civilization has two aspects, one of which is useful and one of which is harmful to humanity. The hadiths of our Prophet clearly allow and encourage the adoption of useful innovations of Western civilization by Muslims: "If one person invents something beautiful and this invention becomes useful to the people, this inventor would be blessed by God until the Day of Judgment," and, "You (people) know better the worldly matters."[37]

Mehmed Âtıf was therefore not completely hostile toward the fact that certain inventions or discoveries are borrowed from other civilizations. He also believed that these "civilisation cross-fertilisations" proved the importance of the East, and more particularly of the Muslim civilization, in the cultural development of Europe. However, he acknowledged the question that was raised by the Ottomans in their quest to implement a reform that would restore the Empire to all its glory since it had become the "sick man of Europe." What could be causing Muslim civilization to stagnate? The answer lies in one single point: Muslims ceased to focus on living a simple life and instead engaged in trade. In his own way, İskilipli demonstrated his difficulty in positioning himself in relation to Europe and the West. While he asserted that the Muslim civilization could incorporate elements considered to be good on the one hand, his final judgment remained very negative. As such,

> Islam prohibits the immoral aspects of Western civilization, such as bars, theaters, brothels and gambling dens. Therefore, it is strictly forbidden in Islam to imitate the Western lifestyle and live like non-Muslims. In fact, *Western civilization is far from being a model civilization for humanity to adopt*, since it does not take an interest in the moral aspects and spiritual happiness of humanity, but focuses only on material gains and encourages mankind's animal instincts.[38]

Note that Ahmet Şeyhun's translation closely follows the formulation that "Western civilization is far from being a model civilization for humanity to adopt" (as highlighted in italics in the extract above), but the original text concisely expresses the idea that "the bad aspects of Western civilisation are not acceptable."[39] Behind this notion hides the more refined legal expression *gayr-i meşru*, which is better rendered as "beyond Islamic law." There is another paragraph of interest for our purposes between the two translated sentences, in which the author mentions "fashion" as one of the aspects of a Western, and in particular European, civilization that is unacceptable:

> It is forever impossible to allow a Muslim to imitate the bad things or adopt the horrors, i.e. the fashion of the time, gambling and arcades, in order to act as a non-Muslim, in other words to become Westernised or Europeanised.[40]

The chapter concludes with an anecdote he witnessed of an American, Mr William Johnson, claiming that Westerners would achieve the political project of westernizing Oriental cultures if they succeeded in making Orientals dress as Westerners.

The next chapter covers the foundations of faith. Addressing the status of faith, *imân* and its opposite, *küfür*, which can be simply translated as "idolatry" or "blasphemy," allows the author to define the clothing accessories leading to ungodliness. If believing in one God, in angels, and in the Day of Judgment is the object of the Muslim religion, then anything to the contrary falls under the category of blasphemy, which must be regarded as an attack on the truth of the Islamic message. Now, in chapter four, İskilipli describes the "accessories" of blasphemy (*şiar-ı küfür*): the hat; the *gayyar*—a rope that signals that you belong to a minority; the belt (*zünnâr*)—an accessory used particularly by Christians and the Magi of Iran; the ring (*küstiç*), which also signals you belong to these same denominations; the yellow suit for Jews (*gaslî*); and finally, the cross—a distinctive Christian sign. A definition of the *şapka*, a European-style hat, is also given:

> Headwear, i.e. a symbol or sign of separation between Muslims and non-Muslims, is an accessory of godlessness and part of the attire.[41]

It is interesting to note that the definition of a hat is given as a distinctive sign of religious affiliation and, moreover, as part of a binary yes/no relationship. As such, the *şapka* in itself is not headwear worn by a European, or even more simply, just a hat. Instead, it is a sign of godlessness that distinguishes between non-Muslims and Muslims; at least, this is what he claimed. It is clear that any accessories that signify a religion other than Islam should be banned from a Muslim's wardrobe. This chapter is therefore extremely interesting, since the author manages to create a real "doctrine" on the accessories of godlessness, which are negatively linked to the identity of a non-Muslim. Finally, in formulating the answer to a Muslim stagnation, the author states bluntly in the last chapter,

> Since the hat is the accessory of a nation and a religion, those who cover their head with it are simply saying: "I belong to this nation."[42]

A Muslim is absolutely forbidden to put on an accessory that is not already part of their dress culture.

> In dealing with this problem, it is considered that the wearer of the hat has lost all connection with the spiritual mindset and, moreover, with sincerity. What is the reason for this judgement? If sincere, the actions and efforts made to display faith, the incorrect behaviour and ultimately the people themselves are hypocritical and divisive.[43]

We could translate further passages from the pamphlet, but the gist behind the thought is now clear: the European-style hat—that of the Franks—is indeed a sign of ungodly affiliation in regard to Islam.

It was certainly this attitude that the new political regime was against when they condemned İskilipli Mehmed Âtıf to death, who in his pamphlet never refers to the issue of modesty—at least not directly. In other words, the term *hayâ* is never questioned. The teachings in this pamphlet provide the possibility of linking the notion to a field other than sexuality: morality—and more precisely, social morality. While Mehmed Âtıf denounces the degenerate, lascivious behaviors of the West—from theater and prostitution to drunkenness—he never makes a direct link between wearing a hat instead of a turban and a relaxed attitude. We would instead be dealing with another form of modesty that is probably best described as political.

Conclusion: From Modesty to a Politics of Modesty

The absence of a direct reference to modesty in İskilipli Mehmed Âtıf's pamphlet is glaring; the text exposes the entire foundations of the history of Republican Turkey up to the present day in relation to clothing practices—particularly the veil—that supposedly clash with the recommendations of Islam. This is because the question is not directly one of modesty. Although the wearing of hats and, later, the banning of veils in public places undoubtedly demonstrate that the issue involves the affirmation of a sense of modesty as seen in traditional Muslim teachings, the actual issue lies elsewhere. The fight against wearing hats, and indeed the obligation to do so, is first and foremost a political one. It is something that is not only political but also based on state policy. The wearing of hats poses a problem that is nothing less than central in Islam: imitation. Muslims are to avoid imitating behaviors that do not correspond, in their cultural imagination and implementation, with the teachings of the Prophet Muhammad. Thus, modesty is not set at a personal level or the discretion demanded by certain parts of the body (*pudenda*, *avret* in Turkish), which determine both the individual and social aspect. There is a policy of modesty that particularly involves severely criticizing the way others—Westerners, Europeans—dress, mainly to avoid mixing with them. Modesty is therefore political above all: it relates to your choice of identity, forcing you to place yourself in one camp rather than another. Of course, an ethical element still plays a minor role, but it has instead taken on a political form of confrontation. Throughout Republican history, the narrative behind the veil has driven political debates and actions, as well as the motivations of generations of veiled women.[44] However, above all, religious—and therefore political—identity prevails, distinguishing the Kemalist and Westernized part of society in relation to another part in modern Turkey.

It is this "political" modesty or to put it better, this "politics of modesty," that allows us to explore the concept of modesty that is being queried. I would like to end this chapter with these conclusions by making a brief comparison with the European context, which has been studied by different scholars, who have suggested some reflections that can also lead to a philosophical analysis. Norbert Elias,[45] focusing on the development of costumes or moral etiquette in social European space, has demonstrated that modesty plays an important role since it shapes individuality, just as Michel Foucault analyzed the same in his work on the History of Sexuality.[46] In fact, according to Foucauldian theory, the development of self-awareness of sexuality shapes also the experience of intimacy, which is a part of modesty's inner elements. As such, we are dealing with a highly political level of modesty here. In more philosophical terms, as Levinas[47] pointed out, modesty evolves as part of a relationship, an intimate dialogue between the I and the You, that shape social relations. In these three European philosophers, modesty appears not exclusively in dress moral appearances, but in its political role of constructing communities and society. So, with regard to the defining moments of Republican Turkey, we could well conclude by saying that in a political relationship with the other—the Westerner, the European—a new way of understanding modesty in terms of dress was being developed. Indeed, the case of dress reform in Republican Turkey, and the absence of any real debate on modesty but rather on the regulations of a "dress code," demonstrates that the very idea of modesty needs to be reconsidered in Turkish and Muslim contexts, against the background of constructing social and political spaces.

Notes

1. In the Turkish vocabulary, *hayâ* has the same meaning as the Arabic term, *ḥayāʾ*, from which it originates. The transcription will follow modern Turkish as it is used in Turkey today, including for any Ottoman terms.
2. Dror Ze'evi, *Producing Desire: Changing Sexual Discourse in the Ottoman Middle East, 1500–1900* (Berkeley: University of California Press, 2006).
3. Iclal Cetin, "Veiled Representations: Political Battles around Female Sexuality in Turkish Print Media," *Feminist Media Studies* 10, no. 4 (2010), 409–19; N. Göle, *Musulmanes et modernes: voile et civilisation en Turquie* (Paris: La Découverte, 2003).
4. Mehmet Erdoğan, *Tesettür meselesinden Türban sorununa* (Cağaloğlu, Istanbul: İz Yayıncılık, 2008).
5. Charlotte Jirousek and Sara Catterall, *Ottoman Dress and Design in the West: A Visual History of Cultural Exchange* (Bloomington: Indiana University Press, 2019), 79–108.
6. Fatma Koç and Emine Koca, "The Westernization Process in Ottoman Women's Garments: 18th Century–20th Century," *Asian Journal of Women's Studies* 13, no. 4 (2007), 62.
7. Madeline C. Zilfi, "Women, Minorities and the Changing Politics of Dress in the Ottoman Empire, 1650–1830," in *The Right to Dress: Sumptuary Laws in a Global Perspective, 1200–1800*, edited by Giorgio Riello and Ulinka Rublack (Cambridge: Cambridge University Press, 2019), 394.
8. Nora Şeni, "Un empire que des firmans habillent. Normes et réformes vestimentaires en Turquie," *Modes pratiques. Revue d'histoire du vêtement et de la mode* 1 (2015), 241.
9. Ibid.
10. Richard Cooper Repp, *The Müfti of Istanbul: A Study in the Development of the Ottoman Learned Hierarchy* (London: Ithaca Press for the Board of the Faculty of Oriental Studies, Oxford University, 1986).
11. Nora Şeni, "Ville ottomane et représentation du corps féminin," *Les Temps Modernes* 41 (1984), 66–95.
12. John P. Dunn, "Clothes to Kill For: Uniforms and Politics in Ottoman Armies," *Journal of the Middle East and Africa* 2, no. 1 (2011), 86–7.
13. Nora Şeni, "La mode et le vêtement féminin dans la presse satirique d'Istanbul à la fin du XIXe siècle," in *Presse Turque et Presse de Turquie*, edited by Nathalie Clayer, Alexandre Popovic, and Thierry Zarcone (Istanbul: ISIS Press, 1992), 198–200.
14. Aysel Morin and Ronald Lee, "Constitutive Discourse of Turkish Nationalism: Atatürk's *Nutuk* and the Rhetorical Construction of the "Turkish People," *Communication Studies* 61, no. 5 (2010), 501.
15. Arif Olgun Közleme, "Şapka İnkılâbı ve Şapka İnkılâbının Türk Toplumu Üzerindeki Tramvatik Etkileri," *Journal of International Social Research* 68, no. 12 (2019), 434.
16. Mehmet Semih Gemalmaz, *Türk Kıyafet Hukuku ve Türban: Tarihçe, İdeloloji, Mevzuat, İçtihat, Siyaset: AİHK ve AİHM Kararları ve Değerlendirilmesi* (Istanbul: Legal, 2005), 149.
17. Alberto Fabio Ambrosio, *Soufis à Istanbul, hier, aujourd'hui: des Hommes et des lieux xiiie–xxie siècle* (Paris: Éd. du Cerf, 2014), 125.
18. Gemalmaz, *Türk Kıyafet Hukuku ve Türban*, 151.
19. Ibid.
20. Joseph Chelhod, "La face et la personne chez les Arabes," *Revue de l'histoire des religions* 151, no. 2 (1957), 236.

21. Loi 671 du 25/11/192, https://www.mevzuat.gov.tr/MevzuatMetin/1.3.671.pdf. Last visited November 11, 2020.
22. Faruk Bilici, "Révolution française, Révolution turque et fait religieux," *Revue du monde musulman et de la Méditerranée* 52, no. 1 (1989), 175.
23. Özlem Sandikci and Güliz Ger, "Veiling in Style: How Does a Stigmatized Practice Become Fashionable?," *Journal of Consumer Research* 37, no. 1 (2010), 21–2.
24. Ayten Sezer Arığ, *Atatürk Türkiyesi'nde kılık kıyafette çağdaşlaşma* (Ankara: Siyasal Kitabevi, 2007), 120.
25. Lorenzo Botrugno, "La diplomazia pastorale di Mons. Roncalli tra Sofia e Istanbul," in *Fede e diplomazia: le relazioni internazionali della Santa Sede nell'età contemporanea*, edited by Massimo de Leonardis (Milan: EDUCatt, 2014), 133–51.
26. Luciano Rocchi and Filippo Argenti, *Ricerche sulla lingua osmanli del XVI secolo: il corpus lessicale turco del manoscritto fiorentino di Filippo Argenti (1533)* (Wiesbaden: Harrassowitz, 2007), 228.
27. Ahmet Şeyhun, *Islamist Thinkers in the Late Ottoman Empire and Early Turkish Republic* (Boston, MA: Brill, 2014), 36–43.
28. Doğan Gürpinar, "The Politics of Memoirs and Memoir-Publishing In 20th Century Turkey," *Turkish Studies*, 13, no. 3 (2012), 537–57.
29. İskilipli Mehmet Âtıf Hoca, *Frenk Mukallitliği ve Şapka*, edited by Yunus Coşkun (Trabzon: 40, Kulübü Yayınevi, 2019).
30. The Turkish language reform law was proclaimed in 1928.
31. Yasin Aktay, "Halife Sonrası Şartlarda İslamcılığın Öz-Diyar Algısı," in *Modern Türkiye'de siyasî düşünce*, edited by Yasin Aktay (Cağaloğlu, Istanbul: İletişim 2001), 73.
32. İskilipli Mehmed Atıf, "Tesettür ve Kadınların Erkekler ile İhtilâtı," *Mahfil* 3, no. 29 (1922), 93–5.
33. İskilipli Mehmed Atıf, "Tesettürün Hikmet-i Şer'iyyesi," *Mafhil* 3, no. 30 (1922), 118.
34. İskilipli Mehmed Atıf, "Tesettür-i Şer'înin Fuâdı," *Mafhil* 3, no. 34 (1923), 149–50.
35. İskilipli Mehmed Atıf, "Aḥkām ve Hakâik-i Dîniyyenin Cümlesini Ma'rifette Aklın Adem-i Kifâyeti," *Mafhil* 4, no. 39 (1923), 41–2.
36. Şeyhun, *Islamist Thinkers*, 41; İskilipli Mehmet Âtıf Hoca, *Frenk Mukallitliği ve Şapka*, edited by Yunus Coşkun (Trabzon: 40 Kulübü Yayınevi, 2019), 5–6.
37. Şeyhun, *Islamist Thinkers*, 42; Âtıf Hoca, *Frenk Mukallitliği ve Şapka*, 9.
38. Şeyhun, *Islamist Thinkers*, 43; Âtıf Hoca, *Frenk Mukallitliği ve Şapka*, 13–14 (emphasis added).
39. "Binaenaleyh medeniyet-i garbın raziyet-i cihetleri gayr-i meşrudur," 13.
40. Âtif Hoca, *Frenk Mukallitliği ve Şapka*, 12 du texte ottoman.
41. Ibid., 27.
42. Ibid., 34.
43. Âtif Hoca, *Frenk Mukallitliği ve Şapka*, 34.
44. Alimen Nazlı, *Faith and Fashion in Turkey: Consumption, Politics and Islamic Identities* (London: I.B. Tauris, 2018).
45. Norbert Elias, *La civilisation des mœurs*, translated by Pierre Kamnitzer (Paris: Pocket, 2017).
46. Michel Foucault, *Histoire de la sexualité*, 1: *La volonté de savoir* (Paris: Gallimard, 1997).
47. Emmanuel Levinas, *Totalité et infini: essai sur l'extériorité* (Dordrecht: Kluwer Academic, 2009).

Bibliography

Ambrosio, Alberto Fabio. *Soufis à Istanbul, hier, aujourd'hui: des Hommes et des lieux (XIIIe–XXIe siècle)* (Paris: Cerf, 2014).

Aktay, Yasin (ed.). *Modern Türkiye'de siyasî düşünce*. Cağaloğlu, Istanbul: İletişim, 2001.

Arığ, Ayten Sezer. *Atatürk Türkiyesi'nde kılık kıyafette çağdaşlaşma*. Ankara: Siyasal Kitabevi, 2007.

Âtıf Hoca, İskilipli Mehmet. *Frenk Mukallitliği ve Şapka*, edited by Yunus Coşkun. Trabzon: 40 Kulübü Yayınevi, 2019.

Aysel, Morin, and Lee Ronald. "Constitutive Discourse of Turkish Nationalism: Atatürk's *Nutuk* and the Rhetorical Construction of the 'Turkish People'." *Communication Studies* 61, no. 5 (2010): 485–506.

Azak, Umut. *Islam and Secularism in Turkey: Kemalism, Religion and the Nation State*. London: I.B. Tauris.

Bilici, Faruk. "Révolution française, Révolution turque et fait religieux." *Revue du monde musulman et de la Méditerranée* 52, no. 1 (1989): 173–85.

Bologne, Jean-Claude. *Histoire de la pudeur*. Paris: O. Orban, 1986.

Botrugno, Lorenzo. "La diplomazia pastorale di Mons. Roncalli tra Sofia e Istanbul." In *Fede e diplomazia: le relazioni internazionali della Santa Sede nell'età contemporanea*. Edited by Massimo de Leonardis, 133–51. Milan: EDUCatt, 2014.

Cetin, Iclal. "Veiled Representations: Political Battles around Female Sexuality in Turkish Print Media." *Feminist Media Studies* 10, no. 4 (2010): 409–19.

Chelhod, Joseph. "La face et la personne chez les Arabes." *Revue de l'histoire des religions* 151, no. 2 (1957): 231–41.

Delaney, Carol, "Untangling the Meanings of Hair in Turkish Society." *Anthropological Quarterly* 67, no. 4 (1994): 159–72.

Dumont, Paul. *Mustafa Kemal invente la Turquie moderne: 1919–1924*. Brussels: Éd. Complexe, 1983.

Dunn, John P. "Clothes to Kill For: Uniforms and Politics in Ottoman Armies." *Journal of the Middle East and Africa* 2, no. 1 (2011): 85–107.

Elias, Norbert. *La Civilisation des mœurs*, translated by Pierre Kamnitzer. Paris: Pocket, 2017.

Erdoğan, Mehmet. *Tesettür meselesinden Türban sorununa*. İnceleme, araştırma dizisi 197. Cağaloğlu, Istanbul: İz Yayıncılık, 2008.

Foucault, Michel. *Histoire de la sexualité*, 1: *La Volonté de savoir*. Paris: Gallimard, 1997.

Gemalmaz, Mehmet Semih. *Türk Kıyafet Hukuku ve Türban: Tarihçe, İdeoloji, Mevzuat, İçtihat, Siyaset: AİHK ve AİHM Kararları ve Değerlendirilmesi*. Istanbul: Legal, 2005.

Göle, Nilüfer. *Musulmanes et modernes: voile et civilisation en Turquie*. Paris: La Découverte, 2003.

Gürpinar, Doğan. "The Politics of Memoirs and Memoir-Publishing in 20th Century Turkey." *Turkish Studies* 13, no. 3 (2012): 537–57.

Iacub, Marcela. *Par le trou de la serrure: une histoire de la pudeur publique, XIXe–XXIe siècle*. Paris: Fayard, 2008.

Jevakhoff, Alexandre. *Kemal Atatürk: Les chemins de l'Occident*. Paris: Tallandier, 1989.

Jirousek, Charlotte A., and Sara Catterall. *Ottoman Dress and Design in the West: A Visual History of Cultural Exchange*. Bloomington: Indiana University Press, 2019.

Kiliç, Selâmi. "Şapka Meselesi ve Kılık Kıyafe İnkılâbı." *Ankara Üniversitesi Türk İnkilap Tarihi Enstitüsü Atatürk Yolu Dergisi* (1995): 530–47.

Kinross, Patrick. *Ataturk*. London: Phoenix, 2001.

Kister, Michael J. "'The Crowns of This Community' ... Some Notes on the Turban in the Muslim Tradition." *Jerusalem Studies in Arabic and Islam* 24 (2000): 217–45.
Koç, Fatma, and Emine Koca. "The Westernization Process in Ottoman Women's Garments: 18th Century-20th Century." *Asian Journal of Women's Studies* 13, no. 4 (2007): 57–84.
Levinas, Emmanuel. *Totalité et infini: essai sur l'extériorité*. Paris: Grasset, 2009.
Nazlı, Alimen. *Faith and Fashion in Turkey: Consumption, Politics and Islamic Identities*. London: I.B. Tauris, 2018.
Orazi, Massimiliano. *Del pudore: per una filosofia dell'alterità e della sua misura*. Turin: G. Giappichelli, 2020.
Özlem, Sandikci, and Ger Güliz. "Veiling in Style: How Does a stigmatized Practice Become Fashionable?" *Journal of Consumer Research* 37, no. 1 (2010): 15–36.
Repp, Richard Cooper. *The Müfti of Istanbul: A Study in the Development of the Ottoman Learned Hierarchy*. Oxford Oriental Institute monographs 8. London: Ithaca Press for the Board of the Faculty of Oriental Studies, Oxford University, 1986.
Rocchi, Luciano, and Argenti Filippo. *Ricerche sulla lingua osmanli del XVI secolo: il corpus lessicale turco del manoscritto fiorentino di Filippo Argenti (1533)*. Wiesbaden: Harrassowitz, 2007.
Şaziye Karlıklı, Defne Tozan, and Orhan Koloğlu, *Cumhuriyet kıyafetleri*. Istanbul: GSD Holding, 1998.
Selz, Monique. *La Pudeur, un lieu de liberté*. Paris: Buchet & Chastel, 2003.
Şeni, Nora. "La mode et le vêtement féminin dans la presse satirique d'Istanbul à la fin du XIXe siècle." In *Presse Turque et Presse de Turquie*. Edited by Nathalie Clayer, Alexandre Popovic, and Thierry Zarcone, 189–209. Istanbul: ISIS, 1992.
Şeni, Nora. "Un empire que des firmans habillent. Normes et réformes vestimentaires en Turquie." *Modes pratiques. Revue d'histoire du vêtement et de la mode* 1 (2015): 237–47.
Şeni, Nora. "Ville ottomane et représentation du corps féminin." *Les Temps Modernes* 41 (1984): 66–95.
Şeyhun, Ahmet. *Islamist Thinkers in the Late Ottoman Empire and Early Turkish Republic*. Boston: Brill, 2014.
Soylu, Sümeyye Gülşen. "Anlaşılmayan Anlam: İskilipli Atıf Hoca." *Uluslararası Bütün Yönleriyle Çorum Sempozyumu, 28–30 Nisan 2016: Bildiriler Kitabı* (2016): 653–67.
Zarcone, Thierry. *La Turquie moderne et l'islam*. Paris: Flammarion, 2004.
Ze'evi, Dror. *Producing Desire: Changing Sexual Discourse in the Ottoman Middle East, 1500–1900*. Berkeley: University of California Press, 2006.
Zilfi, Madeline C. "Women, Minorities and the Changing Politics of Dress in the Ottoman Empire, 1650–1830." In *The Right to Dress: Sumptuary Laws in a Global Perspective, 1200–1800*. Edited by Giorgio Riello and Ulinka Rublack, 393–415. Cambridge: Cambridge University Press, 2019.

9

Heshima and Sexuality beyond Marriage: Gendered Interpretations of Morality in Zanzibar

Marloes Hamelink

"For many years I believed my mother could see from the way I walked if I have had sex. I was very scared, but did it anyway. Much later than my peers. I was really surprised I could keep it a secret all that time."—Amal[1]

Introduction

Amal, in her twenties, describes during our conversation her memories of her first sexual relationship as a late teenager. She explains how her mother made her conscious and worried about the visibility of her sexual behavior to prevent her from getting involved in a sexual relationship. Even though she was scared, she decided to risk it and become sexually active. She does not remember what made her take that decision: "It was probably a mix of being convinced by my boyfriend and curiosity." Sexuality is both an important and controversial part of the lives of Zanzibari Muslim women, in which secrecy plays a crucial part. Islam is often portrayed as constraining women's sexuality. Women in Zanzibar do, however, show flexible notions on how to deal with their gendered roles in sexual relationships in and beyond their legal marriage status. Gender is constructed, performed, negotiated, or rejected within and outside marriage, and Islam plays an important role in the perception of gender roles in relation to marriage along the Swahili coast.[2]

Zanzibar has a prominent position in the Indian Ocean along the East African coast. The archipelago has been a major trade port over the last two thousand years. Swahili language and culture evolved, and Islam emerged because of the interaction between several societies in the Indian Ocean region.[3] Zanzibar, as part of the United Republic of Tanzania, is semiautonomous and has its own government and its own Islamic law system. The archipelago has a long history of being a cosmopolitan place with a heterogeneous ethnic population with African, Asian, Arab, and Indian backgrounds.[4] A history of slavery and being conquered by the Omani and the British brought Zanzibar a multiethnic population with fluid notions of identity. Unlike the mainland of Tanzania, where over a hundred different ethnic groups maintain their respective identities and are religiously divided into about one-third Christians, one-third Muslims, and one-third that practice other religions,[5] the population of Zanzibar consists of 97 percent Muslims. Islam has spread on the islands and the rest of the East African coast since the thirteenth century and plays a big role in all spheres of current life. Zanzibar town is the capital and the research location on which this chapter is based.

Gender relations in Zanzibar and ideas around sexuality are reflected in the legal system. Women's status in Zanzibar is greatly influenced by the interplay between law and culture. The legal system enforces the everyday morality women deal with.[6] There is a need for studying women from a perspective that goes beyond a patriarchal binary system, in which often the dominant position of men is underlined.[7] Men are often portrayed as sexual agents, both by men and women. It is important to create a more nuanced interpretation of this image.[8] Even though Islamic marriage can contain disadvantages for women, for example, their right to divorce,[9] there is a need to focus on the agency women have in those systems.[10] The concept of agency is based on the tension between a set structure that involves laws and rules and the way in which individuals deal with these structures. The interaction between human actions and structure is a dynamic process in which social structures get challenged by the agency of people.[11] The Western approach to agency has the danger of lacking the opportunity for women to express a form of agency in which they can embrace their religion. Anthropologist Saba Mahmood urges for a more nuanced understanding of agency based on ideas of resistance and oppression.[12] This understanding is less individualistic and suits the lives of Muslim women better.[13] Women include their communities in their approach to agency and empower themselves as religious agents.[14] Religion, and particularly Islam, has often been perceived as a constraint on sexuality, being rigid, controlling, and intolerant of any form of sexual expression outside of heterosexual marriage. This essentialist view does not reflect how sexuality is experienced and practiced and does not give a nuanced picture of individual agency.[15] By emphasizing sexual pleasure, women express their feminine identity and negotiate their sexual agency.[16] Feminist and socialist Signe Arnfred argues that behind any façade of wifely submissiveness, power relations of sexuality may well differ from what patriarchs in power might want to believe, and she underlines sexuality as a female domain of expertise and autonomy among women in Northern Mozambique.[17] This is in line with the study on sexual instruction rituals in Zanzibar, where sexuality plays an important role in portraying women as religious agents, as debates on piety are central in sexual instruction rituals.[18]

Marriage is key in ideas about sexual relationships in Zanzibar. Within marriage, sexuality is encouraged and seen as a right and a form of pleasure.[19] Outside of marriage, sexuality is seen as illegitimate and a sin. In everyday life, however, interpretations and lived experiences of sexuality go far beyond this duality. In line with this argument, anthropologist Lila Abu-Lughod suggests looking beyond debates about stereotypes in feminism in Islam on oppression and patriarchy and creating a deeper understanding of what it means to be a woman and Muslim beyond all stereotypes.[20] In Dakar, for example, like in Zanzibar, sex before or outside of marriage is for many unacceptable, but the interpretation and way to deal with it can be very flexible. In the hegemonic construction, boys are expected to embody active sexuality, in which they seek bodily satisfaction of their "natural" and "uncontrollable" desires. Girls, however, are also agents who do not just subordinate to dominant discourses. Girls and women find ways to challenge the gender dynamics by refusing sex to remain respectable or by showing agency by being seductive and satisfying the needs of themselves and their partners. The acknowledgment of the coexistence of silence, pleasure, and agency allows for a more nuanced and more dynamic picture of power processes in sexuality and intimate relationships.[21]

Islamic orthopraxy, the emphasis on correct behavior, plays an important role for Zanzibari women.[22] The concept of *heshima* is central in understanding how women deal with sexuality. *Heshima* is often translated as honor or respectability. It determines the moral position women take in their communities. For Zanzibari women, an understanding of *heshima* should focus on "respectability" rather than "honor." Honor is seen as determined by men and imposed on women, while the idea of respectability gives women the opportunity to have agency over the way they are seen and how they portray themselves. It gives women a greater amount of control over their individual reputations and their positions in social life.[23] Limiting movements, sexual purity, speaking softly, and covering parts of the body as well as limiting contact with men help women to gain and maintain *heshima*.[24] Historian Elisabeth McMahon underlines the importance of *heshima* on Pemba, an island in the Northern part of the Zanzibar archipelago, and emphasizes the religious background of the concept. Respectful behavior and honor are rooted in Islam. The link between moral behavior and religion is important for women in Pemba, which also applies to women in urban Zanzibar. Children are raised with *heshima* in a way which involves respecting their parents and people of their parent's generation.[25] This translates into obedience and appropriate behavior around adults and being discrete about any extramarital sexual activity.[26]

In the context of Zanzibar, modesty and secrecy are seen as positive traits as they help women to keep their *heshima* intact. Only secrets that are exposed can cause shame. Well-kept secrets are part of women's *heshima*.[27] Sexual relationships outside of marriage are religiously illegitimate and interpreted as shameful. As a result, women hide both their love relationships and their sexual affairs. Secrecy is key in love and sexual relationships in the African Islamic context and offers a way for women to maintain their respectability and status and guards them from shame.[28] Anthropologist Eileen Moyer argues in a different context that sexuality is related to morality, honor, and respect.[29] Sexuality, and particularly extramarital sex, can be described as a public secret. People are aware that it happens but won't openly discuss it. Anthropologist Liv Haram uses the term illicit sexual behavior for the way people deal with the gap between values and ideas, and the tolerance they allow themselves in everyday life. Young people in northern Tanzania manage multiple love affairs in a morally acceptable way by keeping them secret. Disciplining one's sexual desires applies both to men and women. Men, however, do have more freedom regarding premarital and extramarital affairs. Both men and women manage to create a wide sexual network in a morally acceptable way,[30] which increases the agency of women.

To contribute to a more nuanced view of practiced sexualities of Muslim women, I will elaborate on the role *heshima* plays in sexual relationships. Women use creative ways to deal with cultural–religious moral standards, specifically concerning sexuality. Retaining their *heshima* strengthens the position of Zanzibari women in society and their roles within the family and helps in creating a discourse in which they become sexual agents. Through stories and experiences of sexuality, women express the role respectability plays in the picture they portray of themselves. They make sure a certain image of them is expressed to the people around them and hide the interactions they do not want to make known. Further, women protect others and the *heshima* of others. Women are responsible for their children and younger family members and play a role in their sexual relationships and secrets around them. I will focus on the role of secrecy in dealing with *heshima* by being discrete and controlling which images and stories will be revealed and which ones women will keep to themselves. The empirical data was collected during sixteen months of ethnographic fieldwork in urban Zanzibar between 2010 and 2013. The main method I used was participant observation, which varied from one-on-one conversations to wedding functions with hundreds of women. Informal conversations have been key, and I further held focus group sessions with university students and interviews with women of different age groups.

This chapter will first emphasize the moral and gendered background of women in urban Zanzibar and ideas that revolve around sexual relationships. It will address social norms and how they are often not lived and the fears of men around the theme of women's sexual agency. Secondly, family and societal responsibilities will be addressed through the story of Maryam. Maryam's niece got pregnant, and she explains how it is the responsibility and task of the family members to deal with this issue. Thirdly, I will address which kind of secrets related to *heshima* revolve around marriage. Nayla expresses her desire to live her life in a way that she considers to be religiously right. She only wants a sexual relationship if it is part of a marriage. After one challenging marriage, she is, however, not interested in a conventional marriage and chooses to get married in secret. Hardly anyone, including the first wife, knows about this marriage. Nayla constructed a relationship that she morally and religiously approved of and in which she could retain the freedom that she gained as a divorced woman. Lastly, I address a different kind of multiple wife marriage, in which secrets and societal expectations play an important role. In this marriage, extramarital affairs are used for reproduction, which is a clear example of how secrecy helps maintain the *heshima* of the different family members. Through these empirical stories, the diversity of negotiating sexuality and the way women deal with a sexual agency is emphasized.

Moral Challenges and Public Appearance

"Having sex with someone other than your husband is the worst sin," Maryam explains, "that is maybe why it causes a lot of problems if people decide to have a sexual relationship anyway. Women get pregnant or get diseases. God tells us we should not do this, but many people do not listen. This is very problematic." Maryam explains her vision of extramarital affairs. Ideas about sexual relationships are strongly gendered and rooted in Islamic moral ideas. Mainly women are held responsible for sexual relationships, as men "cannot naturally control themselves."[31] Men feel attraction toward women and are not supposed to act upon it. However, it is perceived as part of a man's identity to feel attracted to women. Since this attraction is seen as natural, men are often not blamed for it. Salma adds, "For women, it is different. They might get convinced by a boyfriend to have a sexual affair. She should be the one who resists."[32]

Women who think different from the general perception are often much more careful expressing it and especially do not want others to find out if they do not act upon it. Yamina argues not all women live up to the moral ideal. Yamina's eyes scan the room to see if no one is entering and says in a quiet voice,

> Unlike men think, women decide if they do or do not have an affair. A man is easy to seduce because of their lack of control. Women do abuse that if they want to. And if they do not want an affair, they will never have one. Sometimes it is easier for a woman to act like men are in control. It will make them feel prouder.

When I ask her about her own experience, she smiles and looks away. But she is happy to talk about her friend:

> My friend's husband is away a lot. He does not tell her what he does or when he comes back, so she must be careful. But she knows at which times she is not necessarily expected to be home. The man she visits is also married, and they have a good agreement together. They enjoy each other's company, and he even helps her out financially when she is in need.[33]

Women's sexuality is interpreted more as a public domain than men's since their sexuality is linked to the public honor of both men and women.[34] This makes women's sexuality morally more problematized than men's. The honor of female and male relatives is related to the behavior of their female relatives. The conversation with Yamina shows that the role of women can be interpreted in different ways. Women do not always act upon these moral standards, but they often still express themselves as if they do. They navigate the expectations of others and their own desires. *Heshima* of women is not merely related to their deeds, but also to the way they come across and the image people get of them. If a woman manages to maintain a proper public image, she can negotiate her actual behavior in many more flexible ways.

During my ethnographic work (2010–13), I was confronted with many girls and young women who claimed they would never be in sexual relationships, as was expected from them. They explained that only "bad girls" who are not well raised or educated would get involved in such an affair. Yet others ensured me almost every woman does have a sexual relationship before she gets married. "All my friends did it. I did it, even though I was much later than most of them. My boyfriend really cared about me and wanted to wait," Aisha explains to me.[35] Many unmarried women see sexual relationships as normal since almost everyone is involved in sexual relationships.[36] Some are curious themselves, and others are convinced by their boyfriends to do it, for example, because he promises to marry her, or he buys her something nice. Girls and unmarried women are very selective about who they trust to talk with about their love relationship since the information can be harmful to them. Some of them felt safe with me, as I was an outsider and did not have family within the community, so their secrets would be safe with me. Others never opened up about their personal affairs, even when there were signs that there were more things going on than we were talking about. These constant negotiations and discrete behavior are part of women's daily realities.

Some men feel threatened by the idea that women can start affairs and have agency over their sexual experiences. Hussein (19) is a student who is originally from a village and now stays in the town for his studies. He feels intimidated by the women in the town and prefers the way he sees relationships in the village where he is from. "Eventually, I want to marry a girl from the village," Hussein explains:

> The problem with educated girls here in town, and the ones who have jobs, is that they will give you a hard time. They want to go out, and they want to do things. And they might not agree if you want to marry a second wife. I want to take the decisions at home. I want my wife to stay home with the kids. That is how I am raised, and I like it. Here the husbands have no ideas what their wives are up to.[37]

Nassor, a retailer who is in his early thirties and lives in town with his wife and their baby, recognizes himself in the struggle Hussein fears. Nassor sighs when his wife leaves to prepare tea in the kitchen. "Why does it have to be so difficult? Nobody told me this." He just had an argument with his wife because he thinks she should be home. One of her friends has a bad influence on her:

> Her friend goes to all these bars, where there are men drinking and all that. That is not the place for my wife to be. Men tend to forget these women might be someone's wife and mother. I know how they talk and go after them. I don't want my wife to be part of it. I don't understand why she wants to be out in public exposing herself.[38]

A few days later, I had a discussion with his wife. "He is so unreasonable," she claims. She continues,

> He is always out and just expecting me to be home. And the funny thing is that many of the women he thinks about as the proper wives are cheating on their husbands and doing all sorts of things their husbands would never allow. They are just way sneakier about it. If you live the proper life and make a stop somewhere on the way to the shop, there is no issue. If you don't do anything really wrong, but you want to go out and have fun with a friend, you are suddenly a big scandal. It is ridiculous. And don't trust him. He pretends he is the proper one, but meanwhile, he parties all the time.[39]

Nassor and his wife stress the gendered patterns of relationships on *heshima*, expectations, and sexuality. While his wife is in constant need to express where she is going and in constant negotiation, she often does not know where her husband is when he is out, and her husband expresses that he has more specific ideas about what proper moral behavior means for women than for men.

Family and Societal Responsibilities

Family members and neighbors help women protect their moral reputations by keeping an eye on what they do and reminding them when needed about how they should behave. Unmarried young women are seen as a family responsibility, and problems are discussed as such. Maryam is a middle-aged woman who lives in a women's household. Her husband remarried and moved in with his new wife. She calls herself a divorcee but is not actually divorced. Her husband refused to divorce her, as he was afraid she would marry someone else. She thinks he moved away as she never got any children of her own. She does take on a mother's role if it involves her nieces and children of other family members. She takes full responsibility and is the main breadwinner of the household. The situation Maryam explains below stresses that honor and morality are not merely linked to an individual, but involve the entire family. Maryam explained to me, "I have a meeting about one of my nieces. She is very difficult; we do not know what to do with her. She ran off with her boyfriend and got pregnant. Now we are going to sit together and see if she can marry him or if we have to take her back." The niece will not be at this meeting, as it is up to her more mature relatives to decide upon her life. Maryam refers to her as "our daughter," and with "our" she means the women in the family. She deeply cares about her and is very worried about her future. The niece is staying at home currently, and they took away her phone, so she cannot get in touch with the boyfriend or others. The meeting is secret, and nobody from outside of the family is informed. The women feel it is better not to inform others until the decision is taken. "She is very young and might not be able to make a decision that is eventually best for her. That is why we help her. She is trouble now, but I don't want her entire future to be ruined."[40] Not the niece as an individual, but several members of the community around her will negotiate about what will happen with her life. The family is involved, as their moral worlds are related to that of family members. When someone's daughter is known to be in a nonmarital sexual relationship, family members are blamed for raising their daughter without good morals and behavior and therefore interpreted as lacking morals themselves.

Marriage Secrets

"Freestyle," the dance teacher calls out, and Nayla, a businesswoman from the Michenzani neighborhood who is in her mid-thirties, increases the speed at which she is moving her hips while she puts one hand in the air. Her smile gets bigger while she moves to the center of the circle of dancing ladies. She grabs one of them to join her in the circle, and their hips move closely while the ladies around them cheer with a high "ayayayayay." A drop of sweat is making its way down Nayla's face. After the exercise class, Nayla puts her hijab and *buibui*[41] on top of her sweaty clothes, and I join her on her walk home. She is not in a rush, as she will likely be home alone this evening. Her teenage sons from her previous marriage are more often out than not at this time of the day. "And my husband is not around that often," she explains while she looks into my eyes with a smile on her face. Nayla recently got married and is the second wife of her husband. He spends most of the time with his first wife, who is not aware he married someone else as well. She explains,

> For me, this is ideal. I do not want to be the wife that always sits at home and has the food ready for whenever he decides to come home. I have done that in my first marriage, and it is not my thing. Having his food ready, his laundry done, the house clean and all the domestic stuff is pretty boring to me. Now the first wife can have that duty. We make appointments when we see each other and then we spend time together. I have a much better relationship with him than with my ex-husband. I really do not want the first wife to find out; that is why I hardly tell anyone whom I married. It is a bit difficult, as people try to find out anyway who it is. My mother is upset I didn't tell her. I actually only told one friend the full story. Anybody else can just assume, and that is fine. I can deny it when I have to.

She pulls out her phone and shows me her picture. She wears a colorful dress and a lot of makeup. Her hijab is made of green lace and tied back. She smiles, looking at the picture. "This is my wedding picture. I celebrated the day with some women, and he went to the mosque with a few male relatives and friends. He had to be sure nobody who came would tell his wife. We only saw each other the day after, just to be safe." Her sons know she got married and did have their suspicion about who it is because he sometimes passes by when they are around. She says,

> But I won't tell it to them as a fact. You know how kids are; they can tell anyone. I told them it was none of their business, and I would explain when they were older. I don't think they really care. They just want to be able to do their thing. And for me, it is important the first wife doesn't find out what is going on. If she finds out and does not agree, she might ask for a divorce. In that case, he might want me to take over her duties. And that is absolutely not what I am looking for.[42]

Nayla's situation shows that not only extramarital affairs but even entire marriages are kept secret. This is not uncommon in Zanzibar. Like Nayla, many men and women prefer to get married if they want to get involved with each other, as they see it as the only acceptable way to have a sexual relationship, as discussed earlier. Marriage to them is a religious approval to be together. A reason to keep the marriage secret, as Nayla shared, is another wife who does not approve of the situation:

> And for me, marriage is a must to be in a relationship. I am a religious woman; I don't have boyfriends or illegitimate relationships. This might not be what the first wife wants, but we don't do anything wrong as we get married in the eyes of God. In secret, but we are married.

Under Islamic law, men can marry up to four wives in Zanzibar. This does not mean all parties always fully agree with this situation. It varies from woman to woman what kind of marriage they agree with. Nayla explains she prefers being the second wife of her husband, as it gives her the opportunity to be in a relationship with a man, not having to worry about the domestic duties but getting the affection she is looking for. Both she and her husband prefer to keep it secret:

> We never meet in public. He mainly visits me at home, or I go to his place when his wife is not around. We chat a lot by phone. His first wife does not even know about the existence of this phone. He owns two phones that look exactly the same. One phone is for his first wife and business. She can access it, and he leaves it lying around. Therefore she feels confident that he has nothing to hide. His other phone is always silent and tucked away carefully when he is home. If he does not reply for hours, I know he is home with her. He calls it his "outside phone." I know other women in similar situations get frustrated about being ignored. I honestly do not mind. I am very happy with the freedom in this marriage. I am not looking for the traditional partnership marriage often comes with, and I enjoy the excitement of feeling love and attention.

Nayla surprised me when she revealed she had remarried. The year before, we talked several times about her relationship status, and she had very different ideas: "My mom tries to convince me to get married to someone," she told me during a coffee in the shade on a sunny afternoon.

> I won't do it again. My first husband was my mom's proposal, and it was a very bad experience. I never really was into the idea, but she kept pushing me until I agreed. It was a big mistake. He never treated me well; he had high demands from my side and didn't do anything in return. He didn't even support me financially with the kids. Since we are divorced, I am relieved. I am happy to live on my own with my sons. Nobody is telling me to be home, to cook or to clean for them.

The experience of living alone after her divorce was very different for Nayla than the time prior to her marriage, when she lived at home with her mom.

> My mom often had all sorts of chores for me, which kept me busy and didn't allow me to go out much. This was exactly her goal, as she didn't like me to wander around the streets. She told me it was inappropriate for a young woman to roam around. She was always on top of me. I didn't know my husband before we got married, but I was hoping for more freedom. The freedom I was longing for, I only managed to get after my divorce. My family handed me over to my husband, and I was definitely not going to move back. My husband was a very poor choice; he never really cared about me. I decided I had listened enough to my mom, and I found my own place. I did a lot of small jobs until I was able to open my own business and support myself and the kids. That is what gave me freedom. I will

> not move back to the place I was at that point. When my mom recently came up with another man who wanted to marry me, I declined. I do not want to remarry.[43]

At this time, Nayla was not aware yet that she could have both: her freedom to move around and be in a legal relationship with a man. She had several discussions with her current husband to make sure he understood her role in the relationship, and they mutually agreed on this unorthodox form of partnership within their marriage.

Divorced women often have to deal with a stigma, and their families are afraid of the inability of these women to remarry.[44] There are several family constructions and ways of living for women after divorce. Nayla showed that there is suddenly the option to live alone, which is morally seen as very inappropriate prior to marriage. This is, however, an exception, as most women do not have the financial means to do so. Maryam's family chose another construction, in which they share an apartment with five women and their children. They are all family members, divorced, widowed, or left by their husbands without having an official divorce. Within this household, the women keep an eye on each other, and mainly the younger household members are monitored and questioned by their older housemates.

Co-wives

Women give numerous reasons for having extramarital affairs, for example, financial or material benefits, the enjoyment of the male attention, sexual pleasure, and making their husband jealous. The following example expresses how secrecy helps different family members to retain their *heshima*. Mwanakhamis, a woman who runs a small catering business from home, saw what happened at her neighbor's place, a family she has a tight relationship with. They often look after each other's children and help each other out when needed. She became friends with Aafiya and was surprised her friend was quite fine when her husband Juma was going to get married again.

> Earlier, we discussed this possibility because I can at times be scared my husband will run off and marry a new and probably younger wife. It is a fear I need to live with, and you never know for sure what will happen. I don't want it, but what can I do? It is allowed in our religion, so I don't have anything to say. For now, we have been fine, but I know and see often enough that it can change any minute. And your marriage will never be the same if there is a second wife involved.[45]

Aafiya did not seem too worried about that. The day her husband came home and told her he was marrying again, she did not make a scene.

> She even welcomed the second wife of her husband in their lives. They got along well and became very close. Juma challenged his luck and decided to marry again. Both women did not like the third wife. I am not sure if Aafiya did not want to share their husband with a third wife or if they could not get along for other reasons. She just said she was fed up with him and explained he couldn't even support his two

> families; why would he think he could support a third wife? It didn't help that the husband seemed to be particularly keen on his newest and youngest wife.

The third wife had issues getting pregnant, so she went with her husband to the doctor to find out what was going on with her. The other wives both had received multiple children, so they were convinced she had an issue. They came home very surprised, as the doctor had told them Juma is the one who cannot reproduce. The first and second wives were not surprised at all, even though they did not share that with their husbands. Mwanakhamis explains,

> Aafiya had shared a secret only with the second wife of Juma. She did not get pregnant in three years of marriage. She was really keen on becoming a mother, and she decided to get pregnant with somebody else without informing her husband. Aafiya did not discuss the fertility issues with her husband, as she knew women always get blamed when they do not have children. Another friend was sent to a witch doctor to get treated and was told somebody had cursed her. She went through a scary experience. Aafiya did not want this and tried something else.

She shared her knowledge with the second wife, who followed her advice and managed to get children in an extramarital relationship as well. As they did not like wife number three, they never talked about it with her. Mwanakhamis continues,

> When the third wife did not manage to get pregnant, she went to the hospital with her husband. There he found out that he was infertile, and both his wives had been cheating on him. They continued living together as he probably did not want to deal with the embarrassment of telling the truth to people around them. Men never admit they cannot have children. They always blame their wife. He has no other choice than to deny what has happened and that he doesn't have children of his own.

Conclusion

The experiences of Zanzibari in this chapter underline how women navigate sexual relations between their own desires on an individual level, societal expectations, and the practical possibilities in the situations they are facing. Flexible notions of gender roles are included in the way women experience and deal with *heshima*. Yamina states that women are the ones to decide if they have an affair or not, even though men are often assumed to have more sexual drive and a more decisive role. Hussein and Nassor reflect on the fears they have regarding women's sexual agency and Hussein underlines his preference for more conservative gender roles, even though he thinks they are uncommon among the more educated women in urban Zanzibar. Women show diverse ways of dealing with gender roles beyond the patriarchal binary system. They take different roles in the family: for example, Maryam as the head and breadwinner of an all-female household and having a leading position in the decisions that are being taken within the family. Her niece did not take the responsibility her family expected of her, and therefore they find a reason to take over the responsibility for the life of the niece. The fact that she is not married does mean for the family that they are held responsible for what happens to the niece. It underlines *heshima* is not merely an individual, but a family or societal responsibility in which others can negotiate secrecy to maintain *heshima* on behalf of others, in this case the niece.

Women incorporate secrecy to maintain their respectability and yet be able to express forms of sexual agency. Secrecy is an essential part of *heshima* for women in Zanzibar and enables women to move in directions beyond the hegemonic gender discourse. Secrecy and being discrete play a big role for many in their attempt to live a life they morally approve of. Nayla finds it important to be married from a religious perspective, and by marrying in secret she maintains her *heshima* and increases her sexual agency at the same time. Becoming a second wife in secret seems the best solution for her, as she can have a flexible approach toward societal expectations while following her own religious beliefs. Through marriage on her own conditions, she gained agency in several aspects of life and feels in charge of her household and social and sexual relations. Nayla's story underlines how secrecy, *heshima*, and sexual agency can be related in very diverse ways. Juma's wives use their sexual agency for a different target: reproduction. Secrecy plays an important role for both Juma and his wives, as they all benefit from keeping these extramarital affairs secret to maintain their *heshima*. The gendered expectations involve the assumption that as a man Juma has his own biological children. Revealing to the larger society that he did not get one of his wives pregnant would hurt his respectability. The wives are not expected to have extramarital sexual relationships and, therefore, also benefit from this joint secret or illicit sexual behavior. Secrecy plays a key role in relation to sexuality and *heshima*, especially beyond traditional forms of marriage.

Notes

1. Participant observation in Michenzani, Zanzibar Town, August 12, 2012.
2. Katrina Daly Thompson and Erin E. Stiles, "Introducing Gender, Sexuality, and Marriage into the Study of Islam in the Western Indian Ocean," in *Gendered Lives in the Western Indian Ocean: Islam, Marriage, and Sexuality on the Swahili Coast* (Athens: University of Ohio Press, 2015), 30.
3. Akbar Keshodkar, *Tourism and Social Change in Post-socialist Zanzibar: Struggles for Identity, Movement, and Civilization* (Oxford: Lexington Books, 2013), 4.
4. William Cunningham Bissel, *Urban Design, Chaos, and Colonial Power in Zanzibar* (Bloomingtion: Indiana University Press, 2011) and John G. C. Blacker, "Population Growth and Differential Fertility in Zanzibar Protectorate," *Population Studies* 15, no. 3 (1962), 258–66.
5. Kelly Askew, *Performing the Nation: Swahili Music and Cultural Politics in Tanzania* (Chicago: University of Chicago Press, 2002), 271.
6. Salma Maoulidi, "Between Law and Culture: Contemplating Rights for Women in Zanzibar," *Gender and Culture at the Limit of Rights* (2011), 32–54.

7. See, among others, Tom Boellstorff, "Domesticating Islam: Sexuality, Gender, and the Limits of Pluralism," *Law & Social Inquiry* 31, no. 4 (2006), 1035–53; Elke Stockreiter, *Islamic Law, Gender, and Social Change in Post-Abolition Zanzibar* (Cambridge: Cambridge University Press, 2015).
8. Rachel Spronk, "The Idea of African Men: Dealing with the Cultural Contradictions of Sex in Academia and in Kenya," *Culture, Health & Sexuality* 16, no. 5 (2014), 504–17.
9. Women use the court system to file divorce, an act men can do outside of court as well. See: Erin Stiles, "'There Is No Stranger to Marriage Here!': Muslim Women and Divorce in Rural Zanzibar," *Africa* 75, no. 4 (2005), 582–98.
10. See also Susan Hirsch, *Pronouncing and Persevering: Gender and the Discourses of Disputing in an African Islamic Court* (Chicago: University of Chicago Press, 1998).
11. Anthony Giddens is the founder of the debate on agency and structure; Anthony Giddens, "Agency, Structure," in *Central Problems in Social Theory* (London: Palgrave, 1979), 49–95. His theory has been developed further by many others. Baber Zaheer, "Beyond the Structure/Agency Dualism: An Evaluation of Giddens' Theory of Structuration," *Sociological Inquiry* 61, no. 2 (1991), 219–30. Steven Loyal. *The Sociology of Anthony Giddens* (London: Pluto Press, 2003).
12. Saba Mahmood emphasizes to include piety and submission to religion in interpretations of agency. Saba Mahmood, *Politics of Piety* (Princeton, NJ: Princeton University Press, 2011).
13. See, among others: Lila Abu-Lughod, "The Romance of Resistance: Tracing Transformations of Power through Bedouin Women," *American Ethnologist* 17, no. 1 (1990), 41–55; Adeline Masquelier, *Women and Islamic Revival in a West African Town* (Bloomington: Indiana University Press, 2009).
14. Lila Abu-Lughod, *Dramas of Nationhood: The Politics of Television in Egypt* (Chicago: University of Chicago Press, 2008).
15. Andrew Kam-Tuck Yip, "Islam and Sexuality: Orthodoxy and Contestations," *Contemporary Islam* 3, no. 1 (2009), 1–5.
16. Rosabelle Boswell, "Sexual Practices and Sensual Selves in Zanzibar," *Anthropology Southern Africa* 31, nos. 1–2 (2008), 70–83.
17. Signe Arnfred, "Sex, Food and Female Power," in *Sexuality and Gender Politics in Mozambique: Rethinking Gender in Africa* (Woodbridge, Suffolk: James Currey, 2011), 165–87.
18. Katrina Daly Thompson, "How to Be a Good Muslim Wife: Women's Performance of Islamic Authority during Swahili Weddings," *Journal of Religion in Africa* 41, no. 4 (2011), 427–48.
19. Nadine Beckmann, "Pleasure and Danger: Muslim Views on Sex and Gender in Zanzibar," *Culture, Health & Sexuality* 12, no. 6 (2010), 619–32.
20. Lila Abu-Lughod, *Do Muslim Women Need Saving?* (Cambridge: Cambridge University Press, 2013).
21. Anouka van Eerdewijk, "Silence, Pleasure and Agency: Sexuality of Unmarried Girls in Dakar, Senegal," *Contemporary Islam* 3, no. 1 (2009), 7–24.
22. Angela R. Demovic, "Where Are the Women When the Tourists Arrive?: Bodies, Space, and Islamic Femininity in Rural Zanzibar," *Journal of Africana Religions* 4, no. 1 (2016), 6.
23. Elisabeth McMahon, *Slavery and Emancipation in Islamic East Africa: From Honor to Respectability* (Cambridge: Cambridge University Press, 2013).
24. For the concept and interpretation of *heshima*, see, among others: Demovic, "Where Are the Women," 1–27; Altaïr Despres, "The Arrival of White Women: Tourism

and the Reshaping of Beach Boys' Masculinity in Zanzibar," *Ethnography* 24, no. 2 (2023), 217–39; Laura Fair, *Pastimes and Politics. Culture, Community, and Identity in Post-abolition urban Zanzibar, 1890–1945* (Athens: Ohio University Press, 2001); Ayesha M. Imam, "The Muslim Religious Right ('Fundamentalists') and Sexuality," in *Women and Islam: Critical Concepts in Sociology. Volume 2: Social Conditions, Obstacles and Prospects*, edited by Haideh Moghissi (Oxon: Routledge, 2005); Kjersti Larsen, "Pleasure and Prohibitions: Reflections on Gender, Knowledge, and Sexuality in Zanzibar Town," in *Gendered Lives in the Western Indian Ocean*, edited by Erin E. Stiles and Katrina Daly Thompson (Athens: Ohio University Press, 2015), 209–41.

25. Elisabeth McMahon, " 'A Solitary Tree Builds Not': *Heshima*, Community, and Shifting Identity in Post-emancipation Pemba Island," *International Journal of African Historical Studies* 39, no. 2 (2006), 197–219.
26. Joyce Wamoyi, Daniel Wight, and Pieter Remes, "The Structural Influence of Family and Parenting on Young People's Sexual and Reproductive Health in Rural Northern Tanzania," *Culture, Health & Sexuality* 17, no. 6 (2015), 718–32.
27. Katherine Kingsford, *Learning to Be a woman: Negotiating Gender and Identity in Zanzibar*, PhD diss. (University College London, 2016), 32–5.
28. Nadine Beckman, "Pleasure and Danger: Muslim Views on Sex and Gender in Zanzibar," *Culture, Health & Sexuality* 12, no. 6 (2010), 619–32; Corrie Decker, "Love and Sex in Islamic Africa: Introduction," *Africa Today* 6, no. 4 (2015), 1–10; Kjersti Larsen, *Where Humans and Spirits Meet: The Politics of Rituals and Identified Spirits in Zanzibar* (New York: Berghahn, 2008).
29. Eileen Moyer emphasizes on the urge for concealment around sexuality, in relation to HIV/AIDS, in: "Faidha gani? What's the Point: HIV and the Logics of (non)-disclosure among Young Activists in Zanzibar," *Culture, Health & Sexuality* 14, suppl. 1 (2012), 70.
30. Liv Haram, "'Eyes Have No Curtains': The Moral Economy of Secrecy in Managing Love Affairs among Adolescents in Northern Tanzania in the time of AIDS," *Africa Today* (2005), 59–60.
31. Participant observation in Michenzani, May 16, 2011.
32. Participant observation in Michenzani, May 18, 2011.
33. During an informal conversation in Kwaboko, August 9, 2012.
34. Elisabeth McMahon, "'A Solitary Tree Builds Not': Heshima, Community, and Shifting Identity in Post-emancipation Pemba Island," *The International Journal of African historical studies* 39 no. 2 (2006), 197–219.
35. During a long conversation in the Jamhuri gardens, January 9, 2012.
36. Several informal conversations during my fieldwork with young women.
37. Focus group conversation Mnazi Mmoja, February 16, 2011.
38. Participant observation in Vuga, August 23, 2011.
39. Informal conversation in Vuga, August 29, 2011.
40. Informal conversation, May 31, 2013.
41. Long black dress that fully covers, worn outside on top of women's clothes. Also known as *abaya*.
42. Informal conversation at Forodhani Gardens, March 13, 2018.
43. Informal conversation at Forodhani Gardens, April 14, 2017.
44. This issue came up in numerous informal conversations with women throughout my fieldwork (2011–13).
45. Participant observation in the neighborhood Vuga, March 8 and 9, 2011.

Bibliography

Abu-Lughod, Lila. *Do Muslim Women Need Saving?*. Cambridge: Cambridge University Press, 2013.

Abu-Lughod, Lila. *Dramas of Nationhood: The Politics of Television in Egypt*. Chicago: University of Chicago Press, 2008.

Abu-Lughod, Lila. "The Romance of Resistance: Tracing Transformations of Power through Bedouin Women." *American Ethnologist* 17, no. 1 (1990): 41–55.

Arnfred, Signe. *Sexuality and Gender Politics in Mozambique: Rethinking Gender in Africa*. Woodbridge: James Currey, 2011.

Askew, Kelly. *Performing the Nation: Swahili Music and Cultural Politics in Tanzania*. Chicago: University of Chicago Press, 2002.

Baber, Zaheer. "Beyond the Structure/Agency Dualism: An Evaluation of Giddens' Theory of Structuration." *Sociological Inquiry* 61, no. 2 (1991): 219–30.

Beckmann, Nadine. "Pleasure and Danger: Muslim Views on Sex and Gender in Zanzibar." *Culture, Health & Sexuality* 12, no. 6 (2010): 619–32.

Bissell, William Cunningham. *Urban Design, Chaos, and Colonial Power in Zanzibar*. Bloomington: Indiana University Press, 2011.

Blacker, John G. C. "Population Growth and Differential Fertility in Zanzibar Protectorate." *Population Studies* 15, no. 3 (1962): 258–66.

Boellstorff, Tom. "Domesticating Islam: Sexuality, Gender, and the Limits of Pluralism." *Law & Social Inquiry* 31, no. 4 (2006): 1035–53.

Boswell, Rosabelle. "Sexual Practices and Sensual Selves in Zanzibar." *Anthropology Southern Africa* 31, nos. 1–2 (2008): 70–83.

Decker, Corrie. "Love and Sex in Islamic Africa: Introduction." *Africa Today* 61, no. 4 (2015): 1–10.

Demovic, Angela R. "Where Are the Women When the Tourists Arrive?: Bodies, Space, and Islamic Femininity in Rural Zanzibar." *Journal of Africana Religions* 4, no. 1 (2016): 1–27.

Despres, Altaïr. "The Arrival of White Women: Tourism and the Reshaping of Beach Boys' Masculinity in Zanzibar." *Ethnography* 24, no. 2 (2023): 217–39.

Van Eerdewijk, Anouka. "Silence, Pleasure and Agency: Sexuality of Unmarried Girls in Dakar, Senegal." *Contemporary Islam* 3, no. 1 (2009): 7–24.

Fair, Laura. *Pastimes and Politics. Culture, Community, and Identity in Post-abolition Urban Zanzibar, 1890–1945*. Athens: Ohio University Press, 2001.

Giddens, Anthony. *Central Problems in Social Theory. Action, Structure and Contradiction in Social Analysis*. London: Palgrave, 1979.

Haram, Liv. "Eyes Have No Curtains: The Moral Economy of Secrecy in Managing Love Affairs among Adolescents in Northern Tanzania in the Time of AIDS." *Africa Today* 51, no. 4 (2005): 57–73.

Hirsch, Susan F. *Pronouncing and Persevering: Gender and the Discourses of Disputing in an African Islamic Court*. Chicago: University of Chicago Press, 1998.

Imam, Ayesha M. "The Muslim Religious Right ('Fundamentalists') and Sexuality. In *Women and Islam: Critical Concepts in Sociology. Volume 2: Social Conditions, Obstacles and Prospects*. Edited by Haideh Moghissi. Oxon: Routledge, 2005.

Keshodkar, Akbar. *Tourism and Social Change in Post-socialist Zanzibar: Struggles for Identity, Movement, and Civilization*. Oxford: Lexington Books, 2013.

Kingsford, Katherine. *Learning to Be a Woman: Negotiating Gender and Identity in Zanzibar.* PhD Diss., University College London, 2016.
Larsen, Kjersti. *Where Humans and Spirits Meet: The Politics of rituals and Identified Spirits in Zanzibar*. New York: Berghahn Books, 2008.
Larsen, Kjersti. "Pleasure and Prohibitions. Reflections on Gender, Knowledge, and Sexuality in Zanzibar Town." In *Gendered Lives in the Western Indian Ocean. Islam, Marriage, and Sexuality on the Swahili Coast*. Edited by Erin E. Stiles and Katrina Daly Thompson, 209–41. Athens: Ohio University Press, 2015.
Loyal, Steven. *The Sociology of Anthony Giddens*. London: Pluto Press, 2003.
Mahmood, Saba. *Politics of Piety*. Princeton, NJ: Princeton University Press, 2011.
Maoulidi, Salma. "Between Law and Culture: Contemplating Rights for Women in Zanzibar." In *Gender and Culture at the Limit of Rights*. Edited by Dorothy L. Hodgson, 32–54. Philadelphia: University of Pennyslvania Press, 2011.
Masquelier, Adeline. *Women and Islamic Revival in a West African Town*. Bloomington: Indiana University Press, 2009.
McMahon, Elisabeth. "A Solitary Tree Builds Not: Heshima, Community, and Shifting Identity in Postemancipation Pemba Island." *The International Journal of African Historical Studies* 39, no. 2 (2006): 197–219.
McMahon, Elisabeth. *Slavery and Emancipation in Islamic East Africa: From Honor to Respectability*. Cambridge: Cambridge University Press, 2013.
Moyer, Eileen. "Faidha gani? What's the Point: HIV and the Logics of (non)-Disclosure among Young Activists in Zanzibar." *Culture, Health & Sexuality* 14, suppl 1. (2012): S67–S79.
Spronk, Rachel. "The idea of African Men: Dealing with the Cultural Contradictions of Sex in Academia and in Kenya." *Culture, Health & Sexuality* 16, no. 5 (2014): 504–17.
Stiles, Erin. "'There Is No Stranger to Marriage Here!': Muslim Women and Divorce in Rural Zanzibar." *Africa* 75, no. 4 (2005): 582–98.
Stiles, Erin E., and Katrina Daly Thompson (eds.). *Gendered Lives in the Western Indian Ocean: Islam, Marriage, and Sexuality on the Swahili Coast*. Athens: Ohia State University, 2015.
Stockreiter, Elke. *Islamic Law, Gender and Social Change in Post-Abolition Zanzibar*. Cambridge: Cambridge University Press, 2015.
Thompson, Katrina Daly. "How to Be a Good Muslim Wife: Women's Performance of Islamic Authority during Swahili Weddings." *Journal of Religion in Africa* 41, no. 4 (2011): 427–48.
Wamoyi, Joyce, Daniel Wight, and Pieter Remes. "The Structural Influence of Family and Parenting on Young People's Sexual and Reproductive Health in Rural Northern Tanzania." *Culture, Health & Sexuality* 17, no. 6 (2015): 718–32.
Yip, Andrew Kam-Tuck. "Islam and Sexuality: Orthodoxy and Contestations." *Contemporary Islam* 3, no. 1 (2009): 1–5.

Part III

Shame, Modesty, and Honor in Non-Muslim Countries

10

Coping with Honor, Shame, and Modesty: Muslims Undergoing Biomedical Treatments in Italy

Federica Sona

Introduction

While assisting at the passage from "Islam in Europe" to "European Islam,"[1] shariʿa-compliant routes to parenting are spreading across Europe. Parallel to the constantly growing (indigenous) European Muslim population,[2] novel and creative forms of filiation, including those benefiting from biomedical techniques, are becoming more common for intended parents.[3] Among the markets for medically assisted reproductive and procreative technologies, European countries are nowadays the largest one,[4] and, among patients requiring fertility treatments, the number of Muslims intending to be parents is persistently increasing. An analysis of prospective parents accessing Italian fertility clinics documents a similar scenario and thus becomes a privileged observatory of ethno/religious dynamics in multicultural contexts.[5]

In contemporary healthcare environments, various conceptions of the human body coexist and diverse lexicons of permissibility of medical actions on human beings interact on a daily basis. In the incessant flux between continuity and transformations, a happy middle ground has therefore to be found in the midst of biomedical technologies, legal provisions, and religious normativity. The notion of "the cultural construction of clinical reality" has indeed clarified that clinical social science is capable of translating concepts from cultural anthropology into clinical language for practical applications.[6] Individuals perceive their illness and then identify their favored cultural domain among the health care systems—namely, professional, popular, and folk—also depending upon their religious affiliation.[7] Particularly in Mediterranean countries, religious moralities play a key role in shaping the boundaries of legally permitted and socially acceptable medically assisted reproductive methods.[8]

Building upon ethnographic researches,[9] the chapter explores the feelings of shame, modesty, and honor among Muslim intended parents accessing fertility clinics. Voice is thus given to Muslim prospective mothers and fathers as well as to religious authorities. Attention is also paid to the perceptions of Muslim patients as articulated by the non-Muslim healthcare personnel. Accordingly, elaborating on the traditionally given importance of procreation in Islam and the growing recourse to a medicalized approach to infertility, the proposed analysis discusses Muslim patients' engagement with the lexicon of *ḥayā'*.[10]

Naturally, the concept of female modesty appears to be extensively stressed in customs and traditions, but it acquires specific characteristics when adopting the viewpoint of Islamic provisions and Muslim cultures. Furthermore, the broader articulation of *ḥayā'* also encompasses an additional interpretation specifically impacting on masculinity and family honor, as elucidated in the following three subsections.

It should be stressed, in effect, that this concept is "an essential constituent" in the life of every believer, and therefore, it cannot be confined to the female universe only; rather it can be defined as "a wide-ranging modesty and decency, based mainly on the *abstention of sight* and not only *from sight*, and also on the reticence of speech, corresponding to a respect for oneself and for one's neighbour."[11] And this very concept of *ḥayā'*—being strongly interconnected with the idea of privacy—can explain undisclosed family planning aimed at protecting prospective parents' extended kindred as well as their (possibly, still unborn) offspring, as the paper intends to clarify. In real terms, in the pursuit of "Islamic modesty," Muslim patients' conducts disclose the interplay among the idea of (anticipatory or hypothetical) shame and the fear for ethical, moral, or social disapprobation as reconstrued in a minority context.

The above-mentioned dynamics will be unpacked in the next sections. First of all, I address the process of medicalization of infertility and sterility in light of the importance of procreation in traditional Islam. Secondly, the three main areas I identified in which the theme of *ḥayā'* is applied, (re)interpreted, and self-understood by Muslim intended parents undergoing fertility biomedical procedures are explored in-depth by specifically addressing gender seclusion rules, family honor, masculinity, and social stigmatization.

Procreation and Medicalization of Infertility

Islam is conventionally categorized as a pro-natalist religion and ascribes great value and significance to human reproduction. Children are highly valued, and Islamically married adult Muslims are invited to procreate. The desire of parenthood is described as an innate component of human nature in some analyses of contemporary Islamic bioethics. By way of illustration, it has been highlighted that the wish for offspring plays a decisive role in Islam, a religion that "gives strong and unequivocal emphasis to high fertility."[12] Scholars have indeed broadly underlined the pro-natalist attitude of Islamic and Muslim law.[13]

In point of fact, procreation is regarded as an act of worship.[14] When adopting a spiritual viewpoint, pregnancy is compared to the fullness of spirit Muslims acquire during the pilgrimage to the holy city of Mecca or when they fast during the ninth month of the Islamic lunar calendar (Ramadan). Embracing a more pragmatic viewpoint, procreation is related to two main factors. First of all, Islam encourages the growth of an "Islamic multitude"[15] and the numerical increase of the worldwide Muslim population (*umma*). Secondly, procreation is strongly intertwined with the issue of care within the extended kindred networks; to put it differently, bearing children is important since, once adults, they will be responsible for taking care of their elderly parents.[16]

When looking at classical sources, the Qur'an exhorts Muslims to produce offspring, and the shari'a favors high birth-rates among Muslim married partners.[17] Accordingly, birth control is usually prohibited or highly limited by some Islamic scholars. By way of illustration, a resolution issued by the Islamic Fiqh Council designates this practice as being contrary to human nature and violating the provisions of the Qur'an and sunna.[18] The European Council for Fatwa and Research, however, permits some methods of contraception provided reproduction is only temporarily prevented.[19] It should also be mentioned that, differently from other religious denominations, procreation is not the sole and the highest purpose of marriage in Islam;[20] nonetheless, childbearing is constantly described as a natural act and frequently perceived as a sort of "religious duty" by European Muslim communities.[21]

In real terms, statistics confirm that Muslims are, and are projected to be, the world's fastest-growing major religious group in the decades ahead.[22] Muslim parents living in European environments may however adjust the above-described sort of "shari'a based natural procreative imperative" to their daily needs, and in actual fact, the ideal family size is decreasing among Muslim households, in line with the European trend. Infertility and sterility are nonetheless perceived as critically problematic matters, and exceptionally contentious issues arise when adopting Islamic perspectives. Accordingly, some fertility treatments have been gradually included in the list of Islamically permitted alternative routes to parenting also in the Muslim world,[23] and medically assisted procreation is regularly resorted to by Muslim intended parents.

Traditional Islamic sources such as the Qur'an and the sunna are therefore relied upon by Muslim jurists (*fuqahā'*) operating in Islamic bioethics bodies and by the so-called Islamic fatwa institutes.[24] Since the 1970s, these Islamic authorities have been actively issuing deliberations, guidelines, and recommendations mostly on the (non) permissibility of the usage of biomedical technologies at the beginning and the end of life (e.g., abortion, medically assisted reproduction and procreation, organ donation and transplant) following a "casuist pattern."[25] With regard to methodology, the Islamic scholars tend to rely upon traditional *fiqh* concepts to justify the usage of medically assisted procreative and reproductive techniques.[26] As a result, homologous treatments among Islamically married partners are permitted; the intervention of third parties (in terms of gametes, embryos, or surrogate mothers) in conceiving a child is instead problematic for some Muslim denominations.[27]

The medicalization of infertility or sterility has thus fostered a process of interpretation of shari'a in searching for Islamically compliant solutions to Muslim couples' procreative problems. As a result, old provisions are construed in a new light by (some) Islamic scholars and Muslim intended parents.[28] When specifically investigating the manners in which Muslims are coping with involuntary childlessness, the idea of *ḥayā'* appears to be contextualized, reinterpreted, and, sometimes, even transformed. Muslim prospective parents willing to undergo medically assisted procreative procedures are indeed autonomously and resourcefully interpreting shariʿa-compliant provisions in order to embrace their—as well as their extended families'—desire for offspring, possibly within the boundaries of appropriate Islamic behavior.

The idea of parenthood appears therefore to be molded by the prospective fathers' and mothers' religious conceptions and cultural belonging; however, in Muslim-minority contexts, a balance between individual self-determination and socially recognized status is constantly searched for. As further clarified in the following paragraphs, a fluid scenario emerges beyond stereotypes and misconceptions. On the one hand, modesty and gender seclusion rules can affect doctor–patient relationships; on the other hand, traditional Islamic provisions can be creatively enacted or interpreted by Muslim intended parents.

In particular, the interplay of two main attitudes—stigmatization and medicalization—sheds light on concurrent dynamics. The stigmatization of sterility or infertility may urge Muslims to resort to biomedical procreative and reproductive techniques in order to avoid recurring to traditional Islamic remedies for involuntary childlessness, such as polygynous unions or marital dissolutions—namely, the divorce of the (supposedly or gender-selectively) infertile wife. The medicalization of sterility can imply the creation of halal multi-parent families, where the involvement of third parties (such as surrogate mothers, or donors of female or male gametes) can be Islamically supported and socially legitimized. In other case scenarios, on the opposite end of the spectrum, the recourse to medically assisted procedures can be condemned with shame by Muslim parents.

Muslim couples' power dynamics are also affected by masculinity, honor, and shame, particularly in migratory contexts. The spatial division (internal versus external) concretizes the social perception of gender relationships in Islam, and a broad understanding of "the Islamic veil" defines its boundaries also in clinic environments and medical matters. The following sections explore three main areas I identified in which the theme of *ḥayāʾ* is applied, (re)interpreted, and self-understood by Muslim intended parents undergoing medical treatments. In reality, gender seclusion rules, family honor, masculinity, and social stigmatization interact and become markers of lived *ḥayāʾ* in Western environments.

Al-ḥayāʾ and Gender Seclusion

At the crossroads between Western and Islamic biomedical ethics, a number of (potentially) problematic aspects emerge. In particular, when specifically addressing shariʿa-compliant medical treatments, one of the most pressing issues is the protection of female modesty during medical examination. In fact, strict rules of conduct to be adopted with respect to the gender of healthcare professionals involved in medical examination of Muslim patients have been raised within the Muslim world by Islamic bodies. By way of illustration, the Islamic Fiqh Academy stated that "as a general rule, if a female specialist doctor is available, then she should be one to examine the female patient. In the absence of such a specialist, the patient may be examined by a trustworthy non-Muslim female doctor, if not then by a Muslim male doctor, and if not, then by a non-Muslim male doctor."[29]

The quoted resolution encapsulates the hierarchy of doctors' choice by a Muslim patient to avoid personal and familial *ḥayāʾ*. Ideally, a Muslim woman should be treated by a shariʿa-trained Muslim female health care professional. In case this is not a feasible option—particularly, in migratory or minority contexts—then exceptions can be made in an orderly manner. These requirements are deemed necessary to preserve the patient's modesty and honor during medical examinations. There are two main issues at stake: abiding by shariʿa-compliant gender proximity rules and also being conversant with Islamic principles.

In actual terms, Islamic clerics require Muslim physicians to be conversant with Islamic law "related to health, disease, and treatment."[30] Accordingly, in Muslim majority countries, the curricula of medical sciences should thus encompass "an orientation to the Sharia and Law provisions for their rights, duties, competence and responsibilities in regard to the practice of the health professions."[31] In a Western minority context, ideally, physicians and nurses should similarly be well versed in dealing with multicultural and multireligious scenarios in order to avoid problematic issues specifically linked to different perceptions of human bodies and their boundaries.[32]

An additional requirement to be implemented in daily medical practice aimed at avoiding *ḥayāʿ* concerns the manner in which medical examinations are to be performed. It has indeed been stressed that

> ... the doctor should see only the minimum necessary of the patient's body and to the extent possible divert his look, and that the doctor's treatment of the female patient should be in the presence of a *maḥram* (blood relation and certain other persons who, in the eyes of *sharīʿah* are ineligible for marriages with the patient, such as brother and uncle ...) or a husband or a trusted woman, to avoid "*khalwa*" (two persons of opposite sex being together in a remote place).[33]

And, when specifically looking at the recommendations of the Seminar on Human Reproduction in Islam, it is declared that "it is lawful for a medical member of one sex to look at the *ʿawra*[34] of a member of the other sex for purposes of medical examination, treatment, and medical education. Exposition, however, should be limited to what the need calls for."[35]

The medical examination should not last longer than what is strictly necessary and should involve exclusively relevant bodily parts, including intimate body parts (*'awra*). Exclusively necessary medical examinations are therefore to be performed on patients and within the gender seclusion boundaries precisely drawn by Islamic provisions. In order to avoid (supposed) intimacy with the opposite gender, it is also recommended that the female patient, who is to be examined by a male doctor, has to be accompanied by another woman, or her husband, or a person who is Islamically prevented from marrying the patient (*maḥārim*).[36] The pinpointed key concepts appear to be stressed specifically to protect both the physicians' and the patients'—as well as their families'—reputation and honor. Avoiding *zināʾ*, and even just the anticipatory shame linked to the possibility of unlawful sexual intercourse, is thus the foremost goal.

When embracing this viewpoint, two possible articulations of the idea of *ḥayā'* can be identified. First, being familiar with shariʿa, Muslim physicians are to be preferred to non-Muslim ones. The traditional (and sometimes conservative) division between the public and private sphere—which are the domain of men and women, respectively—therefore can be pushed forward to include the public space when a Muslim physician enters into it.[37] *Ḥayā'* is preserved because, although being a male, the Muslim healthcare professional is expected not to violate the Islamic etiquette, being familiar with the shariʿa-compliant understanding of modesty, honor, and shame. Secondly, building upon Islamic rules preserving Muslim women's modesty and prohibiting the exposure of (intimate) bodily parts to marriageable partners, female healthcare practitioners are to be favored by Muslim patients.

Local Islamic scholars corroborate the principles described above aimed at avoiding an infringement of the parties' honor and shame. The ethnographic investigations I conducted, in effect, unveiled that gender proximity norms are to be carefully implemented to the extent that the enactment of *ḥayā'* remains a feasible option.[38] This implies that, although a Muslim female doctor is preferable, exceptions can be made, particularly in clinical emergencies. Furthermore, Muslim patients are not to be singled out and problematized: the needs they voice are sometimes not religious-specific but ethnocultural. In contemporary postmodern times, healthcare professionals can therefore be asked to manage a broader concept of medical ethics encompassing a diverse understanding of the human body and its boundaries, thus leading to different articulations of the idea of modesty and decency.

Facing present contingencies, however, a compromise is to be found between practical everyday needs and the ideal implementation of shariʿa. In particular, the need to deal with the insufficient number of (Muslim) female medical doctors was voiced by local religious figures and also accepted by Muslim patients. Furthermore, Muslims tend not to expect clinicians and nurses to be conversant in Islamic law, including gender dynamics and modesty seclusion roles.[39]

Al-ḥayā', Family Honor, and Masculinity

An additional interesting enactment of the principle of *ḥayā'* can be singled out when examining the strategies Muslim prospective parents referred to fertility clinics developed to cope with Islamic principles in non-Muslim majority environments. For practical reasons,[40] indeed, women might be attending medical appointments alone, with their husbands accompanying and assisting them only on a few occasions during the fertility procedures. And this can happen even if there is the possibility that the clinical tests and examinations can eventually be performed by non-Muslim male doctors.

In order to cope with potential controversial issues related to family honor and masculinity in the patient–doctor relationships, *ad hoc* strategies have been specifically developed by Muslim intended mothers. The first solution consists in requiring the intervention of a so-called cultural mediator.[41] The majority of cultural mediators for Arab-speaking patients available in public hospitals tend to be women and, rather frequently, Muslim women or Muslim men. As a result, seclusion with the opposite gender can be avoided by the intervention of a trusted (most possibly Muslim female) third party. In order to be able to rely upon this service, however, the patient needs to declare not to be fluent in the Italian language and not to be familiar with the environment, thus being a recently settled migrant.

Empirical evidence disclosed that, in a consistent number of cases, language and cultural barriers do exist. Accordingly, the presence of a person bridging the linguistic and cultural gap is of pivotal importance for the clinical examination and for the medical treatments to be successful.[42] In other situations, however, this intervention was relied upon as an *escamotage* to avoid potential violation of Islamic provisions. A cultural mediator—most frequently a (Muslim) Arab-speaking woman—was thus (involuntarily) playing the role of the third party, avoiding Islamically inappropriate vicinity and intimacy between a Muslim female patient and a male doctor. In the examined scenario, a service provided by the Italian public healthcare system is thus indirectly catering for a specific need of Muslim patients—coping with *ḥayāʾ*—without this effect being specifically verbalized or known to the non-Muslim medical personnel.

The second way in which the lexicon of modesty and honor is construed by Muslim women consists in leaving the prominent role to their husbands during the fertility process. Whereas this attitude was perceived by healthcare professionals as a power imbalance between the Muslim couple, an in-depth analysis revealed that, quite often, the embraced rules of conducts were specifically enacted by Muslim women to protect both the male honor and their decency. To put it differently, the adopted behavior was a way to interpret and construe *ḥayāʾ* in minority contexts.

In real terms, when observing doctor–patient relations in hospitals and clinics, it appears that healthcare personnel usually adopt what can be termed a "gender-conscious perspective," independently from the religious and ethnocultural belongings of the patients. The reasons supporting a mentioned frame of mind is that female patients are more affected by medically assisted procreative procedures, and a number of studies indicate that, when compared to intended fathers, prospective mothers' lives are more disrupted by infertility and sterility issues.[43] Accordingly, clinic staff tend to pay specific attention to prospective mothers undergoing fertility treatments, and when interviewed about Muslims, two main behavioral aspects were identified and reported.[44]

The first one was related to the body language of the partners and their usage of space in the hospital premises. A consistent number of fertility clinic personnel declared that the majority of Muslim women tended to enter the clinic facilities following their husbands and staying behind them. While avoiding eye contact with male doctors, Muslim female patients usually left the best seat in front of the member of the clinic personnel to their husbands. Secondly, medical doctors and administrative staff reported that Muslim men showed a tendency to monopolize the conversation, and to them, this behavior was specifically aimed at manifesting what healthcare providers perceived as assertiveness and a dominant family role.[45] Ethnographic observations, while confirming the described gender-based dynamics in the couple accessing the fertility centers and its impact on doctor–patient relations, also shed light on the actual reasons behind certain conducts enacted by Muslim patients.

If in some cases this attitude was justified by the lack of linguistic skills and conversational fluency in the local language by recently (or temporarily) settled Muslim women, in other situations this behavior concealed different issues at stake. When the couple of prospective parents is attending a medical appointment together, Muslim women can in fact decide to abide by customary norms; they thus manifest their respect and submission by choosing not to talk to the physician and leaving the leading role to their husbands. Scholarship has indeed stressed that, particularly during fertility treatments, Muslim women's submission and silent cooperation can also be driven by "the sense of belonging and identity."[46] Women are indeed considered as "the repositories" of patriarchal honor: their (sexual) behavior, their modesty, and veiling indeed highly impact on the reputation of the families (father's and husband's kindred) they belong to.[47] To others, however, the concept of male authority as a legal postulate in Muslim legal tradition is traditionally linked to a patriarchal reading of the sacred texts, specifically in relation to *wilāya* (guardianship) and *qiwāma* (authority). A discursive evolution is thus needed to achieve an egalitarian construction of gender roles and rights in Muslim-minority and -majority contexts.[48] In the examined situations, however, *ḥayāʾ* was also articulated as female patients' reticence of speech.

An additional key factor is to be mentioned: socially, infertility is often conflated with impotency. As a consequence, in order to avoid social stigmatization and de-masculinization of Muslim prospective fathers undergoing fertility treatments, Muslim women might decide to emphasize their modesty and shyness by withdrawing from a leading position when attending medical appointments and during the medically assisted process. Islamic and Muslim principles[49] as well can foster this articulation of *ḥayāʾ*. In actual facts, Inhorn highlights that, when embracing a cultural perspective, Muslim wives are taught to "bear the burden of infertility," upholding their husband's masculinity and sharing their "sterility secret."[50] Infertility and sterility are indeed traditionally linked to women in Islam.[51]

Al-ḥayāʾ and Social Stigmatization

In the fertility field, *ḥayāʾ* can also be interpreted and enacted in such a way that it prevents the stigmatization of all the involved family members—father, mother, and offspring. In addition to the above-described necessity to avoid the de-masculinization of Muslim prospective fathers undergoing fertility treatments, the need to protect the family secret was often voiced among Muslim partners undergoing biotechnological reproductive and procreative procedures. In spite of the fact that Islam supports medically assisted reproduction, it is only rarely that Muslim patients were not embarrassed in disclosing to have opted for medicalization of infertility or sterility.[52] A number of reasons linked to the ideas of modesty and honor support this interpretation, as I clarify in the next paragraphs.

First of all, the need not to reveal the manner in which the (test tube) child was conceived was primarily aimed at protecting the child's lineage (*nasab*). Rumors can indeed spread about the offspring not being actually fathered or mothered by the Muslim parents undergoing the treatments. And this can happen within local communities as well as extended families living abroad. In real terms, some couples can actually undergo heterologous fertility procedures, which are deemed not being compliant with Islamic provisions by Sunni and some Shiʿi interpretations. In other cases, the treatment undergone is regarded as being shariʿa compliant,[53] but the fear of possible social disapprobation and reprehension—even if only hypothetical—impedes the disclosure of this family secret.

Revealing to the spouses' relatives and extended families that the couple's desire for parenthood was eventually satisfied by relying upon fertility techniques can indeed impact not only the offspring, but the parents as well. Fathers might perceive emasculating social attitudes in case the clinical procedure leads to the intervention of a third party (such as a sperm donor) or to the necessity for the couple to adopt an embryo created with the gametes belonging to another couple. Spreading rumors about the woman's infertility can potentially lead to pressure from the extended family on the husband to divorce his (supposedly) sterile wife, jeopardizing the honor of the wife's family and also impacting on the marriageability of other kindred girls.

The control (potentially) exerted by relatives, in addition to the social stigma and ostracism possibly attached to infertile partners and children, explains this narrative of *ḥayāʾ*. In real terms, the interviewed patients undergoing fertility treatments in clinics asserted their need for privacy primarily to protect themselves from kindred pressure and the extended family's interference in the couple's life plan. Muslim women, in particular, repeatedly expressed their desire to avoid family tensions and threats to their matrimonial life. The process of migrant families' nuclearization,[54] alongside a combination of social habits and religious customs, thus prevents open discussion of infertility issues and medically assisted practices among Muslim patients and their familial and social circles.

Conclusions

In exploring Islamic legal thought, Katz suggested the English gloss of *ḥayāʾ* as "shame," "modesty," "bashfulness," and "inhibition." The present chapter took this as the starting point in the definition of *ḥayāʾ* in order to identify the social understanding and enactment of this concept among prospective Muslim parents undergoing medically assisted fertility procedures. More specifically, the unveiled scenario disclosed diverse articulations of the idea of modesty—and its declination as decency, honor, and shame—among Muslim prospective fathers and mothers undergoing fertility treatments.

First of all, patient–doctor relations unveiled the aversion to performing inappropriate actions and enacting unsuitable behaviors, as highlighted by Islamic bodies and Muslim religious authorities. Gender seclusion roles are thus to be followed, while avoiding unnecessary vicinity and intimacy between Muslim female patients and non-Muslim male healthcare professionals. On the one hand, hospitals and clinics can accommodate ethnocultural and religious sensitivities by preponderantly offering the assistance of female clinicians and nurses to Muslim female patients. On the other hand, Muslims can reconfigure and adjust the concept of modesty to non-Muslim majority environments. In this way, a happy medium between patients' religious and ethnocultural necessities and legally permitted medical protocols is achieved by relying upon flexible approaches within the legal threshold of reasonableness and (shariʿa-compliant) medical ethics.[55]

Remarkably, the narrative of *ḥayāʾ* as the importance of avoiding excessive "physical" or "social" self-display is also linked to the honor of all human beings involved in the process. With regard to "the physical component," the honor of the woman, of her husband, and of her family of origin are protected by the fact that the healthcare personnel examine only limited bodily parts and preferably do so in the presence of another person. This approach, specifically aimed at avoiding potential proximity between opposite sexes, safeguards the physician's reputation in addition to the Muslim patient's. In real terms, Islam confers what has been described as the "right to decency" to women in order for their dignity not to be undermined; in effect, the Qurʾan identifies women's garments that have a character of protection of the common sense of modesty.[56] When this protective "veil" is to be removed—for instance, because of medical examinations—the concept of *ḥayāʾ* intervenes to avoid (potential) illegitimate sexual intercourse (*zinā*), thus preventing the Muslim from committing wrong actions and sins.[57]

As per "the concept of social self-display," this specifically regards the Muslim couple undergoing a fertility procedure. Social ostracism and stigmatization are indeed to be avoided by modestly protecting the "family secret"—namely, the fertility procedure undergone. Not disclosing the manner in which the offspring was actually conceived, in effect, safeguards the child's lineage, the father's masculinity, and the mother's honor. Rumors concerning the possible illegitimacy of the child, the father's impotence, or the mother's sterility are therefore prevented. The fear of social and moral disapprobation is thus dealt with and eventually precluded. An extended understanding of *ḥayāʾ*, indeed, implies that disapprobation or disgrace can be exercised by some audiences, at least a hypothetical one.

Social constraints and emotional discomfiture can also be linked to masculinity and male honor. As it happens, Muslim prospective mothers presenting at fertility clinics developed a number of strategies to abide by the Islamic principle of *ḥayāʾ* when living in non-Muslim majority environments. As a first solution, Muslim female patients can ask for the intervention of a cultural mediator, therefore enacting a fresh articulation of the Islamic gender seclusion rule. As a second strategy, Muslim women can express the lexicon of modesty by leaving the leading role to their husbands during the medically assisted procedures. This attitude confirms the traditional perception according to which Muslim women live in a private space as opposed to the public one, which sees a predominance of Muslim men and is a space dedicated to them. In actual fact, in Muslim societies, Islamic jurists "gendered the space" in order to maintain some boundaries between men and women. As a result, traditionally, the interaction between opposite genders is strongly regulated by the clear division between public and private spheres, and this division primarily aims at avoiding the family's shame while, at the same time, protecting Muslims' honor and decency. In real life, however, more complex dynamics might affect the male–female dichotomy.[58]

Ḥayā' is to be manifested not only toward others but also toward themselves and, primarily, before Allah.[59] Muslim prospective parents shall therefore refrain from following the path of non-Islamically permitted biomedical fertility treatments. In real terms, empirical investigations revealed that Sunni Muslim prospective parents can *de facto* resort to heterologous fertility treatments, particularly when settled on European soil. In this case, the newly created family is regarded as being halal on the grounds that some Islamic religious denominations (e.g., some Shiʿi clerics) partly permit the involvement of third parties in the couple's procreative process, and the involved parties' *ḥayā'* is protected by not disclosing this family secret. In the painted scenario, what can be described as a transposed concept of the term *ḥayā'* is thus subjected to a discursive evolution in its understanding and implementation.

Notes

1. This sentence seems to echo Abdullahi Ahmed An-Na'im, "Global citizenship and Human Rights: From Muslims in Europe to European Muslims," in *Religious Pluralism and Human Rights in Europe: Where to Draw the Line?*, edited by M. L. P. "Titia" Loenen, and Jenny E. Goldschmidt (Antwerpen: Intersentia, 2007), 13–55. In actual terms, whereas some literature used to investigate the phenomenon of "Islam in Europe"—see *inter alia*, Felice Dassetto, *L'Islam in Europa* (Torino: EFGA, 1994); Silvio Ferrari (ed.) *L'Islam in Europa* (Bologna: Il Mulino, 1996); Jack Goody, *Islam in Europe* (Cambridge: Polity Press, 2004); Aziz Al-Azmeh and Effie Fokas (eds.), *Islam in Europe: Diversity, Identity and Influence* (Cambridge: Cambridge University Press, 2007). Attention was gradually paid also to the "Euro-Islam," for example, Nezar Al-Sayyad and Manuel Castells (eds.) *Muslim in Europe or Euro-Islam* (Oxford: Lexington Books, 2002)—or the (new) "European Islam," for example, Felice Dassetto "The New European Islam," in *Islam and European legal systems*, edited by Silvio Ferrari, and Antony Bradney (Aldershot: Ashgate Publishing, 2000), 31–45—namely the shariʿa practiced and lived by Muslim minorities settled on European soil, for example, Talal Asad, *Formations of the Secular* (Stanford, CA: Stanford University Press, 2003), 159–180. Dassetto and Nielsen, for instance, suggested one of the most well-known classifications of the typologies of European Islam; see Felice Dassetto and Jørgen Nielsen, "Conclusions," in *Muslims in the Enlarged Europe. Religion and Society*, edited by Brigitte Maréchal, Stefano Allievi, Felice Dassetto, and Jørgen Nielsen (Leiden: Brill, 2003), 539–42. For an introduction on the presence of Muslims in Europe, see for instance Jørgen S. Nielsen, *Towards a European Islam* (London: Macmillan Press, 1999), 1–10 and 79–117.
2. An analysis of statistical data can be found in Egdūnas Račius, *Islam in Post-communist Eastern Europe* (Leiden: Brill, 2020), 34–73, in addition to Pew Research Center, *The Future of the Global Muslim Population. Projections for 2010–2030* (Washington, DC: PRC, 2011); Pew Research Center, *The Future of the Global Muslim Population. Projections for 2010–2050* (Washington, DC: PRC, 2015); Pew Research Center, *The Changing Global Religious Landscape* (Washington, DC: PRC, 2017).
3. Definitions of multiple procedures related to medically assisted reproductive technologies and medically assisted procreative technologies—for example, assisted reproductive technology (ART) and medically assisted reproduction (MAR)—can

be found in Fernando Zegers-Hochschild, et al. "International Committee for Monitoring Assisted Reproductive Technology (ICMART) and the World Health Organization (WHO) Revised Glossary of ART terminology," *Fertility and Sterility* 92, no. 5 (November 2009a), 1520–4; Fernando Zegers-Hochschild et al. "International Committee for Monitoring Assisted Reproductive Technology (ICMART) and the World Health Organization (WHO) revised glossary of ART terminology," *Human Reproduction* 24, no. 11 (2009b), 2683–7; Fernando Zegers-Hochschild et al. "The International Glossary on Infertility and Fertility Care," *Human Reproduction* 32, no. 9 (September 2017), 1786–1801.

4. See for instance The European IVF-monitoring Consortium (EIM) for the European Society of Human Reproduction and Embryology (ESHRE), C. Wyns, C. Bergh, C. Calhaz-Jorge, Ch. De Geyter, M. S. Kupka, T. Motrenko, I. Rugescu, J. Smeenk, A. Tandler-Schneider, S. Vidakovic and V. Goossens, "ART in Europe, 2016: results generated from European registries by ESHRE," *Human Reproduction Open*, 2020, no. 3 (2020).
5. For further details, see Federica Sona, *New Parenthood and Childhood Patterns: Principles and Praxes in Muslim Realities*. Series Fundamental Rights Laboratory No. 7 (Bologna: Il Mulino, 2019). On statistics, see Centro Studi e Ricerche IDOS, *Dossier Statistico Immigrazione* 2020 (Roma: IDOS, 2021). On the nature and significance of ethnographic study of Muslims, see *inter alia* Seán M. McLoughlin, "Islam(s) in Context: Orientalism and the Anthropology of Muslim Societies and Cultures," *Journal of Beliefs & Values* 28, no. 3 (2007), 273–96.
6. See Arthur Kleinman, Leon Eisenberg, and Bryron Good, "Culture, Illness, and Care: Clinical Lessons from Anthropologic and Cross-Cultural Research," *Annals of Internal Medicine*, Feb., 88, no. 2 (1978), 251–8.
7. For further details, see Arthur Kleinman, *Patients and Healers in the Context of Culture: An Exploration of the Borderland between Anthropology, Medicine, and Psychiatry* (Berkeley: University of California Press, 1980).
8. See *inter alia* Marcia C. Inhorn, *The New Arab Man: Emergent Masculinities, Technologies, and Islam in the Middle East* (Princeton, NJ: Princeton University Press, 2012); Alfredo M. Rabello, Daniela Milani, and Dariusch Atighetchi, *Intorno alla vita che nasce: Diritto ebraico, canonico e islamico a onfront* (Torino: Giappichelli, 2013); and M. Hemayatkhah et al., "A Review of Ethical Issues Involved in Fertility Treatments in Different Religious Frameworks: Cases in Judaism, Christianity, and Islam," *Journal of Jahrom University of Medical Sciences*, 11 (2014), 65ff.
9. The present chapter is based on empirical qualitative and quantitative data—for example, group discussions, semi-structured interviews, fieldwork (non)participant observations, and document examination—which were conducted in Italy in three stages in the years 2016 and 2017. The contacted research subjects included: patients of fertility clinics, namely prospective (Muslim) mothers and fathers; Islamic figures active at local, national, and international levels; leaders of Islamic and Muslim associations active at local and national levels; administrative staff of medical centers and clinics offering fertility treatments; clinic staff of medical centers and clinics offering fertility treatments; and local cultural mediators operating in the medical field. Thirty Muslim patients—whose countries of origin were Morocco, Egypt, Tunisia, Bangladesh, and Pakistan—were interviewed at least one time. As per quantitative data, examining the list of couples willing to undergo fertility procedures in a MAR center established in a public hospital in Turin, from January 2009 to March 2017, a total of 8,014 patients were identified and studied. For further details on the

employed methodology and research methods as well as the informants' details, see Sona, *New Parenthood and Childhood Patterns*, 31–40.

10. With regard to the vocabulary used by the research informants when elaborating on the concept of *ḥayā*ʾ, some clarifications are needed. Whereas clinic and administrative staff members relied upon Italian language, Islamic scholars mostly employed the *fuṣḥā* classical Arabic expression *al-ḥayā*ʾ. Muslim patients from South Asian countries would mostly speak in English language, sometimes clarifying words related to Islamic principles recurring to Modern Standard Arabic. Patients from North African countries would follow a similar pattern in relying upon two languages for extra clarity; the language combinations ranged from classical Arabic to Italian, or from local dialects to French language. Cultural mediators for Arabic-speaking patients were originally from Middle Eastern or North African Muslim majority countries; accordingly, although sometimes fluent with local dialects, they tended to use the Italian language and to clarify some expression in Modern Standard Arabic (*fuṣḥā al-ʿaṣr*); only when specifically relevant, or when acting as interpreter between the patients and the clinicians, they would use local dialects. In all the examples and cases reported in the text, the research informants used a combination of the words "shame," "shyness," "modesty," "honor" in a European language (English, French, or Italian) and in Arabic language/dialect (MSA, *fuṣḥā* or mostly *dārija*). Accordingly, the analysis offered by the present chapter identifies and categorizes the different understanding and (re)interpretation of the broad concept of *al-ḥayā*' by Muslim prospective parents resorting to Italian fertility clinics.
11. See Ida Zilio-Grandi, "Modestia, pudicizia e riserbo: la virtù islamica detta ḥayā," *Philologia Hispalensis* 31, no. 2 (2018), 169–83.
12. M. A. Al-Bar and H. Chamsi-Pasha, *Contemporary Bioethics Islamic Perspective* (Dordrecht: Springer, 2015), 173–4.
13. See for instance Abdelaziz Sachedina, *Islamic Biomedical Ethics: Principles and Application* (Oxford: Oxford University Press, 2009), who describes procreation as a divinely ordained obligation, a sort of moral imperative for pious married Muslims.
14. Q. 4:4 and 16:72.
15. See *inter alia* Basim F. Musallam, *Sex and Society in Islam: Birth Control before the Nineteenth Century* (Cambridge: Cambridge University Press, 1986); Marcia C. Inhorn, *Quest for Conception: Gender, Infertility and Egyptian Medical Traditions* (Philadelphia: University of Pennsylvania Press, 1994).
16. The interviewed informants quoted the Qurʾan (17:32; 24:2, 4–5) to express this priority and, embracing a more pragmatic viewpoint, they explained that procreation is also related to the issue of care within the extended family network. See Sona, *New Parenthood and Childhood Patterns*, 75–7.
17. Q. 16:72; 18:46; and 25:74.
18. Resolution 23–30 Rabīʿ al-ʾĀkhir 1400 AH, 1/III.
19. *Fatwā* 10/3, X Ord. Session, Dublin, Dhul al-Qiʿdah 1423 AH 19–26.
20. As clarified by Q. 2:187; 7:189; 30:21.
21. For further details, see Sona, *New Parenthood and Childhood Patterns*, 74–7, and 129–30.
22. Pew Research Center, *The Changing Global Religious Landscape*, 2017.
23. See, for instance, Gamal I. Serour, Mohamed A. Aboul-Ghar, and Ragaa T. Mansour, "Infertility: A Health Problem in the Muslim World," *Population Sciences* 10 (1991), 41–58; Gamal I. Serour, Mohamed A. Aboul-Ghar, and Ragaa T. Mansour, "Bioethics in Medically Assisted Conception in the Muslim World," *Journal of Assisted*

Reproduction and Genetics 12, no. 9 (1995), 559–65; Dariusch Atighetchi, *Islamic Bioethics: Problems and Perspectives* (Dordrecht: Springer, 2007).

24. These bodies are, for instance, the Islamic Fiqh Academies of Mecca and Jeddah, and the Islamic Organization for Medical Sciences.
25. In the present section and further in the text, references to some highly relevant recommendations, resolutions, or *fatāwā*—for example, those issued by the Islamic Fiqh Academy, the Islamic Fiqh Council, the European Council for Fatwa and Research—are reported and analyzed. For a historical summary on the development if Islamic bioethics, see inter alia Thomas Eich, "Bioethics," in *Encyclopaedia of Islam*, III, edited by Kate Fleet, Gudrun Krämer, Denis Matringe, John Nawas, and Everett Rowson (Leiden: Brill, 2009), consulted online on January 22, 2021, at http://dx.doi.org/10.1163/1573-3912_ei3_COM_23420.
26. For instance, Mahmoud refers to "equitable solution," whereas Houot mentions "necessity" and "public interest." See, respectively, Farouk Mahmoud, "Controversies in Islamic evaluation of assisted reproductive technologies," in *Islam and Assisted Reproductive Technologies: Sunni and Shia Perspectives*, edited by Marcia C. Inhorn and Soraya Tremayne (New York: Berghahn, 2012), 70–97; Sandra Houot, "Des usages éthiques du droit islamique: une réponse aux enjeux posés par la reproduction médicalement assistée," *Droit et cultures* 59 (2010), 331–55; Sandra Houot, "Islamic Jurisprudence (*fiqh*) and Assisted Reproduction: Establishing limits to Avoid Social Disorders," in *Islam and Assisted Reproductive Technologies: Sunni and Shia Perspectives*, edited by Marcia C. Inhorn and Soraya Tremayne (New York: Berghahn, 2012), 53–69.
27. For an introduction, see *inter alia* Marcia C. Inhorn, "Fatwas and ARTs: IVF and gamete donation in Sunni v. Shi'a Islam," *Journal of Gender, Race & Justice* 9, no. 2 (2005), 291–318; Marcia C. Inhorn, "Making Muslim Babies: IVF and Gamete Donation in Sunni Versus Shi'a Islam," *Culture, Medicine and Psychiatry* 30, no. 4 (2006a), 427–50; Cathy Harrison, "Who Is Your Mother? Who Is Your Father? Assisted Reproductive Technologies in the Light of Sunni and Shi'a Law," *Journal of Shi'a Islamic Studies* 7, no. 1 (2014), 23–37; Zeynep B. Gürtin, Marcia C. Inhorn, and Soraya Tremayne, "Islam and Assisted Reproduction in the Middle East: Comparing the Sunni Arab World, Shia Iran and Secular Turkey," in *The changing world religion map*, edited by Stanley D. Brunn (Dordrecht: Springer, 2015), 3137–53; Marcia C. Inhorn and Soraya Tremayne (eds.), *Islam and Assisted Reproductive Technologies: Sunni and Shia Perspectives* (New York: Berghahn, 2012). By way of illustration, see the explanation of "artificial insemination" given by Rispler-Chaim on *Encyclopaedia of Islam*; namely Vardit Rispler-Chaim, "Artificial Insemination," in *Encyclopaedia of Islam*, III, edited by Kate Fleet, Gudrun Krämer, Denis Matringe, John Nawas, and Everett Rowson (Leiden: Brill, 2007), consulted online on January 22, 2021, at http://dx.doi.org.ezproxy.eth.mpg.de/10.1163/1573-3912_ei3_SIM_0227.
28. For instance, the surrogate mother can be regarded as the baby's wet-nurse, therefore the Islamically compliant milk-bond can be created between the offspring and the surrogate mother.
29. Resolution No. 81/12/8, Fiqh Academy. For a comment, see also Dariusch Atighetchi, "Human Rights and Bioethics, an Islamic Overview," in *Religious Perspectives on Human Vulnerability in Bioethics*, edited by Joseph Tham, Alberto Garcia, and Gonzalo Miranda (Dordrecht: Springer, 2017), 237–8.
30. See Recommendation No. 8, Session chaired by Abd Al-Aziz Kamel, May 24, 1983 AD - 11 Sha'bān 1403 H.

31. Recommendations of the Third Symposium on "The Islamic Vision of Some Medical Practices," April 18–21, 1987.
32. As disclosed by ethnographic research, local Islamic clerics require physicians and nurses to be conversant with some principles of Islamic and Muslim law to protect Muslim patients' modesty and honor during medical examinations. For further details, see Sona, *New Parenthood and Childhood Patterns*, 113–17.
33. Resolution No. 81/12/8, as above.
34. The Arabic word *ʿawra* is used to indicate intimate body parts.
35. See, for instance, the Recommendation No. 8 as above.
36. On this see further section IV *Al-ḥayāʾ*, family honour and masculinity.
37. An analysis on the interaction between public and private spheres is beyond the scope of the present work. For a broad introduction, see Jürgen Habermas, Sara Lennox, and Frank Lennox, "The Public Sphere: An Encyclopaedia Article (1964)," *New German Critique*, no. 3 (1974), 49–55. On Islamic law, see *infra* note No. 58 and section IV *Al-ḥayāʾ*, family honour and masculinity.
38. See Sona, *New Parenthood and Childhood Patterns*, 113–17.
39. For further details and an analysis of field-collected data, see for instance Sona, *New Parenthood and Childhood Patterns*, 142–6.
40. For instance, because of work commitments or child care-related responsibility.
41. For a definition of (inter-)cultural mediation in theory and in practice, see Marta Castiglioni, *La mediazione linguistico-culturale: principi, strategie, esperienze* (Milano: Franco Angeli, 1997); Laura Gavioli, *La mediazione linguistico culturale: una prospettiva interazionista* (Perugia: Guerra, 2009); David Katan, "La mediazione linguistica interculturale: il mediatore culturale e le sue competenze," *Lingue e Linguaggi*, no. 16 (2015), 365–91. A comparative analysis across six European countries can be found in Simone Casadei and Massimiliano Franceschetti (eds.), *Il mediatore culturale in sei paesi europei. Italia, Francia, Germania, Grecia, Regno Unito e Spagna—ambiti di intervento, percorsi di accesso e competenze* (Roma: Isfol, 2009).
42. Sona, *New Parenthood and Childhood Patterns*, 129–75, 190–5, and 223–7.
43. See, for instance, Antonia Abbey, Frank M. Andrews, and L. Jill Halman, "Gender's Role in Responses to Infertility," *Psychology of Women Quarterly* 15, no. 2 (1991), 295–316; Katerina Lykeridou, Kleanthi Gourounti, Anna Deltsidou, Dimitrios Loutradis, and Grigorios Vaslamatzis, "The Impact of Infertility Diagnosis on Psychological Status of Women Undergoing Fertility Treatment," *Journal of Reproductive and Infant Psychology* 27, no. 3 (2009), 223–37. On the male and female diverse rights and responsibilities in medically assisted procedures, see Rosa M. Limiñana-Gras, "Health and Gender Perspective in Infertility," in *The Psychology of Gender and Health: Conceptual and Applied Global Concerns*, edited by M. Pilar Sánchez-López and Rosa M. Limiñana-Gras (Amsterdam: Elsevier, 2017), 364–400; Maeve Dooley, Tim Dineen, Kiran Sarma, and Aonghus Nolan, "The Psychological Impact of Infertility and Fertility Treatment on the Male Partner," *Human Fertility* 17, no. 3 (2014), 203–9.
44. For further details, see Sona, *New Parenthood and Childhood Patterns*, 129–46.
45. Muslim men, for instance, frequently gave only their own telephone numbers (instead of their wives') to the administrative staff in local fertility clinics. This happened despite the fact that it is usually women who need to communicate regularly with the fertility center when undergoing hormonal stimulation cycles. In several cases, the health care professionals tended to interpret this behavior of Muslim men as a way of gaining power and exercising control over their wives.

46. See Soraya Tremayne, "The 'Down Side' of Gamete Donation: Challenging 'Happy Family' Rhetoric in Iran," in *Islam and Assisted Reproductive Technologies: Sunni and Shia Perspectives*, edited by Marcia C. Inhorn and Soraya Tremayne (New York: Berghahn, 2012), 136.
47. As clarified by Duderija, Alak, and Hissong, sociospatial mechanisms such as gender segregation, veiling, and seclusion of women are thus aimed at managing the social, economic, and political consequences of female (sexual) behaviors. See Adis Duderija, Alina Isac Alak, and Kristin Hissong, "Chapter Three: The Logic of Patriarchal Honour and Its Manifestations in Muslim Contexts: Veiling, Female Genital Cutting, and Honor Based Violence," in *Islam and Gender. Major Issues and Debates*, edited by Adis Duderija, Alina Isac Alak, and Kristin Hissong (London: Routledge, 2020), 45. For further details, see also Eli Alshech, "Out of Sight and Therefore Out of Mind: Early Sunnī Islamic Modesty Regulations and the Creation of Spheres of Privacy," *Journal of Near Eastern Studies* 66, no. 4, October (2007), 267–90; Adis Duderija "The Custom (ʿurf) Based Assumptions Regarding Gender Roles and Norms in the Islamic Tradition," *Studies in Religion/Sciences Religieuses* 45, no. 44, July (2016), 581–99.
48. See *inter alia* Ziba Mir-Hosseini, Kari Vogt, Lena Larsen, and Christian Moe (eds.), *Gender and Equality in Muslim Law: Justice and Ethics in the Islamic Legal Tradition* (London: I.B. Tauris, 2013) and Ziba Mir-Hosseini, *Men in Charge? Rethinking Authority in Muslim Legal Tradition* (London: OneWorld, 2015). For further details on the role of women in the Arab world, see the seminal work of Fatima Mernissi, *Beyond the Veil: Male-female Dynamics in Modern Muslim Society* (Bloomington: Indiana University Press, 1987).
49. The adjectives Muslim and Islamic are often used as synonyms but, building upon the IV form of the Arabic root *s-l-m*, it becomes clear that this is not entirely correct. The adjective "*muslim*" indeed identifies the person professing *Islām*, whereas "*islāmī*" identifies anything related to *Islām*. Accordingly, when addressing specific normativities, "Islamic" is properly used when referring to Islamic sources, whereas the adjective "Muslim" identifies the rules endorsed by and enacted in Muslim majority countries and Muslim believers.
50. This is corroborated by the empirical investigations conducted by Inhorn. See Marcia C. Inhorn, "The Worms Are Weak: Male Infertility and Patriarchal Paradoxes in Egypt," *Men and Masculinities* 5, no. 3 (2003), 236–56; Inhorn, *The New Arab Man*.
51. See *inter alia* Aref Abu-Rabia, "Infertility and Surrogacy in Islamic Society: Socio-Cultural, Psychological, Ethical, and Religious Dilemmas," *The Open Psychology Journal* 6 (2013), 54–60.
52. For further analysis of field-collected data, see Sona, *New Parenthood and Childhood Patterns*, 157–9; 169–75; 179–84; 227–32.
53. For instance, an Islamically married couple is subjected to a homologous fertility procedure.
54. For further discussion on the fragmentation of family relations between extended families and migrant nuclear families, see Talcott Parsons and Robert Freed Bales, *Family Socialization and Interaction Process* (London: Routledge, 2001/1956).
55. Marion H. Katz, "Shame (*Ḥayāʾ*) as an Affective Disposition in Islamic Legal Thought," *Journal of Law, Religion and State* 3, no. 2 (2014), 139–69. For an in-depth study of this matter, see Federica Sona, "Reasonable Accommodation in Fertility Clinics: The Case of Muslim Patients," *Revista General de Derecho Público Comparado*, no. 28, December (2020), 1–25.

56. By way of illustration, see Q. 24:31 and 33:59.
57. A child born out of a shari'a-compliant wedlock is considered a *walad al-zinā*. See for instance Jenny Teichman, *Illegitimacy: An Examination of Bastardy* (Ithaca, NY: Cornell University Press, 1982).
58. See, *inter alia*, Giorgio Vercellin, *Istituzioni del mondo mussulmano* (Torino: Piccola Biblioteca Einaudi, 1996) and Judith E. Tucker, *Women, Family, and Gender in Islamic Law* (Cambridge: Cambridge University Press. 2008).
59. Muhammad Ismail Al-Muqaddam, *Fiqh al Haya' Understanding the Islamic Concept of Modesty* (Riyad: International Islamic Publishing House, 2015).

Bibliography

Abbey, Antonia, Frank M. Andrews, and L. Jill Halman. "Gender's Role in Responses to Infertility." *Psychology of Women Quarterly* 15, no. 2 (1991): 295–316.

Abu-Rabia, Aref. "Infertility and Surrogacy in Islamic Society: Socio-Cultural, Psychological, Ethical, and Religious Dilemmas." *Open Psychology Journal* 6 (2013): 54–60.

Al-Azmeh, Aziz, and Fokas Effie (eds.). *Islam in Europe: Diversity, Identity and Influence*. Cambridge: Cambridge University Press, 2007.

Al-Bar, M.A., and H. Chamsi-Pasha. *Contemporary Bioethics Islamic Perspective*. Dordrecht: Springer, 2015.

Al-Muqaddam, Muhammad Ismail. *Fiqh al Haya' Understanding the Islamic Concept of Modesty*. Riyad: International Islamic Publishing House, 2015.

Al-Sayyad, Nezar, and Manuel Castells (eds.). *Muslim in Europe or Euro-Islam*. Oxford: Lexington Books, 2002.

Alshech, Eli. "Out of Sight and Therefore Out of Mind: Early Sunnī Islamic Modesty Regulations and the Creation of Spheres of Privacy." *Journal of Near Eastern Studies* 66, no. 4 (2007): 267–90.

An-Na'im, Abdullahi Ahmed. "Global Citizenship and Human Rights: From Muslims in Europe to European Muslims." In *Religious Pluralism and Human rights in Europe: Where to Draw the Line?*. Edited by Maria Laetitia Petronella Loenen and Jenny E. Goldschmidt, 13–55. Antwerpen: Intersentia, 2007.

Asad, Talal. *Formations of the Secular. Christianity, Islam, Modernity*. Stanford, CA: Stanford University Press, 2003.

Atighetchi, Dariusch. *Islamic Bioethics: Problems and Perspectives*. Dordrecht: Springer, 2007.

Atighetchi, Dariusch. "Human Rights and Bioethics, an Islamic Overview." In *Religious Perspectives on Human Vulnerability in Bioethics*. Edited by Joseph Tham, Alberto Garcia, and Gonzalo Miranda, 231–42. Dordrecht: Springer, 2017.

Casadei, Simone, and Massimiliano Franceschetti (eds.). *Il mediatore culturale in sei paesi europei. Italia, Francia, Germania, Grecia, Regno Unito e Spagna - ambiti di intervento, percorsi di accesso e competenze*. Roma: Isfol, 2009.

Castiglioni Marta. *La mediazione linguistico-culturale: principi, strategie, esperienze*. Milano: Franco Angeli, 1997.

Centro Studi e Ricerche IDOS. *Dossier Statistico Immigrazione* 2020. Roma: IDOS, 2021.

Dassetto, Felice. *L'Islam in Europa*. Torino: EFGA, 1994.

Dassetto, Felice. "The New European Islam." In *Islam and European Legal Systems*. Edited by Silvio Ferrari and Antony Bradney, 31–45. Aldershot: Ashgate Publishing, 2000.

Dooley, Maeve, Tim Dineen, Kiran Sarma, and Aonghus Nolan, "The Psychological Impact of Infertility and Fertility Treatment on the Male Partner," *Human Fertility* 17, no. 3 (2014): 203–9.

Duderija, Adis. "The Custom (ʿurf) Based Assumptions Regarding Gender Roles and Norms in the Islamic Tradition." *Studies in Religion/Sciences Religieuses* 45, no. 44, July (2016): 581–99.

Duderija, Adis, Alina Isac Alak, and Kristin Hissong. "The Logic of Patriarchal Honour and Its Manifestations in Muslim Contexts: Veiling, Female Genital Cutting, and Honor based Violence." In *Islam and Gender. Major Issues and Debates*. Edited by Adis Duderija, Alina Isac Alak, and Kristin Hissong, 44–58. London: Routledge, 2020.

Eich, Thomas. "Bioethics." In *Encyclopaedia of Islam* III. Edited by K. Fleet, G. Krämer, D. Matringe, J. Nawas, and E. Rowson. Leiden: Brill, 2009. Consulted online on January 1, 2021 at http://dx.doi.org/10.1163/1573-3912_ei3_COM_23420.

Ferrari, Silvio (ed.). *L'Islam in Europa*. Bologna: Il Mulino, 1996.

Gavioli, Laura. *La mediazione linguistico culturale: una prospettiva internazionista*. Perugia: Guerra, 2009.

Goody, Jack. *Islam in Europe*. Cambridge: Polity Press, 2004.

Gürtin, Zeynep B., Marcia C. Inhorn, and Soraya Tremayne. "Islam and Assisted Reproduction in the Middle East: Comparing the Sunni Arab World, Shia Iran and Secular Turkey." In *The Changing World Religion Map*. Edited by Stanley D. Brunn, 3137–53. Dordrecht: Springer, 2015.

Habermas, Jürgen, Sara Lennox, and Frank Lennox, "The Public Sphere: An Encyclopaedia Article (1964)." *New German Critique*, no. 3 (Autumn, 1974): 49–55.

Harrison, Cathy. "Who is Your Mother? Who Is Your Father? Assisted Reproductive Technologies in the Light of Sunni and Shi'a Law." *Journal of Shi'a Islamic Studies* 7, no. 1 (2014): 23–37.

Hemayatkhah, M., Z. Hemayatkhah, and E. Jahromi Farahi. "A Review of ethical Issues Involved in Fertility Treatments in Different Religious Frameworks: Cases in Judaism, Christianity, and Islam." *Journal of Jahrom University of Medical Sciences* 11 (2014): 65ff.

Houot, Sandra. "Des usages éthiques du droit islamique: une réponse aux enjeux posés par la reproduction médicalement assistée." *Droit et Cultures* 59 (2010): 331–55.

Houot, Sandra. "Islamic Jurisprudence (*fiqh*) and Assisted Reproduction: Establishing limits to Avoid Social Disorders." In *Islam and Assisted Reproductive Technologies: Sunni and Shia Perspectives*. Edited by Marcia C. Inhorn and Soraya Tremayne, 53–69. New York: Berghahn, 2012.

Inhorn, Marcia C. *Quest for Conception: Gender, Infertility and Egyptian Medical Traditions*. Philadelphia: University of Pennsylvania Press, 1994.

Inhorn, Marcia C. "Fatwas and ARTs: IVF and Gamete Donation in Sunni v. Shi'a Islam." *Journal of Gender, Race & Justice* 9, no. 2 (2005): 291–318.

Inhorn, Marcia C. "Making Muslim babies: IVF and Gamete Donation in Sunni versus Shi'a Islam." *Culture, Medicine and Psychiatry* 30, no. 4 (2006a): 427–50.

Inhorn, Marcia C. "The 'Worms are Weak': Male Infertility and Patriarchal Paradoxes in Egypt." In *Islamic Masculinities*. Edited by L. Ouzgane, 217–37. London: Zed Books, 2006.

Inhorn, Marcia C. "'The Worms Are Weak': Male Infertility and Patriarchal Paradoxes in Egypt." *Men and Masculinities* 5, no. 3 (2006c): 236–56.

Inhorn, Marcia C. *The New Arab Man: Emergent Masculinities, Technologies, and Islam in the Middle-East.* Princeton, NJ: Princeton University Press, 2012.

Inhorn, Marcia C., and Soraya Tremayne (eds.). *Islam and Assisted Reproductive Technologies: Sunni and Shia Perspectives.* New York: Berghahn, 2012.

Inhorn, Marcia C., P. Patrizio, and Gamal I. Serour. "Third-party Reproductive Assistance around the Mediterranean. Comparing Sunni Egypt, Catholic Italy, and Multisectarian Lebanon." In *Islam and Assisted Reproductive Technologies: Sunni and Shia Perspectives.* Edited by Marcia C. Inhorn and Soraya Tremayne, 223–60. New York: Berghahn, 2012.

Katan, David. "La mediazione linguistica interculturale: il mediatore culturale e le sue competenze." *Lingue e Linguaggi* 16 (2015): 365–91.

Katz, Marion H. "Shame (*Ḥayā'*) as an Affective Disposition in Islamic Legal Thought." *Journal of Law, Religion and State* 3, no. 2 (2014): 139–69.

Kleinman, Arthur, Leon Eisenberg, and Bryron Good. "Culture, Illness, and Care: Clinical Lessons from Anthropologic and Cross-Cultural Research." *Annals of Internal Medicine* 88, Feb., no. 2 (1978): 251–8.

Kleinman, Arthur. *Patients and Healers in the Context of Culture: An Exploration of the Borderland between Anthropology, Medicine, and Psychiatry.* Berkeley: University of California Press, 1980.

Limiñana-Gras, Rosa M. "Health and Gender Perspective in Infertility." In *The Psychology of Gender and Health: Conceptual and Applied Global Concern.* Edited by M. Pilar Sánchez-López and Rosa M. Limiñana-Gras, 364–400. Amsterdam: Elsevier, 2017.

Lykeridou, Katerina, Kleanthi Gourounti, Anna Deltsidou, Dimitrios Loutradis, and Grigorios Vaslamatzis. "The Impact of Infertility Diagnosis on Psychological Status of Women Undergoing Fertility Treatment." *Journal of Reproductive and Infant Psychology* 27, no. 3 (2009): 223–37.

Mahmoud, Farouk. "Controversies in Islamic Evaluation of assisted Reproductive Technologies." In *Islam and Assisted Reproductive Technologies: Sunni and Shia Perspectives.* Edited by Marcia C. Inhorn and Soraya Tremayne, 70–97. New York: Berghahn, 2012.

Maréchal, Brigitte, Allievi Stefano, Felice Dassetto, and Jørgen Nielsen (eds.) *Muslims in the Enlarged Europe. Religion and Society.* Leiden: Brill, 2003.

McLoughlin, Seán M. "Islam(s) in Context: Orientalism and the Anthropology of Muslim Societies and Cultures." *Journal of Beliefs & Values*, 28, no. 3 (2007): 273–96.

Mernissi, Fatima. *Beyond the Veil: Male-female Dynamics in Modern Muslim Society.* Bloomington: Indiana University Press, 1987.

Mir-Hosseini, Ziba. *Men in Charge? Rethinking Authority in Muslim Legal Tradition.* London: OneWorld, 2015.

Mir-Hosseini Ziba., Kari Vogt, Lena Larsen, and Christian Moe (eds.). *Gender and Equality in Muslim Law. Justice and Ethics in the Islamic Legal Tradition.* London: I.B. Tauris, 2013.

Musallam, Basim F. *Sex and Society in Islam: Birth Control before the Nineteenth Century.* Cambridge: Cambridge University Press, 1986.

Nielsen, Jørgen S. *Towards a European Islam.* London: Macmillan Press, 1999.

Parsons, Talcott, and Robert Freed Bales. *Family Socialization and Interaction Process.* London: Routledge, 2001/1956.

Pew Research Center. *The Future of the Global Muslim Population. Projections for 2010–2030*. Washington, DC: Pew Research Center, 2011.
Pew Research Center. *The Future of the global Muslim Population. Projections for 2010–2050*. Washington, DC: Pew Research Center, 2015.
Pew Research Center. *The Changing Global Religious Landscape*. Washington, DC: Pew Research Center, 2017.
Rabello, Alfredo M., Daniela Milani, and Dariusch Atighetchi. *Intorno alla vita che nasce: Diritto ebraico, canonico e islamico a confronto*. Torino: Giappichelli, 2013.
Račius, Egdūnas. *Islam in Post-communist Eastern Europe*. Leiden: Brill, 2020.
Rispler-Chaim, Vardit. "Artificial insemination." In *Encyclopaedia of Islam*, III. Edited by Kate Fleet, Gudrun Krämer, Denis Matringe, John Nawas, and Everett Rowson (2007). Consulted online on January 22, 2021 at http://dx.doi.org.ezproxy.eth.mpg.de/10.1163/1573-3912_ei3_SIM_0227
Sachedina, Abdelaziz. *Islamic Biomedical Ethics: Principles and Application*. Oxford: Oxford University Press, 2009.
Serour, Gamal I., Mohamed A. Aboul-Ghar, and Ragaa T. Mansour. "Infertility: A Health Problem in the Muslim World." *Population Sciences* 10 (1991): 41–58.
Serour, Gamal I., Mohamed A. Aboul-Ghar, and Ragaa T. Mansour. "Bioethics in Medically Assisted Conception in the Muslim World." *Journal of Assisted Reproduction and Genetics* 12, no. 9 (1995): 559–65.
Sona, Federica. "Griglie di lettura ed analisi dell'Islam europeo. Diritto interculturale e relazioni sciaraitiche." *Stato, Chiese e pluralismo confessionale*, issue 40 (2016): 1–33.
Sona, Federica. *New Parenthood and Childhood Patterns: Principles and Praxes in Muslim Realities*. Series Fundamental Rights Laboratory No. 7, Bologna: Il Mulino, 2019.
Sona, Federica. "Reasonable Accommodation in Fertility Clinics: The Case of Muslim Patients." *Revista General de Derecho Público Comparado* 28, December (2020): 1–25.
Teichman, Jenny. *Illegitimacy: An Examination of Bastardy*. Cornell University Press: Ithaca, 1982.
The European IVF-monitoring Consortium (EIM) for the European Society of Human Reproduction and Embryology (ESHRE), C. Wyns, C. Bergh, C. Calhaz-Jorge, Ch. De Geyter, M. S. Kupka, T. Motrenko, Ị. Rugescu, J. Smeenk, A. Tandler-Schneider, S. Vidakovic, and V. Goossens, "ART in Europe, 2016: results generated from European registries by ESHRE." *Human Reproduction Open* 2020, issue 3, 2020.
Tremayne, Soraya. "The 'Down Side' of Gamete Donation: Challenging 'Happy Family' Rhetoric in Iran." In *Islam and Assisted Reproductive Technologies: Sunni and Shia Perspectives*. Edited by Marcia C. Inhorn and Soraya Tremayne, 130–156. New York: Berghahn, 2012.
Tucker, Judith E. *Women, Family, and Gender in Islamic Law*. Cambridge: Cambridge University Press, 2008.
Vercellin, Giorgio. *Istituzioni del mondo mussulmano*. Torino: Piccola Biblioteca Einaudi, 1996.
Zegers-Hochschild, F. et al. "International Committee for Monitoring Assisted Reproductive Technology (ICMART) and the World Health Organization (WHO) revised glossary of ART terminology." *Fertility and Sterility* 92, no. 5, November (2009): 1520–4.

Zegers-Hochschild, F. et al. "International Committee for Monitoring Assisted Reproductive Technology (ICMART) and the World Health Organization (WHO) revised glossary of ART terminology." *Human Reproduction* 24, no. 11 (2009): 2683–7.

Zegers-Hochschild, F. et al. "The International Glossary on Infertility and Fertility Care." *Human Reproduction* 32, no. 9, September (2017): 1786–1801.

Zilio-Grandi, Ida. "Modestia, pudicizia e riserbo: la virtù islamica detta ḥayā." *Philologia Hispalensis* 31, no. 2 (2018): 169–83.

11

Between Family and Friends: Honor, Shame, and the Politics of Eating and Drinking among South Asian British Muslims

John Lever and İrem Özgören Kinli

Introduction

The *Oxford Dictionary of Islam* calls attention to the diverse usage of Arabic terms for honor, which is expressed by the display of "ownership of land and resources, family solidarity, the chastity of women and the personal characteristics of courage, generosity, hospitality, independence, wisdom, honesty, self-control" and other personal qualities.[1] According to Mansoor, collective honor is regarded as more important than personal identity for South Asian British communities from Pakistan, India, and Bangladesh.[2] This is why family members are expected to accept their community's values to maintain their family's collective honor system. Weston argues that the protection of collective honor, within South Asian British communities, is considered a "central framework of social control, encouraging the masking of shameful private behaviour with a public veneer of conformity."[3] In her exploration of honor culture in this context, Metlo emphasizes the fact that Pakistani communities use the notion of *sharam* to identify shame, shyness, and modesty.[4] In complement to this additional conceptual clarification, for Metlo, the idea of honor is best described by the terms *ʿizza* (honor, prestige, respect) and *ghairat* (protection of honor, courage).[5]

In their study exploring the underlying components of an honor system composed of control, shame, and a reference community, Baker, Gregware, and Cassidy suggest that honor cannot be evaluated by reference to a person's own behavior.[6] Since the honor of an individual is dependent on the actions of other people, these behaviors are always being kept under control by others. Correspondingly, Mansoor asserts that honor is a relational concept, which consists of spoken and unspoken rules.[7] Honor is described in a relative manner, and a religious person might feel ashamed because of distasteful behavior by a family or a community member. Dishonorable acts have more serious consequences for women compared to men among South Asian British Muslims, with shame being seen as an emotion that is described as a response to a sense of losing of honor. In this context, feelings of shame might appear in the case of disapproval of certain actions or accomplishments. The main features of honor and shame are acknowledged mostly by sociocultural and familial expectations among members of the community.

According to Peristiany, honor and shame are "social evaluations."[8] They reflect "social ideals" since they might be considered as standards to measure representative types of personalities in a given society. All societies have their own unique forms of honor and shame. In her PhD thesis about the perception of honor among the British–Pakistani community in Watford in southern England, Metlo notes that honor serves to construct a person's individual and communal identity.[9] Additionally, she argues that honor helps an individual to regulate his/her own behaviors in various social contexts. For Moore, honor is generally understood with reference to community and family relations in a South Asian context.[10] As a gender-related concept, it is mainly centered on male authority. Besides, the notion of female honor is constructed by both men and women. At this point in her study on Asian women in Britain, Wilson suggests that community norms reinforce women's inferior position.[11] According to her, women's lives are affected the most by these norms. A woman may have *ʿizza*, but it is usually a woman's husband or father who owns this *ʿizza*. Moreover, Wilson argues that a woman's *ʿizza* is the reflection of the male pride of the family.

As Shahani confirms,

> Honour is ultimately seen as being men's responsibility, while shame is viewed as being women's "burden." Honour is thus actively achieved, while shame is often passively defended, leading to an entirely different set of expectations for men and women. Men are expected to protect women's honour, while women are expected to preserve it.[12]

Recently there has been an upsurge in research studies that seek to explore the lives of second- and third-generation South Asian British Muslims.[13] Fransceschelli, for example, asserts that identity is an ambivalent and multifaceted issue among South Asian British Muslim families.[14] It is claimed that their identity involves reconciliation of continuity and change, difference and closeness, between British values, South Asian cultures, and Islam. The younger generation's identity is thus shaped, in this context, it is argued, by the negotiation of individual and family dispositions, which are accompanied by social impacts where religion, gender, cultures, and class all play a role.

Islam has developed its own distinctive practices and local forms in different parts of the world. In his analysis of production of Islamic knowledge, van Bruinessen argues that diasporic communities constituted by Muslim communities of Western Europe maintain diverse kinds of relations with their countries of origin and with similar communities in other countries.[15] Given the vast diversity of Islamic understandings around the world, we focus solely on South Asian British Muslims' interpretation of Muslim practices in the United Kingdom. Drawing on empirical material from studies of halal food consumption and practice in Manchester in the north of England, we look to insights from figurational sociology to explore the complex networks of social and cultural interdependence through which second- and third-generation South Asian British Muslims encounter the prism of honor–shame culture.

Interviews were conducted over a five-year period in consecutive research projects. In general, we asked questions about halal consumption and practice, and while most interviewees talked about the politics of eating and drinking in their communities, a small number also spoke more specifically about honor and shame culture. It is this smaller group that we draw on in this chapter, all of whom have been interviewed more than once. Focusing on changes in the threshold of shame and honor in their everyday lives, we draw on some key figurational concepts to explore to what extent family honor as an "external social control" and shame as an "internal control" have on the "we-I balance," and on levels of awareness and self-control among South Asian British Muslims. This allows us to explore how South Asian men and women attempt to handle shame and maintain family honor in complex cultural settings where they may be presented with opportunities to consume non-halal food and drinks containing alcohol. The chapter proceeds by initially exploring some of the key figurational concepts that we draw on, before turning to our empirical insights. We conclude with some reflections on our relational figurational analysis for wider understandings of shame and honor culture among South Asian British Muslims.

Insights from Figurational Sociology

According to Norbert Elias, social life should be envisioned as a network of interweaving and interdependent social relationships, which he refers to as figurations. Individuals do not exist independently of figurations, nor do figurations exist independently of individuals. The dynamic and ever-changing nature of figurations is characterized by ever-changing, asymmetrical relations of power, which function as a "structural characteristic of the flow of every figuration."[16] In this context, Elias uses the notion of the We–I balance to explore shifting relations between personal identity and group identity using personal pronouns "I," "you," "we," "they" as a figurational model.[17] These pronouns are functional and relational: "I" can only be understood with reference to all other positions to which "you," "we," "they" signify.

For Elias,

> One's sense of personal identity is closely connected with the "we" and "they" relationships of one's group, and with one's position within those units of which one speaks as "we" and "they." Yet the pronouns do not always refer to the same people. The figurations to which they currently refer can change in the course of a lifetime, just as any person does himself.[18]

In this respect, we-groups, such as local communities, kinship groups or families provide security and receive support if required, while more complicated levels of integration "favour individualization" and "greater emphasis on the I-identity of the individual person, and the detachment of that person from the traditional groupings."[19]

Evolution from an earlier phase of development to a more complicated level of integration is also evident in a long-term shift within increasingly complex figurational settings, in the balance between external social constraints (control by other people and external institutions) and internal self-restraints (control by oneself). Elias treats evolving fears of personal shame and embarrassment by demonstrating how self-control is related to embarrassment. As people become more tightly bound to each other, they develop greater degrees of self-discipline and increasing aversion to certain aspects of human behavior.[20] The feeling of shame, according to Elias, is "a kind of anxiety which is automatically reproduced in the individual on certain occasions by force of habit" in line with the violation of group rules and norms with which one may identify.[21] Since perceptions of South Asian shame and honor are closely tied to one's family, kinship group, or local community, we argue, in this chapter, that concepts of shame and honor among South Asian British Muslims are defined by changing figurational relations between I and We groups. This approach, as we shall see, provides useful insights into the ways in which South Asian men and women attempt to maintain family honor and deal with shame in complex figurational settings in Manchester, where the politics of halal food and alcohol can facilitate complex social relations within families and the wider community.

The Politics of Food and Drink in South Asian Communities

In Arabic, the word halal literally means "permissible" or "lawful," and in relation to food, it signifies "purity" and is protected by certain Islamic principles, most notably the avoidance of pork and alcohol; there are also important considerations about the slaughter of animals for food.[22] In what follows, drawing on the experiences of a small number of second and third generation Pakistani Muslims living and working in South Manchester, we illustrate the complex cultural contradictions South Asian men and women encounter negotiating the politics of eating and drinking.

Imran is around forty years old, and he grew up in Whalley Range in central Manchester. Married with three children, he is employed as a community worker in a multicultural inner-city neighborhood. We spoke with Imran twice during our research, once in 2017 and again a few years later. Although he was brought up in a Muslim household of Pakistani origin, where eating halal food and the avoidance of alcohol were very important, Imran admits that he is not as strict as his parents about what his own children eat. Although their eating habits attract attention, Imran allows his children to eat whatever they want to eat, although he recognizes this can be difficult. He also emphasizes the need to take account of the prevalence of alcohol consumption, and the religious implications of being drunk and intoxicated vis-à-vis using alcohol for other useful purposes (in medication, for example).

Imran often drinks alcohol, and he likes to eat a wide variety of cuisines, particularly if some of his less religiously strict friends visit the house. Things are completely different with his extended family and their friends, however, as Imran confirms:

> If say, for instance, I have my Mum over or my friends, I'll make sure all the food's halal. So there's no alcohol there, it's all halal.

As may be observed by this statement, Imran's Pakistani origin parents and community, as his we-group, impose a strict form of social control by relating halal eating and drinking practices to the protection of family honor. This can be tricky, and Imran is aware that he treads a fine line maintaining the honor of the family on many social occasions.

This manifests itself in different ways. When the children of his more strictly religious friends come to the house to play with his children, they often express concerns about what food their children may be offered, but Imran says that he always respects their wishes and doesn't give the children anything not considered halal. Imran is well aware of the pressure to conform with Pakistani culture, but he also admits that his upbringing and working life in multicultural Manchester has presented challenges, and that while "you don't have to conform … you know there is peer pressure."

Imran clearly feels the responsibility of maintaining family honor, yet his life balance has moved away from an overarching focus on the "*we- identity*" of his South Asian family and community toward the *individualized* life encouraged in England, and he attempts to manage the tensions involved the best he can. His individualistic life patterns within Manchester to some extent release him from some of the mechanisms of social control within the South Asian British Muslim community and the we-feeling with whom the majority identify. Some of the women in our study had similar experiences, although in slightly more nuanced ways, as we shall see.

Rabia is a single British Pakistani woman aged thirty-seven; she is also bisexual. Originally from Leicester, she completed a degree in the History of Art at the University of Birmingham before moving to Manchester about ten years ago. We spoke with her once in 2017 and again in 2021. For most of this time, Rabia has worked in catering, including a long period as a waitress in a multicultural café in south Manchester (which served halal food) and latterly, in the past few years, at a Michelin Star restaurant outside the city (that did not).

The move to the restaurant appears to have coincided with Rabia developing a less strict attitude toward food and drink. While in her previous job in the multicultural café, Rabia would only eat halal meat, in her new role, she suddenly found herself encountering non-halal food more regularly and being encouraged to try it by new colleagues and friends. She admits that this was initially disconcerting and that over time influenced her in different ways. Surrounded by lots of new and interesting foods and flavors, Rabia admits that she soon came to think and feel she was missing out.

Rabia talked openly about how, as she eventually succumbed and tried a "non-halal burger," she was really proud of herself, not least because it tasted so good. This in turn had a more profound impact on her life, and she admits that she became more relaxed about going out and frequenting different types of restaurants. She explained the wider change in her outlook in the following way:

> I think it's made it a little bit easier … going into restaurants and stuff cos sometimes I just don't wanna be that person that's, kind of like, oh, is that halal? Do you know

> what I mean? Not to say … that's a bad thing … But I think it's just a bit more laid back … more personal choice and I wanna try that food.

Rabia now believes that her own individual tastes should determine what to eat, rather than the wider community culture or religion. The process through which she has become detached from her Muslim we-group, we could say, and more integrated into British culture, has led to a greater emphasis on Rabia's individuality and less shame in relation to the violation of Islamic food and drink principles. The fact that Rabia still has the tendency not to consume non-halal food and drink in the presence of her community might be evaluated as an illustration that she used to feel shame when violating community principles.

Rida, another young woman of Indian/Pakistani heritage in her twenties, related similar experiences when eating out. Although she did not talk directly about shame and honor, when we spoke with Rida in 2017, she stated that when she socializes with her non-Muslim friends, she only eats fish or vegetarian options, thus reducing the possibility of shaming herself and violating community honor. Indeed, restaurants present particular difficulties for Muslims. In the context of a globalizing halal food market, where halal food is often available alongside non-halal food on the same restaurant menus, Lever argues that power and status of differentials[23] between established social and cultural groups and those classed as outsiders can decline rapidly, thus leading to unintended social and cultural consequences for those involved.[24]

While Rabia admits that she now eats non-halal meat regularly, she says that she draws the line at eating pork. Eating pork is totally prohibited in Islam, as outlined in the Qur'an in various places. Beyond that, the Qur'an does not explain further or give any other reasons for the prohibition of pork. There were, however, negative attitudes toward pigs and pork before the advent of Islam, and scholars have argued that it was Jewish law that inspired the Prophet Mohammad to ban the flesh of pigs, which in effect distinguished Muslims from their Christian adversaries.[25] This absolute prohibition, which is learned and internalized from childhood, is usually ingrained among Muslim adults, and unlike alcohol, pork has alternatives. Thus, the avoidance of eating pork among Muslims seems to a distinctive measure of being Muslim, a source of distinction compared to other religious identities. Compared to other food restrictions, we could argue that the prohibition on pork appears to be transformed into a visible self-control rather than an external social control.

Rabia's attitude toward food in general seems to be related to what is practical at a particular time and place, at particular moments in her life. Around her friends in Manchester, she can be open, but around her family and in her home community in Leicester, this is more difficult, and it appears that many things remain unsaid. At times, Rabia justifies her everyday practice by stating that she doesn't feel the need to openly express the way she leads her life when she's in Leicester: "I'm just saying the fact that I eat non halal, but it's nothing for me to shout about." This quotation demonstrates that the transgression to non-halal eating and drinking practices might escalate both feelings of shame for the individual and be perceived as a threat to community honor. At times, it appears that Rabia feels like an "outsider" in Leicester:

> I think sometimes culturally ... when I come to Leicester and I visit people and sometimes even with my siblings or people like friends and family and stuff like that, sometimes I'm just a bit like, you know, it's this separate world a bit sometimes, culturally.

Rabia explains this double life usefully when comparing attitudes toward alcohol at the family home in Leicester with her new lifestyle in Manchester:

> You wouldn't really touch on it [in Leicester] cos it's not in our culture. It's not part of our everyday life ... Whereas when I go back to Manchester ... It's different ... I'd be ... bursting to go over and have a pint with my mates ... because ... I've kind of adopted a different kind of lifestyle.

In small groups in private spaces, away from the family home and the South Asian British community, Rabia is more at ease challenging or moving beyond tradition. It should also be noted here that the consumption of alcohol has never been a rare phenomenon among Muslims despite its formal religious prohibition.[26] It also seems that drinking alcoholic beverages does not generate the same degree of self-control and self-discipline that is observed in the case of eating pork products. This is why, perhaps, alcohol use in private gatherings is not accompanied by feelings of embarrassment, while it is accompanied by feelings of shame and honor in the presence of others who might impose external control.

Rabia expresses some interesting reflections on gender, particularly to the way she was treated in relation to her brother growing up. She recollects how her older brother often went nightclubbing when he was quite young in places that served alcoholic beverages and how he came home late at night without informing his parents. Rabia notes that this was much more difficult for her because she was female:

> It was obvious what he was doing ... you know, he didn't ask my parents or anything like that, he just did his own thing so that was fine. Whereas with me, it was ... not acceptable.

Rabia also discusses numerous male friends who date non-Muslim women without disclosing these relationships. Recalling a discussion with a male friend about their dual lives, Rabia noted how, although her friend was comfortable hiding his non-Muslim wife from his family over many years, he was very uncomfortable with Rabia's suggestion that her sexuality doesn't hinder her faith. As she noted,

> I was having a conversation with him a couple of weeks ago and he was so uncomfortable with ... me saying what I like about my religion.

There is an interesting tension at play here, related to shame and honor, through which having a double life seems to be more acceptable, or justifiable, particularly for men, if the nonreligious aspects of life are not mixed with the religious. Men, it appears, are much less willing than women to connect and discuss the religious and the nonreligious aspects of their everyday lives.

Shamana is a single British Pakistani woman aged forty-three, who was born and raised in Manchester. Again, we spoke with here twice, once during 2019 and again in 2020. While she seems closer to British culture, it appears that Shamana doesn't want to call herself British, and perhaps more than Imran and Rabia, she has a dual identity that oscillates between Pakistani and British culture. When she was younger, Pakistani culture influenced Shamana greatly, as she pointed out:

> Growing up I only ever ate halal food, particularly in the household. And even when I broke the rules by drinking and smoking, eating halal food was the one rule I never broke.

Most of the Pakistani Muslim friends she attended school and college with are still like this, Shamana suggests, whether they are devout, strictly or moderately religious, and most will still only eat halal food. They might drink, they might smoke, they might do all sorts of other things they shouldn't do, but for most, the requirement to eat halal food is the single most important rule they won't break.

Things changed for Shamana, it appears, when she started high school, which involved instant immersion into Manchester's wider multicultural communities. Shamana remembers the time fondly:

> I remember my primary school was all Asian, there was like one white individual and one black individual, all literally ... Pakistani. And then when I went to high school it was mixed. I remember liking that mix, you know.

This was a life-changing experience that slowly started to pull Shamana away from Pakistani culture. Things intensified went she traveled abroad for the first time. First of all, she started eating non-halal food, but drew the line at eating pork. A few years later, this changed when she started eating bacon. She now also smokes (cigarettes and cannabis) and drinks alcohol, all of which she describes as a process: "It was a change. It was a process."

Interestingly, while Shamana believes that there are other Pakistanis living similar lifestyles, she suggests that most either keep it to themselves, don't talk about it, or don't socialize with others living in this way. She elaborates,

> I'm not a practising Muslim, as in ... devout or anything, but I've not met another ... that eats pork, and I'm sure they exist, or if they do, they just don't talk about it.

This demonstrates that "outsiders" tend to be invisible, although as we shall see, this invisibility appears to manifest itself in different ways in different social contexts and to have different reactions among different family members and social groups in relation to eating and drinking practices. Moreover, it could be argued that avoidance of haram behavior in the presence of another Muslim signifies a type of external control among South Asian British Muslims, which helps to solidify Muslim identity as identity by the protection of family honor. The consumption of haram (non-halal [not permitted]) food and drink while being away from Muslim communities does not create a sense of shame in that person, whose I-identity matters more than his or her We-identity. In such cases, when the We–I balance tilts toward the I-identity, it could be claimed that abstention from *haram* eating and drinking does not transform from external constraints to internal self-control.

While alcohol is strictly forbidden, Shamana suggests that attitudes are more relaxed about alcohol than they are about pork, and in general, she seems more relaxed about alcohol consumption, even though she now eats pork. This is not the same for everyone, however, and Shamana recalls an interesting story about drinking alcohol along with her brother-in-law. Shamana admits that she likes it when her brother-in-law visits *because* they can go to a pub (a Public House, which is licensed to sell alcohol) together, which is unusual in the family. What she finds strange, however, is his attitude toward these trips, which he likes to hide from his wife:

> When he comes and drinks, he says don't tell your sister. I was like, my sister knows I drink. He says, yeah, but your sister wouldn't like me drinking and I'm like, what the hell! That doesn't even make sense … Very strange.

Shamana believes that in general Pakistani men get away with much more than women in Pakistani culture, and it is her attitude to this fact, in some way, that makes her who she is. This discrepancy is probably related to different gender role expectations and social control for men and women that are widely recognized by Muslim communities. As can be seen, the failure to abstain from unlawful eating and drinking, perceived as a dishonorable act, results in dissimilar outcomes for each gender and imposes distinct sanctions.

Shamana argues that she would not have been vilified to the extent growing up if she had been a boy. She notes that although her brother married a white Irish Protestant girl, when her father visits the brother's house, he still hides certain things to make himself feel better about marrying a non-Muslim, which Shamana feels is ingrained cultural behavior. Shamana argues that such behavior is also common among her married friends:

> They all hide it. Some of their wives know that they drink and stuff, but they hide it from their parents, definitely. Whereas I just think that's a bit pointless at this point.

Shamana has difficulty explaining why spouses prefer to hide their consumption of pork and alcohol, even though their non-halal eating and drinking practices are already known by their partners. She has the tendency to interpret her eating and drinking practices as individual decisions, which are influenced by a variety of personal factors. These individual peculiarities might be the reasons why her choices are significantly different from dominant patterns. Yet from a community perspective, family members are expected to conform to community values for the maintenance of collective honor. Drinking alcohol and eating *haram* food should be treated, for the Muslim community, as an assault on collective honor. It is possible to argue, however, that for South Asian British Muslims, when it appears as a potential threat against the value system of family members, the protection of collective honor more significant than the self-expression of their personal identity. Therefore, family members and parents encourage a kind of social control by imposing Muslim eating and drinking standards and restrictions to maintain this collective honor system.

Things are different again across Shamana's extended family, however, where these issues can be much more complex and controversial. Shamana provides numerous examples. One involves an uncle that no one speaks to anymore because he thinks the family live a haram lifestyle. She also recounts a recent incident when a religiously strict aunt visited the family home and started looking through cupboards in the kitchen for haram food items:

> My aunty, she was saying it was pretty much dishonourable, that it was wrong to have that [product] in my house, and it was wrong to give that to my nieces and nephews.

Shamana reacted strongly when her aunt started disposing of certain products in the rubbish bin, suggesting that she had gone too far.

Compared to Imran and Rabia, Shamana seems more confident and she is clearly tilted more toward the I-identity on the We–I balance. At the same time, however, it appears that she also wants to hide some of her activities or at least not speak about them. Most people are like this she suggests, with people obeying rules to prevent quarrels or conflict. Obeying halal practices thus seems to be an honorable practice in this Muslim community, even if more secular than religious; not obeying halal practices seems to be accepted as a dishonorable practice.

Saeed moved to the UK from Bangladesh over forty-six years ago as a young child. He is married with three children and lives in Longsight in South Manchester. We spoke with him twice, once in 2017 and again more recently. Saeed now works for a Muslim charity, although he previously worked as an academic researcher specializing in Islamic issues. For Saeed, ideas about food and drink lie at the heart of his identity, but he points out that he also has other layers that are informed by his ethnicity, his childhood experiences, and his encounter with the British education system through which he was integrated into British culture.

Saeed is quite critical of the industrialization of halal food. While it has become widely available through an ongoing process of commercialization during his lifetime, he thinks that this expansion has disturbed many Muslims. This has led to concerns, he believes, about whether food sold as halal is halal. Consequently, while some people, including his daughter, have adopted vegetarian diets to avoid the implications of eating non-halal meat, others, as we have seen above, have been compelled to try a variety of new cuisines. Saeed makes some interesting observations about the extent to which South Asian British Muslims avoid shame and dishonor in this changing cultural context. Although younger generations, particularly millennials, are more open about drinking alcohol, he suggests that not so long ago,

> there was a time when people, if they wanted to do that kind of stuff, the naughty stuff or taboo stuff, they'd do it quietly indoors or out of sight, because it wasn't publicly or socially acceptable, so you just didn't do that.

Today things are different, Saeed suggests, and he notes that many of the people he grew up with in a mixed South Asian (Bangladeshi and Pakistani) community now go to great lengths to rationalize their nonreligious behavior. These people, he argues, engage in a kind of "spiritual balancing act" through which they put particular aspects of their faith into "some kind of abeyance" in the belief that they can make it up later in life.

This is an interesting observation, which demonstrates how religion, culture, and daily life intersect to determine not only eating and drinking choices, but many other everyday practices for South Asian British Muslims. Saeed argues that while subtle cultural differences exist, there is no real difference between Bengalis, Pakistanis, or any other South Asian group when it comes to such things and that, ultimately, this kind of behavior is

> a negotiated personalised secularisation, or a form of formal secularism if you like, a compartmentalization of your faith from your everyday life.

Saeed's observations might reveal the fact that the less a person identifies with his/her Muslim community, the less he/she feels pressure to follow halal eating for the sake of protection of community honor. Eating vegetarian due to concerns about whether food sold is actually halal might be interpreted as internal self-control helping to solidify his I-identity for the protection of self-honor. The more he/she appears to follow internal self-controls to conform to religious rules, the more abstention from *haram* eating, we could argue, appears to be related to his/her I-identity.

It is worth stressing again that nonconformity to Islamic dietary laws is characterized as unpleasant behavior, which makes Muslims ashamed not only of their own behaviors, but also those of their family or community members. Special mention should be made here to the figurational sociology perspective that emphasizes the interdependency between individual identity and community identity. It is also worth mentioning the figurational concept of *compartmentalization* at this juncture, which highlights (alongside their interdependence) the psychological, social, and spatial separation of individuals and groups within contemporary societies.[27] Among South Asian British Muslims, we contend, honor is thus relatively described in terms of the practices of other Muslims in their close circle. Thus, it is possible to argue that the relationship between identities is relational among South Asian British Muslims, a situation in which their personal identity might be better understood in most cases with reference to their Muslim identity.

It is interesting to note, and perhaps not surprising, that our interviewees might express a personally flexible attitude toward disobeying some halal food practices when differentiating themselves from their community members. Following halal codes in their food and drinking choices, specifically in a community context, thus demonstrates that South Asian British Muslims sometimes make these decisions by negotiating the competing demands of the public and private sphere. While they may eat non-halal food and drink alcohol in social gatherings away from the eyes of their Muslim community, when socializing at restaurants where *haram* food and drinks are served in the midst of complex cultural gatherings, they may experience an acute sense of embarrassment.

Concluding Thoughts

From the standpoint of figurational sociology, the politics of eating and drinking among South Asian British Muslims seems to be closely linked to their identification with We-groups and the question of I-identity. The more they identify with their Muslim community, the more they feel pressure to follow halal eating and drinking practices and the more they appear to follow external social controls in relations with those who violate religious rules and cultural norms. As we have seen, men are entitled to hold responsibility for the protection of collective honor, while women encounter more serious consequences.

Adherence to religion and Islamic communities clearly determines the everyday eating and drinking practices of second- and third-generation South Asian British Muslims to a lesser or greater extent. Indeed, the more they socialize with people from other cultures and religions, and the more they become detached from their family and community, the less anxiety and shame they feel when indulging in haram eating and drinking practices. Taken together, these findings help to support the conclusion that food plays an important role in the formation and maintenance of religious identities. In the introduction to his book on the physiology of taste, or meditations of transcendent gastronomy, Brillat-Savarin wrote a series of aphorisms, one of which became popular: "Dis-moi ce que tu manges, je te dirai ce que tu es." [Tell me what you eat, I'll tell you what you are.][28] Looking to Brillat-Savarin, we conclude that "What and why we do not eat and drink, might also define who we are"!

Notes

1. John L. Esposito, ed. *The Oxford Dictionary of Islam* (Oxford: Oxford University Press, 2003), 117.
2. Nasreen Mansoor, "Exploring Honour and Shame for South Asian British Muslim men and Women" (PhD diss., University of Manchester, 2017), 52–3.
3. Henry Jeffray Weston, "Public Honour, Private Shame and HIV: Issues Affecting Sexual Health Service Delivery in London's South Asian Communities," *Health & Place* 9, no. 2 (2003), 112.
4. Zubaida Metlo, "The Perception of Honour among the British-Pakistani Community in Watford, United Kingdom" (PhD diss., University of Leeds, 2012), 27.
5. Ibid., 46.
6. Nancy V. Baker, Peter R. Gregware, and Margery A. Cassidy, "Family Killing Fields: Honor Rationales in the Murder of Women," *Violence Against Women* 5, no. 2 (February 1999), 165.

7. Nasreen Mansoor, "Honour and Shame. Through the Eyes of South Asian British Muslim Women and Men," in *Photography in Educational Research. Critical reflections from diverse contexts*, edited by Susie Miles and Andy Howes (London: Routledge, 2015), 209.
8. John George Peristiany, ed. *Honour and Shame. The Values of Mediterranean Society* (London: Weidenfeld and Nicolson, 1965), 9–10.
9. Metlo, "The Perception of Honour," 34.
10. Erin Patrice Moore, "Honor: South Asia," in *Encyclopedia of Women & Islamic Cultures. Volume II. Family, Law and Politics*, edited by Suad Joseph (Leiden: Brill, 2005), 216.
11. Amrit Wilson, *Finding a Voice: Asian Women in Britain* (London: Virago, 1978), 5.
12. Lila Ramos Shahani, "A Question of Izzat: Honor, Shame and Ownership among Sunni Muslims in South Asia and the British Diaspora," *Kritika Kultura* 21, 22 (2013), 7.
13. Harriet Becher, *Family Practices in South Asian Muslim Families* (Basingstoke: Palgrave Macmillan, 2008); Michela Franceschelli, "South Asian Young British Muslims: Identity, Habitus and the Family Field" (PhD diss., University of East Anglia, 2013); Michela Franceschelli and Margaret O'Brien, "'Being Modern and Modest': South Asian Young British Muslims Negotiating Multiple Influences on Their Identity," *Ethnicities* 15, no. 5 (October 2015), 696–714.
14. Michela Franceschelli, *Identity and Upbringing in South Asian Muslim Families. Insights from Young People and their Parents in Britain* (London: Palgrave Macmillan, 2016), 241–2.
15. Martin van Bruinessen, "Producing Islamic Knowledge in Western Europe: Discipline, Authority, and Personal Quest," in *Producing Islamic Knowledge: Transmission and Dissemination in Western Europe*, edited by Martin van Bruinessen and Stefano Allievi (New York: Routledge, 2011), 1–27.
16. Norbert Elias, *What Is Sociology?* (New York: Columbia University Press, 1978), 131.
17. Norbert Elias, *The Society of Individuals* (New York: Continuum, 2001), 153–237.
18. Elias, *What Is Sociology?*, 128.
19. Elias, *The Society of Individuals*, 179.
20. Norbert Elias, "On the Process of Civilisation," in *The Collected Works of Norbert Elias. Volume III*, edited by Stephen Mennell, Eric Dunning, Johan Goudsblom, and Richard Kilminster (Dublin: UCD Press, 2012).
21. Ibid., 457.
22. John Lever and Johan Fischer, *Religion, Regulation, Consumption: Globalising Kosher and Halal Markets* (Manchester: Manchester University Press, 2018); Febe Armanios and Bogac Ergene, *Halal Food: A History* (Oxford: Oxford University Press, 2018).
23. Cas Wouters, *Informalisation: Manners & Emotions since 1890* (London: Sage, 2008).
24. John Lever, "Understanding Halal Food Production and Consumption in 'the West'. Beyond Dominant Narrative," *Cambio. Rivista sulle trasformazioni sociali* 9, no. 19 (October 2020), 89–102.
25. Frederick J. Simoons, *Eat Not This Flesh: Food Avoidances from Prehistory to the Present* (Madison: University of Wisconsin Press, 1994), 33.
26. Laurence Michalak and Karen Trocki, "Alcohol and Islam: An Overview," *Contemporary Drug Problems* 33, no. 4 (December 2006), 534–9.
27. John Lever, Ryan J. Powell, R., "Problems of Involvement and Detachment: Norbert Elias and the Investigation of Contemporary Social Process- es. *Human Figurations. Long-Term Perspectives in Human Condition*, 6, no. 2 (2017).

28. Jean Anthelme Brillat-Savarin, *Physiologie du goût, ou Méditations de gastronomie transcendante* (Paris: Garnier Frères, 1867), 1.

Bibliography

Armanios, Febe, and Ergene Bogac. *Halal Food: A History*. Oxford: Oxford University Press, 2018.

Baker, Nancy V., Peter R. Gregware, and Margery A. Cassidy. "Family Killing Fields: Honor Rationales in the Murder of Women." *Violence Against Women* 5, no. 2 (February 1999): 164–84.

Becher, Harriet. *Family Practices in South Asian Muslim Families*. Basingstoke: Palgrave Macmillan, 2008.

Bruinessen, Martin van. "Producing Islamic Knowledge in Western Europe: Discipline, Authority, and Personal Quest." In *Producing Islamic Knowledge: Transmission and Dissemination in Western Europe*. Edited by Martin van Bruinessen and Stefano Allievi, 1–27. New York: Routledge, 2011.

Elias, Norbert. *What Is Sociology?* New York: Columbia University Press, 1978.

Elias, Norbert. *The Society of Individuals*. New York: Continuum, 2001.

Elias, Norbert. "On the Process of Civilisation." In *The Collected Works of Norbert Elias. Volume III*. Edited by Stephen Mennell, Eric Dunning, Johan Goudsblom, and Richard Kilminster. Dublin: UCD Press, 2012.

Esposito, John L. (ed.). *The Oxford Dictionary of Islam*. Oxford: Oxford University Press, 2003.

Franceschelli, Michela. "South Asian Young British Muslims: Identity, Habitus and the Family Field." PhD diss., University of East Anglia, 2013.

Franceschelli, Michela, and Margaret O'Brien. "'Being Modern and Modest': South Asian Young British Muslims Negotiating Multiple Influences on Their Identity." *Ethnicities* 15, no. 5 (2015): 696–714.

Franceschelli, Michela. *Identity and Upbringing in South Asian Muslim Families. Insights from Young People and Their Parents in Britain*. London: Palgrave Macmillan, 2016.

Lever, John, and Johan Fischer. *Religion, Regulation, Consumption: Globalising Kosher and Halal Markets*. Manchester: Manchester University Press, 2018.

Lever, John. "Understanding Halal Food Production and Consumption in 'the West'. Beyond Dominant Narratives." *Cambio. Rivista sulle trasformazioni sociali* 9, no. 19 (2020): 89–102.

Mansoor, Nasreen. "Honour and Shame: Through the Eyes of South Asian British Muslim Women and Men." In *Photography in Educational Research: Critical Reflections from Diverse Contexts*. Edited by Susie Miles and Andy Howes, 208–23. London: Routledge, 2015.

Mansoor, Nasreen. "Exploring honour and shame for South Asian British Muslim men and women." PhD diss., University of Manchester, 2017.

Metlo, Zubaida. "The Perception of Honour among the British-Pakistani Community in Watford, United Kingdom." PhD diss., University of Leeds, 2012.

Michalak, Laurence, and Karen Trocki. "Alcohol and Islam: An Overview." *Contemporary Drug Problems* 33, no. 4 (2006): 523–62.

Moore, Erin Patrice. "Honor: South Asia." In *Encyclopedia of Women & Islamic Cultures. Volume II. Family, Law and Politics*. Edited by Suad Joseph, 216–18. Leiden: Brill, 2005.

Peristiany, John George (ed.). *Honour and Shame: The Values of Mediterranean Society*. London: Weidenfeld and Nicolson, 1965.

Shahani, Lila Ramos. "A Question of izzat: Honor, Shame and Ownership among Sunni Muslims in South Asia and the British Diaspora." *Kritika Kultura*, no. 21/22 (2013): 1–11.

Simoons, Frederick J. *Eat Not This Flesh: Food Avoidances from Prehistory to the Present*. Madison: University of Wisconsin Press, 1994.

Weston, Henry Jeffray. "Public Honour, Private Shame and HIV: İssues Affecting Sexual Health Service Delivery in London's South Asian Communities." *Health & Place* 9, no. 2 (2003): 109–17.

Wilson, Amrit. *Finding a Voice: Asian Women in Britain*. London: Virago, 1978.

Wouters, Cas. *Informalisation: Manners & Emotions since 1890*. London: Sage, 2008.

12

Modesty and Malay/Muslim Women in Singapore: The Impact of Traditionalism and Revivalism

Nur Syafiqah Mohd Taufek and Norshahril Saat

Introduction

In the late 1970s, Southeast Asia witnessed an emergence of religious revivalism among Muslim communities. In Singapore, *dakwah* (preaching) movements inspired by revivalist movements such as the Muslim Brotherhood in Egypt and the Iranian Revolution of 1979 mushroomed until the 1990s. Led by student societies such as the National University of Singapore Muslim Society (NUSMS), these *dakwah* movements sought to increase religious consciousness among the Muslim community. This led to a rise in traditionalist-revivalist orientation, which later became the dominant orientation among the Muslims. Gender relations and modesty, especially for women, was a central theme of the movement to overcome the alleged encroachment of Western influences. Decades have passed since the *dakwah* movement. To what extent have the Malay/Muslim community moved away from the traditionalist-revivalist discourse on gender? This chapter argues that the traditionalist-revivalist ideas on women and modesty not only remain influential within the Singaporean Muslim community, but have also evolved over time. The prevalence of these modes of thinking on women and modesty has perpetuated sexism, enabled continued objectification of women's bodies, and reduced social problems to women's dressing and modesty, instead of addressing problems of gender inequality.

This chapter discusses two issues that reflect the dominance of the traditionalist-revivalist orientation in the discourse on women and modesty. This includes the *hijab* controversies in 2002 and 2014, and the OKLETSGO saga in 2020. These issues elicited much media attention and were widely discussed on social media platforms. Data presented in the chapter will include the postings of religious elites (both *ulama* and *asatizah*—religious scholars and religious teachers) on social media as well as marriage handbooks. The Malay/Muslim religious elites remain influential today. Their ideas and viewpoints continue to circulate and shape the sentiments of the community. Whereas in the past, religious elites utilized platforms such as books, sermons in radio, and columns in newspapers, today, they ride on social media and videos to disseminate their ideas. Although the religious elite is not a homogeneous social group, there is arguably a common mode of thinking underlying their discourse, which resembles a traditionalist–revivalist orientation and is far from being progressive contrary to what they often claim themselves to be.[1]

Dakwah Movement and Modesty

The encroachment of religious revivalism into the region in the late 1970s coincided with the early period of Singapore's independence where the country expanded its economic activities and underwent significant social developments such as urbanization.[2] It was during this period that the Malay/Muslim community, which made up 15 percent of the 5.6 million population, struggled to adapt to these changes and "continued to lag behind non-Malays."[3] The community was especially overrepresented in "educational under-attainment, unemployment, drug abuse, early marriage and divorce."[4] This caused anxiety especially among community leaders who shouldered the burden of elevating the community. However, instead of examining the problems objectively, the society's predicament was dominantly framed as a moral problem, instead of one that was structural. To this, the leaders claimed that the community lacked the "value orientation required for the changing socio-economic conditions of Singapore."[5] The prevalence of drug abuse among Malay youths, loose gender interaction, smoking and alcohol consumption was seen as an encroachment of Western influences, which has caused the alleged moral degeneration that was responsible for the community's malaise.[6] It was against this background that *dakwah* movements emerged and promoted Islam as "a significant solution (if not the solution) for the community's predicament."[7]

The *dakwah* movement portrays Islam as having solutions to all social problems that are distinct from the West. Such an idea was influenced by the views of globally known scholars such as Hassan Al-Banna, Yusuf al-Qaradhawi, and Ismail Faruqi, as well as Malaysian scholars such as Mohamed Nur Manuty and Muhammad Kamal Hassan.[8] For example, al-Qaradhawi's book *The Lawful and Prohibited in Islam* was translated in Malay and became popular reading among revivalist groups. According to Azhar (b. 1971), a lecturer based in Singapore, these revivalists seek to

> "Islamise" the modern sciences, knowledge and technologies that the West has developed … [this] is exploitative, arrogantly taking over the efforts of others and repackaging them in the name of Islam. Essentially, they are only interested in purifying things that are already made, in order to later patent them as "Islamic" with very little mental or physical input from them. Basically, in this discourse, theological certainty and the affirmation of the faith become the revivalists' prime concerns, rather than a scientific attempt to understand mankind and nature.[9]

Modesty became one of the central themes of the *dakwah* movement to overcome the alleged Western influences associated with moral degeneration.[10] Appropriate dressing for both men and women was defined and became an important marker of the Muslim identity. The wearing of *jubah* (garment worn by Arabs) and *serban* (turban worn by Arabs) were associated with men's piety, but this was not made obligatory.[11] However, for women, veiling or the wearing of hijab was considered obligatory and a symbol of religious piety.[12] As Western dressing for women was treated as dangerous, immoral, and a source of vices, molestation, and rape, "veiling became a sign of emancipation from Western secularism."[13]Although modesty is required of both Muslim men and women, the *dakwah* movement emphasized heavily on the disciplining of women's bodies. The Malay women's bodies were regarded as docile and "had to be disciplined into useful, productive and virtuous bodies."[14] Student organizations such as NUSMS, which was at the forefront of the *dakwah* movement, played an important role in shaping the discourse surrounding the hijab. Female Muslim university students were strongly encouraged to don the *tudung* (headscarf) lest they were seen as less Islamic.[15] Such ideas soon contributed to a radical shift in the attitude of Malay/Muslims on the practice of veiling as will be elaborated later.

The association of hijab with women's piety contrasts with the practice of veiling prior to the *dakwah* movement, which was not strictly observed. Then, Muslim women who chose to practice veiling donned a loose headgear known as the "*selendang*" that was usually worn during religious ceremonies and by those who had gone to Mecca to fulfill their pilgrimage.[16] Unlike the "*selendang*," the *hijab* that was imposed on women following the *dakwah* movement is a more tightly secured headgear that covers the women's neck and chest. The *dakwah* movement changed the symbolic nature of the veil from one that was not a fundamental aspect of local Islamic practice to an important marker of a Muslim woman's piety.

Beyond the issue of modesty, the traditionalist-revivalist orientation that emerged out of the *dakwah* movement also sought to entrench traditional gender relations.[17] This is despite more Malay women participating in the workforce due to high educational attainment, occupational opportunities, and the rise in the cost of living.[18] Women have since assumed the role of a co-breadwinner, giving rise to dual-income households and altering the roles that were traditionally assigned to them as homemakers. With women becoming more financially independent and no longer confined to the domestic realm, a "commensurate change in patriarchal mindsets" was necessary.[19] However, instead of considering these developments, revisiting, and altering gender roles according to modern circumstances, the traditionalist-revivalist religious elites entrenched traditional gender roles. The dominant discourse continued to suggest that women's role, ideally, is in the home. Even if they were allowed to work, their roles were mainly to assist their husbands, as the leader of the household. This will be further elaborated in the next section.

The Dominance of the Traditionalist-Revivalist Orientation

The discourse on women, gender roles, and modesty within the community continues to reflect a traditionalist-revivalist orientation, even though some attempts to revise the discourse have been made. There are competing ideas challenging the dominant discourse, but these voices nevertheless remain marginal. Female modesty, veiling, and roles of women continue to be the dominant themes in discussions about women. Religious elites, in particular, play an important role in perpetuating such discourse. Such ideas can be found in the writings and social media posts of religious elite as well as marriage course handbooks.

In a special edition of *Ar-Risalah* (Issue 18, May–August 2015), a publication by Singapore Islamic Scholars and Religious Teachers Association (PERGAS), topics such as the obligation of veiling were reiterated.[20] The publication also included a page containing ten pieces of advice to women, adapted from a book written by Malaysian preacher *Ustaz* Kazim Elias—all of which emphasize a woman's role as a wife.[21] Among others, these include adorning oneself for the husband and a reminder to women that heaven and hell depends on *keredaan suami* (approval of their husbands).[22]

The traditionalist–revivalist orientation also sought to sustain the traditional gender roles as a timeless solution to societal developments. When asked why male Malay youths have become more unreliable over the years, a Singaporean-born *Ustaz* (religious teacher)[23] currently based in Malaysia claimed that modern developments deprived men of roles to play, though the over-disciplining of girls and neglecting discipline for boys is a contributing factor.[24] The *Ustaz* recalled that men used to attend to their family needs such as treating illnesses and protecting them from harm, but better access to clinics and security in today's world meant that they no longer need to play such roles. Further, women's growing independence would ultimately make men feel broken and a "significant part of them dies."[25] Despite recognizing that women now play significant roles beyond the domestic realm, the *Ustaz* proposed that the community return to traditional gender roles as delineated by the Prophet in which a "husband is the leader of the whole family,"[26] while a woman is responsible for her children.

The response of the *Ustaz* reflects a recurring feature underlying traditionalist–revivalist discourses: the lack of contextualizing authoritative text and the lack of engagement with present realities. Even though the *Ustaz* recognized that women today play various roles, he did not critically engage with such development and make religion more adaptable to the current needs of society. Instead, religious elites with such orientation advocate for a return to traditional gender roles that can no longer serve the society. They miss the fact that gender roles have constantly undergone transformations throughout history and will continue to change as new needs arise. While the *Ustaz* was apologetic toward men as they feel unsure of their roles amid modernity, he overlooks the fact that women, on the other hand, are burdened with multiple roles and constantly struggle to balance their time to fulfill their roles as an employee and a leader of the household.[27]

Traditional gender roles are also often perpetuated in marriage handbooks, although the discourse has undergone a slight shift over the years.[28] Unlike older marriage handbooks, more recent guides such as *Bersama Mu* (*Together with You*) (2013) and *Cinta Abadi* (*Eternal Love*) (2014) have become more accepting of the inevitability of dual-income households.[29] However, the idea that household duties are a shared responsibility remains unpopular.[30] Husbands are encouraged to assist with household duties, but the discourse maintains that their main duty is to provide maintenance for the family while a wife's first responsibility is to manage the home.[31] Women who choose to work are also reminded to acquire their husband's permission, dress modestly, and maintain one's self-respect when socializing.[32] The fact that such reminders are not directed to men implies that women continue to be subjects of discipline and modesty apart from being confined to the domestic realm. As a result, Malay women continue to attend "to the bulk of household work."[33] A study found that while husbands now assist with household chores, the wives remain the person-in-charge of the household who "decide what tasks can be transferred and to whom these tasks can be delegated to."[34] The slight shift in the traditionalist–revivalist discourse on gender roles represents an attempt by religious figures to address contemporary issues affecting both genders. However, the lack of critical engagement with the reality in pursuit of sustaining traditional gender roles wherever possible resulted in a maladjustment of the community in adapting to societal developments.

2002 and 2014 Hijab Movements

The radical shift in the community's attitude on the hijab peaked when Muslim parents started demanding "public schools to allow their daughters to wear the headscarf" in the 1990s.[35] There were instances in which schools allowed female Muslim students to modify their school uniforms to cater to the religious dress code. For example, Malay/Muslim girls are allowed to wear long pants during physical education and sporting activities, though the hijab is still not allowed. The movement culminated in 2002 when four Primary One Muslim students wore *tudung* in addition to their school uniform and were suspended for refusing to remove their headscarves. The incident ended with an attempt by a local nongovernmental Muslim organization known as Fateha.com to mount a legal challenge against the government for banning the headscarf in schools by engaging a prominent lawyer from Malaysia.[36]

Underlying the insistence of pushing for the wearing of *tudung* in public schools is the idea that a girl must be disciplined since young so that "she can become a modest person."[37] To some members of the community, the wearing of tudung is one way to help alleviate the fears that their young girls "become wayward" when growing up.[38] The attempt by Muslim parents in imposing their personal beliefs of modesty in public schools by openly defying policies set by the Ministry of Education (MOE) was an act of civil disobedience which sparked a political concern. Religious elites were divided on the matter. In response to the incident, Syed Isa Semait, the former Mufti of Singapore (1970–2011), through a public statement issued by the Islamic Religious Council of Singapore (MUIS) stated his stance "that education was of a higher priority for Muslims"[39] if a choice has to be made between the tudung and education. Meanwhile, Singapore Islamic Scholars and Religious Teachers Association (PERGAS) maintained that the hijab is compulsory, and Muslims should strive to remove obstacles that "obstruct the fulfilment of one's religious duties."[40]

The strict and rigid view held by PERGAS on the tudung reflects a revivalist overtone, which suggests that the tudung must be held in high regard regardless of context. Due to such beliefs, some parents even withdrew their daughters from public schools once they reach puberty—an age at which wearing the tudung is deemed compulsory.[41] Unlike their peers, these girls take an alternative route to complete their education through private tuitions and part-time classes.[42] The demand for the headscarf to be allowed in public schools was a short-sighted move that overlooks the importance of ensuring that young girls have equal access to education as their male counterparts and attain the education they need in a competitive socio-economic environment. Instead, proponents of the hijab were more preoccupied with disciplining young girls through the wearing of the hijab and imposing their exclusive religiosity in secular institutions.

The contradicting stances between MUIS and PERGAS continued to divide the community on the hijab issue. Due to the lack of a common standpoint of religious clerics on the hijab, the topic remains a sticky issue within the community and resurfaces from time to time. Many remain ambivalent towards MUIS's stance on the hijab. In late 2013, the topic resurfaced in a forum when a polytechnic lecturer questioned why Muslim nurses were not allowed to wear the headscarf.[43] Following that, an online petition was created demanding the restriction be lifted and garnered up to 12,405 signatures, but was later taken down.[44] A Facebook page known as "Singapore Hijab Movement" was also set up and garnered over 26,000 likes but was also later removed.[45] Unlike the 2002 hijab movement that demanded that the hijab be allowed in public schools, the second wave of hijab debate saw the Muslim community extending the demand for hijab in the public sector, especially in professions that require the wearing of uniforms, such as nurses and frontline workers. The hijab movement lasted until the 2015 general election campaign where the hijab issue became a tool of the opposition parties to garner more support for their parties such as the case for Singapore Democratic Party (SDP) candidate, Damanhuri Abas.[46]

By this time, proponents of the hijab— some of whom were part of the *dakwah* revivalist movement— had assumed key positions in society, particularly as activists in civil society organizations. They continue to be proponents of the hijab and champion for its use in the public sector. While the 2002 hijab movement was dominated by the narrative of modesty and the need for Muslims to guard its importance, the recent hijab movement sought to enhance multiculturalism in Singapore. Proponents believed that revisiting the policy on the headscarf "to fit the aspirations of the local Muslim community" can improve "Singapore's image as a country that is inclusive and harmonious."[47] Nevertheless, the obligatory nature of the headscarf remains the dominant narrative underlying the push for the cause. In a media statement, PERGAS reiterated its unchanging view that "the tudung is an important religious obligation and one which symbolises a woman's dignity and decency."[48] In a Facebook post, Dr. Fatris Bakaram, former Mufti of Singapore (2011–2020), also expressed a similar stance that the Muslim community in Singapore does not dispute the obligation of women covering the hair in the presence of a non-mahram.[49]

Although modesty is required of both Muslim men and women, the narrative underlying both hijab movements show that the focus has been placed heavily on the modesty of women, which is ultimately reduced to a hijab. In the 2002 hijab movement, while members of the community problematized the banning of headscarf in public schools and demanded a change in school policies, none questioned the attire for male students that consists of shorts and exposed body parts which some believe would require covering. The fact that some Muslim parents believe that girls need to be disciplined since young in covering their *ʿaura* but do not apply the same idea to boys implies the inequality in the discourse of gender.

The *dakwah* movement has indeed redefined modesty, now marked by the wearing of the headscarf as central to the Muslim identity. Today, the hijab issue continues to dominate society. Whether a woman decides to don the hijab remains a topic of conversation among members of the community. The significance of the headscarf has made the Muslim community become reactive toward alternative viewpoints on the hijab despite the varying interpretations and opinions of scholars. Such an attitude stands out when prominent members of the community and global influencers officially announced that they are no longer donning the hijab. In recent years, a few international Muslim icons such as Dina Tokio and Amena Khan announced their decision to "unveil."[50] Singaporean Malay/Muslims were no exception in criticizing the global influencers on their decisions. Some even pressured local *asatizah* (religious teachers) to address the issue and reinforce the obligatory nature of the headscarf. *Asatizah* who refused to address the matter were criticized and had their credibility questioned. In response to the situation, an *ustaz*, through an Instagram post addressed to his daughter, criticized the attitude that confers the self-worth of a Muslim woman through "a piece of cloth" and those who don the headscarf mainly to appease social pressures.[51]

The tudung or hijab has now become an everyday commodity. Discussion on the topic has evolved into a deeper concern for the "proper wearing and handling of the *tudung*."[52] While preachers remain influential in shaping the discourse on modesty, today, celebrities as well as influencers also play a similar role in promoting modest wear and reinforcing the importance of wearing the headscarf. They become the voice that reiterates the obligation of donning the hijab and set certain standards of modest fashion that is only affordable for the upper and middle classes. For instance, when global influencer Amena Khan removed her hijab, a former radio presenter expressed her disappointment and reiterated the obligation of donning the headscarf: "Wearing the hijab is an OBLIGATION. It is not a fashion statement. The religion requires us to cover our *ʿawra* (parts of body require covering)."[53] She also invited a local *asatizah* to discuss the issue in a podcast.[54]

Modest fashion takes center stage with the promotion of abayas—a clothing originally worn by the Arabs. A local *ustaza* once posted on Instagram regarding her contentment at seeing more women "embracing Abayas for a more modest and demurer look. They look amazing, all covered up with long flowy materials, not an inch of figure to be seen."[55] In the post, she tagged her favorite modest fashion stores that sell products at high prices, making the goods affordable only for the middle to upper classes. Whereas the *dakwah* movement elevated the opinion that the headscarf is *wājib* (compulsory), the discourse today is layered with issues on class such that there are different standards of modest fashion for each social class.

The OKLETSGO Saga

In June 2020, the hosts of independent podcast OKLETSGO (OLG), Dyn Norahim, Dzar Ismail, and Raja Razie, came under fire for its "locker room"-style conversations that consisted of misogynistic and sexually objectifying comments against women.[56] Although the hosts had been making such remarks throughout their weekly podcasts, the "locker room"-style conversation only drew public criticisms later when a few members of the community took to their social media accounts to highlight remarks made by the hosts.[57] They caused public outrage nationwide especially within the Muslim community. Many were furious with the comments, while some found them less problematic.[58] The problem, however, was that not only were the remarks made by the hosts but also that community leaders, including politicians and a few *asatizah*—most of whom were male figures—appeared on the podcast.[59] The failure of these prominent figures to identify what was wrong with the comments and the fact that they chose to appear on the platform raised questions as to whether they were aware of such remarks being made and if they had found them problematic at all.

Shortly after the controversy, women's organizations and prominent figures such as President Halimah Yacob issued a statement addressing the issue and asked the hosts of OLG to apologize. Several *asatizah*, including the current Mufti of Singapore, Dr. Nazirudin Nasir, also addressed the issue, but only after the president did so. Responding to the situation, Dr. Nazirudin Nasir underlined the fact that women have often been "deemed to be of less worth than men."[60] They also pointed out the problem of "sexist attitudes and behaviours that have plagued our community for far too long."[61] He stated that "women are equally important and their contributions exceptionally significant"[62] and highlighted the importance of using one's influence to not perpetuate such a narrative. A female religious teacher also reminded the community that the Prophet has conferred rights to women and urged men to "treat them well, with respect and kindness."[63]

However, not all *asatizah* who responded to the issue were able to recognize that OLG's remarks on women is a microcosm of a normalized sexist attitude that is prevalent within the community and one that stems from deeply entrenched ideas on gender. Instead of seeing the issue as part of a wider problem of prevailing misogyny and sexual objectification, other religious teachers who issued statements framed the issue as a problem of morality (or the lack thereof), behaviors that are not representative of Islam, and abusing freedom of speech. For instance, in a joint statement issued through a Facebook post, fifteen *asatizah* addressed the issue of justifying the use of obscene words and labels such as "Adult Content" and "Not Safe for Work" (NSFW) for entertainment as an immoral act that violates the sharia.[64] They noted that a podcast provides space for people to express themselves, but such freedom is not absolute. It is clear from the statement that the issue of OLG's misogynistic and sexually objectifying remarks appeared to the *asatizah* as a problem of not guarding one's speech. By framing the issue as merely a problem of bad speech or an immoral act, the *asatizah* not only failed to acknowledge the main problem that sparked the controversy, but also steered away the conversation from issues affecting women that were being discussed at the time.

Similarly, in another Facebook post that supposedly address the topic of sexual objectification, an *ustaz* expressed that "making improvements (that may benefit society) should not stop at addressing women issues."[65] He noted that other issues such as using vulgarities in speech, defaming others, and sharing personal stories of intimacy in a public space should be tackled. In the same post, he also stated that many have addressed the issue of objectifying women but overlooked the fact that making jokes about the male reproductive organs is equally an act of sexually objectifying men—an act that "needs to be strongly condemned."[66] Urging the public to go beyond women's issues amid the controversy shows that he underplayed the magnitude of the issue at hand, thus neutralizing the importance of discussing misogyny and sexual objectification, which are long-standing issues faced by women in the community. Such a statement also overlooks the reality of power relations between men and women, that they are not always equal, and that the sense of superiority over another gender has yet to dissipate.

Beyond the problem of bad speech that stems from immorality or following a trend, the OLG controversy reflects a deeply entrenched mindset of the society against women: that women can be and have always been sexualized in both private and public spaces. Responses from *asatizah* that did not address how the issue was centered on women or half-heartedly did so shows that they do not recognize women's issues as worthy of discussion. Overall, the *asatizah's* responses regarding the OLG controversy and the prevailing narrative on the *hijab* reveal that ideas on women remain androcentric.

Conclusion

Ideally, religious elites such as the *asatizah* can play a key role in helping the community grapple with the changing social landscape. As Singapore moved from the industrialization phase to the digital age, women's role in the public sphere should be treated as a norm and should even be a subject of theological debate. Nevertheless, as demonstrated within the Singapore Malay/Muslim community—which can be considered as one of the most advanced middle- and upper-class communities socioeconomically when compared to others in the Muslim world—the discourse on women and modesty remains traditionalist, and lately revivalist. Preachers attempt to address challenges faced by women by framing the issue as a religious one, which often ends up perpetuating and entrenching traditional gender roles. Women's issues continue to be tackled via the lens of religion, particularly women's roles in relation to men, by referring to Qur'anic and Prophetic traditions that mention the matter. There is a lack of regard for the changing social and familial landscape in the country, and the elite continue to adopt an uncritical lens (non-sociological) when discussing women's leadership and public participation. The argument that women are better placed in the domestic sphere continues to perpetuate even though in reality, Malay/Muslim women have gone out to work. This shows that the elite are alienated from the realities of the community.

The prevalence of revivalism also means the preference for modern "Islamic" solutions, though this does not mean improving the lives of Malay/Muslim women.

Instead, there is internalization of gender stereotypes and perpetuation of traditional gender roles by female preachers through talks and programs labeled as "empowering." Often, the revivalists, in their eagerness to portray the Islamic perspective as more effective than the Western counterpart, would say that to solve family or social problems such as outrage of modesty, rape, or abuses, women must safeguard their modesty. Such discourse, wrongly described as an Islamic perspective, are merely selections of traditionalist ideas and often result in blaming women for social crimes.

Notes

1. See Noor Aisha Abdul Rahman who makes similar arguments in her writings. Noor Aisha and Abdul Rahman, "Shariah Revivalism in Singapore," in *Islam in Southeast Asia: Negotiating Modernity*, edited by Norshahril Saat (Singapore: ISEAS, 2018), 195–230; Noor Aisha and Abdul Rahman, "Religious Resurgence amongst the Malays and Its impact: The case of Singapore," in *Alternative Voices in Muslim Southeast Asia: Discourse and Struggles*, edited by Norshahril Saat (Singapore: ISEAS, 2020), 33–66.
2. Azhar Ibrahim, "Discourses on Islam in Southeast Asia and Their Impact on the Singapore Muslim Public," in Lai Ah Eng's *Religious Diversity in Singapore* (Singapore: ISEAS, 2008), 88.
3. Abdul Rahman, "Religious Resurgence," 38.
4. Ibid.
5. Ibid.
6. Ibid., 38–9.
7. Ibrahim, "Discourses on Islam," 88.
8. Abdul Rahman, "Religious Resurgence," 39–40.
9. Azhar Ibrahim, *Contemporary Islamic Discourse in the Malay-Indonesian World: Critical Perspectives* (Selangor: Strategic Information and Research Development Centre, 2014), 53.
10. Ibid., 86.
11. Syed Husin Ali, *The Malays: Their Problems and Future* (Petaling Jaya, Selangor: The Other Press, 2008), 72.
12. Sandra Hochel, "To Veil or Not to Veil: Voices of Malaysian Muslim Women," *Intercultural Communication Studies* 22, no. 2 (2013), 41.
13. Ibid., 42.
14. Nurhaizatul Jamila Jamil, "*Perempuan, Isteri, Dan…*: Embodied Agency and the Malay Woman of Contemporary Singapore," Master's dissertation (National University of Singapore, 2009), 18.
15. Said Mahadi Said Iziddin, "The Islamic Resurgence Movement Amongst Muslim Students in University of Singapore in the 1970s," Honours Thesis (National University of Singapore, 2017), 37.
16. Jamie Koh, "Tudung," *Singapore Infopedia*, available online: https://eresources.nlb.gov.sg/infopedia/articles/SIP_2013-09-30_123324.html (accessed May 30, 2021).
17. Noor Aisha and Abdul Rahman, "Religious Resurgence," 34.
18. Suriani Suratman, "Gender Relations in Singapore: Malay Dual-Income Households: (Un)Changing Views and Practices," *Islam and Civilisational Renewal* 3, no. 1 (2011), 93.

19. Women's Action, "Singapore and the Women's Movement," https://www.womensaction.sg/article/overview
20. See PERGAS, *Ar-Risalah,* issue 18 (Singapore: PERGAS, 2015), 4–14, 38–9, https://issuu.com/ar-risalah/docs/ar-risalah_isu_18_fa_single (accessed May-August 2015).
21. Ibid., 39.
22. Ibid.
23. The Ustaz is currently based in Malaysia but remain a popular religious figure among Singaporeans.
24. Faizuddin Fauzan (@faizuddinfauzan). 2020. "BROKEN MUSLIM MEN." Instagram Video, September 20, 2020 https://www.instagram.com/tv/CFXCqEpBo5b/
25. Ibid.
26. Ibid.
27. Debbie Lee, "Survey: 74% of women turn down jobs due to work-life balance concerns," *The Straits Times*, 2013, https://www.straitstimes.com/singapore/survey-74-of-women-turn-down-jobs-due-to-work-life-balance-concerns.
28. See Suriani Suratman, "Skills for 'Marriage of a Lifetime': An Examination of Muslim Marriage Preparation Handbooks in Singapore, 1974–2018," *Religions* 12, no. 1 (2021), 473, https://doi.org/10.3390/rel12070473
29. Ibid., 11.
30. Ibid., 14.
31. Ibid., 11.
32. Majlis Ugama Islam Singapura, *Pedoman Ringkas Berumahtangga* (*Guidelines on Marriage*) (1974), 22.
33. Suratman, "Gender Relations," 91.
34. Ibid.
35. Suzaina Kadir, "Islam, State and Society in Singapore," *Inter-Asia Cultural Studies* 5, no. 3 (2004), 367, available online: https://doi.org/10.1080/1464937042000288660
36. David Chew, "Tempest over Headscarves Ruffles Singapore's Multiracial Calm," *The Japan Times* (2002), https://www.japantimes.co.jp/opinion/2002/03/01/commentary/world-commentary/tempest-over-headscarves-ruffles-singapores-multiracial-calm/.
37. Journeyman Pictures. "Headscarf Controversy in Singapore (2002)," YouTube, December 14, 2018. Video, 3:01–3:40. https://www.youtube.com/watch?v=aTO73Q-bhW0
38. Ibid.
39. Koh, "Tudung."
40. Kadir, "Islam, State and Society," 367.
41. Journeyman Pictures. "Headscarf Controversy in Singapore (2002)," YouTube.
42. Ibid.
43. Kok Xing Hui, "Hjiab Issue: Govt Must 'Balance Community Requirements," *Today,* November 6, 2013, last updated November 7, 2013, https://www.todayonline.com/singapore/hijab-issue-govt-must-balance-community-requirements.
44. Robin Chan, "Personal Attacks on Muslim Leaders over Hijab Issue Uncalled for," *Straits Times*, October 31, 2013, https://www.straitstimes.com/singapore/personal-attacks-on-muslim-leaders-over-hijab-issue-uncalled-for-dr-yaacob-ibrahim
45. Terence Lee, "Singapore 'Hijab Movement' Facebook Page Mysteriously Disappears," *Tech in Asia*, November 14, 2014, https://www.techinasia.com/singapore-hijab-movement-facebook-page-mysteriously-disappears

46. Kharunisya Hanafi, "SDP's Damanhuri Abas Vows to Address Concerns of the Malay Community," September 8, 2015. http://blog.nus.edu.sg/nm3211/2015/09/08/sdps-damanhuri-abas-vows-to-address-concerns-of-the-malay-community/
47. PERGAS, "PERGAS' Response to the Tudung Issue for Female Muslims at the Workplace," Media Statement, November 8, 2013, http://www.pergas.org.sg/media/MediaStatement/Media-Statement-Tudung-Issue-8-November.pdf
48. Ibid.
49. Original post: "... *Sebagai masyarakat Islam Singapura, kita juga tidak berselisih pada prinsip bahawa rambut seorang muslimah adalah termasuk aurat yang wajib ditutup apabila berhadapan dengan orang-orang yang bukan mahram...*" Fatris Bakaram, "Isu Tudung Dan Media Sosial: Membela Maruah Dengan Memijak Maruah?" ("Social Media and the Tudung Issue: Upholding Dignity by Trampling on Dignity?"), Facebook, October 28, 2013. https://www.facebook.com/notes/fatris-bakaram/isu-tudung-dan-media-sosial-membela-maruah-dengan-memijak-maruah/10151948546233480
50. Sophia Gregory, "The Muslim Influencer Who Removed Her Hijab: A Publicity Stunt or a Personal Struggle?," *Religion Media Centre,* published on June 25, 2020. https://religionmediacentre.org.uk/news/the-muslim-influencer-who-removed-her-hijab-a-publicity-stunt-or-a-personal-struggle/
51. Muhammad Zahid Mohd Zin (@zahidzin). 2020. "Nilai sehelai kain mahkotamu..." ("The Value of a Cloth on Your Head..."). Instagram photo, June 8, 2020. https://www.instagram.com/p/CBJztaSA8JP/
52. Johan Fisher, *Proper Islamic Consumption - Shopping Among the Malays* (Copenhagen: NIAS Press, 2008), 96.
53. Nona Kirana (@nonakirana). "Wearing the Hijab Is an OBLIGATION..." Instagram photo, June 4, 2020. https://www.instagram.com/p/CBAfJesjM_2/
54. Syukran Talks, "Hijabku.. Mahkotaku.. bersama Nona Kirana dan Ustazah Nurul 'Izzah Khamsani," ("My *Hijab*, My Crown, with Nona Kirana and Ustazah Nurul 'Izzah Khamsani") Spotify. June 12, 2020. https://open.spotify.com/episode/4AWse36aaKl3X8pmHzmR7D?si=1lK7DofARp6vsAhDFHtXLw
55. Liyana Musfirah (@liyanamusfira). 2018. "My Abaya journey started Way back since 2009," Instagram photo, August 9, 2018. https://www.instagram.com/p/BmOWFjkhkeA/
56. Belmont Lay, Fasiha Nazren and Syahindah Ishak, "Fast & Furious Backlash against OkLetsGo Podcast in S'pore, Explained," *Mothership,* June 16, 2020, https://mothership.sg/2020/06/okletsgo/.
57. Ibid.
58. Ibid.
59. Nabilah Awang and Latasha Seow, "Okletsgo podcast hosts must 'learn and grow' from criticisms over misogynistic comments: Shanmugam," *Today Online*, last updated February 18, 2021. https://www.todayonline.com/singapore/okletsgo-podcast-hosts-must-learn-and-grow-criticisms-over-misogynistic-comments-shanmugam
60. Nazirudin Nasir (@nazirudinmnasir). 2020. "Assalamualaikum friends, we have come far as a community," June 15, 2020. https://www.instagram.com/p/CBb92T0h0CT/
61. Ibid.
62. Ibid.
63. Nadia Hanim AR, "When it gets too noisy, I will listen to soothing musics or recitations," Facebook, June 14, 2020. https://www.facebook.com/nadia.hanim.ar/posts/2824394361017329

64. Mustafa Al-Sagoff, "Wadah baru podcast dan media sosial membuka ruang untuk lebih ramai bersuara" ("Podcast and social media are new platforms for people to express themselves") Facebook, June 16, 2020. https://www.facebook.com/mustafa.alsagoff/posts/10157900245767800
65. Nuzulul Qadar Abdullah, "Objektifikasi Seksual," ("Sexual Objectification") Facebook, June 14, 2020. https://www.facebook.com/nuzul.turun/posts/10157274700022805
66. Ibid.

Bibliography

Abdullah, Nuzulul Qadar. "Objektifikasi Seksual." ("Sexual Objectification") Facebook, June 14, 2020. https://www.facebook.com/nuzul.turun/posts/10157274700022805.

Al-Sagoff, Mustafa. "Wadah baru podcast dan media sosial membuka ruang untuk lebih ramai bersuara." ("Podcast and social media are new platforms for people to express themselves") Facebook, June 16, 2020. https://www.facebook.com/mustafa.alsagoff/posts/10157900245767800 (accessed June 16, 2023).

AR, Nadia Hanim. "When it gets too noisy, I will listen to soothing musics or recitations." Facebook, June 14, 2020. https://www.facebook.com/nadia.hanim.ar/posts/2824394361017329.

Awang Nabilah, Seow Latasha. "Okletsgo podcast hosts must 'learn and grow' from criticisms over misogynistic comments: Shanmugam." *Today Online*, last updated February 18, 2021. https://www.todayonline.com/singapore/okletsgo-podcast-hosts-must-learn-and-grow-criticisms-over-misogynistic-comments-shanmugam.

Bakaram, Fatris. "Isu Tudung Dan Media Sosial: Membela Maruah Dengan Memijak Maruah?." ("Social Media and the Tudung Issue: Upholding Dignity by Trampling on Dignity?"), Facebook, October 28, 2013. https://www.facebook.com/notes/fatris-bakaram/isu-tudung-dan-media-sosial-membela-maruah-dengan-memijak-maruah/10151948546233480.

Bersama Mu ... Kini dan Selamanya (*Together with You ... Now, and Forever*). 2019.

Chan, Robin. "Personal Attacks on Muslim Leaders over Hijab Issue Uncalled for." *Straits Times*, October 31, 2013, https://www.straitstimes.com/singapore/personal-attacks-on-muslim-leaders-over-hijab-issue-uncalled-for-dr-yaacob-ibrahim.

Chew, David. "Tempest Over Headscarves Ruffles Singapore's Multiracial Calm." *The Japan Times,* March 1, 2002, https://www.japantimes.co.jp/opinion/2002/03/01/commentary/world-commentary/tempest-over-headscarves-ruffles-singapores-multiracial-calm/.

Fauzan, Faizuddin (@faizuddinfauzan). 2020. "BROKEN MUSLIM MEN." Instagram Video, September 20, 2020. https://www.instagram.com/tv/CFXCqEpBo5b/.

Fisher, Johan. *Proper Islamic Consumption - Shopping Among the Malays.* Copenhagen: NIAS Press, 2008.

Gregory, Sophia. "The Muslim Influencer Who Removed Her Hijab: A Publicity Stunt or a Personal Struggle?" *Religion Media Centre,* June 25, 2020. https://religionmediacentre.org.uk/news/the-muslim-influencer-who-removed-her-hijab-a-publicity-stunt-or-a-personal-struggle/.

Hanafi, Kharunisya. "SDP's Damanhuri Abas Vows to Address Concerns of the Malay Community," September 8, 2015. http://blog.nus.edu.sg/nm3211/2015/09/08/sdps-damanhuri-abas-vows-to-address-concerns-of-the-malay-community/.

Hochel, Sandra. "To Veil or Not to Veil: Voices of Malaysian Muslim Women." *Intercultural Communication Studies* 22, no. 2 (2013): 40–57.

Hui, Kok Xing. "Hjiab Issue: Govt Must 'Balance Community Requirements." *Today*, last updated November 7, 2013, https://www.todayonline.com/singapore/hijab-issue-govt-must-balance-community-requirements.

Husin Ali, Syed. *The Malays: Their Problems and Future*. Petaling Jaya, Selangor: The Other Press, 2008.

Ibrahim, Azhar. "Discourses on Islam in Southeast Asia and Their Impact on the Singapore Muslim Public." In Lai Ah Eng, *Religious Diversity in Singapore*, 83–115. Singapore, ISEAS: 2008.

Ibrahim, Azhar. *Contemporary Islamic Discourse in the Malay-Indonesian World: Critical Perspectives*. Selangor: Strategic Information and Research Development Centre, 2014.

Iziddin, Said, and Mahadi Said. "The Islamic Resurgence Movement amongst Muslim Students in University of Singapore in the 1970s." Honours Thesis. Singapore: National University of Singapore, 2017.

Jamil, Nurhaizatul Jamila. "*Perempuan, Isteri, Dan…*: Embodied Agency and the Malay Woman of Contemporary Singapore." Master's dissertation. Singapore: National University of Singapore, 2009.

Journeyman Pictures. "Headscarf Controversy in Singapore (2002)." YouTube, December 14, 2018. Video, 3:01-3:40. https://www.youtube.com/watch?v=aTO73Q-bhW0.

Kadir, Suzaina. "Islam, State and Society in Singapore." *Inter-Asia Cultural Studies* 5, no. 3 (2004): 357–71, https://doi.org/10.1080/1464937042000288660.

Kirana, Nona (@nonakirana). "Wearing the Hijab Is an OBLIGATION…" Instagram photo, June 4, 2020. https://www.instagram.com/p/CBAfJesjM_2/.

Koh, Jamie. "Tudung." *Singapore Infopedia*. https://eresources.nlb.gov.sg/infopedia/articles/SIP_2013-09-30_123324.html (accessed May 30, 2021)

Lay, Belmont, Nazren Fasiha, and Ishak Syahindah. "Fast & Furious Backlash against OkLetsGo Podcast in S'pore, Explained." *Mothership*, published on June 16, 2020, https://mothership.sg/2020/06/okletsgo/.

Lee, Debbie. "Survey: 74% of Women Turn Down Jobs due to Work-Life Balance Concerns." *The Straits Times*, March 4, 2013. https://www.straitstimes.com/singapore/survey-74-of-women-turn-down-jobs-due-to-work-life-balance-concerns.

Lee, Terence. "Singapore 'Hijab Movement' Facebook Page Mysteriously Disappears." *Tech in Asia*, November 14, 2014, https://www.techinasia.com/singapore-hijab-movement-facebook-page-mysteriously-disappears.

Majlis Ugama Islam Singapura. *Pedoman Ringkas Berumahtangga* (*Guidelines on Marriage*). 1974.

Mohd, Zin, Muhammad Zahid (@zahidzin). 2020. "Nilai sehelai kain mahkotamu…" ("The value of a cloth on your head…"). Instagram photo, June 8, 2020. https://www.instagram.com/p/CBJztaSA8JP/.

Musfirah, Liyana (@liyanamusfira). 2018. "My Abaya Journey Started Way Back since 2009…." Instagram photo, August 9, 2018. https://www.instagram.com/p/BmOWFjkhkeA/.

Nasir, Nazirudin (@nazirudinmnasir). 2020. "Assalamualaikum Friends, We Have Come Far as a Community…" June 15, 2020. https://www.instagram.com/p/CBb92T0h0CT/.

PERGAS. "PERGAS' Response to the Tudung Issue for Female Muslims at the Workplace." Media Statement, November 8, 2013, http://www.pergas.org.sg/media/MediaStatement/Media-Statement-Tudung-Issue-8-November.pdf.

PERGAS. *Ar-Risalah*. Issue 18 (May-August 2015) (Singapore: PERGAS, 2015), 4–14, 38–39. https://issuu.com/ar-risalah/docs/ar-risalah_isu_18_fa_single.

Rahman, Abdul, and Aisha Noor. "Religious Resurgence amongst the Malays and Its impact: The Case of Singapore." In *Alternative Voices in Muslim Southeast Asia: Discourse and Struggles*. Edited by Norshahril Saat, 33–66. Singapore: ISEAS, 2020.

Rahman, Abdul, and Aisha Noor. "Shariah Revivalism in Singapore." In *Islam in Southeast Asia: Negotiating Modernity*. Edited by Norshahril Saat, 195–230. Singapore: ISEAS, 2018.

Suratman, Suriani. "Gender Relations in Singapore: Malay Dual-Income Households: (Un)Changing Views and Practices." *Islam and Civilisational Renewal* 3, no. 1 (2011): 90–115.

Suratman, Suriani. "Skills for 'Marriage of a Lifetime': An Examination of Muslim Marriage Preparation Handbooks in Singapore, 1974–2018." *Religions* 12 (2021): 473. https://doi.org/10.3390/rel12070473

Syukran Talks. "Hijabku.. Mahkotaku.. bersama Nona Kirana dan Ustazah Nurul 'Izzah Khamsani." ("My *Hijab*, My Crown, with Nona Kirana and Ustazah Nurul 'Izzah Khamsani") Spotify. June 12, 2020. https://open.spotify.com/episode/4AWse36aaKl3X8pmHzmR7D?si=1lK7DofARp6vsAhDFHtXLw.

Women's Action. "Singapore and the Women's Movement," last accessed June 21, 2021. https://www.womensaction.sg/article/overview.

13

Evolving Islamic Modesty in China: Confucianism, Arabization, and Sinicization

Wai-Yip Ho

Introduction

Since the modern period in China, in particular the "Open-Door Policy" starting in 1978, the notion of modesty among the Muslim minority *Hui* (回族) has been closely associated with the Chinese words *Xiuti* (羞體), meaning "Shameful body." This has been well-documented by Western scholarly fieldwork among the Muslim community in China.[1] While respecting these colleagues' insights and observations, this chapter suggests broadening the understanding of Islamic modesty across different periods of Chinese history. The linking of Islamic modesty to the gendered idea of *Xiuti* among China's Muslims is perhaps a modern phenomenon, given that this specific understanding corresponds to the Arabic notion *ʿawra*, referring to the concealment of the female body to protect women's modesty.[2] The notion of Islamic modesty does not necessarily pertain to this narrow, gendered notion. For in the long history of China before the modern era, modesty to Muslims was understood through an enduring influence of Confucianism. Therefore, the chapter argues that Islamic modesty could be understood as an open and highly malleable concept that varies under different political ideologies. In other words, while *Xiuti* has been widely shared as proper personal conduct among Muslim women nowadays, it is only one of its interpretations, but hardly the only interpretation of Islamic modesty throughout generations in China. The conception of Islamic modesty among Muslims is multifaceted and has been evolving in China. It is neither monolithic nor static. The scholarly field on Islam in China has been flourishing in recent decades.[3] In Ben-Dor Benite's words, the field of Chinese Islam is no longer "a neglected problem" as Broomhall first reported to the Christian missionary enterprise,[4] but rather a complete, even if not "harmonious concert."[5] Frankel even pointed out that this field of study has been shifting from depicting Islam as a monolith to describing it as a mosaic.[6] In the nineteenth century, Western Christian missionaries discovered Muslims in China were a potential group to evangelize, and pioneering reports and surveys were conducted by the Christian missionaries.[7] In the 1990s, with a revival of academic interests after China's opening up, time has been devoted to the study of Islam among the people of Hui, often referred as the "Muslim Chinese."[8] More careful and detailed efforts have been recently paid to the internal situation for the diverse groups of Muslims, separated geographically, ethnically, and linguistically in the rich and dynamic history of China. Moreover, increased interest in Islam in China can be attributed to China's global rise, historical and contemporary geopolitical relations between China and the Muslim world,[9] and the external relations of China's Muslims.[10]

Despite the flourishing academic boom of rediscovering Muslim groups and Islam in China, many topics including Islamic modesty, awaits to be revisited due to the changing situations of Muslims living in the dynamic history of China. In his thesis of the civilizing process, Norbert Elias persuasively analyzed the body as a text of sociogenic and psychogenic changes, arguing that "the structure of the body and human psyche, the structure of human society, and the structures of human history are indissolubly complementary and can only be studied in conjunction with each other."[11] This chapter suggests that the evolving notions of Islamic modesty connect with the Muslims' bodies and dispositions regulated under the ideological forces in Chinese history. Analytically Islamic modesty is discussed in three different phases in Chinese history—namely, Confucianism in premodern China (before 1911), the modern China facing Westernization, and Muslims under the influence of the Arab world (particularly 1978 onward)—as well as the resurgence of patriotism under the national program of *Zhongguohua* (中國化) or *Han Hua* (漢化) "Sinicization,"[12] led by the regime of President Xi Jinping since 2016.

Islamic Modesty in Premodern China: Internal Morality under Confucianism

Tracing the premodern Chinese history before the end of the Qing Dynasty in 1911, the conception of modesty has to be understood in reference to the cultural fabric of Confucian China. From the Ming dynasty (1368–1644) to the Qing dynasty (1636–1912), Chinese Muslim scholars, such as Wang Daiyu (王岱輿) (*c.* 1590–1658) and Liu Zhi (劉智) (*c.* 1662–1736), translated and transmitted Islamic thought from Arabian-Persian texts through the intellectual framework and vocabularies of Confucian Chinese tradition. This intellectual thought in Islamic literature was called *Han Kitab* (漢克塔補); Sino-Islamic texts and those thinkers are known as *Hurui* (回儒), Confucian Muslims. While there are emerging studies and growing academic attention recognizing the importance of the field of *Han Kitab*, mainstream studies focus on how Confucian Muslims attempted to translate and transmit Persian-Arabic Islamic texts in Chinese writings as well as the broader intellectual framework of Confucianism.

The current literature demonstrates the successful attempts of Confucian Muslims to harmoniously express and transmit Islamic thought in the Confucian intellectual framework of *Han Kitab* (Sino-Islamic texts). The Confucian Muslims, on the one hand, faithfully preserved doctrinal essences of Islam in the writings of Confucian tradition[13] while, on the other hand, they demonstrated that being Islamic and being loyal to the state without compromising their Chinese identity can go hand in hand.

Islam and Confucianism are not contradictory to each other but can coexist, enlighten, and communicate with each other and share common ground.

Wang Daiyu's work *Zhengjiao Zhenquan* (正教真詮, *Real Commentary on the True Teaching*), published in 1642, has been understood as the earliest and the most significant work written in the Chinese language on Islam.[14] In expounding Islam in Chinese, Wang remains the very essential spirit of Confucian literati, in which he expressed virtue of Islamic modesty in *qian* (謙), humility, or moderation when introducing his work:

> Even though these arguments and writings are strictly matters of my own private person, the principles are the public affairs under heaven. If I were vainly to praise others in order to express my modesty (*qian*), it would ruin the public principles under heaven and not allow them to be transmitted. Truly that is not my first intention.[15]

When discussing the issue of modesty, Wang reminds his Muslim compatriots that the origin of human beings is from above, though the body is from the mud, but the key is to keep the body from the contamination of the "internal dirt," which is pride and disobedience:

> Although the human ancestor often remembered that his origin is pure and clean, when he reflected further on the fact that his body belongs originally to muddy dirt, he kept on hoping to be modest, so pride was not born in him.[16]
>
> They began to wake up to their own disobedience and to become more modest and humble.[17]

Likewise, when explaining true Islamic modesty, Wang emphasizes inward virtue that expresses modesty:

> Moreover, the will of those who are pure and modest while living in a vile place is not disturbed even if they face death. But when those who are greedy and vile dwell in a clean land, they may be outwardly clean, but they will be inwardly vile.[18]

To understand the notion of shame and modesty, Wang did not refer to gendered or bodily dressing but framed the ethical practices in the matrix of human relations and social virtues, guided by the Confucian cosmological framework of three fundamental bonds and five constant virtues:

> It is not only this, however. In all these matters—filial piety and respecting elders, loyalty and faithfulness, propriety and righteousness, modesty and shame—if there is any lack and deficiency, then the way of heaven and the way of man will not be complete.[19]

The cosmological principle, under the shadow of Confucianism, manifests in social order and human relationships, which is rooted in the virtue of modesty and is an internal quality of morality overcoming the evil disposition of pride. It brings Muslims away from arrogance and helps in attaining true virtue, which is purely internal, not external nor visible through a dressing code but extends to one's interior character formation, including *qian*, or "humility or moderation," and *lian* (廉) or "honesty or integrity":

> Knowing self gives birth to modesty and modesty is the fountainhead of the myriad good things. Its streams are humility, veneration, fear, emptying the heart, and submitting to the good. Ignorance of self gives birth to pride, and the pride is the root of various evils. Its branches are bullying, jealously and fishing for praise and reputation. Without modesty, how will you overcome pride?[20]
>
> You should know that when virtue and modesty come together, self-respect dwells in lowness. When honor and nobility come together, arrogance accords with highness. If your do not open up to the fountainhead of modesty and lowness, you will not cut yourself off from the root of honor and highness.[21]
>
> When you become proud of good deeds, this is not equal to modesty and humility as a result of sin and error. When pride dwells together with virtue, the virtue will surely disperse; when it dwells together with sin, the sin will increase. When humility dwells together with sin, the sin perish as a matter of course; when it dwells together with virtue, the virtue will increase.[22]

Retrieving the works of *Han Kitab* on Confucian Muslims from the Ming-Qing period, by considering Wang Daiyu's work *Zhengjiao Zhenquan*, the above texts illustrate how Muslims in the premodern period understood Islamic modesty within the Confucian ethical worldview through internal moral virtues in terms of *qian* (謙), humility, and *lian* (廉), honesty or integrity. Rather than focusing on appearance in front of the external world, the key determinant for one to be modest is through cultivation of internal virtue and by combating the evil desires of pride and arrogance. Obviously, the essence of self-cultivation and mental discipline is clearly characterized by the school of Song-Ming Confucianism, the dominant Confucian thought throughout the Song (960–1279), Yuan (1279–1368), and Ming dynasties (1368–1644), in which Chinese Muslims since the Song period have understood the notion of modesty under the shadow of Confucian ethical framework, which contrasts drastically with the late Qing period.

Islamic Modesty in the Opening-Up Period: Covering the Body under Arabization

Unlike Wang Daiyu's understanding of modesty as an invisible and internal morality, in addition to expressing the cosmological principle in the social networks and human relationships, perception of modesty in the modern era shifts to the external, visible, and gendered divisions and dressing codes. In understanding the contemporary meaning of modesty among the Muslim Chinese, one often refers to the idea of *xiuti* (羞體) "shamed body," as is best illustrated in Tontini's work of *Muslim Sanzijing*.[23]

According to Tontini, one of the most popular and representative individuals of the *Muslim Sanzijing* (穆斯林三字經) is Hu Songshan (虎嵩山) (1880–1956), a famous Imam, scripturalist against the Sufi order as well as a Chinese leader of the Yhhewani order rallying Muslims against the Japanese invasion during the period of the Second Sino-Japanese War (1937–5). His work *Yisilanjiao sanzi keben* (伊斯蘭教三字課本) [*Three Character Primer of Islam*] was published in Ningxia in 1938. In the midst of the crisis of the traditional social and political orders after the end of imperial rule, the wave of modernity, and the newly established republic, the primary motif of Hu Songshan's *Yisilanjiao sanzi keben* is to strengthen the Chinese nation by legitimizing the traditional Confucian authority of the "five sets of relationships" between father and son, ruler and minister, and husband and wife as well as between brothers and between friends.[24] *Muslim Sanzijing* instructs the appropriate management of social relationship between man and woman:

> Modesty [*xiuti*] consists of concealing [the body] from [people's] sight. Men [should conceal themselves] from the navel to both knees, [while for] women the whole body is [considered the object of] modesty—except the palms and the face. Before every prayer, the body must be cleansed, [based upon a] division between minor [*xiaojing*] and major ablutions [*dayu*]. [If there are] faeces or urine, or blood that runs from the skin, or gas that comes from below, the minor ablution process [*xiaojing*] is [regarded as] compromised.[25]

In the majority of cases, the conception of *Xiuti* refers mainly to the Muslim women, as illustrated by Gillette:

> Most residents of the quarter said that skirts violated the Islamic code of modesty—known locally as *xiuti* or "shamed body"—which dictates that women's bodies be covered from ankle to wrist. For most Xi'an Hui, observing modesty dictates.[26]

This understanding of *Xiuti* has been expounded by the ground-breaking book of Chinese Women's Mosques, coauthored by Maria Jaschok and Shui Jingjun.[27] In a book chapter entitled "Xiuti; 'From Head to Toe'—Shaming and Concealment the body,"[28] Jaschok and Shui revolutionized the long-standing cliché of Chinese Muslim women as passive, submissive, and exploited agents. Instead, they represent Chinese Muslim women also as imams, active agents of spiritual leadership in empowering Muslim women to learn and pursue the path of Islam.[29] Nevertheless, Jaschok and Shui define *xiuti* as covering "from Head to Toe," and it refers to shaming and concealing the body. Likewise, Gillette's anthropological fieldwork in Xian[30] shows how economic prosperity reformed understanding of everyday life and shaped a new consumption pattern. In particular, the changing consumption patterns altered Chinese Muslim (Hui) women's taste in appropriate fashion, so that they embraced the Arab-style headscarves and robes. Most importantly, the Arabization of dress also internalized a new standard of modesty.

In the modern period, the new China is governed by the Chinese Communist Party (CCP) led by the majority Han population. Though the country has been mainly led by the majority Han people, the government recognizes that the country is a multiethnic nation. Following Stalin's definition in identifying national minorities, the government officially recognized fifty-five minority groups. Among the fifty-six nationalities and fifty-five ethnic minority groups living in China, the Hui people are one of the officially recognized ethnic minority groups and the largest of the ten official Muslim nationalities (*minzu*). The other nine Muslim nationalities are Uyghur, Kazakh, Dongxiang, Kyrgyz, Salar, Tajik, Uzbek, Bonan, and Tatar. Language is the key dividing line among the various Muslim ethnic groups when differentiating between Hui and the other nine Muslim nationalities. Unlike the Chinese speaking Hui, the nine other Muslim nationalities use a wide range of languages such as Turkic, Turkic-Mongolian, and Indo-Persian dialects, and Chinese is not their native language.[31] Chinese Hui scholar Wang Xiaoyan observes that the practice of veiling and the symbol of headscarf is the main clothing difference between Hui Muslims and other nationalities, mainly a distinctive mark to differentiate Hui Muslims from Han Chinese.[32] Wang argues that Hui Muslim women traditionally wore a white hat or traditional *Gaitou* (蓋頭) in rural areas where labor is strictly gendered: Hui men work outside the home earning money, and woman are responsible for the domestic duties at home. But since the 1990s, more urban Hui Muslim women began covering their hair, neck, ears, and forehead, which had not been common earlier. Apart from veiling, Hui Muslims distinguished themselves from the Han Chinese in other Islamic customs, such as halal food. Having said that, Hui Muslims' distinctive and visible white cap, the *Gaitou*, and headscarves have become markers of Hui identity that distinguishes them from Han people. To explain how the headscarf became fashionable indicating a new sense of religious life, Wang suggests that there are several factors in explaining the increased veiling among Hi woman—namely as a Hui cultural psychological phenomenon, mainstream cultural context, and the changes in government policy.

Wang observes a new phenomenon that emerged in urban China in the 1990s—namely, increasing number of Muslim ladies regardless of age and marital status, determined to wear headscarf covering their head, ears, and forehead in the street, university campuses, and workplace.[33] Internally, Muslim dressing is a fundamental marker for minority Muslims to uphold the identity from the non-Muslim Han-Chinese population. Yet the emergence of headscarf fashion has to be interpreted as the consequence of China's Open Policy in 1978, improving ties between China and the Muslim Middle Eastern Governments as well as the Chinese Muslims' affiliation to the global Islamic revival movement, rooted in the Middle East, starting from Egypt.[34] Therefore, the Islamic revival in China began in the 1980s when the central government permitted freedom of worship and the reconstruction of damaged mosques, thus correcting government policies that led to extreme anti-religious struggles and persecution that occurred during the Cultural Revolution in the early 1970s.

The opening-up policy and closer China–Middle East ties reinitiated the Muslim pilgrimage (*hajj*) to Mecca in Saudi Arabia. Chinese Muslims were also sent to study Islam, learning Arabic and the Quran, and some Chinese Muslim merchants started doing business in Egypt, Saudi Arabia, Pakistan, and so on. Meanwhile, the *ṣaḥwa* movement was thriving in Egypt, and headscarf fashions spread from the Middle

East to China, through people who had gone to work or study in Egypt, Saudi Arabia, and Malaysia.[35] This opening-up policy also explains how the veiling practice also spread to some university colleges, where Muslim women in China started wearing the headscarf, as a new wave of consumerism and female fashion began in the urban context. Muslim women deliberately chose the headscarf because of the city culture. Wang points out the headscarf emerged in China as a new fashion from abroad, and the Hui women adopt it and follow wearing headscarf, showing that they are modern, not backward, popular, and identify their religious solidarity with the Muslim *umma*:

> One of my relatives, who was educated at a university in Tunisia, and who worked in the United Arab Emirates and toured Egypt, told me that in the late 1990s he often saw Egyptian women wearing scarves, including many university teachers. The more education they had, the more enthusiastically they included scarves in their wardrobes. In this way, the message of contemporary practices in Arabic society was brought and spread throughout Chinese Hui areas by these students, Hajjis, and others.[36]

Apart from examining veiling in the urban and coastal areas of China, Ha's insightful ethnographic work[37] in the rural northwest China suggests that the shifting of styles regarding rural Hui Muslims' headscarf use is connected to its transnational politico-economic origins when China was moving from a socialist to a neoliberal economy. Veiling is seen as a hallmark and assertion of Islamic identity and modesty of living in a non-Muslim majority China. This subtle shift in the meaning of veiling has to be understood within the wider context of China's opening up and shift from a socialist to neo-liberal economic order.

Summing up the modern period in China, the collapse of the Imperial Qing Dynasty marked the fall of feudalism in 1911. The traditional Chinese value system was under severe threat, the nation subsequently confronted by military invasions as well as the challenges of Western modernization. At the crossroads of national crisis, Muslims struggled together with non-Muslim nationals to stand up to the modern challenges. Imam Hu Songshan's work of *Yisilanjiao sanzi keben* attempted to reinstate the traditional Confucian authority of the social hierarchy. More specifically, the conception of *Xiuti* was highlighted reordering Islamic-acceptable relationships between man and woman. After China's opening up and reconnecting to the world since 1978, Muslims in China faced the challenges of Western modernity as well as the influence of the Muslim Arab world. Veiling became a social practice that not only delineates gender relations among ethnic Muslims from the Han majority, but Muslim women often express religious identity through veiling with a sense of pride.

Veiling became a mark of expression of ethnic and religious identity through which Muslims defend modesty and Islamic identity by differentiating themselves from the Han majority. In connecting with a larger Muslim community (*umma*), Muslims living in China struggle to protect their own religious heritage and modesty by standing in solidarity with other parts of the Muslim world by identifying the meaning of modesty of dressing, following in the footsteps of majority Muslim societies in the Middle East.

Islamic Modesty in China's Rise: Ethnic Religion under Sinicization

Although the Chinese government affirms the open-door policy of welcoming the international community, China has opposed external interference in domestic affairs. In the recent policy of "Sinicization," the concerned foreign powers intervening in the hearts and minds of Chinese nationals includes *Yangjiao* (洋教)—foreign religions such as Christianity and Islam.[38] One example of this is that the Chinese government requested Amazon to remove Qur'an and Bible apps from the Apple store in Mainland China.[39] In 2016, President Xi Jinping called for the program of "Sinicization of Religion,"[40] by which religious faiths, practice, and rituals have to be indigenized and made compatible with Chinese culture and society. In fact, the "Sinicization of Religion" is only one part of the Sinicization campaign in reeducating the public by refilling the spiritual and cultural vacuum in the neo-liberal economy, a soul-searching and relocating of Chinese identity under the ideology and leadership of the CCP. Under the guidance of state socialism, Chinese people have to be reoriented from religions to socialist ideology, and religious leaders and institutions have to comply with the CCP leadership.[41] In guarding the national security and the rise of religious extremism, the Chinese government, like other countries, combats terrorism and separatism that prompts the Chinese government to differentiate between "good" religious practices from "bad" illegal activities,[42] while preventing the infiltration of extremist ideology from overseas through new social media.[43]

In response to the Chinese government's announcement of a national plan to sinicize religion through a "five-year plan," representatives of Islamic associations from eight Chinese provinces discussed how to align Islam with Chinese norms, aiming at shielding China's Muslim community from foreign influence. The international community has been paying attention to the situation of Uyghur Muslims in Xinjiang, and the local authority has been persistently suppressing religious radicalism in the Xinjiang region and the Uyghur people. In the name of fighting against religious radicalism, extremism, and terrorism resulting from foreign intervention, it is reported that strict measures of counterterrorism prohibit Uyghur Muslims from fasting and praying in the mosque, children from attending religious schools, men from growing "abnormal" beards, and women from wearing the veil.[44] Although the government does not give a clear guideline regarding the precise style of headscarf and dressing policy, Leibold and Grose analyzed the struggle between the Chinese government and Xinjiang's Uyghur Muslims over defining what is "appropriate" and "normal" female adornment, which has been intensifying when new styles of veiling enter China from abroad and the Chinese government strives to control and standardize Uyghur Muslim dressing.[45]

In the midst of China's rise in the 2000s, the government assimilated Muslim minorities by defining the norm of Islamic modesty and by sanctioning the "abnormal" or "extreme" practices in accordance with the Sinicized or Chinese characteristics. Stressing the regime's role of unifying of China's *shaoshu minzu* (少數民族) ethnic minorities, under the leadership of the CCP in addition to the official coverage of global

Islam emphasizing the religion Islam as dangerous and prone to extremism, Stroup explains the rising Islamophobia sentiments in terms of harassment and suspicions regarding China's Muslims in Han-majority China.[46] The increasing visibility of veiling among Muslim women in various parts of China, in particular in Xinjiang, is considered as a threat in the eyes of Chinese government because it is seen as a sign of "foreign" Arabic culture and is even linked to religious extremism and terror. Therefore, various observers explain why, since 2006, Arabic scripts of halal food labels were removed, de-Islamification of the public sphere occurred, and a surveillance system was employed in ethnic politics.[47]

In the eyes of the Chinese government, Sinicization of Islam standardizing the norm of veiling style is aimed to restore the social order and peace from the disorderly social practices such as the Arabization of Chinese Muslim women veiling. Because of international concerns about human rights and religious freedom of Uyghur Muslims in Xinjiang, the Chinse government continues to attract scholarly attention and research on political Islam in China for the future. However, it should be noted that Xinjiang has been a highly politicized and sensitive target of Beijing. Since 2018, numerous Western news reports state that at least one million Muslim Uyghurs were sent to be reeducated, tortured, and forced into labor in Xinjiang. Some claim Uyghur women were sexually abused, and they faced the threat of "genocide."[48] The veil has emerged as a key battleground in the struggle to regain stability in Xinjiang. Having said that, the Chinese government denies use of forced labor claims and other accusations of "crimes against humanity" as pure fabrications, because it is a card played by anti-China forces in the West, which are attempting to disrupt the region's stability and to contain China's development.[49]

Other than Uyghur Muslims, the campaign of Sinicization of Islam obviously extends to other Muslim groups beyond Xinjiang, also including the Hui, the largest Muslim group in China.[50] Many reports and analysis exist on how Arab-influenced mosques, dressing, and religious practices are being replaced, in accordance with the leadership of the CCP.[51] One startling example of this is that, in 2021, the "Arab-style" dome and minarets of Dongguan mosque in Xining, one of the largest mosques in China in the Qinghai Hui Autonomous Region, were removed and renovated with Chinese characteristics on the front gate, followed by similar removal and renovation changes on the Nanguan Mosque in Yinchuan in Ningxia in 2020. Loudspeakers and Arabic signs in Gansu mosques of Linxia were removed and three mosques in Yunnan were demolished in 2018; similar changes happened in Henan and Shangdong in 2019.[52] In the national campaign of Sinicization, it is observed that measures of de-radicalization do not necessarily target only Uyghur Muslims in Xinjiang area, but the underlying rationale of Sinicization is to define and impose state-acceptable Han-leading norms of religions and ethnicity. In one precise understanding of "sinicization"—*Han Hua*—religions and ethnic groups go through the process of indigenization, led by Chinese characteristics or according to Han-defined norms.[53]

Moving from internal politics to foreign affairs, the Chinese Consul in Pakistan Zhang Heqing published a provocative video song, "Off your hijab," in his tweet in March 2021. The video showed a Chinese lady dancing without the hijab, which resulted in uproar, and many Muslims in Pakistan criticized Zhang for insulting Islam and spreading news to Pakistani Muslims of women taking off the hijab.[54] Though it might be an individual diplomatic dispute, it clearly shows the Chinese official stance that appropriate and modest dressing for Muslim ladies is without the veil or headscarf. While China's treatment of Muslim minorities in Xinjiang, Northwest China, receives global attention, the government's restrictions of Islamic practices have extended to other regions of the country as well as different Muslim minorities in China. The restriction of the headscarf was also imposed on Hui Muslims. *South China Morning Post* (2020) reported that traditional Muslim dress is banned in schools and government offices, and Arabic architecture is now strictly censored in Sanya, the southern part of China.[55] As a result of tightening measures with respect to Muslim rights, a group of veiled Hui school girls holding textbooks staged a protest outside a primary school.

Conclusion: Changing Islamic Modesty under China's Sovereign Ideologies

Surveying the notion of Islamic modesty across three different periods of Chinese history, this chapter attempts to show the conceptual changes in views of Islamic modesty under ideological thoughts in different periods of Chinese history. The chapter argued that the notion of Islamic modesty is highly malleable, negotiated, and defined by dominant social forces in specific periods of Chinese history: Cultivation of internal mental discipline under Confucianism in the Song-Ming Period, Muslim women's veiling under Arabization since the fall of the Qing Dynasty, and recently upholding patriotic spirit in segregating good from external religious influence under the national campaign of Sinicization. Islamic and China's Muslims' understanding of modesty has been evolving far beyond the exclusive understanding of gendered and external dressing codes. In terms of Chinese Islamic intellectual history, the notion of Islamic modesty points to the interior and underlying ethical requirement to both Muslim men and women, which is highly influenced by the Islamic thought embedded within the moral fabric of Confucian culture in the premodern period. Under the shadow of anti-China forces targeting the Xinjiang issue, veiling becomes a socially contested and stigmatized issue in the Sinicization campaign.

This chapter suggests that the Muslim meaning of Islamic modesty has been made compatible to the Confucian moral order in the Imperial period, as the Islamic concept of modesty can also be translated to internal dispositions of *qian* (humility or moderation) and *lian* (honesty or integrity). However, after the Imperial collapse and the crisis of Islamic identity living with Han-majority rule in modern China, the meaning of modesty focused on the notion of *xiuti* (shamed body). Here, Chinese Muslims' understanding of modesty reconnected and corresponded more closely with Arab Muslims' understanding of Islamic modesty that emphasizes female veiling. However, under the national assimilation campaign, the "Sinicization of religion," Muslim practice and mosque architecture have to be sinicized (*Zhongguohua* or *Han Hua*) and approved by the Chinese state, which includes the interpretation and practice of Islamic modesty. Veiling is banned in some parts of China, for it is considered as a foreign, Arabic way of life that is alien to Han-leading practice or the Chinese norm. Some mosques, with their Arabic-style tall minarets and domes, are also considered incompatible with the Chinese style.[56] Specifically, CCP's anti-veiling campaign is due to the state authority's determination to break the direct link between veiling, radical Islam, and even terrorism.

This chapter reviewed the Islamic notion of modesty in three different periods and distinguishes between the following: an emphasis on internal morality in the Imperial period, the greater importance of gendered dressing in the opening-up modern period, and finally, the banning of the hijab with the state's targeting of separatism and Sinicization. Muslims' notion of modesty in China is neither monolithic nor static, and it may be read as an empirical indicator of shifting conditions of sovereign power and dominant ideologies in Chinese history.

Notes

1. See, for instance, Maria Jaschok and Shui Jingjun, "Purity, Sexuality and Faith: Chinese Women *Ahong* and Women's Mosques as Shelter and Strength," in *Sexuality in Muslim Contexts: Restrictions and Resistance*, edited by Anissa Hélie and Homa Hoodfar (London: Zed, 2012), 151–81; Maris Boyd Gillette, *Between Mecca and Beijing: Modernization and Consumption among Urban Chinese Muslims* (Stanford, CA: Stanford University Press, 2000); Maris Boyd Gillette, "Fashion among Chinese Muslims," *ISIM Review*, 15 Spring (2005), 36–7.
2. Maria Jaschok, "Religious Agency and Gender Complementarity: Women's Mosques and Women's Voices in Hui Muslim Communities in Central China," *Review of Religion and Chinese Society* 5 (2018), 201.
3. For example, Ho Wai-Yip, "From Neglected Problem to Flourishing Field: Recent Developments of Research on Muslims and Islam in China," in *Concepts and Methods for the Study of Chinese Religions I: State of the Field and Disciplinary Approaches*, edited by André Laliberté and Stefania Travagnin (Berlin: De Gruyter, 2019), 93–114.
4. Marshall Broomhall, *Islam in China: A Neglected Problem* (New York: Paragon Book, 1910).
5. Zvi Ben-Dor Benite, "Chinese Islam: A Complete Concert," *Cross-Currents: East Asian History and Culture Review* 23 (2017), 199.
6. James D. Frankel, "From Monolith to Mosaic: A Decade of Twenty-First Century Studies of Muslims and Islam in China," *Religious Studies Review* 37, no. 4 (2011), 249–58.
7. Alimu Tuoheti, *Islam in China: A History of European and American Scholarship* (Piscataway: Gorgias Press, 2021).
8. Dru Gladney, "The Study of Islam in China: Some Recent Research," *Middle East Studies Association Bulletin* 27, no. 1 (1993), 23–30.
9. James D. Frankel, *Islam in China* (London: I.B. Tauris, 2021).
10. For instance, please see Kelly Hammond, *China's Muslims & Japan's Empire: Centering Islam in World War II* (Chapel Hill: University of North Carolina Press, 2020).
11. Norbert Elias, *The Society of Individuals* (Oxford: Blackwell, 1991), 36.

12. Yang Fenggang, "Sinicization or Chinafication?: Cultural Assimilation vs. Political Domestication of Christianity in China and Beyond," in *The Sinicization of Chinese Religions*, edited by Richard Madsen (Boston: Brill, 2021), 16.
13. Please see Sachiko Murata, *Chinese Gleams of Sufi Light: Wang Tai-yu's Great Learning of the Pure and Real and Liu Chih's Displaying the Concealment of the Real Realm; with a New Translation of Jami's Lawaih from Persian by William C. Chittick* (Albany: SUNY Press, 2000); Sachiko Murata, *The First Islamic Classic in Chinese: Wang Daiyu's Real Commentary on the True Teaching; translated with an Introduction and Notes by Sachiko Murata* (Albany: SUNY Press, 2018); Sachiko Murata, William Chittick, and Weiming Tu. *The Sage Learning of Liu Zhi* (Cambridge: Harvard University Press, 2009).
14. Murata, *The First Islamic Classic in Chinese.*
15. Ibid., 37.
16. Ibid., 56.
17. Ibid., 58.
18. Ibid., 98.
19. Ibid., 163.
20. Ibid.
21. Ibid., 190.
22. Ibid., 194.
23. Roberta Tontini, *Muslim Sanzijing: Shifts and Continuities in the Definition of Islam in China* (Leiden: Brill, 2016).
24. Ibid., 157.
25. Ibid., 164.
26. Gillette, *Between Mecca and Beijing*, 209.
27. Maria Maria Jaschok and Shui Jingjun, *The History of Women's Mosques in Chinese Islam* (Richmond: Curzon, 2001).
28. Ibid., 211–36.
29. Jaschok and Jingjun, "Purity, Sexuality and Faith."
30. Gillette, *Between Mecca and Beijing*; Gillette, "Fashion among Chinese Muslims."
31. Wang Jianping, "Islam and State Policy in Contemporary China," *Studies in Religion* 45, no. 4 (2016), 566–80; Dru Gladney, "Islam in China: Accommodation or Separatism?," *China Quarterly* 174 (2003), 451–67; Jacqueline Armijo, "Islam in China," in *Asian Islam in the 21st Century*, edited by John Voll, John Esposito, and Osman Baker (Oxford: Oxford University Press, 2007), 151–81.
32. Wang Xiaoyan, "The Headscarf and Hui Identity," *Fashion Theory* 15, no. 4 (2011), 481–501; Wang Xiaoyan, "Hui Women and The Headscarf in China," in *The Routledge International Handbook to Veils and Veiling Practices*, edited by Anna-Mari Almila and David Inglis (Abingdon: Routledge, 2017), 255–66.
33. Xiaoyan, "The Headscarf and Hui Identity," 487.
34. Ibid., 488.
35. Xiaoyan, "Hui Women and the Headscarf in China," 261.
36. Xiaoyan, "The Headscarf and Hui Identity," 489.
37. Ha Guangtian, "The Silent Hat: Islam, Female Labor, and the Political Economy of the Headscarf Debate," *Signs: Journal of Women in Culture and Society* 42, no. 3 (2017), 743–69.
38. Richard Madsen, "Introduction," in *The Sinicization of Chinese Religions*, edited by Richard Madsen (Boston, MA: Brill, 2021), 3.

39. *VOA*, "Amazon Removes App for Quran, Bible from Apple Store in China," *VOA*, October 16, 2021. https://www.voanews.com/a/amazon-removes-app-for-quran-bible-from-apple-store-in-china/6273518.html (accessed October 19, 2021).
40. James Dotson, "Propaganda Themes at the CPPCC Stress the 'Sincization' of Religion," *The Jamestown Foundation*, 2019. https://jamestown.org/program/propaganda-themes-at-the-cppcc-stress-the-sinicization-of-religion/ (accessed October 18, 2021).
41. Thomas Harvey, "The Sinicization of Religion in China: Will Enforcing Conformity Work? Lausanne Global Analysis," 8, no. 5 (September 2019). https://lausanne.org/content/lga/2019-09/sinicization-religion-china (accessed June 22, 2021).
42. Zhang Chi, "'Illegal Religious Activities' and Counter-Terrorism in China," *Politics and Religion* 14, no. 2 (2021), 269–93.
43. Ho Wai-Yip, "Reporting Religions with Chinese Characteristics: Sinicizing Religious Faith, Securitizing News Media," in *The Routledge Handbook of Religion and Journalism*, edited by Kerstin Radde-Antweiler and Xenia Zeiler (London: Routledge, 2021), 311–22.
44. Aljazeera, "China Uighurs: Ban on Long Beards, Veils in Xinjiang," *Aljazeera*, April 1, 2017. https://www.aljazeera.com/news/2017/4/1/china-uighurs-ban-on-long-beards-veils-in-xinjiang (accessed June 22, 2021), *The Economist*, "An American Agency Denounces the Treatment of Muslims in China," *The Economist*, July 7, 2017. https://www.economist.com/erasmus/2017/07/07/an-american-agency-denounces-the-treatment-of-muslims-in-china (accessed June 22, 2021).
45. James Leibold and Timothy Grose, "Islam Veiling in Xinjiang: The Political and Societal Struggle to Define Uyghur Female Adornment," *China Journal* 76, no. 1 (2016), 78–102.
46. David Stroup, "Han-Hui Relations and Chinese Regime Legitimation in the Xi Jingping Era: God Is a Drug," *Asian Survey* 60, no. 4 (2020), 659–84; David Stroup, "Good Minzu and Bad Muslims: Islamophobia in China's State Media," *Nations and Nationalism* 27 (2021a), 1231–52.
47. David Stroup, "The De-Islamification of Public Space and Sinicization of Ethnic Politics in Xi's China," *Middle East Institute*, September 24, 2019. https://www.mei.edu/publications/de-islamification-public-space-and-sinicization-ethnic-politics-xis-china (accessed October 20, 2021); James Leibold and Timothy Grose, "Islam Veiling in Xinjiang: The Political and Societal Struggle to Define Uyghur Female Adornment"; Timothy Grose, "Veiled Identities: Islam, Hu Ethnicity, and Dress Codes in Northwest China," *Journal of Islamic and Muslim Studies* 5, no. 1 (2020), 35–60; James Leibold, "Surveillance in China's Xinjiang Region: Ethnic Sorting, Coercion, and Inducement," *Journal of Contemporary China* 29, no. 121 (2020), 46–60.
48. BBC, "'Their Goal Is to Destroy Everyone': Uighur Camp Detainees Allege Systematic Rape," *BBC*, February 2, 2021. https://www.bbc.com/news/world-asia-china-55794071 (accessed July 3, 2021); Reuters, "EXCLUSIVE China Policies Could Cut Millions of Uyghur Births in Xinjiang," *Reuters*, June 7, 2021. https://www.reuters.com/world/china/exclusive-amid-accusations-genocide-west-china-polices-could-cut-millions-uyghur-2021-06-07/ (accessed July 3, 2021); Aljazeera, "China Commits 'Genocide' against Uighurs: State Department," *Aljazeera*, March 31, 2021. https://www.aljazeera.com/news/2021/3/30/china-genocide-uighurs-xinjiang-state-department-report-human-rights (accessed July 3, 2021).
49. Global Times, "How Blood-Stained West Orchestrated 'Genocide; Defamation against Xinjiang Step by Step,'" *Global Times*, June 8, 2021. https://www.globaltimes.cn/page/202106/1225747.shtml (accessed July 3, 2021); South China Morning Post,

"Xinjiang Government Criticises US, Says Forced Labour Claim Is 'Card Played by Anti-China Forces,'" *South China Morning Post*, June 3, 2020. https://www.scmp.com/news/china/politics/article/3135897/xinjiang-government-criticises-us-says-forced-labour-claim-card (accessed July 3, 2021).

50. David Stroup, "The De-Islamification of Public Space and Sinicization of Ethnic Politics in Xi's China," *Middle East Institute*, September 24, 2019. https://www.mei.edu/publications/de-islamification-public-space-and-sinicization-ethnic-politics-xis-china (accessed October 20, 2021).
51. DW, "What Does China Want to Achieve by 'Modifying' Islam," *DW*, June 8, 2019. https://www.dw.com/en/what-does-china-want-to-achieve-by-modifying-islam/a-46995813 (accessed June 22, 2021).
52. David Stroup, "Sinicization Erasing 'Arab-Style' Mosques in China," *Asia Times*, October 1, 2021. https://asiatimes.com/2021/10/sinicization-erasing-arab-style-mosques-in-china/ (accessed October 20, 2021).
53. Leibold, "Surveillance in China's Xinjiang Region."
54. Charles Dunst, "China Is Repeating U.S. Mistakes with Its Own Global Arrogance: Racism and Hubris are Marring Beijing's Image Globally," *Foreign Policy*, August 13, 2021. https://foreignpolicy.com/2021/08/13/china-arrogance-reputation-racism-united-states-mistakes/ (accessed October 19, 2021).
55. South China Morning Post, "Tiny Muslim Community in China's Hainan Becomes Latest Target for Religious Crackdown," *South China Morning Post*, September 28, 2020. https://www.scmp.com/news/china/politics/article/3103253/tiny-muslim-community-chinas-far-south-becomes-latest-target (accessed June 22, 2021).
56. Lloyd Ridgeon, "The Problems of Sinicizing Beijing's Mosques," *Journal of Muslim Minority Affairs* 40, no. 4 (2020), 576–96.

Bibliography

Aljazeera. "China Uighurs: Ban on Long Beards, Veils in Xinjiang." *Aljazeera*, 2017. https://www.aljazeera.com/news/2017/4/1/china-uighurs-ban-on-long-beards-veils-in-xinjiang (accessed June 22, 2021).

Aljazeera. "China Commits 'Genocide' against Uighurs: State Department." *Aljazeera*, 2021. https://www.aljazeera.com/news/2021/3/30/china-genocide-uighurs-xinjiang-state-department-report-human-rights (accessed July 3, 2021).

Armijo, Jacqueline. "Islam in China." In *Asian Islam in the 21st Century*. Edited by John Voll, John Esposito, and Osman Baker, 151–81. Oxford: Oxford University Press, 2007.

BBC. "'Their Goal Is to Destroy Everyone': Uighur Camp Detainees Allege Systematic Rape." *BBC*, February 2, 2021. https://www.bbc.com/news/world-asia-china-55794071 (accessed July 3, 2021).

Benite, Zvi Ben Dor. "Chinese Islam: A Complete Concert." *Cross-Currents: East Asian History and Culture Review* 23 (2017): 170–203.

Broomhall, Marshall. *Islam in China: A Neglected Problem*. New York: Paragon Book, 1910.

Dotson, James. "Propaganda Themes at the CPPCC Stress the 'Sincization' of Religion." *The Jamestown Foundation*, 2019. https://jamestown.org/program/propaganda-themes-at-the-cppcc-stress-the-sinicization-of-religion/ (accessed October 18, 2021).

Dunst, Charles. "China Is Repeating U.S. Mistakes with Its Own Global Arrogance: Racism and Hubris Are Marring Beijing's Image Globally." *Foreign Policy*, August 13, 2021. https://foreignpolicy.com/2021/08/13/china-arrogance-reputation-racism-united-states-mistakes/ (accessed October 19, 2021).
DW. "What Does China Want to Achieve by "Modifying" Islam." *DW*, June 8, 2019. https://www.dw.com/en/what-does-china-want-to-achieve-by-modifying-islam/a-46995813 (accessed June 22, 2021).
Elias, Nobert. *The Society of Individuals*. Oxford: Blackwell, 1991.
Frankel, James D. "From Monolith to Mosaic: A Decade of Twenty-First Century Studies of Muslims and Islam in China." *Religious Studies Review* 37, no. 4 (2011): 249–58.
Frankel, James. *Islam in China*. London: I.B. Tauris, 2021.
Gillette, Maris Boyd. *Between Mecca and Beijing: Modernization and Consumption Among Urban Chinese Muslims*. Stanford, CA: Stanford University Press, 2000.
Gillette, Maris Boyd. "Fashion among Chinese Muslims." *ISIM Review*, 15 Spring (2005): 36–7.
Gladney, Dru. "The Study of Islam in China: Some Recent Research." *Middle East Studies Association Bulletin* 27, no. 1 (1993): 23–30.
Gladney, Dru. "Islam in China: Accommodation or Separatism?" *China Quarterly* 174 (2003): 451–67.
Global Times. "How Blood-Stained West Orchestrated "Genocide; Defamation against Xinjiang Step by Step." *Global Times*. June 8, 2021. https://www.globaltimes.cn/page/202106/1225747.shtml (accessed July 3, 2021).
Grose, Timothy. "Veiled Identities: Islam, Hu Ethnicity, and Dress Codes in Northwest China." *Journal of Islamic and Muslim Studies* 5, no. 1 (2020): 35–60.
Ha, Guangtian. "The Silent Hat: Islam, Female Labor, and the Political Economy of the Headscarf Debate." *Signs: Journal of Women in Culture and Society* 42, no. 3 (2017): 743–69.
Hammond, Kelly. *China's Muslims & Japan's Empire: Centering Islam in World War II*. Chapel Hill: University of North Carolina Press, 2020.
Harvey, Thomas. "The Sinicization of Religion in China: Will Enforcing Conformity Work?" *Lausanne Global Analysis*. 8, no. 5 (September 2019). https://lausanne.org/content/lga/2019-09/sinicization-religion-china (accessed June 22, 2021).
Ho, Wai-Yip. "From Neglected Problem to Flourishing Field: Recent Developments of Research on Muslims and Islam in China." In *Concepts and Methods for the Study of Chinese Religions I: State of the Field and Disciplinary Approaches*. Edited by André Laliberté and Stefania Travagnin, 93–114. Berlin: De Gruyter, 2019.
Ho, Wai-Yip. "Reporting Religions with Chinese Characteristics: Sinicizing Religious Faith, Securitizing News Media." In *The Routledge Handbook of Religion and Journalism*. Edited by Kerstin Radde-Antweiler and Xenia Zeiler, 311–22. London: Routledge, 2021.
Jaschok, Maria. "Religious Agency and Gender Complementarity: Women's Mosques and Women's Voices in Hui Muslim Communities in Central China." *Review of Religion and Chinese Society* 5 (2018): 183–207.
Jaschok, Maria, and Shui Jingjun. *The History of Women's Mosques in Chinese Islam*. Richmond: Curzon, 2001.
Jaschok, Maria, and Shui Jingjun. "Purity, Sexuality and Faith: Chinese Women *Ahong* and Women's Mosques as Shelter and Strength." In *Sexuality in Muslim*

Contexts: Restrictions and Resistance. Edited by Anissa Hélie and Homa Hoodfar, 151–81. London: Zed, 2012.

Leibold, James. "Surveillance in China's Xinjiang Region: Ethnic Sorting, Coercion, and Inducement." *Journal of Contemporary China* 29, no. 121 (2020): 46–60.

Leibold, James, and Timothy Grose. "Islam Veiling in Xinjiang: The Political and Societal Struggle to Define Uyghur Female Adornment." *China Journal* 76, no. 1 (2016): 78–102.

Madsen, Richard. "Introduction." In *The Sinicization of Chinese Religions*. Edited byRichard Madsen, 1–15. Boston, MA: Brill, 2021.

Murata, Sachiko. *Chinese Gleams of Sufi Light: Wang Tai-yu's Great Learning of the Pure and Real and Liu Chih's Displaying the Concealment of the Real Realm; with a New Translation of Jami's Lawaih from Persian by William C. Chittick*. Albany: SUNY Press, 2000.

Murata, Sachiko. *The First Islamic Classic in Chinese: Wang Daiyu's Real Commentary on the True Teaching*. Translated with an Introduction and Notes by Sachiko Murata. Albany: SUNY Press, 2018.

Murata, Sachiko, William C. Chittick, and Tu Weiming. *The Sage Learning of Liu Zhi*. Cambridge, MA: Harvard University Press, 2009.

Reuters. "EXCLUSIVE China Policies Could Cut Millions of Uyghur Births in Xinjiang." *Reuters*, June 7, 2021. https://www.reuters.com/world/china/exclusive-amid-accusations-genocide-west-china-polices-could-cut-millions-uyghur-2021-06-07/ (accessed July 3, 2021).

Ridgeon, Lloyd. "The Problems of Sinicizing Beijing's Mosques." *Journal of Muslim Minority Affairs* 40, no. 4 (2020): 576–96.

South China Morning Post. "Tiny Muslim Community in China's Hainan Becomes Latest Target for Religious Crackdown." *South China Morning Post*, September 28, 2020. https://www.scmp.com/news/china/politics/article/3103253/tiny-muslim-community-chinas-far-south-becomes-latest-target (accessed June 22, 2021).

South China Morning Post. "Xinjiang Government Criticises US, Says Forced Labour Claim is 'Card Played by Anti-China Forces.'" *South China Morning Post*, June 3, 2020. https://www.scmp.com/news/china/politics/article/3135897/xinjiang-government-criticises-us-says-forced-labour-claim-card (accessed July 3, 2021).

Stroup, David. "The De-Islamification of Public Space and Sinicization of Ethnic Politics in Xi's China." *Middle East Institute*, September 24, 2019. https://www.mei.edu/publications/de-islamification-public-space-and-sinicization-ethnic-politics-xis-china (accessed October 20, 2021).

Stroup, David. "Han-Hui Relations and Chinese Regime Legitimation in the Xi Jingping Era: God Is a Drug." *Asian Survey* 60, no. 4 (2020): 659–84.

Stroup, David. "Good Minzu and Bad Muslims: Islamophobia in China's State Media." *Nations and Nationalism* 27 (2021a): 1231–52.

Stroup, David. "Sinicization Erasing 'Arab-Style' Mosques in China." *Asia Times*, October 1, 2021b. https://asiatimes.com/2021/10/sinicization-erasing-arab-style-mosques-in-china/ (accessed October 20, 2021).

The Economist. "An American Agency Denounces the Treatment of Muslims in China." *The Economist*, July 7, 2017. https://www.economist.com/erasmus/2017/07/07/an-american-agency-denounces-the-treatment-of-muslims-in-china (accessed June 22, 2021).

Tontini, Roberta. *Muslim Sanzijing: Shifts and Continuities in the Definition of Islam in China*. Leiden: Brill, 2016.
Tuoheti, Alimu. *Islam in China: A History of European and American Scholarship*. Piscataway: Gorgias Press, 2021.
VOA. "Amazon Removes App for Quran, Bible from Apple Store in China." *VOA*, October 16, 2021. https://www.voanews.com/a/amazon-removes-app-for-quran-bible-from-apple-store-in-china/6273518.html (accessed October 19, 2021).
Wang, Jianping. "Islam and State Policy in Contemporary China." *Studies in Religion* 45, no. 4 (2016): 566–80.
Wang, Xiaoyan. "The Headscarf and Hui Identity." *Fashion Theory* 15, no. 4 (2011): 481–501.
Wang, Xiaoyan. "Hui Women and the Headscarf in China." In *The Routledge International Handbook to Veils and Veiling Practices*. Edited by Anna-Mari Almila and David Inglis, 255–66. Abingdon: Routledge, 2017.
Yang, Fenggang. "Sinicization or Chinafication? Cultural Assimilation vs. Political Domestication of Christianity in China and Beyond." In *The Sinicization of Chinese Religions*. Edited by Richard Madsen, 16–43. Boston, MA: Brill, 2021.
Zhang, Chi. "'Illegal Religious Activities' and Counter-Terrorism in China." *Politics and Religion* 14, no. 2 (2021): 269–93.

14

The Headscarf and Modesty in Multicultural Aotearoa New Zealand: A Post-Christchurch Attack Story

Eva F. Nisa

Introduction

It began as a regular Friday. Friday was my weekly teaching-free day when I often spent hours enjoying the university library. On that day, however, things changed. During the Friday prayer time, I received a call from my husband.

Faried:	[panting] Where are you?
Eva:	I'm in the library as usual; why? Why aren't you praying now?
Faried:	Have you heard about the mosque shootings?
Eva:	[My heart sunk; panic took over] Where? Where are you? Are you okay?
Faried:	Yes, I'm okay. Can you please go back to your office and stay there? Do not go anywhere until I pick you up, okay?! Now, please.
Eva:	Okay, I'll go back to my office now.

My office was merely 70 meters from the library. As I walked the short journey back and waited at the traffic lights, cars passed me with open windows. The passengers smiled and/or looked sympathetic. I was confused. Later that day, after trying to process the tragedies that occurred, I began to understand their "looks." My female Muslim colleagues, friends, and students had received the same warm look from people on the street. The commonality among us: we were all Muslim women who wore veils. One colleague told me, "We want to assure you that we welcome you here in New Zealand. We do not see your veil as a sign of terrorism, but as the way you perceive your religion—Islamic women's modesty." Departing from my story and the stories of other Muslim women in Aotearoa, New Zealand, this chapter focuses on the way the notion of Muslim women's modesty has been perceived in multicultural New Zealand settings after the Christchurch Mosque shootings of March 15, 2019, which killed fifty-one people.

The study is based on seven months of fieldwork conducted in Wellington, New Zealand. I interviewed Muslims and non-Muslims from diverse backgrounds, including citizens, residents, students, and community leaders. In addition, I conducted a survey among Muslim women and organized two focus group discussions on issues pertaining to modesty. When non-Muslims adopted veiling after the Christchurch Mosque attacks to show solidarity, the topic of the veil and Islamic modesty generated debate not only among veil wearers themselves, but also within the multicultural New Zealand public context, including those who see veiling as an archetypal sign of women's oppression and lack of self-determination. Both the policing of women's bodies about veil wearing and showing solidarity by donning the headscarf remain areas of contestation in the New Zealand public sphere.

Revisiting Veiling in Western Nations

Those who focus on the modesty of Muslim women and veiling in Western nations often discuss it in the context of the religious–secular divide and issues pertaining to gender equality.[1] Veiling is often conceptualized as an Islamic expression of Muslim women's modesty.[2] It is perceived as a sign of women's oppression and lack of agency. The wearers and narratives often mentioned in re-veiling movements, which are particularly evident in some Muslim countries, depict the veil as liberating—a claim which has also caused discomfort for secular feminists.[3] In some European nations, the headscarf is also seen as "an emblem of radical Islamist politics."[4] This kind of rhetoric is evidenced in the banning of veiling in some European countries. Perceiving veiled women from this perspective is part of the process of othering or Orientalism, to borrow Edward Said's (1935–2003) (1978) concept. Said defines Orientalism as "the corporate institution for dealing with the Orient—dealing with it by making statements about it, authorizing views of it, describing it, by teaching it, settling it, ruling over it: in short, Orientalism as a Western style for dominating, restructuring, and having authority over the Orient."[5]

The process of othering veiled women by viewing them entirely through the lens of oppression and lack of self-determination or agency has led to the working assumption that veiling and the modesty attached to it are incompatible with the concept of gender equality. This has resulted in the ideological construct that these Muslim women need to be saved.[6] Lila Abu-Lughod calls this ideological construct "colonial feminism."[7] In New Zealand, at the moment, the ideological construct to "save" veiled women by unveiling them is fortunately nonexistent.

Questioning Gendered Modesty

Modesty in Islamic tradition is often referred to using varied terms, including *ḥayāʾ* (literally means shyness, timidity, and modesty) and *al-tawāḍuʿ* (freedom from vanity). The two terms have varied meanings, and modesty is one of them.[8] The concept is not only about women, but also men, as mentioned in the Qurʾan 24:30–31. The verses call for both women and men to behave modestly. From these two verses and other verses, which are often considered as part of "the veil verses," discussions of modesty in Muslim majority contexts are often linked to women's bodies and women's attire, their hijab (literally means a screen or curtain. It usually refers to a body covering including veil), headscarf, or even face veil. The emphasis is often on modesty in dress rather than modesty in manner. Modernists and Muslim feminists, however, have criticized this understanding. In Egypt, for example, Qasim Amin (1863–1908), known, especially in the Arab world, as the first Muslim feminist, emphasized that there is no direct link between veiling and modesty. Amin focused on face covering as he believed that religious texts do not stipulate face veils as a manifestation of Islamic modesty.[9]

In patriarchal understandings, modesty becomes inexorably gendered. This can be seen in both Muslim majority and minority contexts.[10] Modest dress, for example, is often equated with Islamic clothing, especially for women. In many discussions of modesty in Islam, the keywords are often heavily linked to women's covering, such as *ʿawra* (linguistically means "weakness," "imperfection," "genitalia"; in this context refers to body parts that need to be covered) and *zīna* (adornment or natural beauty, as mentioned in the two verses above: 24:30–31), which in the case of women are both linked to the concept of *fitna* (temptation which is considered as a destructive element in society).[11] Fatima Mernissi argues that *fitna* links to women's sexuality, which is "uncontrollable" and thus highly dangerous to men.[12] In her discussion of women's modesty and segregation in Egypt, Valerie J. Hoffman-Ladd mentioned two opposing camps: traditionalist and modernist views. The traditionalist camp believes that

> Key concepts relating to the Islamic ideology of female modesty are contained in the words *ʿaura*, *fitna*, and *zīna*. That is, the entire body of a woman (except her face and hands) is to be treated as *pudenda*; it is a vulnerable, weak object that must be covered to avoid embarrassment and shame. … Her appearance causes *fitna* (chaos or discord), and she, therefore, must be covered for the protection of men. … These two oppositional concepts lie behind a modesty code that interprets the Qurʾanic passages on *zīna* to mean that all of the woman should be hidden from view, except her face and hands.[13]

This kind of view indeed is not uncommon in other religious traditions. Besides humility and a humble attitude, the concept of modesty in other religious traditions and in Western contexts is also often linked to dress, especially women's dress to preserve public morality and moral values.[14] For example, Adeline Masquelier argues, "While Christian theologians advocated modesty and concealment at times to the point of obsession—in some European Catholic families, children until World War I wore gowns while bathing, lest they engage in the sinful contemplation of their nudity."[15] Ronit Irshai argues that the concept of modesty in Jewish tradition, "encompasses many broad spheres, including norms related to the relationship between the sexes before and after marriage … and rules governing the covering of the body."[16] Samuel Morris Brown and Kate Holbrook define it as "a set of notions about how the body should be presented."[17] Adding to theological studies, Jessica Rey, an actress and designer known for modest swimwear products and her version of modesty, says, "Modesty isn't about covering up our bodies because they're bad. Modesty isn't about hiding ourselves. It's about revealing our dignity."[18]

The laws of modesty in some religions might overlap. In the Jewish tradition, for example, the law of modesty enjoined "that married women cover their heads; forbid women to sing in the presence of men; and mandate the wearing of non-revealing clothing."[19] Annelies Moors analyses an important initiative in modest fashion across religious traditions, which can be seen in Dana Becker's Modest Clothing Directory.[20] It was initiated in the United States in 1998, featuring not only Islamic styles of modest dress but also brought together "different faith communities as well as regional style through the lens of modesty."[21]

Muslim fashion designers and people in the business of Muslim fashion have popularized the term "modest fashion," referring to fashion deemed to be in accordance with Islamic teachings. Therefore, modest fashion is often related to dress that covers women's bodies and often but not always includes women's head coverings. The term modest fashion, however, is often perceived, especially by those opposing the concept, as *contradictio in terminis* (contradiction in terms). Reina Lewis, in the edited volume *Modest Fashion*, states, "Simply putting the terms 'modest' and 'fashion' together immediately invites questions, comments, criticism and, not infrequently, incredulity."[22] Earlier, Banu Gökariksel and Anna J. Secor discussed the concept of "veiling-fashion," which is deemed to be controversial, especially for conservatives who see veiling as a "powerful set of religious, cultural and political references, and fashion, an unmoored system of self-referential change associated with capitalism, modernity and a particular kind of consumer subject."[23] Following Lewis and other scholars focusing their studies on modesty and modest fashion, this chapter does not offer a specific definition of modesty. Modesty and modest fashion are fluid concepts. Lewis argues, "modesty is a mutable concept that changes over time and is diversely adopted, rejected, altered by or in some cases imposed on different groups of women (and, to a lesser extent, men) in different times and places."[24]

Muslims in Multicultural New Zealand

The number of Muslims in New Zealand is relatively small, with only 57,276 of a total 4,699,755 of the population identifying as Muslims, according to the 2018 census released in September 2019. However, as evidenced in historical documentation, Muslims were present in New Zealand as early as 1769.[25] Like many other countries, global tensions, such as the 9/11 terror attacks and the spread of Islamophobia, have led Muslims to be continuously under the spotlight.[26]

New Zealand, however, has consistently been named as the most "Islamic country in the world" in the Islamicity Indices overall index from 2016 until 2021.[27] The index, with its relative obscurity, refers to how the country fits Islamic principles and best reflects Islamic values in the domains of economy, legal system and governance, human and political rights, and international relations. In 2021, New Zealand ranked particularly high in the areas of economy (including poverty alleviation) and legal system and governance (prevention of corruption). The country differs from other non-Muslim minority and Western nations, where the presence of Muslims is often politicized and used for "political mobilisation," to borrow anthropologist Erich Kolig's term.[28] The type of Islamophobia mixed with political interests, which can be seen in the policies and statements issued by leaders of European countries such as France, remains thin in New Zealand. Kolig argues in this context, "New Zealand is fortunate insofar as the Muslim presence has not been politicised and become an ideological issue to the degree that it has, for instance, in neighbouring Australia."[29]

In addition, social hostilities, including religious hostilities, in New Zealand remain low. Pew Research recorded that in 2016, New Zealand had a "Social Hostilities Index score of 0.9 out of 10."[30] Indeed, the tolerant nature of New Zealand was clearly witnessed during the aftermath of the Christchurch attacks. The nation honored the victims of the terrorist attack during the Islamic Friday prayer by broadcasting *adhān* (the call to prayer) and the Friday prayer live. Additionally, a couple of weeks after the shootings, all of the country's mosques opened their doors to non-Muslims, inviting them to join the Friday congregants and listen to the Friday sermon in remembrance. Suddenly, Friday sermons across the country were inundated by spontaneous applause—not a traditional occurrence during Muslim worship. A Muslim organization in Wellington, the International Muslim Association of New Zealand, also recorded that there had been an increase in conversions to Islam after the Christchurch attacks.[31]

The concept of multiculturalism as one of the characteristics of New Zealand when acknowledging the presence of the country's multicultural profile is often mentioned in this context. Responding to the country's multicultural profile, the initial approach was minorities needed to assimilate into the mainstream culture, which led to the suppression of cultural differences.[32] When multiculturalism as a government policy—first introduced in Canada in the 1970s—traveled to New Zealand, the initial assimilation effort was then replaced by the concept of multiculturalism.[33] Kolig argues that "Internationally, New Zealand is cited as a beacon of multiculturalism and enlightened pluralist tolerance in a globalising world."[34]

The concept of multiculturalism, however, does not guarantee that differences can be celebrated fully in public. Ian Clarke, in this context, contends, "Minorities are expected to conform to the values of the *de facto* normal group, except in the limited areas in which they are allowed to differ. … State multiculturalism may be seen as being based on the same assimilative presumptions as to the nation-state model they seek to replace, only manifested in a more refined and subtle manner."[35] This kind of state multiculturalism signifies the power of the state to tolerate differences.[36] Scholars often connect this approach to multiculturalism to what Stanley Fish calls "boutique multiculturalism."[37] Fish explains,

> Boutique multiculturalism is characterized by its superficial or cosmetic relationship to the object of its affection. Boutique multiculturalists admire or appreciate or enjoy or sympathize with or (at the very least) "recognize the legitimacy of" the traditions of cultures other than their own; but boutique multiculturalists will always stop short at approving other cultures at a point where some value at their

> center generates an act that offends against the canons of civilised decency as they have been either declared or assumed. (emphasis mine)[38]

Drury and Pratt use the term "incorporated multiculturalism" for New Zealand with its "multicultural diversity within the bi-cultural context."[39] This is unique to New Zealand, making the multiculturalism prevalent in New Zealand relatively different from that of other Western nations. New Zealand's multicultural policies have received significant criticism due to the risk of undermining the commitment of the government to biculturalism, which pertains to the rights of Māori.[40]

Veiling and Modesty in Multicultural New Zealand

Multicultural New Zealand is not immune from issues pertaining to the acceptance of Muslims. However, responses surrounding issues of modesty, which are often tied to wearing proper Muslim dress in New Zealand, remain nonviolent—indeed, the public tends to "politely ignore" them.[41] According to Kolig, this is indicative of New Zealand's "populist multiculturalism," referring to pragmatic multiculturalism that is an "officially undeclared kind, based on a diffuse sense of tolerance—or, perhaps better, indifference to—cultural Otherness."[42] One of the many expressions of populist multiculturalism according to Kolig can be seen through the way New Zealanders politely ignore "saris and hijabs in the streets."[43] Generally, wearing a veil in public does not create problems, with the exception of the face-covering *burqa* (face veil). The "*burqa* affair" in New Zealand was considered a problem.[44] The case of two *burqa* wearers who appeared at the Auckland District Court and refused to take off their *burqa* raised public debate about the nature of New Zealand's secular state.[45] During the case, the judge Lindsay Moore asked the women to remove their *burqa*; however, he did not ask the women to remove the veils covering their hair.[46] The judge permitted the two *burqa* wearers to witness behind a screen, allowing only the judge and counsel to see their full faces. This signifies a limit of tolerance: covering the hair is acceptable but covering the face is not. In analyzing this case, David H. Griffiths emphasized the permissive New Zealand's type of secular state.[47] This permissive secular state refers to "a state that does not favour the religious beliefs of any particular group, but which attempts to avoid acting in ways that hinder religious activities which do not harm others or threaten important public policy goals (a 'negative secular'—or 'substantively neutral'—state)."[48]

Muslim modesty that involves covering one's hair has been accepted by most New Zealanders. In November 2020, the country introduced the veil as part of the official police uniform for female Muslim officers. Zeena Ali, who was inspired to join the police force after the Christchurch terror attacks, became the first officer to wear this uniform. In addition, the acceptance of the veil can also be seen in the fact that some cases pertaining to the refusal of accepting the headscarf have often resulted in apologies and raised sympathy from the public, especially when covered by the media. Sympathy toward veiled women—from the public, mainstream media, and alternative media—has become even stronger in the aftermath of the Christchurch attacks.

Headscarf Movement and Modesty

In the weeks after the Christchurch tragedy, waves of sympathy and support for Muslim communities were visible daily. The influx of support peaked on Friday, March 22, which marked the first week after the mosque attacks in the country. The question of how to support the most affected Muslim communities in the aftermath of one of the deadliest mass shootings in history has been raised several times. Supports to New Zealand Muslims were displayed in various different ways. Many Muslims attest that the hearts of their Kiwi compatriots have made it easier to face the tragedy and begin to heal. A female Muslim Victoria University student, for example, shared her thoughts as follows: "We do not have to teach our fellow New Zealanders how to support us [Muslim communities]; you can see how they support us from the simple smile to their attendance to vigils."[49] Her view has been echoed by Muslims throughout New Zealand. A tsunami of solidarity, love, and support toward Muslim communities has inundated the country. The flow of donations in the form of time, goods, and money continues. Vigils and marches have been held across New Zealand. At the same time, although New Zealand generally remains tolerant of Muslims,[50] citing former Race Relations Commissioner Susan Devoy, the Chief Human Rights Commissioner at the New Zealand Human Rights Commission, Paul Hunt, mentioned that in recent years, there had been an increase in hatred and abuse toward Muslim communities in New Zealand.[51] Thus, there is still an ongoing concern, especially relating to the safety of veiled Muslim women who are visibly more recognizable as Muslims.

In the wake of the Christchurch tragedy, some Muslim women have felt unsafe, scared, and vulnerable because they have felt targeted as Muslims. Samia, a new young convert, says, "Post-Christchurch is a bit different. I am not worried about myself, but my parents are very worried about me. My father often asks me not to go out because I am wearing a veil. He is worried that I will be targeted by those who do not like us to be part of New Zealand."[52] Across the country, some veiled students avoided attending university for a couple of days after the attacks. Adding to the fearful atmosphere, two days after the attacks, two veiled Muslim women were verbally abused at Auckland Railway Station.[53] The question of how to support veiled Muslim women and create a safe and hospitable space for them has therefore become a main concern for the nation.

Street-level Islamophobia targeting veiled Muslim women has been prevalent in many Western contexts, especially after the attacks of 9/11.[54] Unfortunately, those who have been concerned with hate crime and Islamophobia have often neglected the more specific type of gendered Islamophobia perpetrated against Muslim women with their increased visibility due to veils. Barbara Perry[55] has argued that public violence related to gendered Islamophobia has often been neglected. At the same time, the impacts of gendered Islamophobia have positioned women to feel insecure regarding safety, mobility, and belonging to the public sphere. Conversely, after the attacks, New Zealand has been reenergized in wanting to identify the existence of Islamophobic violence and, more specifically, gendered Islamophobic violence.

Marking the first week of the tragedy, medical doctor Thaya Ashman and other New Zealanders initiated the Headscarf for Harmony movement on Friday, March 22.

Ashman and the Islamic Women's Council of New Zealand invited New Zealanders to wear scarves on Friday. They wrote,

> Let's show our love and support for our Muslim communities grieving the loss of 50 amazing mothers, fathers, children, friends and colleagues in the terrorist attack last Friday.
>
> THIS FRIDAY, 22 March, you're invited to wear a headscarf or head covering at work, school, or play—to peacefully show your love and support for the Christchurch, New Zealand, and worldwide Muslim communities.[56]

In conjunction with this, an initiative called "Scarves in Solidarity" was launched. Anna Thomas, one of the organizers of the event, contended that "Scarves in Solidarity" was launched after learning that veiled Muslim women are fearful of racial abuse in public. Thomas's message aims to help Muslim women facing gendered Islamophobia because of their veils. She says, "Women especially who wear the hijab [veil] are fairly regularly fearful when they go out in the streets and what a better way to show support and walk alongside them than to wear one."[57] These initiatives were shared extensively offline and online through #scarvesinsolidarity, #headscarfforharmony, #weareone, and #theyareus.

Before these initiatives were launched, one of the most famous pictures linked to the Christchurch attacks had been the picture of New Zealand's Prime Minister Jacinda Ardern wearing a headscarf. The image went viral after the shootings and was shared by millions of people around the world.[58] Indeed, that was not the first time Ardern had worn a veil, and the action attracted varied opinions. Many believed that it was an expression of empathy "rather than an endorsement of any particular religious symbol."[59]

Modesty, Veiling, and Their Muslimness

Any type of clothing is polysemic and "open to interpretation by different wearers and observers."[60] In the New Zealand context, the veil, modesty, and Muslimness are a package. This was particularly evident after the Christchurch attacks, when many non-Muslims showed their solidarity by wearing the headscarf, including female police officers, reporters, and presenters. The appearance of the prime minister wearing the headscarf several times in public as a sign of solidarity, respect, and tolerance also signifies the interconnectedness of these three elements in the perspective of many New Zealanders who still think that the veil is the sole identifiable element of Muslim women.[61]

However, Ardern's public appearance with a veil was perceived with mixed responses. It became one of the country's hotly debated topics for weeks. Belinda, a 47-year-old New Zealander, argues,

> I understand that there are conflicts relating to Jacinda's appearance with the headscarf. For me, one thing that I know is these Muslim women who wear a headscarf like you are at least part of their way of presenting themselves as modest

> dresser. Those with the headscarf, for example, will not wear miniskirts or show cleavage.[62]

One day after the attacks, on March 16, 2019, New Zealand's national television channel interviewed me about this topic on their morning news program. The newscaster asked for my thoughts about non-Muslims wearing modest Muslim dresses, especially the headscarf. The reason behind this question was that many New Zealanders were still unsure about the feelings of their Muslim compatriots regarding their wish to show solidarity by wearing the headscarf. This was due to some negative comments, especially on social media, regarding this kind of gesture.[63] Dominique, a 25-year-old activist, for example, says,

> I love Thaya Ashman's Headscarf for Harmony. I wanted to wear a headscarf, but I did not know whether my whole outfit, my pants and blouse, were modest enough by Islamic modesty standards. I tried to remember church modesty rules which I thought the principle was quite similar in general. Before I wore my headscarf, I double-checked it with my Muslim friend because I did not want to offend Muslims.[64]

Expressions of solidarity and campaigns for supporting veiled women in the Western context are not new. In Sweden in 2013, there was a Hijab Call-to-Action to support Muslim women's rights.[65] The Hijab Call-to-Action—which called all women, religious and non-religious, to veil for one day—was initiated after an incident where a veiled woman was verbally harassed by someone who shouted, "people like you should not be here."[66] The initiative aimed to show solidarity with Muslim women, especially veiled women who are perceived as wearing a religious symbol.

Opponents of these initiatives, including some Internet users, found the solidarity movements problematic. They claimed that the veil is a sign of women's oppression, powerlessness, backwardness, and religious conservatism and a symbol of sexualizing women, patriarchal hegemony, and men's harassment, especially due to the imposition of wearing the veil by some governments and Muslim families. They believe the veil is contradictory to women's rights. Therefore, for many "colonial feminists," for example, a veiled Muslim woman is often regarded as someone who needs "saving" from their religion and their patriarchal husbands.[67]

When a head of government, like Ardern, wears the veil, opponents believe this might iconize the headscarf as the sole identifier of their Muslim identity and normalize the practice that is deemed to oppress women. In the context of New Zealand's secular nature, Ardern's symbolic gesture was perceived by some as a disruption to secularism. Those in opposition believe this symbolic gesture contests the secular–religious divided or the state–church divide. Feminists who initiated Hijab Call-to-Action in Sweden were also questioned because the initiative was seen as not in accordance with the feminist spirit.[68] Responding to the criticism, Ardern emphasized the context of her gesture, saying, "If in wearing the hijab, as I did, gave them a sense of security to continue to practice their faith, then I'm very pleased I did it."[69]

Those who oppose the veil also mention that solidarity can be expressed by denouncing anti-Muslim rhetoric. Shenila Khoja-Moolji states, "Solidarity ... can begin with donning the hijab, but it should not end there. It must evolve into a deeper engagement with the causes of Islamophobia, racism and bigotry, along with oppression of women."[70] It was pointed out that there are many Muslims who do not wear a headscarf and that the movement might harm them. For example, their families and other social circles might compare their appearance to the initiative by asking them to embrace modest Muslim clothing because even non-Muslims understand that veiling is a sign of Muslim women's modesty and identity. As a result, this might lead to some Muslim women being forced to wear the veil. Sociologist Marnia Lazreg also raised this issue in her explanation of why women should not wear the veil.[71] Lazreg emphasizes, "A Muslim woman is not more modest than another woman for wearing a veil. Modesty is not reducible to the veil."[72] She argues when wearing a veil is considered a guarantee of "modesty" and a pious act, this implies that Muslim women who do not wear it are less moral or modest.

Another argument against the movement was issues pertaining to cultural appropriation. A woman who holds this view said, "As a Muslim woman myself, I think this is nothing but cheap tokenism. It's a gimmick and pretty distasteful."[73] The majority of Muslim women in New Zealand, however, did not share her position. Responding to this argument, a member of a Muslim woman's WhatsApp group said, "These people are trying to do whatever they can to make us feel better, make us feel we are one of them. They are going the extra mile to understand our culture and religion. So please, sister, take it in a positive way and look at their intention." These interpretations highlight the diversity within New Zealand's Muslim communities. However, it is noteworthy that the success of and public response toward the Headscarf for Harmony initiative signifies a predominantly moderate voice of Muslims in New Zealand.

Headscarf movements to show solidarity should not lead to fetishizing the headscarf as an Islamic identity and the only expression of female modesty in Islam. Lazreg, in her critique on veiling, raises this issue by posing the question, "But why is the veil a mark of modesty? Can a woman not dress modestly without wearing a long coat that flaps between her feet?"[74] She argues, "a key chapter (sura) in the Qur'an referring to dress does not mention 'modesty,' for which the Arabic word is *istihsham*."[75] This argument is problematic, especially given that many Muslim scholars ranging from the most conservative to the most progressive have offered various translations and interpretations on verses of the veil, including Qur'an 24:30–31, and have connected them to the concept of modesty.[76]

Despite the varied reasons mentioned by modest dressers, religion often becomes the main reference. Lewis, for example, explained some of these diverse reasons:

> For some women, modest dressing is clearly motivated by their understanding of their religion. ... For others, modest dressing is less about faith or spirituality than about pragmatic options for achieving social or geographical mobility, or for responding to changes in their lifecycle (such as having children, getting older, going to a new job). (2013: 3)

These reasons signify that the iconization of the veil as the sole identifier of Muslim women's identity is misleading. The belief of some New Zealanders that wearing a modest dress is aligned with religious teaching across religious traditions has also led them to assume that Muslim women wear a modest dress as an expression of Islamic identity.

Conclusion

Modesty does not only refer to modesty in dress, but also in deeds. In the discussion of Muslim women, however, modesty is often referred to as veiling or *proper* covering. Indeed, across religious traditions, although modesty in manners, including humility and dignity, is often mentioned, the domain of modesty in dress is often exclusively referring to modesty in women's dress. In the Western context, the term "Islamic modesty" pertaining to women is commonly linked to veils and identity. This can be seen clearly in the headscarf movements, which aim to show solidarity with Muslims, especially Muslim women.

After the Christchurch attacks, the wearing of headscarves in solidarity has been both celebrated and criticized. The presence of non-Muslim New Zealanders wearing the headscarf suggests that some consider the veil as the sole identifier of Muslim identity. Ardern's veiled appearance and the subsequent debates signal that many non-Muslim New Zealanders have begun to understand that some Muslims think that the veil is not the sole identifier of their Muslim identity. However, at the very minimum, they know that it is one of the expressions of Islamic female modesty. However, it should also be emphasized that modesty for Muslim women should not be reduced to wearing a veil, and veiling does not guarantee its wearer's modesty.

Those who criticized the headscarf movement argue that the most important act is to fight against anti-Muslim rhetoric in the country. One aspect that is often neglected by those who oppose this kind of movement is the fact that veiled women often become the main targets of verbal and physical abuse in Western contexts. Headscarf for Harmony and Scarves in Solidarity can play a significant role in obliterating many painful memories relating to Muslim women and their chosen dress. These headscarf movements are indeed the opposite of the well-rooted colonial feminists' ideological construct to "save" veiled women by unveiling them. Instead, headscarf movements allow veiled women to celebrate their perceived Islamic modesty. It is important to note that not all Muslim women wear veils in New Zealand or elsewhere. There are diverse opinions among Muslim scholars regarding whether wearing veils is obligatory.

Acceptance of the face veil remains an ongoing debate in many Western settings. Acceptance of the standard veil (which does not cover the wearer's face), however, has been prevalent. Unfortunately, general acceptance does not make veil wearers immune from gendered Islamophobic violence and the unceasing process of othering. In many countries where Muslims are in the minority, veiling often serves as a test of the country's tolerance. Headscarf for Harmony and Scarves in Solidarity in New Zealand, however, are not so much a test of New Zealand's multiculturalism. During the events, issues pertaining to New Zealand's core secular values, whether a religious expression can create problems in Aotearoa's secularist societies, or whether wearing the veil conflicts with other civil liberties, were thinly present in the public debates, as can be seen from Ardern's veiled appearance. Indeed, the ongoing concern is mostly related to cultural appropriation—many non-Muslim women feared they could cause harm by wearing the veil as they did not want to offend veiled Muslim women and their upheld notion of Islamic modesty.

Notes

1. John R. Bowen, *Why the French Don't Like Headscarves: Islam, the State, and Public Space* (Princeton, NJ: Princeton University Press, 2008), 14. See also Joan Wallach Scott, *The Politics of the Veil* (Princeton, NJ: Princeton University Press, 2007); Lena Gemzöe, "Solidarity in Head-scarf and Pussy Bow Blouse: Reflections on Feminists Activism and Knowledge Production," *Social Inclusion* 6 (2018), 70.
2. Fadwa El Guindi, *Veil: Modesty, Privacy and Resistance* (Oxford: Berg, 1999).
3. Cécile Laborde, *Critical Republicanism: The Hijab Controversy and Political Philosophy* (Oxford: Oxford University Press, 2008), 143. See also Saba Mahmood, *Politics of Piety: The Islamic Revival and the Feminist Subject* (Princeton, NJ: Princeton University Press, 2005). On criticism against this liberating aspect, see Bronwyn Winter, *Hijab and the Republic: Uncovering the French Headscarf Debate* (Syracuse: Syracuse University Press, 2008), 43.
4. Scott, *The Politics of the Veil*, 3.
5. Edward W. Said, *Orientalism* (New York: Pantheon Books, 1978), 3.
6. Lila Abu-Lughod, "Do Muslim Women Really Need Saving? Anthropological Reflections on Cultural Relativism and Its Others," *American Anthropologist* 104 (2002), 783–90.
7. Abu-Lughod, "Do Muslim Women Really Need Saving?," 784.
8. Ibn Manzur, *Lisan al-ʿArab* (Beirut: Maktaba Tahqiq al-Turath, 1993), vol. 3, 429 and vol. 15, 327.
9. Qasim Amin, *Tahrir al-Marʾa [The Liberation of Women]* (reprinted in Muḥammad ʿImara: *Qasim Amin: Al-Aʿmal al-Kamila*) (Beirut: Dar al-Shuruq, 1976), 45.
10. Frances Raday, "Modesty Disrobed—Gendered Modesty Rules under the Monotheistic Religions," *Feminism, Law, and Religion*, edited by Marie Failinger, Elizabeth Schiltz, and Susan J. Stabile (Surrey: Ashgate, 2013), 283.
11. Valerie J. Hoffman-Ladd, "Polemics on the Modesty and Segregation of Women in Contemporary Egypt," *International Journal of Middle East Studies* 19 (1987), 29; Fatima Mernissi, *Beyond the Veil: Male-Female Dynamics in a Modern Muslim Society* (Cambridge, MA: Schenkman Publishing Company, 1975), 81.
12. Mernissi, *Beyond the Veil*, 68.
13. Hoffman-Ladd, "Polemics on the Modesty and Segregation of Women in Contemporary Egypt," 43.
14. See Reina Lewis, "Introduction: Mediating modesty," in *Modest Fashion: Styling Bodies, Mediating Faith*, edited by Reina Lewis (London: I.B. Tauris, 2013), 4–5; Khadijeh Zolghadr and Lynda Clarke, "Social and Individual Impacts of Veiling on Muslim Women: The Views of Mortaza Mutahhari and Qasim Amin," *International Journal of Humanities* 23 (2016), 34; in Judeo-Christian tradition see Adeline Masquelier, "Dirt, Undress and Difference: An Introduction," in

Dirt, Undress and Difference: Critical Perspectives on the Body's Surface, edited by Adeline Masquelier (Indianapolis: Indiana University Press, 2005), 1–33; in Jewish tradition see Ronit Irshai, "Judaism," in *The Oxford Handbook of Theology, Sexuality, and Gender*, edited by Adrian Thatcher (Oxford: Oxford University Press, 2014), 413–31. https://www-oxfordhandbooks com.virtual.anu.edu.au/view/10.1093/oxfordhb/9780199664153.001.0001/oxfordhb-9780199664153-e-022 (accessed March 3, 2021); in Mormon see Samuel Morris Brown and Kate Holbrook, "Embodiment and Sexuality in Mormon Thought," in *The Oxford Handbook of Mormonism*, edited by Terryl L. Givens and Phillip L. Barlow (Oxford: Oxford University Press, 2015), 292–306. https://www-oxfordhandbooks-com.virtual.anu.edu.au/view/10.1093/oxfordhb/9780199778362.001.0001/oxfordhb-9780199778362-e-20?rskey=toTVuY&result=2 (accessed February 19, 2021).
15. Masquelier, "Dirt, Undress and Difference," 2.
16. Irshai, "Judaism".
17. Brown and Holbrook, "Embodiment and Sexuality in Mormon Thought".
18. Quoted in Katelyn Beaty, "Toward a New Understanding of Modesty," *The Atlantic*, August 20, 2013. https://www.theatlantic.com/sexes/archive/2013/08/toward-a-new-understanding-of-modesty/278652/ (accessed February 9, 2021).
19. Irshai, "Judaism."
20. Annelies Moors, "'Discover the Beauty of Modesty': Islamic Fashion Online," *Modest Fashion: Styling Bodies, Mediating Faith*, edited by in Reina Lewis (London: I.B. Tauris, 2013), 17–40.
21. Ibid., 18.
22. Lewis, "Introduction," 1.
23. Banu Gökariksel and Anna J. Secor, "New Transnational Geographies of Islamism, Capitalism and Subjectivity: The Veiling-Fashion Industry in Turkey," *Royal Geographical Society* 41 (2009), 7.
24. Lewis, "Introduction," 3.
25. Abdullah Drury, "Mostly Harmless: A Short History of the First Century of Muslim Settlement in New Zealand," *Waikato Islamic Studies Review* 1 (2015), 25–49; Eva Nisa and Faried F. Saenong, "From Mahometan to Kiwi Muslim: History of NZ's Muslim Population," *The Conversation*, 2019. https://theconversation.com/from-mahometan-to-kiwi-muslim-history-of-nzs-muslim-population-114067 (accessed February 21, 2021); Stats NZ, "Losing Our Religion," *Stats NZ* 3 (October 2019), https://www.stats.govt.nz/news/losing-our-religion (accessed February 19, 2021).
26. Douglas Pratt, "Secular New Zealand and Religious Diversity: From Cultural Evolution to Societal Affirmation," *Social Inclusion* 4 (2016), 62.
27. Islamicity Indices, "Islamicity Indices: 2021," *Islamicity Index*, 2021. http://islamicity-index.org/wp/latest-indices-2021/ (accessed June 11, 2022).
28. Erich Kolig, "Muslim Traditions and Islamic Law in New Zealand: The 'Burqa Case' and the Challenge of Multiculturalism," in *Asia in the Making of New Zealand*, edited by Henry Johnson and Brian Moloughney (Auckland: Auckland University Press, 2006), 160.
29. Erich Kolig, "Whither Cultural Acceptance? Muslims and Multiculturalism in New Zealand," in *Asians and the New Multiculturalism in Aotearoa New Zealand*, edited by Gautam Ghosh and Jacqueline Leckie (Otago: Otago University Press, 2015), 161.
30. Katayoun Kishi, Stephanie Kramer, Joey Marshall, and Aleksandra Sandstrom, "4 Facts about Religion in New Zealand," *Pew Research Center*, March 21, 2019. https://

www.pewresearch.org/fact-tank/2019/03/21/4-facts-about-religion-in-new-zealand/ (accessed March 3, 2021).

31. Ayca Arkilic, "What Is Islam's Appeal to Māori?," *Newsroom*, August 19, 2020. https://www.newsroom.co.nz/ideasroom/what-is-islams-appeal-to-maori (accessed January 3, 2021).
32. Ian Clarke, "Essentialising Islam: Multiculturalism and Islamic Politics in New Zealand," *New Zealand Journal of Asian Studies* 8 (2006), 69–96.
33. Clarke, "Essentialising Islam," 73–4.
34. Kolig, "Whither Cultural Acceptance?" 181.
35. Clarke, "Essentialising Islam," 74.
36. Ibid.
37. Stanley Fish, "Boutique Multiculturalism, or Why Liberals Are Incapable of Thinking about Hate Speech," *Critical Inquiry* 23 (1997), 378–95.
38. Fish, "Boutique Multiculturalism," 165.
39. Abdullah Drury and Douglas Pratt, "Islam in New Zealand—A Mixed Reception: Historical Overview and Contemporary Challenges," *Journal of College of Sharia & Islamic Studies* 39 (2021), 165.
40. Jo Smith, "Post-cultural Hospitality: Settler-Native-Migrant Encounters," *Arena Journal* 28 (2007), 64–86.
41. Kolig, "Whither Cultural Acceptance?," 173.
42. Ibid.
43. Ibid.
44. Ibid., 176; see also Kolig, "Muslim Traditions and Islamic Law in New Zealand."
45. David H. Griffiths, "Defining the 'Secular' in the New Zealand Bill of Rights Era: Some Cases and Controversies," *Otago Law Review* 12 (2011), 499–500.
46. Griffiths, "Defining the 'Secular' in the New Zealand Bill of Rights Era," 505.
47. Ibid.
48. Ibid., 504.
49. Interview with Farida (pseudonym), Victoria University of Wellington, March 19, 2019.
50. Drury and Pratt, "Islam in New Zealand—A Mixed Reception," 149.
51. Paul Hunt, "We Must Give Nothing to Racism and Islamophobia," *Stuff*, March 19, 2019. https://www.stuff.co.nz/national/christchurch-shooting/111395470/we-must-give-nothing-to-racism-and-islamophobia (accessed February 17, 2021).
52. Interview with Samia (pseudonym), Victoria University of Wellington, March 27, 2019.
53. In addition to this verbal attack, in February 2017, veiled women experienced a similar racist attack in the Waikato town of Huntly.
54. Chris Allen, "Exploring the Impact of Islamophobia on Visible Muslim Women Victims: A British Case Study," *Journal of Muslims in Europe* 3 (2014), 137–59.
55. Barbara Perry, "Gendered Islamophobia: Hate Crime against Muslim Women," *Social Identities: Journal for the Study of Race, Nation and Culture* 20 (2014), 74–89.
56. https://www.instagram.com/p/BvK-gJYh77n/ (accessed February 11, 2020).
57. Alice Webb-Liddall and Scott Palmer, "Scarves in Solidarity Urges Kiwis to Wear Scarves on Friday," *Newshub*, March 20, 2019. https://www.newshub.co.nz/home/new-zealand/2019/03/scarves-in-solidarity-urges-kiwis-to-wear-scarves-on-friday.html (accessed February 9, 2021).
58. Glenn McConnell, "Face of Empathy: Jacinda Ardern Photo Resonates with the World after Terror Attack," *Stuff*, March 18, 2019. https://www.stuff.co.nz/

entertainment/arts/111361303/face-of-empathy-jacinda-ardern-photo-resonates-with-the-world-after-terror-attack (accessed March 1, 2021).
59. Ali Shakir, "Don't Let Jacinda Ardern's Headscarf Send the Wrong Message," *Stuff*, October 2, 2019. https://www.stuff.co.nz/national/christchurch-shooting/116195738/dont-let-jacinda-arderns-headscarf-send-the-wrong-message (accessed March 11, 2021).
60. Lewis, "Introduction," 3.
61. Nesrine Malik, "With Respect: How Jacinda Ardern Showed the World What a Leader Should Be," *The Guardian*, March 28, 2019, https://www.theguardian.com/world/2019/mar/28/with-respect-how-jacinda-ardern-showed-the-world-what-a-leader-should-be (accessed March 1, 2021).
62. Interview with Belinda, Wellington, April 9, 2019.
63. Zane Small, "Christchurch Terror Attack: Judith Collins PRAISES Jacinda Ardern for Wearing Hijab," *Newshub*, March 21, 2019. https://www.newshub.co.nz/home/politics/2019/03/christchurch-terror-attack-judith-collins-praises-jacinda-ardern-for-wearing-hijab.html (accessed March 3, 2021).
64. Interview with Dominique, Victoria University of Wellington, March 22, 2019.
65. Gemzöe, "Solidarity in Head-Scarf and Pussy Bow Blouse," 67.
66. Ibid., 68.
67. Abu-Lughod, "Do Muslim Women Really Need Saving?"
68. Gemzöe, "Solidarity in Head-Scarf and Pussy Bow Blouse," 68.
69. Malik, "With Respect."
70. Shenila Khoja-Moolji, "Muslims Need More Than Just Symbolic Solidarity," *New York Times*, January 6, 2016. https://www.nytimes.com/roomfordebate/2016/01/06/do-non-muslims-help-or-hurt-women-by-wearing-hijabs/muslims-need-more-than-just-symbolic-solidarity (accessed February 11, 2021).
71. Marnia Lazreg, *Questioning the Veil: Open Letters to Muslim Women* (Princeton, NJ: Princeton University Press, 2009).
72. Ibid., 23.
73. Anonymous, "Headscarves Movement Means Well, but it Is 'Cheap Tokenism,'" *Stuff*, March 22, 2019. https://www.stuff.co.nz/national/christchurch-shooting/111473440/headscarves-movement-means-well-but-it-is-cheap-tokenism.x (accessed September 3, 2020).
74. Lazreg, *Questioning the Veil*, 20.
75. Ibid.
76. See, for example, Muhammad Asad, *The Message of the Quran* (Gibraltar: Dar Al-Andalus, 1980), 760; Asma Barlas, *Believing Women in Islam: Unreading Patriarchal Interpretations of the Qur'an* (Austin: University of Texas Press, 2019), 57.

Bibliography

Abu-Lughod, Lila. "Do Muslim Women Really Need Saving? Anthropological Reflections on Cultural Relativism and Its Others." *American Anthropologist* 104 (2002): 783–90.

Allen, Chris. "Exploring the Impact of Islamophobia on Visible Muslim Women Victims: A British Case Study." *Journal of Muslims in Europe* 3 (2014): 137–59.

Amin, Qasim. *Tahrir al-Mar'a [The liberation of Women]* (reprinted in Muhammad ʿImara: *Qasim Amin: Al-Aʿmal al-Kamila*). Beirut: Dar al-Shuruq, 1976.

Anonymous. "Headscarves Movement Means Well, but It Is 'Cheap Tokenism.'" *Stuff*, March 22, 2019. https://www.stuff.co.nz/national/christchurch-shooting/111473440/headscarves-movement-means-well-but-it-is-cheap-tokenism.x (accessed September 3, 2020).

Arkilic, Ayca. "What Is Islam's Appeal to Māori?" *Newsroom*, August 19, 2020. https://www.newsroom.co.nz/ideasroom/what-is-islams-appeal-to-maori (accessed January 3, 2021).

Asad, Muhammad. *The Message of the Quran*. Gibraltar: Dar Al-Andalus, 1980.

Barlas, Asma. *Believing Women in Islam: Unreading Patriarchal Interpretations of the Qur'an*. Austin: University of Texas Press, 2019.

Beaty, Katelyn. "Toward a New Understanding of Modesty." *The Atlantic*, August 20, 2013. https://www.theatlantic.com/sexes/archive/2013/08/toward-a-new-understanding-of-modesty/278652/ (accessed February 9, 2021).

Bowen, John R. *Why the French Don't Like Headscarves: Islam, the State, and Public Space*. Princeton, NJ: Princeton University Press, 2008.

Brown, Samuel Morris, and Holbrook Kate. "Embodiment and Sexuality in Mormon thought." In *The Oxford Handbook of Mormonism*, edited by Terryl L. Givens and Phillip L. Barlow (Oxford: Oxford University Press, 2015), 292–306. https://www-oxfordhandbooks-com.virtual.anu.edu.au/view/10.1093/oxfordhb/9780199778362.001.0001/oxfordhb-9780199778362-e-20?rskey=toTVuY&result=2 (accessed February 19, 2021).

Clarke, Ian. "Essentialising Islam: Multiculturalism and Islamic Politics in New Zealand." *New Zealand Journal of Asian Studies* 8 (2006): 69–96.

Drury, Abdullah. "Mostly Harmless: A Short History of the First Century of Muslim Settlement in New Zealand." *Waikato Islamic Studies Review* 1 (2015): 25–49.

Drury, Abdullah, and Douglas Pratt. "Islam in New Zealand—A Mixed Reception: Historical Overview and Contemporary Challenges." *Journal of College of Sharia & Islamic Studies* 39 (2021): 149–70.

Fish, Stanley. "Boutique Multiculturalism, or Why Liberals Are Incapable of Thinking about Hate Speech." *Critical Inquiry* 23 (1997): 378–95.

Gemzöe, Lena. "Solidarity in Head-Scarf and Pussy Bow Blouse: Reflections on Feminists Activism and Knowledge Production." *Social Inclusion* 6 (2018): 67–81.

Gökariksel, Banu, and Anna J. Secor "New Transnational Geographies of Islamism, Capitalism and Subjectivity: The Veiling-Fashion Industry in Turkey." *Royal Geographical Society* 41 (2009): 6–18.

Griffiths, David H. "Defining the 'Secular' in the New Zealand Bill of Rights Era: Some Cases and Controversies." *Otago Law Review* 12 (2011): 497–524.

El Guindi, Fadwa. *Veil: Modesty, Privacy and Resistance*. Oxford: Berg, 1999.

Hoffman-Ladd, Valerie J. "Polemics on the Modesty and Segregation of Women in Contemporary Egypt." *International Journal of Middle East Studies* 19 (1987): 23–50.

Hunt, Paul. "We Must Give Nothing to Racism and Islamophobia." *Stuff*, March 19, 2019. https://www.stuff.co.nz/national/christchurch-shooting/111395470/we-must-give-nothing-to-racism-and-islamophobia (accessed February 17, 2021).

Ibn Manzur. *Lisan al-ʿArab*. Vols. 3 and 15. Beirut: Maktaba Tahqiq al-Turath, 1993.

Irshai, Ronit. "Judaism." In *The Oxford Handbook of Theology, Sexuality, and Gender*, edited by Adrian Thatcher (Oxford: Oxford University Press, 2014), 413–31. https://www-oxfordhandbooks-com.virtual.anu.edu.au/view/10.1093/oxfordhb/9780199664153.001.0001/oxfordhb-9780199664153-e-022 (accessed March 3, 2021).

Islamicity Indices. "Islamicity Indices: 2021." *Islamicity Index* (2021). http://islamicity-index.org/wp/latest-indices-2021/ (accessed June 11, 2022).
Khoja-Moolji, Shenila. "Muslims Need More Than Just Symbolic Solidarity." *New York Times*, January 6, 2016. https://www.nytimes.com/roomfordebate/2016/01/06/do-non-muslims-help-or-hurt-women-by-wearing-hijabs/muslims-need-more-than-just-symbolic-solidarity (accessed February 11, 2021).
Kishi, Katayoun, Stephanie Kramer, Joey Marshall, and Aleksandra Sandstrom. "4 Facts about Religion in New Zealand." *Pew Research Center*, March 21, 2019. https://www.pewresearch.org/fact-tank/2019/03/21/4-facts-about-religion-in-new-zealand/ (accessed March 3, 2021).
Kolig, Erich. "Muslim Traditions and Islamic Law in New Zealand: The 'Burqa Case' and the Challenge of Multiculturalism." In *Asia in the Making of New Zealand*. Edited by Henry Johnson and Brian Moloughney, 204–24. Auckland: Auckland University Press, 2006.
Kolig, Erich. "Whither Cultural Acceptance? Muslims and Multiculturalism in New Zealand." In *Asians and the New Multiculturalism in Aotearoa New Zealand*. Edited by Gautam Ghosh and Jacqueline Leckie, 159–92. Otago: Otago University Press, 2015.
Laborde, Cécile. *Critical Republicanism: The Hijab Controversy and Political Philosophy*. Oxford: Oxford University Press, 2008.
Lazreg, Marnia. *Questioning the Veil: Open Letters to Muslim Women*. Princeton, NJ: Princeton University Press, 2009.
Lewis, Reina. "Introduction: Mediating Modesty." In *Modest Fashion: Styling Bodies, Mediating Faith*. Edited by Reina Lewis, 1–16. London: I.B. Tauris, 2013.
Mahmood, Saba. *Politics of Piety: The Islamic Revival and the Feminist Subject*. Princeton, NJ: Princeton University Press, 2005.
Malik, Nesrine. "With Respect: How Jacinda Ardern Showed the World What a Leader Should Be." *The Guardian*, March 28, 2019. https://www.theguardian.com/world/2019/mar/28/with-respect-how-jacinda-ardern-showed-the-world-what-a-leader-should-be (accessed March 1, 2021).
Masquelier, Adeline. "Dirt, Undress and Difference: An Introduction." In *Dirt, Undress and Difference: Critical Perspectives on the Body's Surface*. Edited by Adeline Masquelier, 1–33. Indianapolis: Indiana University Press, 2005.
McConnell, Glenn. "Face of Empathy: Jacinda Ardern Photo Resonates with the World after Terror Attack." *Stuff*, March 18, 2019. https://www.stuff.co.nz/entertainment/arts/111361303/face-of-empathy-jacinda-ardern-photo-resonates-with-the-world-after-terror-attack (accessed March 1, 2021).
Mernissi, Fatima. *Beyond the Veil: Male-Female Dynamics in a Modern Muslim Society*. Cambridge, MA: Schenkman Publishing Company, 1975.
Moors, Annelies. " 'Discover the Beauty of Modesty': Islamic Fashion Online." In s*Modest Fashion: Styling Bodies, Mediating Faith*, edited by Reina Lewis, 17–40. London: I.B. Tauris, 2013.
Nisa, Eva, and Faried F. Saenong. "From Mahometan to Kiwi Muslim: History of NZ's Muslim Population." *The Conversation*, 2019. https://theconversation.com/from-mahometan-to-kiwi-muslim-history-of-nzs-muslim-population-114067 (accessed February 21, 2021).
Perry, Barbara. "Gendered Islamophobia: Hate Crime against Muslim Women." *Social Identities: Journal for the Study of Race, Nation and Culture* 20 (2014): 74–89.

Pratt, Douglas. "Secular New Zealand and Religious Diversity: From Cultural Evolution to Societal Affirmation." *Social Inclusion* 4 (2016): 52–64.

Raday, Frances. "Modesty Disrobed—Gendered Modesty Rules under the Monotheistic Religions." In *Feminism, Law, and Religion*. Edited by Marie Failinger, Elizabeth Schiltz, and Susan J. Stabile, 283–306. Surrey: Ashgate, 2013.

Said, Edward, W. *Orientalism*. New York: Pantheon Books, 1978.

Scott, Joan Wallach. *The Politics of the Veil*. Princeton, NJ: Princeton University Press, 2007.

Shakir, Ali. "Don't Let Jacinda Ardern's Headscarf Send the Wrong Message." *Stuff*, October 2, 2019. https://www.stuff.co.nz/national/christchurch-shooting/116195738/dont-let-jacinda-arderns-headscarf-send-the-wrong-message (accessed March 11, 2021).

Small, Zane. "Christchurch Terror Attack: Judith Collins Praises Jacinda Ardern for Wearing Hijab." *Newshub*, March 21, 2019. https://www.newshub.co.nz/home/politics/2019/03/christchurch-terror-attack-judith-collins-praises-jacinda-ardern-for-wearing-hijab.html (accessed March 3, 2021).

Smith, Jo. "Post-Cultural Hospitality: Settler-Native-Migrant Encounters." *Arena Journal* 28 (2007): 64–86.

Stats NZ. "Losing Our Religion." *Stats NZ*, October 3, 2019. https://www.stats.govt.nz/news/losing-our-religion (accessed February 19, 2021).

Webb-Liddall, Alice, and Scott Palmer. "Scarves in Solidarity Urges Kiwis to Wear Scarves on Friday." *Newshub*, March 20, 2019. https://www.newshub.co.nz/home/new-zealand/2019/03/scarves-in-solidarity-urges-kiwis-to-wear-scarves-on-friday.html (accessed February 9, 2021).

Winter, Bronwyn. *Hijab and the Republic: Uncovering the French Headscarf Debate*. Syracuse: Syracuse University Press, 2008.

Zolghadr, Khadijeh, and Lynda Clarke. "Social and Individual Impacts of Veiling on Muslim Women: The Views of Mortaza Mutahhari and Qasim Amin." *International Journal of Humanities* 23 (2016): 27–44.

Index

www.ingramcontent.com/pod-product-compliance
Lightning Source LLC
Chambersburg PA
CBHW071850270326
41929CB00013B/2177
9781350386143